UNIVERSITY OF NOT

10 0812579 7

WITHDRAWN
FROM THE LI

D1758524

THE MARKET LOGICS OF CONTEMPORARY FICTION

PAUL CROSTHWAITE

University of Edinburgh

University of Nottingham
Hallward Library

CAMBRIDGE
UNIVERSITY PRESS

CAMBRIDGE
UNIVERSITY PRESS

University Printing House, Cambridge CB2 8BS, United Kingdom

One Liberty Plaza, 20th Floor, New York, NY 10006, USA

477 Williamstown Road, Port Melbourne, VIC 3207, Australia

314–321, 3rd Floor, Plot 3, Splendor Forum, Jasola District Centre,
New Delhi – 110025, India

79 Anson Road, #06–04/06, Singapore 079906

Cambridge University Press is part of the University of Cambridge.

It furthers the University's mission by disseminating knowledge in the pursuit of
education, learning, and research at the highest international levels of excellence.

10 0812579~7

www.cambridge.org
Information on this title: www.cambridge.org/9781108499569
DOI: 10.1017/9781108583787

© Cambridge University Press 2019

This publication is in copyright. Subject to statutory exception
and to the provisions of relevant collective licensing agreements,
no reproduction of any part may take place without the written
permission of Cambridge University Press.

First published 2019

Printed in the United Kingdom by TJ International Ltd, Padstow Cornwall

A catalogue record for this publication is available from the British Library.

ISBN 978-1-108-49956-9 Hardback

Cambridge University Press has no responsibility for the persistence or accuracy of
URLs for external or third-party internet websites referred to in this publication
and does not guarantee that any content on such websites is, or will remain,
accurate or appropriate.

For Mel, Poppy, and Violet

Contents

Acknowledgements   *page* ix

Introduction: Neoliberalism, Financialization, and the
Contemporary Literary Marketplace   1

PART I THE EMERGENCE OF MARKET METAFICTION

1 Market Metafiction and the Varieties of Postmodernism   37

PART II THE PHANTASMAGORIAS OF CONTEMPORARY FINANCE

2 Trading in the As If: Fiduciary Exchangeability and
   Supernatural Financial Fiction   71

3 "The Occult Logic of 'Market Forces'": Iain Sinclair's
   Post-Big Bang London   92

PART III THE MARKET KNOWS

4 The Price Is Right: Market Epistemology, Narrative Totality,
   and the "Big Novel"   129

5 Fully Reflecting: Knowing the Mind of the Market in DeLillo
   and Kunzru   154

PART IV THE MOMENT OF MARKET METAFICTION

6 Putting Everything on the Table: Markets and Material
   Conditions in Twenty-First-Century Fiction   187

7 Between Autonomy and Heteronomy: Exchanging
Capital in Zink, Cohen, and Heti   218

Coda: Basic Income, or, Why Barbara Browning's
The Gift Is Not a Gift   256

Notes   262
Index   302

Acknowledgements

This book is concerned with novels that incorporate a recognition of the material conditions that shaped their production into their own narratives. A different way to put this would be to say that the authors of such works turn their acknowledgements pages into the subject matter of their books themselves. My own acknowledgements of the many forms of support that have made the writing of this book possible are confined to their customary place, but, in truth, proper recognition of that support could easily fill an entire volume.

I must offer thanks, first of all, to my colleagues in the Department of English Literature at the University of Edinburgh for the friendship, good humour, and enthusiasm for ideas that make 50 George Square such a pleasurable and stimulating place to work. For clarifying conversations, reading tips, and loans (sometimes gifts) of relevant texts, special thanks are due to Benjamin Bateman, Sarah Carpenter, Simon Cooke, David Farrier, Penny Fielding, James Loxley, Simon Malpas, Andy Taylor, Lee Spinks, Randall Stevenson, Alex Thomson, Rebecca Tierney-Hynes, and Greg Walker. True to its Enlightenment traditions, Edinburgh upholds a strong sense of the interwovenness of the various disciplines and a commitment to fostering research that bridges such (seemingly) disparate fields as literature and finance. In this spirit, it's been a pleasure to discuss shared areas of interest with the likes of Nathan Coombs, Karen Gregory, Donald MacKenzie, Michael Northcott, Paolo Quattrone, Tamara Trodd, and Arno Verhoeven. I've also learnt much from the brilliant PhD students whose research I've been lucky enough to supervise (Sarah Bernstein, Sarah Humayun, Iain McMaster, Brandon Jenvey, and Tomás Vergara), and I've benefited from the opportunity to discuss ideas that figure in this book with students on my Modernism and the Market course and the MSc in Literature and Modernity.

Further afield, numerous friends and colleagues have encouraged and assisted my work on this project, including John Beck, Arthur Bradley, Nina Boy, Dorothy Butchard, Marieke de Goede, Robert Eaglestone, Jane Elliott, Joyce Goggin, Matt Hart, Rob Hawkes, Jennifer Hodgson, David James, Miranda Joseph, Alissa Karl, Arin Keeble, Adam Kelly, Sadek Kessous, Becky Munford, Russell Napier, Peter Nicholls, Tomos Owen, Helen Paul, Mary Poovey, Anindya Raychaudhuri, Joanna Rostek, Stephen Shapiro, Barbara Straumann, James Taylor, Jo Walton, and Patricia Waugh. This book has benefited hugely from invitations to air work in progress at the universities of Brighton, Dundee, Lancaster, Manchester, Nottingham, St Andrews, Strathclyde, Sydney, Uppsala, York, and Zürich, as well as Columbia University, Copenhagen Business School, and New York University. My thanks to all of the colleagues who generously hosted these visits.

Peter Knight, Nicky Marsh, and I have been collaboratively puzzling over what literature and economics have to do with one another for a decade now. Our conversations, as well as their readings of earlier drafts, have enriched this book in innumerable ways, large and small. For their friendship, support, and unflagging enthusiasm, I am deeply grateful.

I would not have been able to complete this book without two semesters of research leave granted by the School of Literatures, Languages, and Cultures at Edinburgh. I'm privileged to belong to an institution that remains so committed to supporting its academics' scholarship.

Cambridge University Press's two anonymous reviewers provided feedback that was exceptionally careful, thoughtful, and rigorous, and the finished book has benefited hugely from their close engagements with its arguments. I was in Peter Boxall's debt long before he suggested that this project might have potential for the new series he was then developing, and I am all the more so now. Peter provides a model of the kind of professionalism, mentorship, and commitment to intellectual work to which we might all aspire. I'm deeply grateful to Ray Ryan for his consistent enthusiasm and support for this project, and to Edgar Mendez for his meticulous attention to detail in guiding it towards publication.

My mother Bernie, father David, and brother Mark remain limitless sources of love, assistance, and encouragement, and I'm deeply grateful, too, for the kindness and affection of my extended family: Cristina, Judith, Les, Keith, Jen, Matilda, and Beau. Melanie Waters' infinite reserves of love, support, humour, and kindness have not only made this book possible, they make everything possible. The time that she has enabled me to have to work on the project has been essential, but it has been equally important to have reasons to stop. Nothing will frustrate the feeling that every moment must be rendered productive, efficient, and economical quite like living with young children; in that, as in so much else, our daughters Poppy and Violet are the truest of gifts.

Portions of Chapters 2 and 3 of this book previously appeared in my essay "Phantasmagoric Finance: Crisis and the Supernatural in Contemporary Finance Culture." Copyright 2011 from *Criticism, Crisis and Contemporary Narrative: Textual Horizons in an Age of Global Risk* edited by Paul Crosthwaite. Reproduced by permission of Taylor and Francis Group, LLC, a division of Informa plc.

Introduction
Neoliberalism, Financialization, and the Contemporary Literary Marketplace

In August 2008, while financial markets were already dominating headlines around the world amid mounting chaos in the global credit system, a singular finance-themed news story appeared in arts pages and on cultural web sites in North America and Europe: the New York-based writer Tao Lin was selling shares in his in-progress second novel (eventually published in 2010 under the title *Richard Yates*) to the public. The quasi-stock prospectus for this offering that appeared on Lin's blog explained that he was selling six shares, each entitling the holder to 10 per cent of the US royalties of his novel, for $2,000 per share, as well as the right to "call yourself a 'producer' of [the] novel if you want to do that." Within six days, Lin announced that all shares had been sold.[1] Online commentators were quick to question the exact nature of the reported transactions, though it was evident that, for Lin, the idea of treating book production "like the stock market" was at least as appealing as the actuality: he was, he explained, drawn to "the experience of being [a] 'publicly-owned company'" – "in some way a corporation instead of a person." Dismissals of the affair as a "mere" publicity stunt (typical of accusations that had long surrounded Lin in New York media circles)[2] also seemed beside the point, since Lin's announcement made no secret of the fact that the sale was at least in part a "publicity thing": not only was his share issue "another thing people can talk about in terms of me and will 'in itself' 'increase sales' in the long term," but "if anyone buys shares they will have concrete motivation to promote me and that also will increase sales."[3]

Though his method was unorthodox, it's perhaps unsurprising that Lin felt the need to boost both his income and his profile. His publisher at the time, Brooklyn's Melville House, could offer only the modest advances typical of smaller independent presses; while already emerging as one of the key outlets for innovative fiction in the United States, its marketing clout was (and remains) only a fraction of that of a major New York house.[4] Lin's ongoing self-promotion campaign seems to have eventually paid

I

dividends: as Frank Guan describes, "Lin's efforts at publicity ... likely helped him secure a high-profile agent [Bill Clegg of William Morris Endeavor] and a book deal ... from a major publisher," Vintage (an imprint of one of the world's largest publishing companies, Random House), which agreed a $50,000 advance for his third novel in 2011.[5] I return to the resulting novel, *Taipei*, which appeared in 2013, later in this book, but I highlight the various transactions that led to its publication here because they so starkly display the relationship that I trace in the following chapters between contemporary fiction and market logics modelled on those of contemporary finance.

* * *

Literature, and especially prose fiction, have long been shaped by their relations to the capitalist marketplace. But fiction published in Britain and the United States over recent decades has increasingly internalized the structures, dynamics, and demands of market systems. More specifically, contemporary authors are inclined to conceive of the literary marketplace in which they operate, and to which they are obliged to be acutely sensitive, as inextricable from the financial markets that exert ever-greater dominance over the global publishing industry and book retail business and the global economy at large. While stock, bond, foreign exchange, and other types of financial markets remain deeply embedded in networks of commodity production and consumption, the "financialization" of advanced capitalist economies since the 1970s has seen crowded trading floors, or, latterly, open plan offices arrayed with ranks of electronic trading terminals, come to define how writers understand the ontology of "the market" as such, and to embody the model of value against which contemporary authors are obliged to measure themselves and their work.

As a matter both of temperamental propensity and structural necessity, the ambitious contemporary novelist's relation to the market activities of Wall Street and the City of London is deeply conflicted. This is the case for two key reasons. Firstly, as the prime mover of social and economic change over recent decades, our present phase of intense financialization defines the horizons of the contemporary novel's political imagination, by turns inspiring utopian visions of a sublime new world of speed-of-light data transfer and value creation, and dystopian images of grotesque excess, inequality, and exploitation. And secondly, the heavily financialized restructuring of the global publishing industry since the 1970s has ratcheted up the commercial pressures on authors, obligating a submission to the literary marketplace that is sharply at odds with an equally strongly felt imperative – mandated by the legacy of modernism and the avant-garde – to maintain one's artistic and intellectual autonomy. While these processes are of course global in scale, they are unsurprisingly felt peculiarly acutely by writers situated in the vicinity of the world's pre-eminent financial and publishing centres – London and New York – and accordingly it is on these twin locations that this study is primarily focused.

Central to my argument in what follows is the twenty-first-century efflorescence of what I call "market metafiction": a mode, evident across a varied array of narratives, which is concerned less with the fictionality of the text as such, and more with the ways in which that fictionality solicits or spurns the approval of the literary marketplace. Time and again in such narratives, this self-consciousness about the text's market positioning is articulated via a profoundly ambivalent reckoning with the power of stock markets, currency exchanges, hedge funds, and trading algorithms – the most spectacular manifestations today of the market mechanisms that contemporary authors must learn to navigate.

This book thus returns in a genealogical vein to the history of literary postmodernism in order to explore how we arrived at the "moment" of market metafiction so vividly exemplified by a figure like Tao Lin. Alongside Lin, the book examines key texts by a wide range of authors, including Iain Sinclair, Don DeLillo, Thomas Pynchon, Kathy Acker, Bret Easton Ellis, Anne Billson, David Foster Wallace, Percival Everett, Chris Kraus, Colson Whitehead, Hari Kunzru, Barbara Browning, Teju Cole, Ben Lerner, Nell Zink, Joshua Cohen, Sheila Heti, and Garth Risk Hallberg. Engaging closely with the work of these and other writers, the book reveals contemporary fiction's signature tensions – between complicity and critique; co-option and autonomy; transparency and self-reflexivity; scepticism and belief – to be inextricable from a preoccupation with the intertwined logics of literary and financial markets and the monetary forms and credit instruments that circulate within them.

This book takes a nuanced approach to the question of literary periodization. In the case of the phenomenon that, in Part II, I call "fiduciary exchangeability" – that is, the capacity of fictional texts and monetary and financial instruments to circulate in the market by virtue of their solicitation of trust or belief – I argue that the mass "engineering" of synthetic new financial instruments over recent decades has heightened the importance of fiduciarity to economic life, and found literary expression in a proliferation of outlandish speculative genre modes. At the same time, however, it is a key premise of that part of the book that these recent developments represent mutations and intensifications of dynamics that extend over a much longer historical arc – one reaching back to the co-emergence of modern finance and the Anglophone novel in eighteenth-century Britain.

In a similar way (albeit on a considerably shorter timescale), I argue that while "market metafiction" – fiction that self-consciously reflects upon its own marketability – has coalesced into a fully constituted and highly visible mode over the past decade, instances of similar practices have been evident in British and American fiction since at least the 1970s. This book is thus founded in the belief that attempting to trace lines of continuity is as important a task for literary history as identifying moments of break or rupture. Indeed, I would go so far as to suggest that work in contemporary literary studies is sometimes hampered by its determination to insist on the stark novelty of the practices it identifies, whereas deeper literary-historical research is always liable to yield evidence of, at the very least, anticipations of the latest forms and styles, thereby necessitating more nuanced and less strident – but, I would argue, richer and more accurate – accounts of literary change. This is one of the ways in which this book aims to make an intervention in the methodological practices of its primary field.

* * *

In 1998, as the economic, political, and literary landscape over which this book will range was still emerging into view, the French sociologist Pierre Bourdieu published an essay that perceptively sketched many of that landscape's key features. "The Essence of Neoliberalism" sets out to identify the core elements of a concept then becoming increasingly prevalent as a means of defining the global drift of social and economic life over the previous two decades. Neoliberalism, Bourdieu argued, was best understood as nothing less than a programme aimed at the destruction of "*any and all collective structures*" that "may impede the pure market logic" – a logic, that is, whereby the value of anything is determined solely in economic terms, by the transactions of buyers and sellers in their shifting relations of demand and supply.[6] Under capitalism, of course, where the means of production of goods and services are in private hands, the more that the allocation of resources falls simply to the market's individualized mechanisms of exchange (rather than being subject to some form of provision, arbitration, or control orientated towards collective needs), the more the capitalist class itself stands to benefit.

Like other important analysts of neoliberalism, Bourdieu stresses that while neoliberals often overtly preach a doctrine of nineteenth-century-style laissez-faire, they are distinguished from their classical liberal antecedents by a more covert recognition that it is not sufficient merely to strip away a set of distorting "collective structures" (trade unions, nationalized industries, the welfare state, and so on) in order to allow the "logic of the pure market" to run its natural course. Instead, this logic must be actively constructed, cultivated, institutionalized, and policed through strong state and international institutions.[7] As he puts it: neoliberalism aims at "constructing, in reality, an economic system conforming to its description in pure theory, that is a sort of logical machine that presents itself as a chain of constraints regulating economic agents."

Bourdieu also points the way to current scholarly discussions of neoliberalism in locating the leading edge of neoliberal restructuring in the global financial sector: the domain of investment banks, hedge funds, treasury departments, and stock, bond, currency, commodity, and derivatives exchanges. "The movement toward the neoliberal utopia of a pure and perfect market," he writes, "is made possible by the politics of financial deregulation ... The globalisation of financial markets, when joined with the progress of information technology, ensures an unprecedented mobility of capital." Under these conditions, investors fixated on their portfolios' short-term performance are liable to punish any dip in firms' growth or profitability, leading those firms to "adjust more and more rapidly to the exigencies of the markets, under penalty of 'losing the market's confidence.'"

A further claim of Bourdieu's essay is that one of the most crucial effects of the "implementation" of neoliberalism is "the progressive disappearance of autonomous universes of cultural production, such as film, publishing, etc. through the intrusive imposition of commercial values." Here, Bourdieu echoes the "Postscript" to the book for which he is best known by literary scholars, *The Rules of Art: Genesis and Structure of the Literary Field* (1992). In that study, as well as other influential texts such as *The Field of Cultural Production* (1993), Bourdieu shows how the Aestheticist, Decadent, Symbolist, and other modernist and avant-garde literary movements of late nineteenth- and early twentieth-century France operated within a "subfield of restricted production," leveraging the "cultural capital" endowed by education and social background to compete for the "symbolic capital" of recognition, notoriety, or academic consecration, while displaying indifference (or even outright hostility) towards the economic capital centrally at stake in the subfield of "large-scale production" – the domain of "commercial" literature "oriented towards the satisfaction of the demands of a wide audience" and "dedicated and devoted to the market and profit."[8]

Contemplating the late twentieth-century literary field at the end of *The Rules of Art*, however, Bourdieu suggests that the relative autonomy from market pressures enjoyed by earlier generations of cultural producers faces an unprecedented challenge in the form of "the increasingly greater inter-penetration between the world of art and the world of money," prompting him to ask "whether the division into two markets characteristic of the fields of cultural production since the middle of the nineteenth century . . . is not now threatening to disappear, since the logic of commercial production tends more and more to assert itself over avant-garde production (notably, in the case of literature, through the constraints of the book market)." For Bourdieu, while the "experimental work" always, necessarily, occupies a marginal position relative to the "bestseller," that position had, by the 1990s, become untenably precarious.[9]

Bourdieu's literary field can sometimes seem like a deeply cynical place, where the cynicism of producing literature purely for the market would be trumped only by the cynicism of those who affect a pose of indifference to the market merely in order to accrue reputation and prestige that will in time yield their own economic payoffs as the processes of consecration and canonization take their course. However, the unmistakable note of alarm that Bourdieu sounds at the end of *The Rules of Art* makes clear that for him there is something more at stake in the presence of a "subfield of restricted production" in the literary field than a mere opportunity for writers to execute a smart opening gambit while playing the "long game" of literary entrepreneurship. While Bourdieu questions whether modernist and avant-garde movements are "radical," "subversive," or "disinterested" in quite the ways or to quite the extents that they claim (and indeed believe themselves to be), it is nonetheless clear that for him the disappearance of a literary sphere that, whatever its conscious or unconscious motivations, does not simply subordinate itself to the logic of the market would be a profound – in fact, an incalculable – loss.

In "The Essence of Neoliberalism" and the wider body of work from which it derives, Bourdieu charts a set of relations – between a logic of pure market exchange, the diffusion of neoliberalism, the reorientation of advanced capitalist economies towards financial trade, and the shrinkage of spaces of autonomy in the literary field – that have grown far stronger and more starkly visible over the past two decades, and which are crucial to the analysis I offer in this book. Where Bourdieu's late work sometimes seems to herald a state of total enclosure by the laws of supply and demand, however, I highlight the inventive and resourceful – if never pure or uncompromised – strategies via which formally ambitious contemporary writers seek to open up spaces of manoeuvre immanent to, but not simply determined by, the market.

* * *

This book makes its primary interventions in a field – the study of contemporary literature and finance – which has emerged as a major site of interdisciplinary scholarship over the past decade, impelled by the explosion of novels, plays, poems, films, and other cultural productions concerned with the topic that followed the global financial crisis of 2007–8.[10] As the following pages will make clear, *The Market Logics of Contemporary Fiction* intersects with and diverges from this existing body of scholarship in numerous ways. Rather than treating this area of study as an already defined and delimited field, however, I instead approach it as still emerging and in formation, and so aim to expand its boundaries and open it to new forms of critical inquiry. Most obviously, this book moves the field into new territory by offering a sustained engagement with the ways in which today's publishing industry and literary marketplace are themselves subject to processes of financialization, and with the effects of these very direct and urgent economic pressures on literary production, especially in the form of the narrative self-reflexivity I call "market metafiction." While recent critical studies of contemporary literature and finance are necessarily concerned in various ways with markets, they rarely address the market for literature itself. I aim to deepen our critical understanding of contemporary "fictions of finance" by examining in detail how the literary marketplace is both materially shaped and also (in many contemporary texts) metaphorically figured by the financial markets.

In ways that I discuss further at the end of this introduction, this book also aims to relocate the field's core focus of inquiry away from the problematics of literary realism and towards more "speculative" genres and experimental forms. Methodologically, too, this project seeks to broaden the horizons of economically orientated contemporary literary studies, by bringing the field's predominantly Marxist theoretical influences into closer contact with burgeoning work on money and finance in various overlapping fields of the social sciences, including economic sociology, economic anthropology, cultural economy, and the social studies of finance. *The Market Logics of Contemporary Fiction* seeks, then, to advance its primary area of study on a range of fronts in the process of developing its overarching argument: that a central challenge for fiction today is negotiating equally compelling imperatives to embrace and resist an ideology of the market whose locus lies in the systems of contemporary finance.

This introduction highlights the main historical and conceptual components of the book by identifying two multiply intersecting sets of developments: the rise and consolidation of neoliberalism and financialization and the late twentieth- and early twenty-first-century transformation of the publishing industry and book trade. The book's analysis of contemporary fiction and the market is situated at the nexus of these momentous economic, political, and cultural transitions.

The Extended Present: Neoliberalism and Financialization

The coalescence of market metafiction into a distinctive, clearly visible, and widespread narrative style is a development of roughly the past decade, but it is one that is only properly intelligible in relation to a longer literary (as well as economic) history. This book on contemporary fiction conceptualizes "the contemporary," therefore, not as a condition of pure immediacy, but as a "long," "thick," or "extended" present; and, on the basis that the contemporary is best defined in terms of the core socioeconomic conditions that shape the experience of the present and recent past, I understand the long contemporaneity that we inhabit to have been forged in the multiple, mutually reinforcing intersections between a neoliberal model of market optimality and efficiency and a shift in the regime of global capital accumulation towards a round of finance-led expansion over the past four decades. Central to my project, then, is the intimate relationship between neoliberalism (as both theory and practice) and late twentieth- and early twenty-first-century financialization. If, in Greta Krippner's influential definition, *finance* refers to "the provision (or transfer) of capital in expectation of future interest, dividends, or capital gains," then *financialization* is "the tendency for profit making in the economy to occur increasingly through financial channels rather than through ... activities involved in the production or trade of commodities."[11]

As Cédric Durand suggests, financialization "is no epiphenomenon. It is a process that gets to the very heart of how contemporary capitalism is organised," affecting areas of the economy ostensibly far-removed from the bastions of "high finance" (not least, as we'll see, the publishing and retailing of books).[12] In Kevin R. Brine and Mary Poovey's words, "finance as we know it today [is] the combination of institutions, regulations, asset categories, theories, models, and infrastructure that manages, creates, and studies money, credit, claims, banking, assets, and liabilities." Finance is a perennial feature of economic life, but it assumes very particular characteristics in the present: "In one sense – as a credit or a hedge against the possibility that a crop might fail – finance seems as old as exchange itself. In another sense – as an algorithm that speeds high-volume trades around the world in a fraction of a second – finance seems like a creature of today."[13]

My other key term – neoliberalism – is often used without sufficient discrimination, but I'd argue that it remains a necessary concept for grasping the common logic and direction of travel of an otherwise diverse set of socio-economic ideas, events, and processes. It can only serve this purpose, however, insofar as that diversity is respected, and the various component elements of a larger neoliberal market logic are treated with due specificity and precision. As Simon Springer, Kean Birch, and Julie MacLeavy suggest, while "most scholars tend to agree that neoliberalism is broadly defined as the extension of competitive markets into all areas of life," "the concept is in need of unpacking."[14]

On the one hand, neoliberalism can be conceived of as a more-or-less coherent body of ideas, theories, proposals, and polemics broadly united by a belief in the inherent desirability of installing market systems in preference to all other forms of resource allocation, and a conviction that the evaluation of "all institutions and spheres of conduct" is reducible "to a single economic concept of value."[15] As an intellectual movement (or "thought collective," as Philip Mirowski has described it)[16] neoliberalism springs from elite discussion forums like the Mont Pelerin Society, university departments (pre-eminently, the Economics Department and Business School at the University of Chicago), and think tanks including the Cato Institute, the American Enterprise Institute, and the Manhattan Institute for Policy Research in the United States and the Adam Smith Institute in the United Kingdom.[17] I engage in detail with core tenets of neoliberal doctrine (relating to ideas of market efficiency, methodological individualism, rational decision-making, and utility maximization) in Part III of this study.

Throughout the book, I also address a second conception of neoliberalism: as a set of practical processes whereby governments, regulators, central banks, international financial institutions, business leaders, and other elites exert their power in order to restructure global flows of capital, systems of welfare provision, corporations' organizational arrangements, the relations between public and private sectors of the economy, and, ultimately, the subjectivities and rationalities of ordinary citizens. These measures, initiatives, and reforms have invariably been informed to some degree by neoliberal theory, but they are just as likely to have been enacted by pragmatists working in a piecemeal, ad hoc manner under the contingent pressures of particular circumstances as by ideologically driven true believers intent on the thoroughgoing rollout of neoliberal orthodoxy; and what is sometimes referred to as "actually existing neoliberalism" has often strayed from the letter of neoliberal commandment, and shown marked regional variation, even as it has consistently adhered to its spirit of expanding the role of market dynamics in economic and social spheres.[18]

As I've already suggested, neoliberalism has an intimate connection to finance. In Chapter 4, I discuss in detail the especially direct relay evident in the financial sector between neoliberal intellectuals and academics and economic actors engaged in the practicalities of constructing and embedding new markets. Much of the ground for the neoliberal restructuring of the global economy, moreover, was cleared by transformations in the international monetary system in the early 1970s, while the privatization, deregulation, and market expansion that we associate with the processes of "neoliberalization" have been nowhere more pronounced than in the financial sphere. In the following chapters, I consider a series of key inflection points that have helped to make ours an intensely, arguably unprecedentedly, financialized age – one of what Arjun Appadurai calls "deep financialization."[19] These include the cascading economic "shocks" (to the gold convertibility of the dollar; to oil prices; and to interest rates) that punctuated the 1970s; the rise of currency futures and other forms of derivatives trading stemming from the shift to floating exchange rates following the 1971 closure of the Bretton Woods "gold window"; the crisis of industrial profitability that increasingly beset the advanced capitalist economies during the 1970s; the Third World debt crisis of the 1980s, and the resulting imposition of jarring "structural adjustment" programmes; the "Big Bang" reforms of 1986 that turned the City of London into arguably the world's leading financial centre; the emergence of High-Frequency Trading technologies; and a series of devastating financial crises – most obviously, of course, the global "credit crunch" of 2007–8.

It's not difficult to see why the period since the credit crisis has seemed to many commentators to have something of the quality of an interregnum. While the near-collapse of the financial system has led to loud questioning of the idea of the self-correcting market so central to neoliberal theory (as I discuss in Part III), the fallout of the crisis in practical and policy terms has been "neoliberalism recharged," as Martijn Konings puts it: "far from a political turning point, the crisis has been the occasion for an entrenchment of neoliberal principles and an extension of its operative mechanisms."[20] During 2008, the Dow Jones Industrial Average fell 34 per cent and the FTSE 100 31 per cent, but the ten-year anniversary of the onset of the crisis, in late 2017, saw both indexes post record highs. If the age of neoliberal financialization is in its death throes, as some have suggested, then it is undoubtedly going down fighting.[21]

* * *

What the upheavals on financial markets over the past decade (and indeed the past several decades) have made abundantly clear is the extent to which, as the communication theorist Tony Sampson puts it, market actors are "mired in the 'interplay' between, on the one hand, a dream of rational freewill and, on the other, an irrational relation to the affects, desires, beliefs, and sentiments of others."[22] One of the key reasons why the credibility of neoliberalism, as a theoretical project, looks severely tarnished in the wake of the global financial crisis is that its idealized model of the human subject as a calculating, utility-maximizing *Homo economicus* is so painfully at odds with the patently irrational behaviour in which many market participants indulged in the run up to, and during, the crash. Conversely, the crisis has enhanced the legitimacy of the economic subfield known as behavioural economics, which attends precisely to the cognitive biases, miscalculations, and distortions that affect economic decision-making. As Annie McClanahan has argued, however, behavioural economics founders on its tendency to understand "even a large-scale and complex event like a financial crisis . . . as no more than the consequence of aggregated individual choices."[23] Such an understanding presents a basic "problem of scale": "how to account for the fact that many individuals must make exactly the same erroneous calculation at exactly the same time for a bubble (or a bust) to happen."[24]

In this book, in contrast to a behaviourialist approach, I argue that a rigorous account of the psychological, affective, imaginative, and libidinal dimensions of financial markets must understand them precisely *not* in individual, atomized terms but rather as constitutively inter-subjective phenomena. To this end, I turn to social-scientific approaches to finance that theorize forms of belief, fantasy, and desire that are operational in financial markets only insofar as they are formed and resonate *between* market actors, drawing them into inter-responsive networks of relations in which no decision is made in isolation but is instead necessarily shaped by the collective imaginary in which actors participate. Of course, to foreground such phenomena is not to downplay the role of "structural, institutional, [and] historical factors"[25] in the operation of financial markets; nor is it to suggest that the markets might somehow be able to run purely on collective confidence, optimism, or euphoria (or, conversely, that their downturns should be understood simply as mass outbreaks of fear, panic, or disillusionment). Rather, it is to suggest that if we understand the subjective aspects of the markets as innately extra-individual, then we are required to reassess a distinction between the structural and the "merely" psychological, recognizing "market psychology" not as mere froth atop a properly objective set of structures, but as immanent to, and exerting its own determining influence within, those very structures. This book makes the case that it is with this notion of permeability to the fore that an economically orientated literary criticism is best able to contribute to a wider understanding of financial phenomena, mobilizing literature's inherent imbrication of formal structure and subjective or characterological content, and its irreducibly inter-subjective formation in the relations between author, text, and reader, to illuminate the ways in which finance hovers uncannily in a space between the straightforwardly objective and the purely subjective.

Jameson, Postmodernism, and the Market

In beginning to consider the relations between contemporary finance and contemporary culture, one can hardly proceed far without reckoning with Fredric Jameson's monumental work in this area. In his landmark essay of 1984, Jameson famously identifies the "cultural dominant" of the age, postmodernism, as the expression of the logic of late capitalism.[26] In more recent work, Jameson has come to the conclusion that what most clearly distinguishes the present stage of capitalism is the dominance of finance capital, and that it is to this dominance that the cultural hegemony of the postmodern attests.[27] Jameson's theorizations of the economic formation of postmodernism are of course based on a particular understanding of modernism. For him, the age of modernism, running from the late nineteenth to the mid-twentieth century, is defined by the persistence of an autonomous (or at least "semi-" or "relatively autonomous") "sphere of culture" that permits "a certain minimal aesthetic distance" and the "possibility of the positioning of the cultural act outside the massive Being of capital."[28]

This notion of modernism is based in Frankfurt School critical theory, and in particular Max Horkheimer and Theodor Adorno's account of the place of serious art amid a dominant "culture industry." For Horkheimer and Adorno, writing as émigrés in California in the early 1940s, the mass-market forms that crowded the cultural landscape – Hollywood movies, radio serials, drugstore paperbacks, celebrity magazines – were formulaically produced to induce passivity and acquiescence on the part of consumers, who could be persuaded that their deepest needs and desires were being met insofar as they availed themselves of these commodities.[29]

The culture industry thesis also, though, allows for the residual presence of cultural spaces not yet saturated by the logic of the market – albeit ones that Horkheimer and Adorno already, in this mid-century moment, position as objects of wistful retrospection. To the extent that, earlier in the century, "intellectual activity" still possessed "a remnant of autonomy," it owed it, they suggest, "precisely to such backwardness": being "still exempt from the market mechanism," still in possession of "a degree of independence from the power of the market," "stiffened the backbone of art in its late phase against the verdict of supply and demand, heightening its resistance far beyond its actual degree of protection."[30] This "late phase" of art is of course the phase of modernism, or what Horkheimer and Adorno tend to refer to as "bourgeois" art ("art was only ever able to exist as a separate sphere in its bourgeois form," they suggest, because bourgeois ideology – the lofty self-conception of nineteenth- and early twentieth-century European civilization, which would be swept away by war, fascism, and the rise of the culture industry – still prized "purposelessness" and "uselessness" as necessary spiritual counterpoints to the "principle of utility" that governed its commercial concerns).[31]

In Horkheimer and Adorno's estimation, it was the case as early as the 1940s that art (that is, what might formerly have been conceived of as modernist or "bourgeois" art) "now dutifully admits to being a commodity, abjures its autonomy, and proudly takes its place among consumer goods" as "the demand for the marketability of art becomes total."[32] Jameson's model of causality and periodization is different, with the mid-to-late-twentieth-century emergence of late capitalism – or, as he argues more recently, finance capitalism – constituting the crucial determinant and phase of transition, but the outcome is the same: by the 1980s, he could confidently declare that in the culture of postmodernism "what has happened is that aesthetic production today has become integrated into commodity production generally."[33] Echoing Horkheimer and Adorno, he perceives in postmodernism the "universal presence" of "an effacement of the older distinction between high and so-called mass culture, a distinction on which modernism depended for its specificity, its Utopian function consisting at least in part in the securing of a realm of authentic experience over against the surrounding environment of middle- and low-brow commercial culture."[34] In the conclusion to *Postmodernism* (1991), he similarly suggests that

> the deepest and most fundamental feature shared by all the modernisms is ... their hostility to the market itself. The centrality of this feature is then confirmed by its inversion in the various postmodernisms, which, even more wildly different from each other than the various modernisms, all at least share a resonant affirmation, when not an outright celebration, of the market as such.[35]

In Jameson's account – still the most powerful and influential theorization of the relations between modernism and postmodernism that we have – a sharp distinction is thus apparent: whereas the modernist cultural sphere retained at least a degree of autonomy from, and displayed an overt antipathy towards, the market, postmodernism is defined by the market's total penetration of culture – a condition that postmodernist aesthetics seems enthusiastically to embrace. If the economic has colonized the cultural, though, then so for Jameson has culture come to suffuse the economy, "the dissolution of an autonomous sphere of culture" being at the same time "an explosion: a prodigious expansion of culture throughout the social realm, to the point at which everything in our social life" – very much including "economic value" – "can be said to have become 'cultural.'"[36] Echoing this claim in "Culture and Finance Capital," Jameson argues that "any comprehensive new theory of finance capitalism will need to reach out into the expanded realm of cultural production," which is "as profoundly economic as the other productive areas of late capitalism and as fully a part of the latter's generalized commodity system."[37] In his "Postmodernism" essay, Jameson describes this merger of culture and the economy as an "original and yet untheorized" phenomenon,[38] and an adequate theorization is not, I think, to be found either in this piece or in other texts, such as "Culture and Finance Capital," where Jameson has made similar claims.

In this book, I'll suggest some ways in which it might be possible to theorize a new intimacy between cultural production and economic value under contemporary conditions of financialization. Yet to suggest that the cultural and the economic have simply collapsed into one another, becoming coterminous and indistinguishable, is to claim – hyperbolically, in my view – that the distinctions between what Jameson himself, in *The Political Unconscious* (1981), calls the various "levels" or "instances" of social life have been erased.[39] It is thus also to do away with the need to understand the relations of mediation and causality between these levels, and to render moot Jameson's own project of "transcoding." Jameson defines transcoding as the use of "a particular code or language ... such that the same terminology can be used to analyze and articulate two quite distinct types of objects or 'texts,' or two very different structural levels of reality." It is premised on the idea that "in its "fundamental reality" social life is "one and indivisible, a seamless web, a single ... transindividual process, in which there is no need to invent ways of linking language events and social upheavals or economic contradictions because on that level they were never separate from one another."[40] Yet if we take Jameson's account of postmodernism at its word, then this deep "underlying unity" has become the surface fact of everyday life: no need for transcoding when the economic and the cultural are now visibly one and the same.

In this book, conversely, I'll suggest that it is precisely something in the line of a critical transcoding that is required to trace the complex causal relations and processes of mediation via which different economic sectors (the financial sector; the book trade) and different areas of the cultural field (popular or mass-market fiction; the "innovative" or "experimental" novel) have entered into greater proximity with one another over recent decades without, for all that, simply undergoing some manner of thoroughgoing interpenetration. In the process, I'll suggest that to conceive of the cultural logic of late or finance capitalism as a uniform tendency towards the folding of culture into commerce is to overlook the existence of a range of market logics within contemporary literary culture, with complex and sometimes contradictory valences. This culture, that is, is very far from offering a consistent, uniform, or uncomplicated affirmation of the market.

The Ambivalence of Critique

While this book departs in significant ways from the substance of Jameson's account of postmodernism, then, its methodology has a strongly Jamesonian inflection. This is true not just of the ways in which I theorize the relations between different social domains, but also of my attempts to identify in contemporary fiction a "political unconscious" that projects onto the financial markets both utopian desires and dystopian anxieties. The authors whose works I examine, that is, respond to the power of stock exchanges and other sites of financial trade in narratives that lurch between reverence, doubt, and renunciation in patterns that mimic the ebbing and flowing rhythms of finance itself. In these texts, financial markets are, by turns, enchanted forces of messianic transformation and manifestations of the most malign necromancy; paradisiacal spaces of collective belonging and totalitarian mechanisms of surveillance and control; and sites where radiant futures are already graspable while the most grinding forms of exploitation still persist.

Part of my argument is that these states of ambivalence or oscillation point the way to an important intervention in contemporary debates concerning the limits of politicized critique and the exhaustion of oppositional or "suspicious" forms of cultural analysis. Recent questioning of critique has taken various forms, but Rita Felski, in *The Limits of Critique* (2015), speaks for many scholars when she takes issue with "a style of interpretation driven by a sprit of disenchantment" and a "mood" of "critical detachment ... tied to the cultivation of an intellectual persona that is highly prized in literary studies and beyond: suspicious, knowing, self-conscious, hardheaded, tirelessly vigilant." In contrast, Felski wishes to know where we might find literary and cultural criticism's "theory of attachment."[41] Reading the work of Felski and others who've embarked on the turn to "postcritique," I share Nico Baumbach, Damon Young, and Genevieve Yue's concern that "at the very moment we most need a political critique of culture, we are busy disavowing the tools that might deliver one," and indeed their assertion that one should not be afraid "to be 'suspicious and aggressive,' under historical conditions that call for nothing less."[42] Nevertheless, I want to suggest that the polarized positions into which participants in this debate have quickly fallen might be productively complicated, and that works of contemporary "financial fiction" embody an alternate form of critical disposition, which mediates between the poles of post- and pro-critique without simply even-handedly balancing them out.

The strategies of the authors I examine have a key precedent, I'd suggest, in the critical writings of Susan Sontag – a surprisingly sidelined figure in the so-called "method" or "reading wars" of recent years. At the opening of her 1964 essay "Notes on 'Camp,'" Sontag offers a compelling rationale for ambivalence as a method of critical inquiry:

> I plead the goal of self-edification, and the goad of a sharp conflict in my own sensibility. I am strongly drawn to Camp, and almost as strongly offended by it. That is why I want to talk about it, and why I can ... To name a sensibility, to draw its contours and to recount its history, requires a deep sympathy modified by revulsion.[43]

Similar models of critical engagement have recently been advocated by scholars in feminist and queer theory. Picking up on Jackie Stacey's assertion that analysts of culture should not "wish away" our "necessarily conflicted relation to objects," Carolyn Pedwell, for example, argues for a "mood work" that requires "inhabit[ing] moods as a means to understand their ambivalence as well as their discursive-material power" and an acknowledgment of how we "grapple with different moods or vacillate between them."[44] I argue that, in a similar way, the narrative engagements with market logics analysed in this book model a critical "mood" in which insights arise not from a studiedly impassive or remorselessly suspicious stance, but rather from fully articulating and exploring one's own complex attachments to the objects of critique themselves. In describing this positionality in terms of "ambivalence," I am not positing a simple interplay of "for" and "against," in which the two sides merely serve to balance one another out. Rather, as Robert Pfaller (following Freud's foundational writings on the topic) suggests, in a state of ambivalence, properly understood, the coexistence of hatred and love correspondingly *intensifies* the libidinal relation to the object.[45] That contemporary fiction's engagement with market logics is so intense is a function, that is, of that engagement's profound ambivalence. Similarly, I argue that what arises from this position of ambivalence is not simply a trade off between critical insight, on the one hand, and unthinking affective attachment, on the other, but rather forms of insight that are only possible precisely at this vexed juncture of disavowal and attraction.

A further important claim in what follows (especially in Part III) is that it is not only broadly left-aligned novelists who have detected the glimmer of a collective or communitarian utopianism in an idealized image of the financial markets, but that a "political unconscious" of this kind is evident, too, in the work of neoliberal market ideologues themselves. In this way, this book seeks to answer Leigh Claire La Berge and Quinn Slobodian's call for literary critics concerned with neoliberalism to "engag[e] with neoliberals' own writings," since "to remain plausible, the invective of neoliberal rationality must not serve only as a dark backdrop against which we watch all that we value vanish"; rather, "a convincing analysis must also acknowledge the many ways that neoliberalization is endlessly productive of its own meanings, life stories, literary modes, and affects beyond – and beside – those of deprivation and loss."[46]

The Literary Marketplace and the Fate of Autonomy

That writers on the left (or, for that matter, neoliberals on the right) should inhabit a deeply conflicted position in relation to contemporary financial markets is perhaps counter-intuitive. But that such writers should occupy a position of this kind in relation to the literary marketplace is far more readily apparent, since this marketplace is the domain that – in order to be a writer (or at least a visible and self-sustaining one) – one must to some degree internalize, but that – in order to be meaningfully on the left – one must renounce (since, as I explain further at the end of this section, it is through their activities in the literary marketplace that writers may work to contest a wider neoliberal ideology of the market that is a crucial mechanism in the ongoing widening of economic inequality). This double bind vis-à-vis the market for literature returns us to Jameson's work on postmodernism. One reason why Jameson's work (as well as that of literary scholars working within paradigms derived from it) doesn't provide a fully adequate account of the relations between contemporary capitalism and contemporary literature is its lack of sustained attention to the crucial ways in which authors' responses to an intensely financialized capitalist system are mediated through the economic spheres whose pressures impose themselves most directly and urgently on the practice of writing: namely, the publishing industry and the book retail business. In this section, then, I turn to consider the making of the contemporary "literary marketplace" – a term which in itself is something of an abstraction, but which, as Evan Brier suggests, "might be defined as the set of linked institutions" – "including but not limited to publishers, agents, authors, and bookstores" – "that collaborate, and compete, to produce books and sell them to a certain population of readers."[47] As I've already intimated, attending closely to these factors will allow us to nuance and complexify the supposed mass capitulation to the market that Jameson associates with postmodernism. In requiring us first to return to the culture of modernism, moreover, such attention will also lead us to reconsider Jameson's view of that culture as offering a flat out rejection of the market.

Recent scholarship has reconstructed a modernist literary culture that occupied a complex position in relation to market forces, one characterized by the varied interplay of economic and symbolic forms of value. This body of research has given us a much clearer understanding of what modernist "relative autonomy" meant in practice.[48] Competing conceptions of value were especially evident in the positioning of modernist authors in the context of mainstream commercial publishing. Presses that were, and remain, among the best-known names in publishing – the likes of Random House, Faber & Faber, Macmillan, Allen & Unwin, Harcourt Brace, Jonathan Cape, Victor Gollancz, and Chatto & Windus – devoted significant resources to publishing modernist work, whether by acquiring manuscripts by untried authors operating in experimental modes, or by taking on writers who had already established a level of critical regard via little magazine and small press publication or bringing out trade editions of renowned but hard-to-come-by titles, as in the case of Random House's publication of the first official American edition of James Joyce's *Ulysses* in 1934. While they tended towards the "serious" or 'high-brow" end of the market, such presses were major business concerns with formidable presences in their industry and significant resources to place behind both the immediate costs of high-standard publication and wide distribution and publicity. They were willing to put these resources at the disposal of challenging work whose market potential was often open to question (especially in the short term) because, as the publishing historian John Thompson puts it, their lists primarily "reflect[ed] the idiosyncratic tastes and styles of their owners and editors."[49]

Of course, these publishers could hardly afford to be indifferent to their bottom lines, even as – free of the need to operate under arbitrary timeframes to satisfy shareholders – they were in a position to evaluate books' success in a relatively long-term perspective. And, as historians of the period stress, we should be wary of romanticizing this lost world of "gentlemanly" publishing precisely because of the social exclusions implied by that affectionately applied term. Moreover, as Andrew Goldstone has stressed, it would be a mistake to see the "modernist and early-twentieth-century ... model of publishing" associated with the likes of Faber and Random House as synonymous with something like "traditional" publishing, however tempting it may be to think of that model as an inveterate norm. Instead, this model flourished within a relatively brief window: emerging in the early decades of the century, when a group of innovators founded or reinvigorated firms that "took advantage of the expansion of the reading public and its fragmentation into taste strata so that 'literary' publishing could be a market for an independent business," it would (as we'll see) not long survive the century's mid-point.[50]

While it lasted, a crucial factor that this publishing and retailing ecology – in which even large publishers were not beholden to shareholders or obliged to pay hefty advances to star authors, and in which bookselling was imbued with the ethos of a cultural and educational vocation – did give rise to was that judgments of immediate saleability could often be subordinated to judgments of quality, interest, or importance. In the mid- to late twentieth century and into the twenty-first, however, publishing and bookselling would undergo their own neoliberal and financial revolutions,

which would see the structures that permitted this degree of semi-
autonomy vis-à-vis the literary marketplace shift and contract.[51]

A crucial early moment that portended the publishing industry's later
neoliberal and financial restructuring came in 1959 when Bennett Cerf and
Donald Klopfer, the founders of Random House, sought to secure the
longevity of their company beyond the ends of their own careers by
engaging a Wall Street investment bank to sell 30 per cent of their stock
to the public. Although public listing imposed new pressures on Random
House and the other publishers that soon followed its lead, the following
decade was a period of considerable buoyancy and optimism in the
industry. The "paperback revolution" (spearheaded by Penguin Books in
London) generated unprecedented growth while enacting a philosophy of
cultural democratization and a commitment to "supporting material considered valuable without necessarily being saleable."[52] At the same time,
welfare state institutions actively sought to foster a sophisticated literary
culture. Both the British Arts Council and the US National Endowment
for the Arts were supportive of experimental writing during the latter part
of the 1960s and into the 1970s, while the post-war expansion of higher
education on both sides of the Atlantic served to broaden the audience for
complex works of literature.[53] As Randall Stevenson describes, however,
the "expansion and new ventures following the 1960s paperback revolution" were curtailed by the economic crises of the 1970s. In the years
following the 1973 oil shock – triggered when OPEC imposed an embargo
in retaliation against the United States and other nations that had supported Israel during the Yom Kippur War – the prices of paper, printing,
distribution, and warehousing all rocketed, "deterr[ing] publishers from
new initiatives, and from taking a risk on any book that could not be sold
fairly quickly."[54]

These pressures were intensified by the acceleration of a "merger mania"
that had first become apparent in the 1960s. This process of conglomeration – the defining phenomenon in the industry over recent decades –
owed much to the wider financial shifts of the period. "Capital's flight into
finance," as Michael Szalay puts it, had been underway since the early
1970s, precipitated by a crisis of industrial profitability as intensifying
global competition led manufacturing firms in the leading capitalist economies into spirals of price-cutting.[55] And by the 1980s and 1990s, when most
major publishers already sat within one media conglomerate or another,
such redirected capital was increasingly being used to make loans "to
consolidating media transnationals prepared to assume huge amounts of
debt."[56]

The upshot of this process of consolidation, which has continued through to the present, is that what were once dozens of independent publishing firms now exist as imprints within a handful of enormous publishing companies – Penguin Random House, Hachette, HarperCollins, Simon & Schuster, and Macmillan being by far the largest. These firms are themselves under the umbrellas of huge parent corporations, the likes of Bertelsmann, Pearson, News Corp, and CBS. These publishers are subject to ever-increasing pressure from their parent companies to reach quarterly and yearly profit and growth targets that will boost stock prices on Wall Street or in the City of London and placate shareholders expecting adequate returns on their investments. In this way, the "pure market logic" (in Bourdieu's terms) that defines the financial markets is extended, to an increasing extent, to a sector that had formerly allowed greater space for other forms of evaluation: it works, that is, to reshape that sector along its own lines.

This drive towards short-term profit maximization was exacerbated by the rise, from the 1980s, of the retail book chains – primarily Barnes & Noble, Waterstones, and – before its collapse in 2011 – Borders, as well as moves by supermarkets and other mass merchandisers into bookselling. These large retailers place a strong emphasis on quick-selling, "frontlist" (i.e. new) books by authors with strong sales track records and significant brand-name recognition, thus squeezing the space available for the backlist titles and more offbeat offerings that are the mainstays of independent bookshops, which have faced intense competition from the chains and increasingly from Amazon and other online retailers. The number of independent stores has fallen markedly since the mid-1990s, though recent years have seen a partial recovery, at least in the United States.

The result of this combination of factors is that the leading publishers increasingly focus on putting out only "big books" – books that will quickly (within weeks or at most months) reach sales figures at least in the mid-tens of thousands. In making acquisition decisions, publishers thus look increasingly to a writer's sales record – their "track" – and to the list of "comps," the comparable titles that the text resembles and that can provide a model for its marketing. Editors are of course always looking for the next big thing, but there are strong imperatives in the industry militating towards "me-too" publishing – towards mimicking the *last* big thing, with a minimal twist. Genre modes, in particular, serve in this context "as indispensible technologies for minimizing risk and targeting readerships, because 'semi-programmed' literature that follows a proven

formula and appeals to a preexisting audience helps combat the unique-
ness, and hence unpredictable sales, of any new book."[57]

Now, it should be stressed that even the corporate publishing companies
still care about the symbolic capital that comes from glowing and prominent reviews or the award of literary prizes, both for its own sake, and
because – as James English has argued – such capital is at least partially
fungible with economic capital, tending to enhance the stature and hence
competitiveness of the company and often translating directly into
increased sales.[58] It's worth noting, though, that the major British and
American literary prizes typically operate according to distinctly conservative criteria of "quality." In Martin Paul Eve's words, "literary prizes . . .
tend towards the reproduction and legitimation of forms that are already
valued, especially in a market context" (though prizes like those run by
Fiction Collective Two in the United States and the recently instituted
Goldsmiths Prize and Republic of Consciousness Prize in the United
Kingdom are expressly designed to encourage and reward more innovative
work).[59]

A degree of differentiation is also maintained in the industry by the
presence within the large corporations of multiple imprints (including
many of publishing's most storied names) with distinct identities; by the
continued existence of a small group of mid-sized, independent trade
publishers (the likes of Faber, Bloomsbury, Canongate, Granta, Atlantic,
and Norton), whose different organizational structures at times allow
greater leeway in list-building; and – perhaps most significantly – by the
appearance over the past two decades (thanks to the reduced costs of entry
to the industry) of numerous small independent publishers, often displaying very different priorities and practices to the corporations. Self-
publishing is easier than ever too, especially in digital form; and in the
United States and United Kingdom anyone can "publish" (in the loose
sense) pretty much whatever they want online at minimal cost to themselves and virtually zero cost to their readers.

Hence, as John Thompson argues, the problem is not so much one of
a lack of diversity per se as a lack of "*diversity in the marketplace*" – a lack of
diversity not simply in what is available but in what is "*noticed, purchased,
and read.*"[60] As the mainstream presses have become less inclined to put
their resources behind a diversity of output, so the potential for a range of
work to garner significant cultural visibility and respectable sales has
decreased. A greater and greater share of the fiction market is now the
preserve of brand-name authors (the Dan Browns, Stephen Kings, and J.K.
Rowlings) and well-established styles, with the rest of the market consisting

of a very long, very thin tail. If "not exactly a winner-takes-all market, it is a *winner-takes-more* market."[61]

Of course, "avant-garde" writing in the strict sense has invariably, almost by definition, registered only on the fringes of the marketplace, at least in the short term – hence the prevalence of self-publishing, patronage networks, and private wealth among the avant-garde groups studied by Bourdieu and others.[62] What the changes of the past few decades have produced, though, is a mainstream industry that is not simply inhospitable to difficulty as such, but which tends more than ever to discourage a writing practice that, while its results may not necessarily be wilfully alienating or rebarbative, is born of a belief that the production of a novel must involve a return to first principles and an approach to novelistic form as a structure to be purpose-built from the ground up, rather than merely adapted from one or other pre-existing blueprint. The narrowing of literary culture's mainstream has a distorting effect on the entire field. If authors and publishers wish to gain visibility and a viable audience for their output in order to build a career or sustain and grow a business, there's increasingly strong pressure for them to tailor their productions to the commercially successful modes. Thus even the two-person, spare bedroom indie press, for whom the idea of being part of a corporation listed on the NYSE or LSE is as fanciful as it is distasteful, is subject to a "logic of the field" determined by the priorities of organizations in precisely that position.[63]

It's true that, as Sarah Brouillette suggests, a text's determinedly "anti-market" stance or wilfully leftfield stylings can ironically be the very conditions of its positive reception among particular niche audiences.[64] This alternative market logic – that of the "marketable antimarket gesture" – is one I consider in several places in this book. And there will surely always be publishing "black swans" whose runaway success is an affront to industry common sense (the *Name of the Rose* phenomenon.) Yet in a market where rewards tend more than ever to accrue to works that refine or minimally innovate within – rather than wilfully frustrate – the conventions of mainstream modes and genres, there's a powerful imperative to smooth off a text's rough edges and sculpt it in line with the more readily accessible and hence bankable forms. As Timothy Aubry writes, in a literary culture dominated by "a market-orientated submission and editorial process designed to maximize profitability," publishers' "ability to gamble on experimental, idiosyncratic, or innovative fiction" is tightly constrained.[65]

In this book, then, I argue that contemporary writers' adoption of non-commercial narrative forms cannot simply be dismissed as mere posturing or position-taking in a prestige economy that is only ever an indirect means of accessing the economy proper (even if something like this dynamic is necessarily implicated, to some extent, in all such cultural production). Not only are conversion rates between "symbolic" and "economic" or "material" forms of capital volatile, unpredictable, and – increasingly – tenuous, but an all-encompassing, imperialist sociology of culture that can only see each and every cultural act as an attempt to accrue another nugget of social distinction or as a move in a "scripted game show"[66] is unable to discern when something more may be at stake – aesthetically, economically, and politically. While this book is strongly informed by sociological approaches to literature and culture, therefore, it insists on the necessity of close textual analysis in order to determine the specific valences of texts' strategies and techniques. Conversely, it is clearly not the case that all writers are now obliged simply to churn out copycat versions of the work of one or other brand-name author or bestselling novel: that move would be wholly counter-productive, for how would new writers differentiate themselves, and establish their own brand-name status, in such a thoroughly homogenized field? It is rather the case that the *spectrum* of positions in which writers can situate themselves has narrowed – at least if they have realistic aspirations of building visible and viable careers as professional authors.

There's strong evidence to suggest that this narrowing – a feature of the publishing industry's decades-long consolidation phase – has been exacerbated by the global financial crisis, the resulting "Great Recession," and their prolonged aftereffects. For one thing, the economic contraction and cuts to funding of core welfare state provisions that followed the crisis have exacerbated structural conditions inimical to "the literary" as such, understood – in Brouillette's words – as "a set of affects and dispositions." Brouillette continues:

> The things that are necessary to the development of the specifically literary disposition, which were always relatively distinguishing and elite, are now decreasingly available ... These include the leisure and focus to read for relatively long periods of time, exposure to the kind of education that inculcates the value of the literary and other aesthetic experiences, [and] available and relatively welcoming public institutions of expressive art and culture.[67]

It is exactly these capacities and opportunities that mid-twentieth-century Western welfare states – and even their residual late twentieth- and early twenty-first-century successors – sought to foster through such programmes as free or low-cost public education, social security protection, and widespread funding for the arts. The erosion of the welfare state in a climate of fiscal austerity is thus (amongst many other things) an erosion of the conditions of the literary.

In view of these broad structural challenges to "the aesthetic field of cultural production and experience,"[68] it's perhaps unsurprising that print book sales fell sharply in the United States and the United Kingdom after the onset of the downturn in 2007–8, and that they remained significantly below pre-crisis levels a decade later.[69] A 2017 report by Arts Council England (ACE) indicates that "literary" fiction was the big loser in the decade following the financial crisis.[70] "Literary fiction" is a notoriously problematic category. In gauging sales, the report's authors are obliged to fall back on the closest proxy offered by the sales tracking service Nielsen BookScan – "General Fiction" – which in practice means everything that does not fall into the other major category of "Genre Fiction." This is of course an unsatisfactory distinction, since, as many exponents of genre fiction (as well as many critics) have pointed out, "lit fic" might itself be understood as a genre – or at least as consisting for the most part of texts operating within a well-defined mode with its own set of conventions, formulas, and stock features. It would be a mistake, too, to view "literary fiction" as in any way synonymous with "experimental" or "innovative" forms of fictional writing (themselves deeply vexed categories, whose meanings in the twenty-first century it is part of the project of this book to explore). The default mode of "literary fiction" over recent decades – perhaps best defined by Zadie Smith as "lyrical realism"[71] – is as convention-bound as any "popular" genre, and for many years proved eminently marketable (the "big book" and the authorial "brand-name" being far from incompatible with "literariness," as a figure like Jonathan Franzen, for example, makes clear). Nor, as this book will emphasize, are "popular genre" and "experimental" tendencies mutually exclusive. Sales of texts of a markedly experimental bent, however, will invariably show up (to the extent that they show up at all) in Nielsen's "General Fiction" category. If, as the authors of the ACE report note, the General Fiction market enjoyed a "boom" or "bull run" between 2002 and 2008,[72] it was lyrical realism that took the spoils; and as General Fiction sales dropped off overall following the crisis, the intensification of the structural factors discussed above curtailed still further the conditions of market diversity conducive to the visible presence of conspicuously innovative or experimental fiction within the market.

The fiction market appears to have shifted decisively post-crisis: "overall the books selling well are not literary – they may be fiction, but they tend to be either commercial genre fiction ... or children's fiction" (J.K. Rowling and her many imitators of course looming especially large in the latter category). The growth of the digital market has done much to compensate for the decline of print sales from their mid- to late-2000s highs, but here the skew away from literary/general fiction is even more marked, with "genre and commercial fiction predominat[ing] in ebook format."[73] Amid the post-crisis contraction of the publishing industry, it has become increasingly difficult to earn a viable living from writing books of any kind.[74] If "for literary writers in particular" these challenges "may be even more extreme," then the same goes doubly for those operating on that fringe of the "literary" that we might define as innovative or experimental.[75] A typical advance from one of the small indie presses that are now almost the only outlets for writers seeking to work outside mainstream conventions might be little more than £1,000.[76]

While it has recently become all the more difficult to make a living as a writer self-consciously operating outside the mainstream, this is of course by its nature a challenging and precarious career path. Hence the "retreat" that "serious" authors of various kinds have been making since the mid-twentieth century from "the open market" to the "economic refuge" that is the university creative writing programme – "the largest system of literary patronage for living writers that the world has ever seen," as Mark McGurl recounts in his landmark study of this phenomenon, *The Program Era: Postwar Fiction and the Rise of Creative Writing* (2009).[77] In this context, McGurl continues,

> even failure as a commodity, for a literary work, might count as (existential) success-in-the-market as long as that failure earned sufficient cultural or spiritual capital for its producer to seem "worth it," and especially if that capital could be converted into credentials for an academic job that could act as a permanent hedge against the low odds of high sales.[78]

Yet the university may no longer represent such a safe haven. As Brouillette suggests, the "de-develop[ment]" of "the aesthetic field of cultural production and experience" has extended to "the English Department and other traditional university humanities courses." In North America, "the existence of tenure" is one of a range of "prosaic factors ... underpin[ning] the autonomous aesthetic" that are being increasingly eroded.[79] As Peter Boxall suggests in *The Value of the Novel* (2015), universities are undergoing their own processes of "rationalization," with the humanities required "to 'account' for themselves, to make claims about their social and economic value that are comically at odds with their own disinterestedness, their own critical detachment from the commodity, the market place, the whole question, indeed, of value."[80]

While often (as we'll see) in possession of some experience of the culture of the creative writing programme, the contemporary authors who have most deeply internalized and interrogated interlocking conditions of publishing sector retrenchment, finance-driven capital accumulation, and neoliberal restructuring are (in the terms influentially formulated by the editors of *n+1*) at least as much NYC (or LON) as MFA,[81] taking their chances in the market and grappling with all of the challenges, contradictions, and compromises that that situation implies. Intimately familiar with these high-cost-of-living cities, where financial and cultural power are both concentrated and unequally distributed, contemporary New York- or London-based writers, I argue, are intensely conscious of their ambiguous class position, one simultaneously of considerable privilege (relative to many forms of industrial and service sector labour) and often of significant marginalization and precarity (especially relative to the high-earning professionals of the finance sector, whose own symbolic and imaginative – but more handsomely remunerated – labour makes them privileged objects of comparison in the narratives I discuss).

While this book has an Anglo-American focus, my analysis of the work of the Nigeria-raised, New York-based writer Teju Cole in Chapter 6 suggests that the kinds of complex creative pressures experienced by Anglophone writers from the Global South are highly conducive to the self-reflexivity of market metafiction. In this and other ways, the book complements research into the institutional and marketing mechanisms via which what's often called "Anglophone world literature" circulates globally and accrues sales and prestige, including critical studies by Graham Huggan, Sarah Brouillette, Amitava Kumar, Pascale Casanova, William Marling, Mads Rosendahl Thomsen, Raphael Dalleo, and Stefan Helgesson and Pieter Vermeulen, among others.[82] In contrast to such studies, however, this book is designed to address a relative (and perhaps surprising) lack of systematic mappings of how the contemporary literary marketplace is reshaping the production of literature in the British and American contexts. I take this approach not out of an urge to reassert the primacy of the "core" in the face of (laudable and vital) scholarly attention to the "periphery", but because it seems to me that if we lack rigorous and sustained accounts of how writers working in the vicinity of the world's leading publishing centres (London and New York) are responding to the transformations of the industry emanating from those same centres, then we are missing a large and important piece of the puzzle in understanding the conditions of literary production in the twenty-first century. Equally, though, I aim in the book to show how writers like Cole and Ben Lerner reflect in their fiction on how the material and intellectual privileges that they enjoy at the metropolitan centre rely upon exploitation at the neocolonial margins.

All of the authors I consider in this book – albeit in different ways and to different extents – seek to resist a narrowing of the literary field whose ultimate endpoint would see it become indistinguishable from the literary marketplace. It is worth emphasizing, though, what is at stake here – and what is not. Firstly, if such resistance derived from nothing more than squeamishness about the taint of commerce entering the pristine world of Literature, then it would be profoundly misplaced, for books (and especially novels) have of course always – whatever other purposes they may have served – been commodities. As Lucien Febvre and Henri-Jean Martin describe in their field-defining work on the rise of print, "from its earliest days printing existed as an industry, governed by the same rules as any other industry," while those involved in the book trade viewed their products primarily (if, it should be stressed, not solely) as "piece[s] of merchandise," "produced before anything else to earn a living."[83]

Secondly, resistance to the dominance of the literary field by the market goes astray if it devolves into a mere denigration of popular narratives as debased or simplistic forms for which the masses have been trained to settle in place of some more authentic mode of popular expression; such disparagement tends merely, as Nicholas Thoburn puts it, "to replicate the tropes of bourgeois distinction."[84] By the same token, there is little that is inherently radical or progressive about resisting such popular forms simply *because* they are popular. The problem, rather, is the way in which the notion of popularity has come to serve as cover for the imposition of the iron law of the market: how (so this ideological argument goes) can there be anything wrong with markets if they are simply an unmediated manifestation of the will of the people? The critiques, deconstructions, or subversions of popular genre forms that I analyse in this book perform meaningful political and cultural work, then, not insofar as they attack those forms per se, nor even insofar as they attack them *as* popular, but insofar as they counter an ideology of the market that has arrogated the category of the popular to itself.[85] As Nicholas Brown suggests, assertions of aesthetic autonomy from the market could not be more politicized when, as is the case today, the claim of the universality of the market is . . . the primary ideological weapon wielded in the class violence that is the redistribution of wealth upwards. The upwards redistribution of wealth in the current conjuncture would be unthinkable without this weapon: the entire ideology of neoliberalism hinges on the assertion that this redistribution is what a competitive market both produces and requires as a precondition.

Thus, "if the claim to autonomy is today a minimal political claim, it is not for all that a trivial one," since it partakes of a larger politics that rejects "the politics of acquiescence to the dictates of the market."[86]

This, then, is the radical basis for the assertion of autonomy vis-à-vis the literary marketplace. But one might also offer a liberal version of this rationale that has validity too. This would be the idea that if all literary production today is necessarily profoundly subject to market imperatives, then there is, nonetheless, an obligation to foster and hold open substantial spaces *within* the market for works that are not simply *for* the market, but have other artistic or intellectual priorities. Such, one could argue, is the basic condition of any literary culture worthy of that name. In deliberately, if only partially, resisting the marketplace's dominant signals, then, the texts I discuss in this book also enact this dual imperative of inhabiting the market without being fully determined by the market's norms and prevailing preferences. Such efforts call for a form of critical practice – what we might call "market reading" – that analyses modulations of genre, style, form, and readerly solicitation as self-conscious responses to market norms and demands, and examines how contemporary authors internalize and manifest anxieties about their texts' marketability within their narratives. One of the key goals of this book, then, is to offer a sustained demonstration of the potential of such a methodology for the close analysis of contemporary literature.

Overview of Chapters

This book is divided into four parts, and sub-divided into seven chapters. In the single-chapter first part, I develop my argument that the postmodernist novel is defined by equally strongly felt imperatives to propitiate and renounce the market. I make the case that, under these conditions, a degree of self-consciousness concerning a text's market positioning – what I call market metafiction – is always liable to arise. I point to a series of examples of novels exhibiting this style of reflexivity, which demonstrate that recent texts in this mode are not *sui generis*, but rather make newly visible techniques that have been evident in fiction for some decades. In the process, I address four major – roughly historically sequential, though overlapping – tendencies in fiction shaped by the defining postmodernist double bind vis-à-vis the market. Firstly, I consider market metafiction as an impulse within the wider foregrounding of a narrative's constructedness and manipulation of its reader that is such a feature of the postmodernist novel as it emerged in the 1960s and 1970s, highlighting, in particular, the work of B.S. Johnson and Gilbert Sorrentino. Next, I turn to the mid-1970s to mid-1990s phenomenon of "Avant-Pop" and related collisions of experimental and popular genre forms, showing how these collisions are self-reflexively thematized in novels by Kathy Acker and Martin Amis. I also consider how the narrow range of pop-cultural representations of Black and ethnic minority life presents especially complex challenges for writers of colour, focusing in particular on the work of the African American novelist Percival Everett. The following section considers how a desire to lay bare the economic conditions of a text's production figures in the much-vaunted shift away from experimental postmodernism towards sincerity, "postirony," and renewed forms of realism since the mid-1990s, paying particular attention to the work of Dave Eggers. I then suggest that a widely discussed "genre turn" among "advanced" or "serious" novelists over the past decade gives rise to anxious self-questioning over what appears to be a decisive rapprochement with prevailing marketplace demands: my exemplar here is Colson Whitehead. Finally, I show how the post-financial crisis novel has found itself tempted by this genre turn, but has almost always drawn back from it, and reiterate my view that the most revealing engagements with contemporary market logics are to be found where "speculative" genre modes intersect with experimental forms of postmodernism.

Part II carries forward this concern with the relations between genre and formal innovation. In Chapter 2, I argue that we might better understand postmodernism's ambivalent appropriation of genre models by theorizing it in terms of a logic of quasi- or "as if" belief that cuts across structures of financial and literary market exchange. Taking recent work in economic sociology and the "New Economic Criticism" as jumping-off points, I show how a deep-rooted kinship between fiction and finance as forms of writing that mediate value in the modern credit economy (in Mary Poovey's terms) is becoming newly visible today. As I explain, the shared condition of fictional texts' and financial and monetary instruments' successful market circulation is their solicitation of tacit faith or trust in imaginary things. I argue that a desire both to exploit and to subvert this condition of what I call "fiduciary exchangeability" shapes the experiments in supernatural narrative form offered by Bret Easton Ellis's *American Psycho* (1991) and *Lunar Park* (2005), Anne Billson's *Suckers* (1993), Stephen Marche's *The Hunger of the Wolf* (2015), and Jonathan Coe's *The Terrible Privacy of Maxwell Sim* (2010). In the work of these writers, I argue, we see many of the crucial elements of market metafiction in action.

In Chapter 3, I suggest that a logic of fiduciary exchangeability finds its most sustained and versatile expressions in the work of the celebrated London writer Iain Sinclair. Sinclair's work of the 1990s, I argue, is both a crucial signal of a deepening intimacy between experimental and genre writing that has become all the more pronounced over the past two decades, and a leading-edge example of the techniques of market metafiction so prevalent today. I read Sinclair's novel *Downriver* (1991), published in the wake of the Thatcherite transformation of the City of London's financial services sector, as exploring what happens to structures of fiduciary circulation when they are pushed to – and beyond – their limits. My reading of the ostensibly non-fictional *Lights Out for the Territory* (1997) as an exercise in what I call the "hermeneutics of speculation," meanwhile, argues for the constitutive roles of faith and belief even in texts that apparently ground themselves in the real and material, in the process challenging the homology between literary realism and precious metal that is a basic premise of much key work in the New Economic Criticism.

Having focused intently on fiction's place in the marketplace in parts I and II, Part III turns to consider how an idealized understanding of the market has become a crucial model for fictional form itself in the contemporary novel. Collectively, Part III makes the case that the big, brainy, intricately structured American novel that goes by the name of the "encyclopaedic" or "systems" novel is shaped by an ambivalent relation to the correspondingly capacious, complex, and informationally rich sphere of the financial markets. Chapter 4 begins by tracing the idea of the all-knowing market from Adam Smith to Friedrich Hayek to the "efficient market hypothesis" that continues to dominate the discipline of financial economics today, and shows how this intellectual history has intersected with the history of the novel. In historicizing the contemporary "big novel" in relation to the late twentieth-century rise of efficient market thought, I challenge the critical consensus that reads such texts as defined by the determinism of conspiracy plotting (however sprawling or decentred), and argue that they are more closely aligned, instead, with the random – yet collectively synchronized – movements of the classically "efficient" market. In the latter portion of this chapter, I show how major encyclopaedic or systems texts – by Thomas Pynchon, William Gaddis, Richard Powers, Jonathan Franzen, David Foster Wallace, and Garth Risk Hallberg – position the omniscient financial market as performing at once a redemptive mapping and an oppressive (and aggressively masculine) surveilling of the social totality.

In Chapter 5, I devote extended attention to two novels from either end of the "efficient market era" – Don DeLillo's *Players* (1977) and Hari Kunzru's *Gods Without Men* (2011) – that model their narrative forms on the information-crunching prowess of the financial markets' price mechanisms, only to leave absences in the textual fabric that defy a totalitarian logic of epistemological capture. The juxtaposition of these two novels, I suggest, highlights how changing technological instantiations of efficient market theory have elicited shifting formal responses, and underscores both why the ideology of the efficient market has retained a hold over the imaginations of novelists, and why that hold is subject to increasing self-critique. I argue, moreover, that Kunzru overtly presents his novel's lack of conclusiveness as opposed not only to the market epistemology of contemporary finance, but also to the norms of the literary marketplace, with its own preference for narrative closure and transparency.

In the book's final part, I argue that, particularly in the United States, market metafiction has emerged as the vanguard fictional style of the post-financial crisis period. In Chapter 6, I begin my discussion of the highly visible coalescence of this mode over the past decade by returning to the career of Tao Lin – a figure whose fictional strategies and marketing techniques, as we've already seen, bring logics I discuss throughout this book into exceptionally sharp focus. I then show how twenty-first-century market metafiction intersects with a wider contemporary interest in self-revealing "autofiction," highlighting the widely influential example of Chris Kraus's *I Love Dick* (1997). In the remainder of the chapter, I analyse two recent works of market metafiction that exemplify this paradigm, even as they register and contest differing financial and literary market logics. In Ben Lerner's *10:04* (2014), attempts to deal with risk and uncertainty central to derivatives trading provide models for "hedging" between different forms of literary value, so that underperformance in market terms may be offset against critical approbation. Even as this strategy avoids a state of pure determination by the market, it entails significant contradictions and compromises, all of which Lerner makes fully visible in his narrative. In Teju Cole's *Open City* (2011), meanwhile, the depredations of what David Harvey calls "the Wall Street–IMF–Treasury complex," as they are visited on countries like Nigeria, where

Cole grew up, are seen to be of a piece with the global publishing industry's exploitation of images of African suffering. In his novel, Cole deliberately sidesteps these stereotyped and voyeuristic images, while at the same time acknowledging the privilege that permits him (now a relatively affluent and highly educated New Yorker) to perform precisely such a resistance to market-dictated convention.

In the book's final chapter, I argue that recent examples of market metafiction by Nell Zink, Joshua Cohen, and Sheila Heti stake out a set of key positions that the ambitious novelist (that is, the novelist concerned to expand the possibilities of the form, but also seeking to build a viable career) might adopt in the contemporary literary field. Beginning with an analysis of the improbable rise to literary fame of the long-obscure Nell Zink, I identify a recurrent logic (evident across all elements of the "Zink phenomenon": interviews, profiles, and other media coverage, as well as her 2016 novel *Nicotine*) whereby an embrace of market forces paradoxically enables the very writing that it at the same time threatens to destroy. Turning to the work of Joshua Cohen, I read the sprawling, experimental *Book of Numbers* (2015) as an ambivalent attempt to channel the logic of the iconic "disruptors" of the contemporary tech sector, whose radical new products defy stock market wisdom in the short term, only to force the market to reshape itself to accommodate the innovative offering in the longer term. Finally, I argue that in her memoir-cum-novel *How Should a Person Be?* (2010) Sheila Heti aims to produce a text that circumvents conventional forms of literary valuation by being neither merely *desired* (as a commodity on the market) nor simply *admired* (as an object of critical veneration), but existing instead as an object of *use* – a guide or tool with the potential to be strategically deployed by those who read it with the aim of securing a greater degree of personal agency.

The brief concluding Coda juxtaposes the market logics traced throughout the book with a form of exchange that is often identified as their antithesis: that of the gift. Focusing on Barbara Browning's 2017 novel *The Gift*, I show how this exemplary work of twenty-first-century market metafiction tries to imagine itself into an alternate economy of gift-giving. I explore the tension, however, whereby the publication of this experimental text, with its Occupy Wall Street affiliations, is made possible by the "gifts" of the corporate and financial donors who support its small, nonprofit press. Rather than viewing this situation as a mere contradiction, however, I suggest that it helps us to recognize that the creation of formally ambitious, "autonomous" works of literary art will always be incompatible with the purity of the gift, since such creation demands material and other resources accessible only via some form of financial backing or remuneration. I argue further, though, that there is a crucial debate to be had about the sources of that support. I suggest that a key challenge for cultural practitioners and critics in the twenty-first century is to look beyond market success and the patronage of corporations and financial institutions to imagine a less ends-focused, more democratic structure of support for the arts, one capable of fostering the creative and intellectual autonomy that is the condition not just of a meaningful literary culture but of culture as such.

PART I

The Emergence of Market Metafiction

I now want to find out who's controlling me economically and why.
– Kathy Acker

CHAPTER I

Market Metafiction and the Varieties of Postmodernism

In the Introduction, I offered an account of literary postmodernism as defined by conflicting demands to pander to, and dissent from, the market. This first chapter fleshes out some of the key claims of the Introduction and surveys the literary-historical context in which material discussed in the following chapters is situated. What Claire Squires calls "material conditions and acts of marketing" (which should, I'd suggest, encompass both how a text is positioned in the market and how it unsettles that positioning) are often overlooked in accounting for texts' forms and meanings; but, as Squires argues, they "profoundly determine the production, reception and interpretation of literature." Indeed, for Squires they are nothing less than "the making of contemporary literature."[1] Jeremy Rosen notes that "literary and cultural scholars have barely begun to consider how [the] marketplace transformations" of recent decades "have affected literary production," and this book aims to go some way towards redressing this gap.[2] It should be stressed, though, that even in a heavily marketized literary field, where authors are acutely conscious of the material conditions surrounding their work, their narratives' structures and concerns are not *solely* determined – in some reductive, mechanistic, or "vulgar" fashion – by such factors; indeed, it will be part of my argument that a close attunement to the literary marketplace and the conditions of literary production in contemporary fiction refracts wider intellectual, political, and formal engagements with the power of market logics, especially as they pervade and emanate from the financial sector.

Postmodernism – and postmodernist fiction in particular – is the form of (broadly) contemporary literature, I'd argue, where these various pressures are most energetically worked out. This working out gives rise to the form of self-consciousness that I call "market metafiction": a mode in which authors reflect upon or allegorize contradictory impulses towards the market in the very process of enacting them. Market metafiction has become especially prevalent in recent years in texts that are often associated

37

with a putative "post-postmodern" turn. I argue, however, that such writing represents not so much an abandonment of or movement beyond postmodernism as a coming to widespread self-consciousness of postmodernism's agonizingly conflicted imperatives in its relation to market forces of varying kinds and scales. Here and elsewhere in this book, then, I aim to show how specific material and historical conditions produce and intensify what Linda Hutcheon calls postmodernism's tendency towards "complicit critique": postmodernism "does not pretend to operate outside [the capitalist] system, for it knows it cannot; it therefore overtly acknowledges its complicity, only to work covertly to subvert the system's values from within."[3]

Forming an important building block of the book's larger literary-historical argument, this chapter surveys a set of major currents in postmodernist fiction, and highlights a series of major authors and texts, in order to show that market metafiction is a recurrent feature of the postmodernist novel – that, indeed, it is an impulse always incipient within postmodernism as such because of postmodernism's constitutive ambivalence towards the market. Market metafiction has become a more overt and prevalent mode in British and American fiction as market pressures in the literary field have themselves intensified in ways discussed in the Introduction.

We can see elements of this form of self-reflexivity in a series of styles or tendencies within the extended historical span of postmodern fiction: their major phases follow a sequential pattern, albeit with significant overlaps. In what follows, I first discuss impulses towards market metafiction in what we might think of as "classic" or "high" metafiction as it enjoyed its period of greatest visibility in the United States and the United Kingdom in the 1960s and 1970s. I then show how this kind of self-consciousness figures in the heyday (running roughly from the mid-1970s to the mid-1990s) of splicings between experimental and popular genre modes often defined in terms of a hybrid "Avant-Pop" style and in reckonings with pop-cultural stereotypes of Black life by African American writers. In the next section, I consider how an increasingly acute awareness of market pressures factors into the emergence, through the 1990s and 2000s, of a partial resistance to earlier waves of postmodernism under the banners of sincerity, "postirony," and a retooled realism. And finally I examine how the demands of the literary marketplace have been internalized in the "genre turn" among nominally "advanced" or "literary" authors that has been one of the most marked features of the literary scene post-2008. Of course, all of these movements could be (and have been) the subjects of book-length studies in their own right. While I cover an expanse of literary-historical ground in this chapter – necessarily doing so often only in outline – my main goals are very specific: firstly, to suggest that, while it may be better to speak of a variety of postmodernism*s*, the advanced contemporary novel has been continually shaped by the defining postmodernist challenge of the inescapability of the market after modernism; secondly, to draw attention to key elements of late twentieth- and early twenty-first-century literary history that will be examined in greater detail in subsequent chapters; and finally and most importantly, to demonstrate that today's widespread deployment of "market metafiction" did not come from nowhere but can be connected to important precedents and antecedents in the recent past.

While I would argue that the styles I range over in this chapter constitute the major varieties of postmodernism in fiction (or of fiction produced under the dominance of postmodernist cultural conditions), I certainly would not claim that they exhaust that variety. I should also note straightaway the omission from what follows of two narrative styles that rightly figure prominently in many accounts of the postmodernist novel: magical realism (largely a phenomenon of the 1980s and 1990s in Anglophone literary culture) and the "encyclopaedic" or "systems" novel that has persisted as a recognizable form (especially in the United States) from the 1970s to the present (while intersecting in various ways with the styles I discuss below). I set these topics aside here because I focus upon them elsewhere in this book: Chapter 3 reads Iain Sinclair's work in the context of magical realism, while Part III is devoted to examining a range of examples of the encyclopaedic/systems mode.

"The Indulgent Megalomania of Growth"? "High" Metafiction in the Market

Elements of market metafiction are evident, first of all, in the work of the generation of metafictionists or "surfictionists" who achieved prominence in Britain and the United States in the 1960s and 1970s, forming what is now recognizable as the first wave of Anglophone literary postmodernism: the likes of B.S. Johnson, Muriel Spark, John Fowles, and Christine Brooke-Rose in the United Kingdom; and John Barth, William H. Gass, Raymond Federman, Robert Coover, Gilbert Sorrentino, and Ronald Sukenick in the United States. For these authors, metafiction is primarily an aesthetic and philosophical matter:

fictional writing that (in Patricia Waugh's canonical definition) "self-consciously and systematically draws attention to its status as an artefact in order to pose questions about the relationship between fiction and reality."[4]

The metafictionists' rejections of attempts to create consistent, verisimilar, three-dimensional narrative worlds tended to position the nineteenth-century realist novel as their explicit antagonist (as, most famously, in Fowles' *The French Lieutenant's Woman* [1969]), though they also implicitly reacted to the renewed dominance of realism on both sides of the Atlantic in the 1940s and 1950s. In the immediate post-war period, with most of the major figures of Anglophone modernism dead, modernist experimentation, whose centrality to elite conceptions of the literary had always been at odds with its relatively limited presence in the wider literary field, could no longer even command vanguard status. Instead, it was increasingly seen – by a new generation of novelists and critics – as ultimately trapped (in the words of one major neorealist exponent, the English novelist C.P. Snow) in a "cul-de-sac."[5] Understanding their project as in many ways one of rejuvenating and radicalizing modernist experimentation, the metafictional writers who emerged in the 1960s were shaped not only by an opposition to what they saw as realism's dissembling narrative techniques and faulty philosophical premises, then, but also by an awareness that realism had tightened its grip on literary culture, and the literary marketplace, in the previous two decades.

While realism remained to a large extent the novel's established and accepted mode, the expansionary publishing conditions of the 1960s and early 1970s were relatively hospitable to authors experimenting with alternative narrative forms, especially in the United Kingdom. It was, for example, one of the new paperback presses, Panther Books (in association with the venerable house Secker & Warburg), that published one of the high points of post-war British experimentalism, B. S. Johnson's randomly re-orderable "novel-in-a-box" *The Unfortunates* in 1969. While a succession of mainstream publishers supported Johnson's work throughout his career (Secker & Warburg even, unusually, putting him on a salary for three years), readers were less responsive, and his lack of commercial success was a factor in his depression and eventual suicide in 1973.[6] The last of Johnson's novels to appear in his lifetime, *Christie Malry's Own Double-Entry*, released by another leading publisher, William Collins, in the year of his death, foregrounds these concerns and pushes metafiction as conventionally understood (and as practised by Johnson more militantly, perhaps, than by any of his peers) in the direction of what I have defined as "market metafiction."

Conscious that "economics dictate to an extent sometimes not fully realised the real (as distinct from the imaginary) possibilities open to one," the eponymous protagonist of Johnson's novel seeks to "place himself next to the money," first by working at a bank and later by taking a job as an accountant at a confectionary company; at both places of work, the background chatter is of a "share value which ha[s] oscillated oddly" or "the state of the share market."[7] Christie's elaborate system of revenge based on the methods of double-entry bookkeeping – methods central, as John Lanchester puts it in his introduction, to "the whole structure of capitalism" (vii) – is abruptly curtailed (though not before it has turned mass-homicidal) when he develops cancer and, in short order, dies, bringing the novel to a seemingly premature conclusion. In the closing section of the book, the narrator appears in order to commiserate directly with Christie and gives signs of having the same concerns about "earning a living" (12) as his ill-fated character. In the Introduction to his collection of prose pieces *Aren't You Rather Young to be Writing Your Memoirs?*, also published in 1973, Johnson laments that "just as there seem to be so many writers imitating the act of being nineteenth-century novelists, so there must be large numbers imitating the act of being nineteenth-century readers."[8] Elsewhere in this collection, Johnson imagines a narrator being slipped a copy of the *XLCR Mechanical Plot-Finding Formula*, which guarantees "popular acclaim" provided that one follows a highly conventional set of "XLCR rules."[9] *Christie Malry*, however, draws to a close with an even more despondent view of the possibility of establishing a viable readership for ambitious contemporary fiction. Here, the narrator acknowledges that "it does not seem to me possible to take this novel much further," endorsing Christie's view that, in the face of competition from "the theatre or cinema," the novel should now "try simply to be Funny, Brutalist, and Short" (165). It's fair to say that *Christie Malry* has been all of these things, but it has also – unpromisingly, from a commercial point of view – "been a continuous dialogue with form," as its protagonist notes, meaning that discussions of its effects on its reader are premature, for they assume "there is a reader" for the book, when in fact "most people won't read it" (166, 165).

The novel's pessimism about the extent of its own readership proved to be all-too accurate (at least in the short term), and by 1973 the economic conditions that had made texts like Johnson's viable publishing propositions, even in the absence of large sales, were under strain too. As Randall

Stevenson describes, "English fiction's most innovative or postmodernist phase coincided significantly with publishers' relative freedom from financial pressures, in the 1960s and early 1970s," but "the crisis in the book trade which followed the economic downturn" triggered by the oil shock of 1973 "made publishers reluctant to risk novels-in-boxes or other unfamiliar forms of writing."[10] The critic Bryan Appleyard recalled: "the oil crisis indicated the fragility of our little world"; in these changed economic circumstances, "rarefied" fictional experiment was "the last thing that was required" – "randomly ordered novels reeked of the indulgent megalomania of growth."[11]

Even before the oil crisis, a group of American novelists committed to metafictional and other experimental modes had become frustrated with seeing their books go out of print and with the challenges of finding publishers for new work. So intractable did these problems seem that the group aimed to establish a wholly different platform for their writing, which they named the Fiction Collective. Announcing the launch of the Collective in a 1974 column for the *New York Times Book Review* that would become something of a manifesto, Ronald Sukenick, probably the most prominent member, explained that the new venture would set itself apart from the publishing industry, "a mass market industry that cannot afford to produce small, reasonably priced editions of quality fiction." The Collective was "not a publishing house," he insisted, "but a 'not-for-profit' cooperative," "the first of its kind in this country, in which writers make all business decisions and do all editorial and copy work." Though its university-housed, government grant-supported business model was not always stable (its National Endowment for the Arts [NEA] funding fell victim to a Reagan-era backlash against experimental writing), the Collective would provide an important alternative publication channel for "non-traditional" fiction during the 1970s and for much of the 1980s, bringing out books by Sukenick, Raymond Federman, Russell Banks, Fanny Howe, and Gerald Vizenor, among many others.[12]

The obstacles faced by writers of formally innovative fiction who continued to pursue conventional forms of publication were well testified to by Gilbert Sorrentino's 1979 novel *Mulligan Stew*, an especially overt early exhibitor of the impulses I've defined under the term "market metafiction." Sorrentino had been the beneficiary of NEA support while writing the book but faced considerable difficulties in placing it with a publisher: it was rejected by nearly thirty trade presses, "including all the major New York houses," because they "doubted its commercial viability, fearing that a book so long and so literary would not earn enough profits to justify production costs."[13] The manuscript was eventually accepted by Grove Press (a crucial incubator – if also in certain ways incorporator – of avant-garde impulses in the United States in the period).[14] Grove's legendary owner, Barney Rosset, urged Sorrentino to preface the text with his accumulated rejection letters, but Sorrentino instead composed his own set of parody letters, which allowed him to articulate all the more clearly how he perceived his novel to be positioned in relation to the publishing industry's prevailing norms. One letter, for example, laments that "the sheer *cost* of doing your book is insurmountable for a small, struggling house like this one," which "must show a profit to the parent company" before "even consider[ing] getting behind a project like yours"; in the meantime it must focus on books that "are not only *good*, but have definite market appeal."[15] Another refers to the unshakeable "economic reasons" for not "doing" the book, while a third suggests that "this novel within a novel within a novel . . . would find few readers, I fear" (n.p.) The preface ends with a note, supposedly from Grove's distributor, explaining that it will be exercising its option not to handle the title because it "was not considered by our legal staff to be of sufficient merit to warrant the additional investment in inventory. 'Merit' in this context to be spelled 'bottom line,' if you follow me" (n.p). As Abram Foley suggests, via this preface Sorrentino "turns his novel into a meta-critical reflection on the extraneous pressures – primarily the publishing industry – exerted on the intra- and intertextual working of literary history."[16]

Sorrentino's preface not only foregrounds his novel's self-conscious awareness of its own marginality in market terms but also announces the major theme of the text – its concern with the tension between innovative fictional ambition and commercial imperatives. The main narrative strand presents the literary rivalry between the narrator and his brother-in-law: the former styles himself as a "determinedly avant-garde, experimental" writer who has "labored over my obscure non-selling novels" but is now convinced that his latest work-in-progress "will establish me as the most interesting spokesman for the American avant-garde, and for Sur-fiction, as well as Ur-fiction, and Post-Modern fiction to boot" (58, 225, 358); meanwhile, he disparages his nemesis for "set[ting] his sights on commercial success" and churning out "cash trash" and "pure hackwork" (28, 225, 250). As the extended sections of the narrator's novel-in-progress (which comprise much of *Mulligan Stew*'s 450-page length) make painfully clear, however, the narrator's purportedly "avant-garde," "experimental" project is in fact little more than an inept stab at mimicking the conventions of popular genre fiction – primarily those of the detective or mystery genre.

Sorrentino's writing in these sections is mercilessly parodic and deconstructive, resulting in a surfeit of jarringly off-key pseudo-genre-style prose, which no doubt contributed to publishers' near-consensus on the commercial unviability of the project. At the same time, however, the novel testifies, through the figure of its hapless narrator, to what I'd call a recurrent "will to genre" in postmodern – and more broadly contemporary – fiction. The narrator admits, for example, to his urge to give full rein to a genre impulse and "compose a Gothic romance 'by Viola Tremble' – the moors sullen under lightning, the cold and eerie house, the howling dogs, the shadows, the rain, the secret in the attic, or the cellar, or the greenhouse, or the maze." As Sorrentino's narrator acknowledges, part of what's at stake in this attraction to a reliable set of genre tropes may be "simply" a desire for "financial success" (57–58).

Internalizing the "Great Divide": Avant-Pop and Genre Appropriation

We see more overt evidence of this will to genre in the concerted blurring of boundaries between "advanced" or experimental narrative forms and popular, mass-market modes that is such a feature of what's typically thought of as postmodernism in fiction as it developed between the 1970s and the 1990s. The emergence of this style was impelled, at least in part, by a sense that the commitment to a renewal of modernist difficulty by the leading experimentalists of the 1960s and 1970s risked resulting in fiction that was excessively austere and alienating for its potential readers. Perhaps unsurprisingly, these strategies of genre appropriation and recombination were especially liable to give rise to the kinds of reflexivity I call "market metafiction." Such work also displayed a growing tendency to envisage the literary marketplace through the prism of the financial markets, reflecting the financial sector's mounting influence on the cultural field, and the wider economy, from the 1970s.

For a number of influential theorists (most obviously Fredric Jameson, but also the likes of Andreas Huyssen and David Harvey), the blending of "high" and "low" is nothing less than the defining feature of postmodernism as such.[17] Such foundational theoretical accounts tend to see postmodernism as characterized by a state of giddy, indiscriminate revelry in mass-market genre forms following modernism's (supposed) insistence on a "great divide" between high art and mass or commercial culture. Closer inspection of the kinds of texts that would seem to invite such a reading, however, often reveals the re-inscription of something like this divide *within* the text itself, so that while genre forms are appropriated and exploited for their narrative (and commercial) potential, they are at the same time interrogated, critiqued, and deconstructed. If, as Larry McCaffery argued in the mid-1990s, a postmodernist embrace of mass culture could be seen in its "purest" form in Pop Art, then much post-modernist fiction displayed an *Avant-Pop* sensibility, combining "Pop Art's focus on consumer goods and mass media with the avant-garde's spirit of subversion and emphasis on radical formal innovation."[18] Emblematic writers in this vein would include the likes of Kathy Acker, Bret Easton Ellis (whose work I consider in Chapter 2), Samuel R. Delany, Paul Auster, Mark Leyner, Lynne Tillman, Mark Amerika, and the major cyberpunk exponents William Gibson, Bruce Sterling, and Rudy Rucker. The Avant-Pop aesthetic was spearheaded from the late 1980s by a rebooted Fiction Collective – Fiction Collective Two – under its new Black Ice Books imprint. Envisaged – as the Collective's Managing Director, Curtis White, put it – as "a merging of the avant-garde with the popular," Black Ice's output would go on to achieve considerable success on both critical and commercial fronts during the 1990s.[19]

Kathy Acker – a contributor to the first *Avant-Pop* anthology, published by Black Ice in 1993 – epitomizes this mode especially clearly. Having established a reputation in the New York art world and Downtown literary scene through a series of cryptic self- and small press-published texts, Acker had decided by the mid-1970s that (as Chris Kraus puts it in her recent biography) "she didn't want to be stuck in the ghetto of 'experimental' writing." Instead, "she began looking towards nineteenth-century novels and contemporary mass-market paperbacks as models that might be adapted and then synthesized with her own free-form diary texts."[20] Acker's 1984 novel *My Death My Life by Pier Paolo Pasolini* typifies this strategy, studiedly adopting "the genre conventions of the detective story" while challenging the tendency of "conventional detective novels [to] inscribe a world inherently reasonable, logical, and determinate" – not least by making the eponymous filmmaker and poet the posthumous investigator of his own murder.[21]

In the process, Acker's narrator (of shifting and often indeterminate gender, but – as ever in her fiction – displaying a strongly autobiographical persona) repeatedly reflects on the relationship between the different forms of value to which the text's hybrid narrative form appeals. Posing the question "are art and monetary profit compatible?" for example, the narrative voice suggests that if "writing is the making (of values)" and money a kind of "nonvalue," then it is doubtful whether the two forms of value "can occur simultaneously."²² Later, it asserts that at a time when "a book no longer has anything to do with literary history," "the history of literarture [sic] you're taught in school is for shit" and mere "sellability and control . . . are the considerations that give the art object its value" (251). Elsewhere, it invokes Adorno to define writing as that which "expresses the individual, the unique, the utopian, the critical, the new, the innovative vision" and hence "the opposite of . . . media advertising commerciality or the market" (297). But, turning to Marx, it pessimistically claims: "when I work, there's the actual value of my work and the market value of my work; the problem is that the market value is increasingly, now fully, the determinant of the work's total value" (301). Acker's thinking about art, writing, and the market continually oscillated between these polarized positions in a private philosophical dialogue to which the language of finance readily lent itself. In an essay from 1990, for example, she describes lurching between a conception of art as "an angel miraculously living amid the greed and zombielike behaviors of those outside the art world, the faceless business-suits who crowded into Wall Street every morning," and a realization that "Art was simply stock in a certain stock market."²³

While the Avant-Pop aesthetic was grounded in a specifically American cultural and media landscape, non-American authors attuned to similar influences deployed comparable strategies in the period. The most obvious British example is Martin Amis, whose novels of the 1980s and 1990s demonstrate a particularly deep engagement with the crime thriller genre – especially in its hardboiled, American form – even as they also show the influence of an older generation of metafictional writers. (Another British case would be Anne Billson, whose deployments of the Gothic mode I discuss in Chapter 2.) In Amis's *Money: A Suicide Note* (1984), for example, doubts about the value of money in a disorientating and conspiratorial post-gold window, post-oil crisis world segue into doubts about the value of *Money* – the noirish Amis novel we're reading – and about *Good Money* (later *Bad Money*), the gangland screenplay drafted by a writer-character in the narrative named Martin Amis. The novel becomes, then, a self-conscious meditation on what it takes for a text (whether monetary, literary, or cinematic) to achieve the stability of meaning necessary for its successful circulation in the marketplace (a question to which I return in Part II).²⁴

The characteristic concerns and strategies of market metafiction are all the clearer in Amis's *The Information* (1995). Drawing much of its suspense and narrative drive from an underworld subplot concerning kidnap, extortion, and murder, *The Information* is at the same time a highly self-reflexive exploration of the international publishing industry, in which the two central writer-characters are both, as Amis acknowledges, versions of himself,[25] and the narrator's overtly authorial identity (initials M.A.; nickname Mart) remind us that the text's reflections on writing relate as much to its own form and style as to its characters' literary productions.[26] The novel portrays a publishing world in which, on the one hand, "a little magazine called *The Little Magazine*" (41) sinks into ever deeper penury, while, on the other, a successful novelist attends a lunch party comprised of a "financier, male columnist, female columnist, publisher, newspaper diarist, newspaper profilist, photographer, captain of industry, [and] Shadow Minister for the Arts," where the financier – having left his "fellow sharks and vultures ... shivering over their visual display units" in the City – lays out his vision of "the kind of literary magazine ... he [is] prepared to be the financier of," complete with plans to get "some market research underway" (41, 26, 28).

Rather in the manner of Sorrentino's *Mulligan Stew*, the intimate yet mutually antagonistic writers at the centre of *The Information* enact a dialectic between commercial and artistic ambitions. One writes "cute," "bland," "transparen[t]" bestsellers, in which "everything is smooth and everything fits," and for which the press materials consist of "quotes, not from the critics but from the balance sheets": these are novels in the category that *The Information* calls "trex" – the domain of "fat financial thrillers, chunky chillers and tublike tinglers," books to be consumed on plane journeys in order to "escape from the pressures facing the contemporary entrepreneur" (43, 80, 139, 289). The other writer, meanwhile, is a "marooned modernist" committed to "fanatically difficult modern prose" who surpasses the ultimate "genius novel[ist]," Joyce, in being "a drag" not merely "half the time," but "all the time," the "octuple time scheme and ... sixteen unreliable narrators" of his work-in-progress, *Untitled*, inducing disturbing neurological conditions in the very few readers who attempt to tackle it (170–71, 121, 193, 209–10, 237). A sense that *The Information* – part pacey crime entertainment; part cerebral, elliptical exploration of writing, death, and identity – was enacting its own themes was heightened by the media spectacle surrounding its publication (Amis's controversial change of agents; his half-million-pound advance; the book's huge publicity campaign; its immediate appearance at the top of the *Sunday Times* bestseller list), which offended many commentators' feelings of propriety about the extent of serious fiction's imbrication with market dynamics.[27]

In the United States, the forces shaping the Avant-Pop aesthetic were felt especially keenly – though with a different inflection – by Black and ethnic minority writers. In certain respects, the growing attunement of the publishing industry to market signals over the closing decades of the twentieth century was a boon for writers of colour. Despite the ongoing lack of minority representation at major publishers, the sheer fact that by this time there was plainly a substantial market for multi-ethnic writing – not only among minority readers themselves (spending on books by African Americans increased by an estimated 71 per cent between 1990 and 2000, for example), but also (for books appropriately packaged and presented) among white buyers too – meant that the industry was virtually obligated to diversify its lists (leading to initiatives such as the establishment of imprints at HarperCollins, Random House, and other presses that specifically focused on work by African American writers).[28]

Even for a Black writer who was the very epitome of a ludic postmodernist – Ishmael Reed – the literary marketplace had long represented an opportunity for cultural dissemination, rather than a threat to experimental literary ambition. Reed was instrumental in establishing three significant publishing enterprises in the 1970s and even conceived of a plan (never realized) for an "Afro-American Cultural Bank" that would "make loans" and "investments" supporting "worthwhile projects" in "television, theater, writing, etc." Espousing a philosophy of "free enterprise," Reed urged African American writers to abandon "the myth that business and art do not mix."[29] Of Reed, Cannon, & Johnson Communications Co., the multicultural publishing house he launched with two friends in 1972, Reed remarked unapologetically: "We're a business, we're not trying to change society overnight; we're trying to sell books, discover new talent, and we're not limiting our market."[30] As Nicholas Donofrio has recently argued, Reed's belief in the inherent link between the free circulation of commodities in the market and freedom as such is clearly manifest in his novels of the period (*Yellow Back Radio Broke-Down* [1969], *Mumbo Jumbo* [1972], and *Flight to Canada* [1976]). Donofrio suggests that "Reed's inveterate antiauthoritarianism, coupled with his cheerleading for businesses and cultural diversity, was largely compatible with the antistate, promarket neoliberal policies that would soon restructure the culture industries, along with many other areas of American life," even as he staunchly opposed the creep of corporate conglomeration and advocated the "decentralization" of publishing and the media.[31]

A similarly complex position has been occupied for several decades by an African American novelist whose importance to the development of postmodern fiction is arguably even greater than Reed's: Toni Morrison. As a senior editor at Random House from the late 1960s to the early 1980s (where she was the first Black woman to hold such a position), Morrison used her proximity to the centres of industry power to open up opportunities for publication, media exposure, and wide readership to African American women writers such as Gayl Jones and Toni Cade Bambara. As an author, Morrison also displayed a willingness to enter into the dynamics of the mass media and the mass market, most obviously through her close involvement with the Book Club segment of the internationally syndicated *Oprah Winfrey Show*, a major shaping force on the US literary marketplace during its fifteen-year run from 1996 to 2011. Morrison made three appearances on Oprah's Book Club (while Winfrey produced and starred in the 1998 adaptation of Morrison's 1987 classic *Beloved*). John K. Young suggests that "the alliance between Morrison's canonical status and Winfrey's commercial power ... enable[ed] Morrison to reach a broad, popular audience while also being marketed as artistically important"; successfully combining "'popularity' and 'difficulty,'" Morrison emerged as "the most dramatic example of postmodernism's merger between canonicity and commercialism."[32]

The growing role of market considerations in publishers' decision-making over recent decades has had the welcome effect, then, of opening up new spaces for writers of colour in the literary field; at least some such writers, moreover, have been able to access mainstream commercial success while continuing to produce boldly innovative and challenging work. A problem that many African American writers, in particular, have been quick to register, however, is that while publishers may be newly receptive to their writing, that receptivity is often conditional on their writing conforming to a narrow and reductive set of assumptions about the nature of "Black experience." As Young describes:

> The predominantly white publishing industry reflects and often reinforces the racial divide that has always defined American society, representing "blackness" as a one-dimensional cultural experience. Minority texts are edited, produced, and advertised as representing the "particular" black experience to a "universal," implicitly white (although itself ethnically constructed) audience. The American publishing industry, that is, has historically inscribed a mythologized version of the "black experience" onto all works marked by race.[33]

Novels by leading African American postmodernists such as Clarence Major (*My Amputations* [1986]), Gloria Naylor (*Mama Day* [1988]), John

Edgar Wideman (*Philadelphia Fire* [1990]), and Paul Beatty (*The White Boy Shuffle* [1996], *Tuff* [2000], and *Slumberland* [2008]) show their authors internalizing exactly this issue, as their protagonists reflect on what can be said to constitute "authentic" Black experience, how such experience might be adequately represented, and how these representations are liable to be simplified and distorted as they circulate in the wider culture. (In a pointed footnote, Beatty's *Slumberland* describes Oprah Winfrey as being "in the process of buying the rights to the life story of every black American born between 1642 and 1968 as a way of staking claim to being the legal and sole embodiment of the black experience from slavery to civil rights.")[34]

By the late 1990s, one set of representations of African American life had assumed a cultural centrality out of all proportion to their actual representativeness or typicality – namely those associated with what Rachel Farebrother calls the "ghetto glamour" aesthetic: spectacles of extreme violence, criminality, and familial dysfunction played out among disadvantaged Black inhabitants of the American inner city.[35] In his 2001 satirical novel *Erasure*, Percival Everett highlights (in a manner typical of market metafiction) the pressure on African American cultural producers to exaggerate the social problems of Black urban America to the point of caricature for voyeuristic consumption by a predominantly white audience, and how such pressure militates against the exploration of other forms of literary expression on the part of Black authors.

Erasure's narrator and protagonist, Thelonius "Monk" Ellison, bears the names of two major figures of Black US cultural history, and is (like Everett himself) an African American writer who maintains the support of an academic post (Monk is a professor at UCLA; Everett at the University of Southern California) while writing works of experimental fiction that are generally published by small independent presses and whose success tends to be measured more in prizes and respectful reviews than sales (a list of Monk's honours and awards – closely resembling his author's – appears in the novel).[36] Monk writes novels that are, by his own admission, "dense, obscure," and "often inaccessible" and "not commercial enough to make any real money" (5, 251, 48). His most recent manuscript has accrued no fewer than twenty rejections (49, 69). Like Sorrentino's *Mulligan Stew*, *Erasure* includes rejection notes from unenthusiastic editors. "*Who wants to read this shit?*" one asks; "*It's too difficult for the market . . . Come on, a novel in which Aristophanes and Euripides kill a younger, more talented dramatist, then contemplate the death of metaphysics?*" (48; italics in original). Another considers the book "too dense," and a third avers that "the market won't support this sort of thing" (69). The novel or novel-like work ("I guess you'd call it a novel" [8]) that Monk is embarking upon as *Erasure* opens hardly seems likely to improve his commercial prospects: a "parod[y] of French poststructuralists" that subjects Roland Barthes' *S/Z* to the same obsessively close analysis that Barthes' own book performs on Balzac's *Sarrasine*, the text (an extract from which appears in *Erasure* [18–22] having previously been published under Everett's name in a 1999 issue of *Callaloo*) is a predictably challenging read.

Monk is accustomed to being told that the problem with his novels is that they are "not *black* enough" (4; emphasis in original). One reviewer is quoted as finding an earlier novel of Monk's to be "*finely crafted, with . . . rich language, and subtle play with the plot*" while being at a loss "*to under-stand what this reworking of Aeschylus' The Persians has to do with the African American experience*" (4; italics in original). Monk similarly recalls an agent telling him that he "could sell many books" if he'd "forget about writing retellings of Euripides and settle down to write the true, gritty real stories of black life" (4). Such supposedly "true" and "real" but in fact exaggerated and unrepresentative "stories of black life" appear in a novel that Monk encounters early in *Erasure*: the "runaway-bestseller-soon-to-be -a-major-motion-picture" (247) *We's Lives in Da Ghetto* by Juanita Mae Jenkins. A middle-class Black woman from Ohio who landed a post-college job at a New York publishing house (a winking reference to the Ohio-born Morrison, perhaps), Jenkins has worked up her childhood experience of spending "a couple of days" visiting relatives in Harlem into what she earnestly describes – in an interview on a barely fictionalized version of Oprah's Book Club – as a novel "about our people" (61). Initiating another tale of literary rivalry – in which contempt for a fellow writer's output co-exists with rage and jealousy at their commercial suc-cess – Monk sets out to write a parody of narratives of Black urban crisis (whose most obvious real-life models are Richard Wright's *Native Son* [1940] [see *Erasure*, 70] and Sapphire's *Push* [1996] – both major bestsellers in their time, and producers of templates that many Black writers subse-quently felt pressure to follow).

Monk attributes the resulting text – "a book on which I knew I could never put my name" (70) – to the alias Stagg R. Leigh (after the turn-of-the -century folk hero Stagger Lee). Presented in full (73–150) between Monk's framing narrations, *My Pafology* (later retitled *Fuck*) gratuitously repro-duces every "ghetto glamour" stereotype and cliché as it follows a poor African American teenager, Van Go Jenkins, the unsupportive father of four children by different mothers, as he careers nihilistically around Los

Angeles, spouting a torrent of racist, misogynist, and homophobic rhetoric, getting into violent confrontations with other Black men, sexually assaulting a succession of women, and eventually murdering a Korean grocery store worker. Monk is appalled but – running short of cash – also grudgingly gratified when the publishers to whom his agent has reluctantly sent the manuscript of *My Pafology* "can't see it's a parody" (151) and Random House offers an advance of six hundred thousand dollars (155). Monk's self-described "offensive, poorly written, racist, and mindless" book (289) goes on to receive full page ads in the *New York Times* and *Washington Post* (179), to attract a three-million-dollar bid for movie rights (234), to feature on the Oprah-esque *Kenya Dunston Show* (263, 274–80), and to reach number one on the *Times* bestseller list (287) while being praised by the paper's reviewer as "so honest, so raw, so down-and-dirty-gritty, so real" that it is "more like the evening news" than a novel (288). *Erasure* culminates with *Fuck* winning the "National Book Association" (read National Book Foundation) Book Award, "the most prestigious book award in the nation" (287), and with an unhinged Monk (who has served as a judge for the prize and tried to sway his colleagues away from "his" book) making for the podium for a moment of humiliating and highly public unmasking.

Erasure very clearly draws attention, then, to the especially narrow gateway to mainstream publication that faces writers of colour, and the factors that tend to make gatekeepers resistant to minority writing that appears to privilege formal experimentalism over "gritty" documentary realism. Narrated by a self-described writer of "experimental stories and novels" (251) and written by an author typically described in the same terms, *Erasure* – with its book-within-a-book structure, its extended attempt at a prose style more poststructuralist than poststructuralism itself, and its numerous other opaque and incongruous textual fragments (e.g. 44–45, 56, 68, 176–77, 192–202, 211, 217, 248, 286–87) – seems in many ways to enact the very challenges to conventional narrative form that it endorses. That endorsement isn't uncomplicated, however, as becomes apparent at a meeting of the "*Nouveau Roman* Society" where Monk presents his bid to out-Barthes Barthes. Monk is dismissive of the "circle of *innovative* writers" who make up the bulk of the Society's membership – writers who "survived the sixties by publishing each others' stories in their periodicals and each others' books collectively, thus amassing publications, so achieving tenure at their various universities, and establishing a semblance of credibility in the so-called real world" (14; emphasis in original). The leader of this circle is an absurd character given to quoting the opening line of *Gravity's Rainbow* at random (42) and self-aggrandizingly insistent on himself as the embodiment of "postmodern fiction" understood as a true "avant-garde movement" (43). His puffed-up rhetoric – "I have unsettled [readers'] historical, cultural, and psychological assumptions by disrupting their comfortable relationship between words and things. I have brought to a head the battle between language and reality" (44) – is treated almost as satirically as the stylized "ghetto talk" of Jenkins' *We's Lives in Da Ghetto*.

While *Erasure* looks askance at the kinds of aesthetic and intellectual claims (as well as the publishing practices) associated with the "high" metafiction of groups like the first-generation Fiction Collective, *Everett's* novel also distances itself from the showily populist tendencies of the Avant-Pop style, substituting a Frankfurt School-style contempt for "popular culture" (epitomized by Jenkins' novel and felt by Monk as a deadening weight that "land[s] on me daily, or hourly" [34]) for Avant-Pop's playful push-and-pull of deconstruction and appropriation. *Erasure's* core aesthetic sympathies in fact seem to be most clearly manifest in the sensitively depicted, affecting, and broadly realist portrait of family crisis and upheaval that is interwoven with its literary world satire: a narrative thread that takes in Monk's father's suicide, his mother's worsening Alzheimer's, his sister's murder, his brother's coming out and consequent marital breakdown, and the discovery of an unknown half-sister. In its concern to portray rounded, believable, emotionally involving characters, in the surprising resemblance of its family drama plot to the narrative of Jonathan Franzen's *The Corrections* (published the same year), and in its observation that it was Monk's one "'realistic' novel" that – unlike the rest of his oeuvre – "sold rather well (69), *Erasure* intersects with another key development in contemporary fiction, to which I now turn.

Full Disclosure: Trust, Realism, Sincerity

During the 1990s and 2000s, the forms of market metafiction I have been discussing became increasingly prevalent in British and American novels (as much of what follows in this book will explore). The spread of this mode, though, was accompanied to a significant degree by a movement against both the forbiddingly experimental narratives of the 1960s and 1970s metafictionists and the pop culture-immersed exponents of Avant-Pop and affiliated styles. As a number of critics have suggested, this movement in the advanced or "cutting edge" fiction of the 1990s and 2000s could be understood – paradoxically – as in certain key respects a conservative one, tending in the direction of realism and a concomitant revival of belief or sincerity as categories of literary experience.[37] As we've seen, in the post-war period realism has never been seriously threatened as the dominant form of "literary" fiction in market terms (a dominance entrenched, in the late-twentieth-century United States, by a re-orientation of state funding of literature towards realist – understood as populist – styles).[38] The extent to which realism has been embraced or rejected by writers ambitiously seeking to usher the novel into its next phase of artistic development has varied considerably, however, with the period since the 1990s marking one of its periodic revivals.

This shift is most evident in the work of important recent American novelists such as David Foster Wallace (discussed in Chapter 4), Jonathan Franzen (whose work I address in chapters 4 and 5), Dave Eggers, Jeffrey Eugenides, Dana Spiotta, George Saunders, and Rachel Kushner. Writers' self-conscious dramatization of "a coherent generation's movement away from their ancestors," in Stephen Burn's words,[39] has been more overt in the United States than elsewhere, but a comparable tendency can be seen in the work of some key British novelists, including Zadie Smith (a close affiliate of some of her American contemporaries), Alan Hollinghurst, Nicola Barker, Alan Warner, and Jonathan Coe (who figures in my second chapter). This shift has sometimes been discussed in terms of a "post-postmodern" turn, but Burn's periodization is, I think, more helpful in referring to a group of "second-generation postmoderns" (with meta/surfiction, Avant-Pop, and other related tendencies understood as jointly forming a first or "high" postmodernist generation).[40] Emphasizing the degree of continuity involved in this realignment is important because, as a number of critics have emphasized, the writers in question have clearly internalized the lessons of earlier waves of postmodern fiction, even as they aim to move beyond a knee-jerk self-cancelling narrative reflexivity or a state of cynicism, irony, and exhaustion induced by over-proximity to mass media culture.[41]

Such work also exhibits continuities with earlier forms of postmodern fiction insofar as it defines itself in and through the market. Arguing that it was in the 1990s that neoliberalism entered a *sociocultural phase*, subjecting literature and other forms of art ... to a rigorous economic calculus committed to efficient profit-maximization," Mitchum Huehls and Rachel Greenwald Smith note that "David Foster Wallace, Jonathan Franzen, Dave Eggers, and other writers who came to adulthood during the late postmodern period ... often articulated their formal innovations as responses to the literary marketplace, suggesting that reading and writing were activities that should be evaluated according to a market model" (I discuss Franzen's advocacy of this model in Chapter 5).[42] In this way, such work is compatible with what Smith elsewhere calls "compromise aesthetics" – a position valorizing contemporary literature's "efforts to produce a compromise between experimentalism and convention; difficulty and readability; and the underground and the mass market" – which must, she suggests, "be read in the context of the rise of neoliberalism ... over the past three decades."[43]

For Lee Konstantinou, "postironic" authors such as Wallace and Eggers share a deep investment in the idea of belief: to this way of thinking, writers should be willing to eschew the "self-consciousness and hip fatigue" of "the old postmodern insurgents," even at the "risk [of] accusations of ... over-credulity" (as Wallace puts it in his celebrated essay "E Unibus Pluram: Television and U.S. Fiction" [1993/1997]), while readers should be given every encouragement to believe in the textual worlds they encounter.[44] These strategies, I'd suggest, are central to such writers' rapprochement with the market, for (as I show in Part II) the solicitation of belief is the core condition of a market logic that governs not only the literary marketplace, but contemporary financial markets too.

Postironic authors' "idiosyncratic respect for the suspension of disbelief" is bound up both with their "return to some kind of realism" (as Robert McLaughlin puts it) and with a wider "reality hunger" evident (as David Shields suggests) in a predilection for confessional and memoiristic forms.[45] Thus postironists "try to map fictional narratives onto extratextual foundations" to help readers "believe in a specific reality beyond fiction's fourth wall," in Konstantinou's words.[46] In the process, they deploy "credulous metafiction" – writing that asks "not that we become aware of the fictiveness of [the] fiction, the artifice of the artificer, but rather that we believe in the total, genuine honesty ... of the author" – or, in a similar way, they offer "nonfiction that uses anxious metacommentary to tell the truth."[47]

These forms of credulity-inducing metatextuality are often connected to versions of what I call market metafiction. In Chapter 4, we'll see instances of this convergence in Wallace's *The Pale King* (2011), but we could equally point to another landmark of postirony (or New Sincerity, or second-generation postmodernism): *A Heartbreaking Work of Staggering Genius* (2000), Eggers's bestselling memoir recounting his efforts to raise his younger brother following the deaths, mere months apart, of his parents from cancer. Konstantinou and other critics have attended closely to the ways in which Eggers uses metacommentary not to dispel but to reinforce the truth of his account, as when, in the book's opening "Acknowledgements" section, he intervenes (metatextually) to assure the reader that all of the seemingly "gimmicky" levels of metatextuality in the following pages – levels that recursively signal the author's "aware[ness] of his knowingness about his self-consciousness of self-referentiality" – are there only as "a device, a defense, to obscure the black, blinding, murderous rage and sorrow at the core of this whole story."[48]

What has received less attention, however, is the way in which the text seeks to gain its readers' trust by using metatextual devices to expose the economic conditions of its production and publication.[49] Almost the first words in the Vintage paperback edition, appearing just under the publisher details on the copyright page, for example, insist on making us aware of the text's thoroughly corporate provenance: "Random House [Vintage's parent company] is owned *in toto* by an absolutely huge German company called Bertelsmann A.G. which owns too many things to count or track" (ix). Similarly, in flagging up the book's "themes" in his Acknowledgements section, Eggers admits to the "ECONOMIC, HISTORICAL, AND GEOGRAPHICAL PRIVILEGE" that underwrites the "SOLIPSISM" some readers may detect (xxxvi). This moment is typical of Eggers's attempts to defuse criticism of his project by openly acknowledging aspects of his economic status and motivations that might otherwise be held against him. What is at stake in Eggers's laying bare of his economic position becomes all the clearer when (speaking about himself in the third person) he asserts his view that "not shrinking from the admission of . . . manipulations of his pain for profit . . . immediately absolves him of responsibility for such manipulations' implications or consequences, because being aware of and open to one's motives at least means one is not lying, and no one, except an electorate, likes a liar. We all like full disclosure" (xxxi). In other words, in freely admitting that he is aiming to commodify and capitalize upon his "sorrows" and "suffering" (xxxi), Eggers pre-empts accusations of cynicism or double-dealing, and paradoxically reinforces his and his story's honesty and trustworthiness.

This notion of the desirability of "full disclosure" (a term used in business where a potential conflict of interest may exist) is evident, too, when we're informed that "the author would . . . like to acknowledge what he was paid to write this book" and we're provided with an itemized financial statement consisting of "TOTAL (GROSS) $100,000.00" and various "DEDUCTIONS," including an agent's fee of 15 per cent, as well as taxes, rent, research trips, food, a laser printer, paper and other outgoings, resulting in "NET TOTAL $39,567.68" (xxxix). The inclusion of this list of revenue and expenses furthers Eggers's goal of frankness and transparency concerning the inherently pecuniary nature of his literary enterprise and the mundane material factors on which the pursuit of a "creative" vocation relies: if there's a conflict of interest here between art and commerce, Eggers cannot be accused of not having disclosed it at the outset. At the same time, in highlighting the fact that people (specifically, the hardback publisher, Simon & Schuster) have invested serious money in this book, Eggers bolsters the impression that what he is offering is fundamentally valuable, significant, and worthy of commanding our interest and attention. We are placed in the position of the would-be investor assessing one of the company profit and loss statements that Eggers's inventory so closely resembles, and obliged to conclude that the top line (that $100,000 advance) is solid indeed. Eggers thus assures us that we are justified in our willingness to believe in, and pay for, his book by making it clear that others – whose judgement is presumably informed and discerning – already have.

It is fitting that one of Eggers's "deductions" is "postage" to "send manuscript, for approval, to ... 'Ricky' (San Francisco, investment banker – high-tech IPOs)" (xxxix), for much of the narrative of *A Heartbreaking Work* plays out amid the early stages of the 1990s Bay Area "dot-com" stock market boom. In the book, Eggers describes how the satirical magazine he co-founded, *Might*, occupies office space previously inhabited by the tech bible *Wired* (by this time housed two floors up), and the same South Park neighbourhood as various other "computer rags ... not to mention countless start-up software companies, Web developers, Internet providers" – a combination that leads the press to dub the area "about to explode," this being "1993, when this stuff is new" (169, 170). Eggers vividly describes the optimism and excitement pervading this environment: "the young creative elite of San Francisco are here and only here, do not want to be elsewhere," because "in San Francisco, for better or worse, there are no ideas dumb enough to be squashed" (171). Whether they work at a magazine or "one of these tech start-ups or whatever," Eggers's generation of San Franciscans can't help but "believe" that "this the 'best place on earth'" (171). Here, they "are lucky, feel lucky," perceive "possibility, *prob*ability," a sense "that we are, at least at this point in time ... at the very red molten-hot core of everything, that something is happening here, that ... we are riding a wave, a big wave" (171, 172; emphasis in original). It later occurs to Eggers that San Francisco itself is made of nothing more than "whimsy and faith" (296), and his magazine will eventually try to tap into what the then-Federal Reserve Chairman,

Alan Greenspan, famously called the "irrational exuberance" of the era when it courts investors such as "a guy [who] cashed out of Microsoft and has about three hundred mil he's putting into progressive media" (414).

By the time Eggers was completing his memoir, his own "dumb idea" – his magazine – had folded, but the wider milieu he describes still had a long way to run (not until the spring of 2000, when his book was shooting to the top of the *New York Times* bestseller list, would the Nasdaq Composite index enter into the long nose dive that brought the dot-com boom to its end). *A Heartbreaking Work* is very much a product of this exuberant era – an affirmation that belief in the underlying truth, authenticity, and importance of an undertaking is the key driver of its success in the marketplace. *A Heartbreaking Work* helps us to see, too, how the appeal to belief that is a hallmark of the wider "postirony" or "New Sincerity" generation partakes of what, in Part II of this book, I define as a dominant contemporary market logic of "fiduciary exchangeability" – of faith, trust, and credit as the conditions of circulation in literary and financial markets alike.

Sink or Swim: The Market and the "Genre Turn"

As I also show in detail in Part II, the investment of belief – or at least suspended disbelief – in literature is central to a further key development in contemporary fiction: a renewed turn to genre. As various critics have noted, growing numbers of both established and emerging novelists evidently see opportunities to integrate serious literary ambition with an "eager embrace of the apparatus of once-tabooed genre fiction, in particular the forms of science fiction, horror, and fantasy," as Mark McGurl writes.[50] This convergence is evident in novels by American and British authors including Colson Whitehead, Stephen Marche (a topic of Chapter 2), Jennifer Egan, Junot Díaz, Jonathan Lethem, Chang-rae Lee, Emily St. John Mandel, David Mitchell, Michael Faber, and Kazuo Ishiguro. McGurl suggests that the "genre effects" at work in such texts are the equivalents "of special effects in movies," which remind "distracted readers . . . of fiction's capacity to produce its version of the richly artificial pleasures on offer everywhere else in contemporary mass culture," "show-[ing] off the sheer power of fiction to alter the real."[51]

As Andrew Hoberek suggests, "this phenomenon . . . has its roots in postmodernism's own vaunted openness to mass cultural forms," but "postmodernism's incorporation of such forms into its fundamentally difficult, experimental (that is to say, modernist) project is . . . distinct from the way twenty-first-century novelists have tended to work within popular genres," the latter seeking "to inhabit rather than assimilate" those genres and approaching "genre elements from a realistic rather than an experimental angle."[52] If, in an earlier Avant-Pop mode, the suture between experimental and genre elements was jaggedly visible – a certain antagonism between the two being central to the project of such work – in this more recent wave of fiction the grafting of narrative components often appears close to seamless.

Though initially evident around the turn of the millennium, this trend has gathered considerable momentum over the past decade. Hoberek has suggested that "the 2008 banking collapse and the recession that followed will ultimately prove the most significant events in early twenty-first-century literary history,"[53] and they help to explain this turn to genre in two ways. Firstly, as I'll suggest further shortly, they present representational and narrative challenges that call for the kinds of uncanny forms characteristic of "speculative" genres. And secondly, as we've seen, the economic crises and contractions of the past decade have placed further pressure on writers to tailor their work to market-approved forms. Thus, while it is tempting to suggest (following Hoberek) that with the twenty-first-century conjunction of art fiction and genre fiction we really are beyond postmodernism, we might hesitate about doing so, since the core question of postmodernism as I've been exploring it here – how to deal with the shrinkage of spaces of relative autonomy from the market after the decline of modernism – has only become more pressing in recent years. While the current crop of genre-infused novels may look very different to postmodernist texts as we tend to think of them, then, they're nonetheless shaped, I'd suggest, by this central postmodernist problematic.

Thus, while departing in important ways from the substance of Fredric Jameson's writings on postmodernism, I would very much want to affirm his claim – central to the original "Postmodernism" essay, and reiterated as recently as 2015 – that postmodernism should not simply be understood as a particular set of aesthetic styles and techniques (which some cultural artefacts display and others don't – probably fewer and fewer as time goes on), but rather as a "cultural dominant" that shapes *all* cultural production under its hegemony.[54] The end of postmodernism in this latter sense (Jameson now prefers the term "postmodernity" in order to stress its epochal significance) might not require a transformation as radical as the end of capitalism, but it would I think – for reasons that I've tried to make clear in this book thus far and will underscore in the following chapters – require something like the end of neoliberalism.

McGurl points us towards the question of the market in observing that the recent rise of "genre effects" suggests "a crisis of faith in lyrical realism, in its aesthetic and also, possibly, market potential."[55] As we've seen, the evidence would tend to bear out McGurl's conjecture: if, prior to the late 2000s, to be a "literary" author generally meant being located somewhere between a realist "core" and an experimentalist "margin," then the sharp post-crisis contraction and subsequent flat-lining of the literary/general fiction segment of the fiction market, set against the relative buoyancy of genre fiction sales, provide strong incentives for authors and publishers to re-orientate their output towards genre forms. As an editor at a leading British independent publisher describes the situation, sales "are being pushed to extremes, so that each year there are a handful of runaway hits, a few dozen that sell into five figures, and an increasing majority that feel lucky to reach four figures. Most of the breakout literary books borrow from genre fiction for commercial appeal."[56] Whatever else it is (and, as I've already intimated, it is often able to do significant and interesting formal work) the hybrid literary-genre novel is an effective marketing proposition, because it is able to appeal to both domains while at the same time standing out from the crowd in each.

Such texts' characteristically well-integrated, smoothly consistent narrative forms militate against the overt, frame-breaking self-consciousness of metafiction (in its various forms), yet novels in this vein internalize ambivalence about their relation to the market in other ways. We can see instances of these more sublimated forms of self-consciousness in what is, by common consensus, the exemplary manifestation of the contemporary literary novel's will to genre: Colson Whitehead's 2011 zombie apocalypse narrative, *Zone One*.

The novel's eponymous "zone" is the area of lower Manhattan in which living humans have managed, more or less, to establish a beachhead against the skeletal hordes who elsewhere transmit their zombifying contagion unchecked. Mitchum Huehls suggests that "Whitehead makes it pretty clear that the zombie plague represents, or even allegorizes, the brain-dead homogenization wrought by contemporary capital."[57] At the end of the novel, when Zone One is overrun, for example, the protagonist, a zombie exterminator named Mark Spitz (a nickname – we never learn his real name), sees "the dead [stream] past ... like characters on an electronic ticker in Times Square" and "read[s] their inhuman scroll as an argument: I was here, I am here now, I have existed, I exist still. This is our town."[58] This idea that the zombies – as figures of capitalism (or, more specifically, the finance capitalism of the stock ticker) – are merely reclaiming what was theirs is borne out by numerous features of the text: Zone One occupies an area roughly coterminous with "the crooked streets of the financial district," with its "nerve center" in "an old bank," while in hunting the remaining zombies Mark Spitz and his companions traverse "the floor of a Wall Street conference room" or spaces that were once "great sinks of money and insurance," "global headquarters brimming with junior VPs and heads of accounts," or the meeting places of "coteries of investment bankers" (95, 114, 19, 96). To Mark Spitz, "the dead" are the kind of people he formerly "saw every day" on the Subway – "Wall Street titans," "executive vice presidents in charge of new product marketing," or "devisers of theoretical financial instruments of unreckoned power" (266–67).

As Huehls suggests, however, "even as the novel's language and figures explicitly develop [a] parallel between zombification and contemporary capitalism, the text also suggests the obsolescence of the type of reading method that would identify and reveal such parallels – that is, the mode of reading that wants to see one thing representing, standing in for, or pointing to another thing."[59] Mark Spitz finds it "boring," for example, when other survivors tell him that the "the plague" is an effect of "the calculated brutalities of the global economic system," since for him, tautologically, "the plague was the plague. You were wearing galoshes, or you weren't" (153). Though Whitehead's protagonist has managed, against the odds, to avoid the "deluge" in which "everyone [is] drowning" (312), at the end of the novel he decides to enter it: "Fuck it, he thought. You have to learn how to swim sometime. He opened the door and walked into the sea of the dead" (322). If in one sense, then, the zombies in *Zone One* clearly figure a condition of being consumed by the logics of capital and the market, then there's also a way in which the zombies are just zombies – and in fact for Huehls it's precisely in this tendency towards literalism that "*Zone One* aligns itself so thoroughly – in both content and form – with the modes of contemporary capitalism," understood as tending towards "brain-dead homogenization."[60]

A question implicitly running through *Zone One*, then, might be whether, in order to be a perfect capitalist commodity, this zombie novel should be *just* a generic, standard, formulaic zombie novel? Should it willingly become *one of them*? The answer it arrives at, I think, is *not quite* – and the clue is provided by Mark Spitz's resolution in the final sentence: while (as the narrator puts it earlier) "everyone [is] drowning" in the "deluge" that is the zombie outbreak, Whitehead's protagonist is determined (however optimistically) to "learn to swim" in it – that is, not to be engulfed and overwhelmed by this "sea," but to retain a degree of independence as he navigates within it. Precisely insofar as contemporary capitalism has a strong homogenizing drive, it magnifies the importance of fine distinctions, minor novelties, and slight incongruities – an intertwined logic we see as much in what Ed Finn calls "cultural arbitrage" (as performed, for example, by Amazon's or Netflix's recommendations algorithms) as in techniques of financial arbitrage.[61] The strength of *Zone One* from a marketing point of view, then, is that it enters a well-established and prevalent sub-genre while occupying a distinctive position – what one critic describes as the apparent "oxymoron" of "the literary zombie novel."[62] Rather than drowning in an undifferentiated sea, *Zone One* learned to swim: of the hundreds of zombie novels that have found their way onto the market, only a few have reached the *New York Times* bestseller list (as *Zone One* did quickly after its release in 2011, becoming the first of Whitehead's novels to do so).

For Huehls, *Zone One*'s ending hints at the idea that "neoliberal capital has such a totalizing grasp on our contemporary moment that more might be gained by speaking its language than resisting it."[63] In his recent study *After Critique: Twenty-First-Century Fiction in a Neoliberal Age* (2016), Huehls locates Whitehead's novel squarely in a postcritical camp: "instead of critiquing and resisting, instead of imagining alternatives external to neoliberal totality" we should join "Mark Spitz in saying, 'Fuck it,' let's see what happens when we swim with zombies."[64] I would argue that the novel adopts a much more ambivalent position, however, its affirmation of neoliberal logics co-existing with an intensely melancholy tone, which registers profound regret over the loss of an autonomy that – beyond the most minimal form of differentiation-within-sameness – no longer seems possible.

The Post-Crisis Novel: Naturalism or Supernaturalism?

Zone One might be considered something of a "limit text" for this project, then, both in the extent of its disquiet at the pressures of the market on contemporary novelistic production, and in the extent of its apparent acknowledgement of those pressures' irresistibility. As I've suggested, Whitehead's novel also revealingly highlights the key contemporary fault line between literary fiction and genre fiction. In British and American fiction dealing directly with the financial markets, literary fiction of a decidedly realist kind was already the predominant mode prior to 2008, and it has been all the more prevalent since, with what Annie McClanahan calls "the credit-crisis realist novel" or what Katy Shaw has identified as a corpus of realist "crunch lit" novels far outnumbering other forms of fictional response to the global financial crisis.[65]

Much of this work places itself more or less overtly in a lineage of financial representations stretching back to the High Victorian "Condition of England" or "state of the nation" novel or to the later nineteenth- and early twentieth-century "economic novel" central to the canons of American literary realism and naturalism.[66] As Alison Shonkwiler suggests, in the face of the "capitalist unreality" so troublingly manifest in recent decades, "it is perhaps no surprise that contemporary fiction turns for its representational needs to the supposedly 'grounding' strategies of realism" – namely its "accumulation of detail, its commitment to social description, and its narrative authority."[67] Even as they seek such grounding, however, post-credit crunch realist novels time and again betray an urge to register the logic of financial forms whose imaginative and temporal projections always place them crucially out of step with existing empirical conditions. And in grasping at the complex ontology of the as-if, not-quite, or not-yet real that is essential to an understanding of the crisis, they repeatedly resort to a rhetoric of virtuality, illusion, myth, magic, and the sacred – to language, that is, native to the forms of super-natural genre fiction known collectively (and aptly) as "speculative fiction." This recent example of what I've called a recurrent "will to genre" in contemporary fiction might be read as displaying anxieties not only over realism's formal purchase on processes of financialization, but also over realist literary fiction's loss of ground to popular genre fiction in the marketplace. Indeed, the two sets of anxieties may be inseparable insofar as contemporary financial and monetary instruments' and contemporary genre texts' conditions of market circulation are themselves (as I've already intimated, and as I discuss in detail in Part II) closely aligned – both formed by what Edward LiPuma calls "ontologically real social fictions" that "agents quasi-automatically produce through the grace of collective belief."[68]

We see this will to genre, for example, early in Sebastian Faulks's paradigmatic crunch lit novel *A Week in December* (2009), when the wife of a London hedge fund manager reflects on the ways in which, in the run up to the crisis, banking came to operate in a "semi-virtual world," trading "new products" whose "joy" was "their magical self-sufficiency, the way they appeared to eliminate the risk of any final reckoning." In order for such a system to persist as long as it did, she surmises, "there must be a passionate faith: they had to believe that theirs was the true system and that earlier beliefs had been heretical . . . A breed of fanatic was born."[69]

Numerous other examples of "crunch lit" feature similar moments that foreground the seemingly paranormal power of finance from which the narratives are retreating in their formal (and often thematic) flights to the real. The narrator of C.K. Stead's *Risk* (2012), for instance, observes of the impact of the credit crisis on the City of London:

> It was fairy-tale, it was myth, but it was real; and the banks, those great castles that had created these possibilities, were shaking now, as if in an earthquake, their towers wobbling, threatening to come down. This was *Götterdämmerung*, "the twilight of the gods." Loge the fire-god was at work – except that Valhalla was too big to fail and panicky governments were hurrying to prop it up.[70]

Similarly cosmic and apocalyptic rhetoric surrounds the financial system in Martha McPhee's *Dear Money* (2010). The book's narrator is a novelist-turned-mortgage-backed securities trader, who, in the run up to the financial crisis, swaps making up stories for administering "the fabulously spinning non-correlated assets we'd invented, those curious cycles and epicycles derived from dreams." She is conscious, though, of "the One Percent Chance" that "the galaxy we'd created – the substance of our dreams, our deals" might come apart: "that the supercollider experiment would somehow form antimatter that would fuse everything . . . into a solid, ever-expanding ball of destruction. The one percent was Kali, destroyer goddess, riding on a theoretical comet of the apocalypse." "The One Percent" is likewise the "realm of the dragons" and the "terrible, wholesale destruction the dragons could do."[71] Utilizing a similar fantastical language, the protagonist of Paul Torday's *The Hopeless Life of Charlie Summers* (2010) reflects ruefully on how as the "Client Relations Director" for a Bloomsbury hedge fund, he has had "the high priest's job of making this new religion comprehensible, irrefutable, and irresistible" for potential investors, convincing them of the credibility of "the magical rates of return that only we, and a charmed few like us, could produce."[72] The narrator of Zia Haider Rahman's *In the Light of What We Know* (2014) likewise suggests that in designing the opaque instruments that fuelled the subprime boom, the bankers were creating a "monster" while attempting to preserve "the mystique of the priesthood." He describes his friend, a Wall Street derivatives trader, as "quickly establish[ing] a reputation as a bright though erratic financial wizard."[73] In Talitha Stevenson's *Disappear* (2010), set at the peak of the boom, the father of the manager of (yet another) London hedge fund admonishes his son for his firm's reckless practices: "You lot go and sing a pretty song to the bank and they chuck credit at you as if they've been hypnotised by it . . . It's not possible to sustain a business model that relies on debt and rumour: two *illusions*. At some point one has to face reality." Later, when the son's firm gets into difficulties, the father decries "banks lending as if they're immortals with great pots of gold."[74]

A similar language of the divine and the supernatural features in financial narratives set, and at least partly written, prior to 2008, but which appeared later, and were hailed on publication as astute commentaries on the culture of excess that eventually culminated in the crash. In Aifric Campbell's *On the Floor* (2012), for example, the protagonist, a young investment banker working in London in the early 1990s, pictures the stock warrants of companies listed on the Nikkei as "little scraps of torch paper, magical promises that can evaporate like those fortune cookie wrappers that ignite and dissolve on the tongues of fire, the incantation of holy words." She characterizes the analysts at her bank as "clairvoyant"; describes one client as "unkillable, a post-apocalyptic spectre that will stalk the financial wastelands for all eternity"; and refers to another as a "near-mythical presence from the land of wizardry and omnipotence."[75] The New York hedge fund at the centre of Jonathan Dee's *The Privileges* (2010) (set at a deliberately ill-defined point in the recent past) is likewise described as having "put up numbers" in its four years of existence that have pushed its manager "into shamanistic territory, where people earnestly [believe] that he [is] performing a kind of magic."[76]

A sense that finance is nigh on sacred in its mysteriousness and its elevation above the tangible and the material is captured particularly forcefully by a scene in Adam Haslett's early 2000s-set *Union Atlantic* (2010). In this scene, an administrator at the titular Union Atlantic Bank pays a visit to the New York Federal Reserve – "the undying realm of the central bank"[77] – and is treated to a tour of the gold vault in the company of no less a personage than the Bank's President:

> "It's the largest accumulation of monetary gold in the world," he said. "In fact, it's a decent-size chunk of all the gold ever mined. . . .
>
> "The tours come to the outer gate here every day. I think last year we had twenty-five thousand visitors. People love to look at it." . . . "And yet this," he said, indicating with a sweep of his hand the whole contents of the vault, "barely matters. Add it up and it's no more than eighty or ninety billion worth. The wires clear more than that in an hour. All anchored in nothing but trust. Cooperation. You could even say faith, which sometimes I do, though it's certainly of an earthly kind. Without it you couldn't buy a loaf of bread . . .

"The system has to work. People have to trust the paper in their wallets. And that starts somewhere. It starts with the banks."[78]

In including this – in plot terms – somewhat gratuitous and unmotivated scene, it is almost as if Haslett wishes to register his nostalgia for a time in which the mimetic aspirations of the realist novelist might have found a warrant in the traceability of monetary transactions to precious metal. This passage is (or wishes to be) a nugget of what Jean-Joseph Goux (as I discuss in Chapter 3) calls "gold-language" – language in and through which "the real would be conveyed without mediation"[79] – in a thematic as well as a stylistic sense. At the same time, though, Haslett is obliged to acknowledge that those monetary transactions rely more on forms of tacit belief akin to those that undergird speculative genre fiction than on appeals to material facticity consonant with realist aesthetics.

Recent book-length studies of contemporary fiction and finance take the question of realism – its capacities, challenges, and limits – as their central problematic, whether in texts produced prior to 2008 (La Berge), after (McClanahan; Shaw), or either side of the crisis (De Boever; Shonkwiler). These works have charted realist fictional representations of finance extensively (covering a number of the novels I have just discussed), and they have considered texts in which an awareness of realism's representational limits gives rise to what Shonkwiler calls "hybrid realist-postmodern forms."[80] They have not, though, explored the propensity of realist financial fictions to flicker (however momentarily) on the verge of morphing into very different – speculative or supernatural genre – forms. Nor, more significantly, have they paid sustained attention to the kinds of hybrid *genre*-postmodern texts that, as I argue in Part II, offer especially revealing narrative analogues for the complex ontologies of contemporary finance.[81] While occasionally addressing individual texts, economically orientated contemporary literary studies has so far also largely overlooked the major phenomenon that is the postmodern encyclopaedic or systems novel – the topic of the third part of this book. The book's final part, meanwhile, is the first attempt to define and analyse the vanguard movement of economically engaged writing in contemporary literary culture, which takes the form of a fully fledged style of market metafiction. Moving the study of contemporary fiction and finance into new areas, while relating the question of fiction and *financial* markets to that of fiction and the *literary* marketplace, the remainder of this study aims, then, both to expand the field of study in which the book is situated and to bring new methodological and analytical perspectives to bear on that field's core concerns. Having deepened my project's literary-historical and conceptual dimensions in this opening part, Part II explores contemporary financial fiction's self-consciously enacted will to genre in greater detail.

The Phantasmagorias of Contemporary Finance

One plausible etymology for phantasmagoria is *phantasma agoreuein*, the ghosts of the public place or marketplace.

– Margaret Cohen

The stock exchange is a poor substitute for the Holy Grail.

– Joseph Schumpeter

CHAPTER 2

Trading in the As If
Fiduciary Exchangeability and Supernatural Financial Fiction

It was a time of great tribulation. In 2007 and 2008, as global credit markets seized up, venerable banking and insurance institutions collapsed, and stock prices around the world slid and then tumbled, desperate financial professionals sought supernatural insights into the unimaginable disaster that had befallen them. In London, psychics experienced a dramatic surge in demand for their advice from City workers.[1] In Paris, Jérôme Kerviel, the rogue trader whose unauthorized market positions resulted in losses of €5 billion for the French bank Société Générale and intensified the stress on global markets, turned to clairvoyants in a futile attempt to predict the future.[2] Across the Atlantic, leading US corporations queued to secure the services of Laura Day, another psychic or, in her preferred term, "intuitive,"[3] and anxious Wall Streeters flocked to the healing hands of the financial planner-cum-Tibetan shaman Larry Ford.[4] Among the fraudsters indicted by the US Securities and Exchange Commission in the wake of the crisis was "America's Prophet" and head of the Delphi Investment Group, Sean David Morton, whose claim to have used a "spiritual remote viewing system" to call "ALL the highs and lows of the market . . . over the last 14 years" persuaded tens of thousands of investors to follow his stock tips, or even, in some cases, to entrust him with their life savings.[5]

More generally, the credit crunch was the occasion of a mini religious revival in downtown Manhattan. At the height of the crisis in the fall of 2008, after the implosion of Bear Stearns and Lehman Brothers, Trinity Church, the neo-Gothic edifice that looms incongruously at the west end of Wall Street, reported that congregations were often more than double their usual size,[6] while extraordinary prayer meetings were held at Merrill Lynch, Goldman Sachs, JPMorgan Chase, Citigroup, Morgan Stanley, Deloitte, and other institutions.[7]

The crisis merely heightened and made publicly visible a long-established tendency for financial professionals to seek supernatural

71

intercession in their working lives. Studies have shown that individuals who trade financial securities for a living harbour levels of superstitious belief that defy theoretical models of economic rationality. There is, for example, substantial evidence of altered trading behaviour on days marked by the eerie darkness of solar eclipse, as well as on inauspicious dates and during ill-omened months – Friday the 13th and October, with its long history of market crashes (not to mention its culmination on All Hallows' Eve), being the chief examples.[8] Numerous reports since the 1990s indicate that astrology plays a significant role in the market analytics used by British high street banks, City investment funds, and major Wall Street institutions.[9] As the business historian Caley Horan comments, "within the world of finance, there's always a superstitious, quasi-spiritual trend to find meaning in markets ...Technical analysts at big banks [are] trying to find patterns in past market behaviour, so it's not a leap for them to go to astrology."[10] Anthropologists who have explored the world of finance paint a picture of the trading floor as a space pervaded by belief in fate, karma, mojo, and the power of magical talismans.[11]

This predisposition towards supernatural structures of belief (what we might think of in terms not so much of the "cultural" as of the "occultural" economy of finance)[12] has a long history. In the Gilded Age and Progressive Era United States, for example, robber barons such as Cornelius Vanderbilt, J.P. Morgan, and Charles M. Schwab are reputed to have regularly sought investment advice from mediums, spiritualists, or astrologers.[13] The dominant City personality of the early twentieth century, Montagu Norman, who became Governor of the Bank of England in 1920, was a theosophist who claimed to be able to walk through walls.[14] Around the turn of the century, many Wall Street operators made their investment decisions by consulting dream books, which "claimed to reveal the numerological significance of dreams and coincidences" and thereby help "stabilize the sorcery of the marketplace."[15] The twentieth century's most celebrated investment gurus, the Americans William D. Gann and Ralph Nelson Elliott, based their systems in astrology and numerology respectively. In 1971, in his book *Wall Street and Witchcraft: An Investigation into Extreme and Unusual Investment Techniques*, the journalist Max Gunther reported encounters with portfolio managers, suburban housewives, paranormal researchers, and the flotsam and jetsam of the 1960s counterculture, all of whom dealt "with psychic and occult phenomena" in their speculations on the stock market (telepathy, astrology, horoscopy, Tarot card reading, crystal ball gazing, Wiccan ceremonies), many boasting major companies and banks among their clients.[16]

In this procession of occult adepts and supernatural schemes, then, we catch glimpses of a shadow history that flits its way through the annals of modern finance. The existence of such a history suggests that the suspension of disbelief that financial workers are obliged to cultivate in order to deal in things "not altogether real" (in the historian J.G.A. Pocock's words)[17] is liable to tip over into belief proper – belief, that is, in entities and agencies whose intangibility and ineffability mirror the properties of finance itself. A history of this kind appeals to the imaginations of contemporary writers, who likewise sense that something in the credit-based logic of finance demands an embrace of the otherworldly and paranormal. In its purest form – as in the work of Iain Sinclair, the focus of the next chapter – this brand of literary occultism appears to place as much faith in the actuality of the supernatural as do some of the financial profession's more ardent believers. Even as it strives to solidify belief, however, such writing also pushes belief to its limits, beyond which it is liable to collapse.

This chapter begins by staging an encounter between recent work on money and finance in the social sciences and the field of contemporary literary studies known as the New Economic Criticism. Taking the accounts of economic and literary belief that emerge from this scholarship as starting points, I build on, develop, and in certain key respects challenge such work in order to theorize the appeals to readerly belief and absorption newly prevalent even (or especially) in the "advanced" fiction and memoir of recent decades. If, as I argued in the Introduction, the contemporary prominence of the genre-literary hybrid, in particular, testifies (at least in significant part) to economic pressures whose ultimate sources lie in the financial markets, then the authors I discuss in this chapter (Bret Easton Ellis, Anne Billson, Stephen Marche, and Jonathan Coe), as well as the works of Iain Sinclair discussed in the next chapter, enable us to understand this connection more clearly by casting their own role as being (as Sinclair puts its) "to deal paper" akin to the "commercial paper" or promissory notes traded on the money markets, plying their wares in a market for books "wild with speculations and futures."[18]

In so doing, they suggest that the turn to genre not only answers to a (financial) market logic of seeking out new profit sources, but also channels the power of a fiduciary logic – a logic of trust or tacit belief – that marketable fictional texts and credit instruments have long shared, and that may even (as some scholars have argued) be a product of a common point of origin in the conjoined "revolutions" that brought modern finance and the modern novel into being. At the same time, these two chapters aim to deepen, enrich, and complexify approaches in economic sociology and anthropology and the social studies of finance that have turned to key literary categories to theorize aspects of financial and economic life, but have not yet begun to tap the potential of actual literary texts for furthering this project. This chapter begins, then, by teasing out the connections between faith, imagination, and the paranormal that tie fictional narrative to the monetary and financial instruments of the "credit economy" – past and present. It then shows how these intertwined concerns animate exemplary contemporary novels by Ellis, Billson, Marche, and Coe.

Making Believe: Fiduciary Exchangeability

It's common, and, on the face of it, quite reasonable, to suppose that money is essentially – or at least originally – metallic in nature. In fact, however, there is strong evidence to suggest that money was "virtual" – having no more material instantiation than, say, a set of tally marks on a stick or tablet – before it was "real." As the anthropologist David Graeber puts it, "history tends to move back and forth between periods dominated by bullion – where it's assumed that gold and silver are money – and periods where money is assumed to be an abstraction, a virtual unit of account. But historically, credit money comes first."[19] The anthropological and historical records suggest that, as Nigel Dodd puts it, "money is not *essentially* metallic but fiduciary" (from the Latin *fidere*: to trust).[20]

The precise forms and structures of these relations of trust are as historically varied as are systems of money themselves, though they are always constitutive factors. Consider, for example, the gold standard regime of "representative" paper money in place in Britain and other industrialized economies by the middle of the nineteenth century. For Karl Marx, writing in *A Contribution to the Critique of Political Economy* (1859), the issuance of such money was an attempted "illusion" whereby the state appeared "to transform paper into gold by the magic of its imprint."[21] Responding to Marx's Gothic brand of political economy in 1993's *Specters of Marx*, Jacques Derrida suggests that in such ways Marx cast "money, and more precisely the monetary sign, in the figure of appearance or simulacrum, more exactly of the ghost." For Marx, Derrida suggests, money entailed a "movement of idealization" that produced "ghosts, illusions, simulacra, appearances, or apparitions."[22] Yet whereas, under the system of gold convertibility that Marx knew, the state's "illusion" sought (not without considerable risks, in his view)[23] to instil confidence that paper money was effectively equivalent to the precious metal that nominally backed it, in today's monetary system a still more audacious act of legerdemain is involved, whereby trust must be cultivated in the absence of any possibility of currency's convertibility into some material – and notionally prior or more authentic – form. Hence the "monetary specter," in Derrida's words, is now more than ever a "fiduciary sign."[24]

Rarely, that is, has trust been installed so centrally as it is in the fiat money regime that assumed *de facto* command of the international monetary system in the early 1970s, following the collapse of the Bretton Woods system of fixed exchange rates pegged to the gold-backed US dollar that had been established in 1944. In theory, fiat money has value because it is proclaimed as such by the state that issues it. Yet in practice its functioning is reliant on ongoing tacit agreement among ordinary people to acknowledge that value. Fiat money is often described as based on "belief," but, as recent work in economic sociology has stressed, it would be a mistake to imagine that the people who use such currency do so in the belief that it is valuable in some absolute, objective sense; instead, they recognize that there are practical benefits to going along with everyone else in behaving *as if* it were truly valuable, or of exercising a kind of voluntary and bounded credulity. Today, moreover, the increasing creation of credit money – which commercial banks perform when they issue loans, and which now far outweighs the issuing of coins and notes by central banks – means that fiat money (in the form of cash deposited in bank accounts) is imagined as "backing" some still less tangible form of value, despite lacking "real" value itself.[25] Money, then, as Philip Goodchild writes, "is an implicit contract": "the social contract of market society involves a willingness to accept money in payment based on the confidence that others will also accept it in payment."[26] It therefore misses the mark to claim – as Arne De Boever recently has – that "the abolition of the gold standard" and the emergence of other key aspects of contemporary financialization have made "psychosis" – in which "human beings disavow existing reality, sometimes in combination with the substitution of another reality" – the "dominant affliction" of "our particular economic moment."[27] The diagnosis of psychosis – of full-blown, thoroughgoing delusion – fails to grasp the way in which belief in the "reality" of contemporary monetary and financial instruments co-exists in complex interplay with a recognition of their underlying "unreality."

As I've just suggested, the fiduciary logic that defines contemporary money – in the narrow sense of currency exchangeable for goods and services – also governs the wider array of credit instruments that makes up the financial economy at large. As Karin Knorr Catina puts it, the buying or selling of stocks, bonds, and other financial assets "initiates an engagement or contract," which takes the form of "claims and commitments exercised over time based on the promise of future outcomes." While such "promissory engagements" in the financial markets are contingent – since "the future is uncertain" and "outcomes cannot be guaranteed" – the risks of investment and speculation are masked, Knorr Catina argues, by narrative appeals to fantasy and the imagination. Indeed, a collective willingness on the part of market actors to "buy into a promise" may itself actively defer risks: hence the way in which – at least for a while – stocks may trade at ever-higher prices regardless of their parlous "fundamentals."[28]

This dynamic is all the more evident in derivatives markets, whose growth has been perhaps the financial system's most significant development of recent decades. Originally, forms of insurance for hedging against risk, options and futures contracts (offering the right or obligation, respectively, to purchase an underlying asset at a set price in the future) – as well as their wider ilk (swaps, forwards, repos, etc.) – have, since the 1970s, emerged as heavily traded instruments in their own right, spawning increasingly "exotic" mutations via the securitization of an ever-widening pool of asset classes (especially forms of consumer debt). This is the process whose logical outgrowths were the synthetic collateralized debt obligations (synthetic CDOs) that combined other derivatives contracts – primarily credit default swaps – to take positions on the mortgage-backed securities market in the run up to the subprime crisis (and played a considerable role in precipitating it). As Cédric Durand remarks, such products seemed to be "limited by nothing other than the imaginations of financial actors themselves," flourishing "in an unregulated grey zone separate from the official finance markets – so-called 'shadow banking.'"[29] A trader involved in building one such product describes "standing in the middle of all these complex, highly levered, exotic trades [I] created without necessarily understanding all the implications of those monstrosities." Invoking the figure of Frankenstein, he refers to a synthetic CDO as "the type of thing which you invent telling yourself: 'Well, what if we created a "thing," which has no purpose, which is absolutely conceptual and highly theoretical and which nobody knows how to price?'"[30]

It is crucial to stress that to highlight the roles played by collectively constituted forms of imagination and tacit belief in the functioning of the monetary system and the financial markets is not in any way to suggest that such belief is sufficient simply to override objective factors or "structural fundamentals" (Annie McClanahan's phrase) in the wider economy (as some poststructuralist-based approaches have implied).[31] As McClanahan notes with regard to the circumstances surrounding the global financial crisis of 2007–8, it would be a mistake to suggest that "some magical shared 'belief' either caused or could prevent the collapse, as if the economy were in the last instance ... fully imaginary" or "as if mere suspension of narrative disbelief could protect us against falling home prices or rising unemployment."[32] Once the income streams to which CDOs and other credit derivatives instruments gave their holders a claim began to dry up, no amount of wishful thinking could stop the market for those instruments crashing. What recent social-scientific analyses of the inter-subjective, fiduciary dimensions of financial and economic life do help us to grasp, though, is how, on a day-to-day or even trade-to-trade basis, markets forestall, circumvent, or defer crisis. That they cannot do so indefinitely is unquestionable; but that they can do so at all often seems to defy all logic.

It is the obligation to solicit belief in intangible entities that gives rise to a rhetoric of monetary and financial enchantment in contemporary culture (and that also, as I suggested at the beginning of this chapter, fosters the occult practices that are surprisingly prevalent features of investment banks and trading floors). In view of the prevalence of this rhetoric, it is perhaps unsurprising that social scientists have recently found insights in the models of imagination, trust, and reciprocity theorized in literary studies.[33] On this view, the complexities of monetary or financial faith may be best captured by Samuel Taylor Coleridge's hoary but still unsurpassed argument on behalf of "poetic faith": his claim that in works of literature even "persons and characters supernatural" may be imbued with "a semblance of truth sufficient to procure for these shadows of imagination [a] willing suspension of disbelief."[34] Critics and theorists of the novel, in particular, have been much concerned with identifying the precise mechanisms via which fictional narratives establish and sustain this state of suspended disbelief (or what Catherine Gallagher, in an important recent reconsideration of Coleridge's celebrated idea, refers to as a condition of "ironic credulity").[35] Fittingly enough, it is to the language of business and commerce ("exchange," "transaction," or – especially – "contract") that literary scholars have most frequently turned in articulating the novelistic trust-building devices that have developed over the form's history.

According to such accounts, the so-called "paradox of fiction" (that in consuming fictional narratives readers or viewers become emotionally attached to entities that they know to be unreal) persists because the overwhelming majority of fictions are premised on an implicit agreement between author and reader that the events depicted are to be treated *as if* they possessed some manner of actuality, and that everything will be done to maintain the consistency of this illusion. In one of the most influential of these accounts, the semioticians A.J. Greimas and Joseph Courtès describe the ideal form of such an agreement:

> We are dealing here with a narrative without surprises, in which relation-ships are regulated by what we shall call a *fiduciary contract*, an act of trust, where no double-dealing can enter ... The exchange is characterized by "truth" [and] a common, tacit, and implicit accord ... shared by the tale teller and the audience.[36]

Of course, the nature of the "fiduciary contract" that underwrites works of fiction (what constitutes "double-dealing"; what is able to pass as "true") varies not only historically, but also generically: critics speak of "generic verisimilitude" to describe how things that would be thoroughly credible in a work of horror would tend to violate the implicit promise of a text located in a realist mode, or within the idioms of the romance or detective novel.[37] Lauren Berlant defines genre as "a loose affectual contract that predicts the form that an aesthetic transaction will take":[38] while genres are far from fixed, they have a relative stability, which makes it possible to assume the cluster of experiences, feelings, and responses that a text identifiably located within a particular genre will activate (and, conversely, those that it will leave largely untouched).

The notion that the shifting forms of trust generated by fiction parallel, and are bound up with, rearrangements in the fiduciary structures of money and finance is a key premise of the strand of contemporary literary studies known as the New Economic Criticism.[39] Such parallelism is often described as being of the order of "homology," but the precise stakes of this method are not always rigorously examined.[40] As Raymond Williams notes, "'homology' is correspondence in origin and development," and a homological mode of cultural analysis identifies "examples of real social relationships, in their variable practice, which have common forms of origin."[41] When foundational works of New Economic Criticism venture to identify a shared origin for literature and money, it is invariably found to lie in some loosely defined, but decidedly ancient, moment of primordial union.[42] More recent work in the field, however, is less sweeping. Exemplary here is Mary Poovey's landmark study *Genres of the Credit Economy: Mediating Value in Eighteenth- and Nineteenth-Century Britain* (2008). Poovey offers a considerably more specific and historically circum-scribed (though still remarkably ambitious) account, in identifying, in the period of the English Financial Revolution of the seventeenth and eighteenth centuries, if not an absolute point of shared origin, then the existence of a "continuum" in which monetary and literary forms of writing were commonly located.

Poovey makes the case that in the late seventeenth century and for much of the eighteenth, the forms of inscription that constituted monetary instruments, such as promissory notes, bank paper, and share certificates, were not consistently differentiated from various kinds of imaginative writing, chiefly the new experiments in prose fiction then beginning their famous rise (the two "kinds" of writing shared formal arrangements, rhetorical tropes, and so on). Nor did one kind enjoy ontological or causal primacy over the other: rather, both performed "variants of [the] single function" of mediating value – that is, facilitating the increasingly intangible forms of exchange essential to an emerging credit economy.[43] During this period, Poovey argues, the forms of value mediated by imaginative literary genres – just as much as by monetary ones – were primarily, if not exclusively, economic: "because these genres – or the continuum of writing from which they would eventually be differentiated *as* genres – mediated the credit economy, all this writing helped make the system of credit and debt usable and the market model of value familiar."[44]

Central to the gradual differentiation of these genres from one another that would occur over the course of the nineteenth century were attempts by successive generations of British Romantic writers, as well as by late-century proto-modernists, to extricate literature from this market model of value and align it, instead, with a "model of aesthetic autonomy" that was "theoretically indifferent to, and protected from, the vicissitudes and dynamics of the market."[45] This latter model (whose centrality to modernism and the early twentieth-century avant-gardes we considered in the Introduction) sought to "challenge the market evaluation registered by *popularity* or *demand*."[46] Poovey argues, however, that traces of the relationship that imaginative writing "had once obviously had with monetary writing" persisted "in the fact that every book written to be sold was a commodity" that "inevitably circulated in the market, where price and demand prevailed."[47] To the extent that certain kinds of imaginative texts – those disparaged as mere "trash" or "print commerce"[48] – embraced, rather than denied, the continued commodity status of literature, they, like the forms of monetary writing with which they had once been closely affiliated, sought to guarantee their successful circulation in the market by eliciting the trust of those through whose hands they passed.

When contemporary writers (like Jonathan Coe or, as discussed in the next chapter, Iain Sinclair) connect present imbrications of fictional and financial fiduciarity to those of previous centuries, then, they do so not because they imagine our own stage of financialized capital accumulation to be straightforwardly continuous with those of past ages (rather, as I've argued, such writers are responding to a specific set of historical conditions, both local and contingent and structural and systemic); rather, they do so precisely because the particular cultural-economic valences of our extended, post-1970s present, in militating so relentlessly against the sites of "nonmarket"[49] aesthetic and cultural value carved out in the epochs of Romanticism and modernism, have rendered an earlier kinship newly visible. The types of "writing" (technical, algebraic, algorithmic) that constitute today's most advanced credit instruments may be further away than ever from the norms of imaginative writing, but in actively homo-logizing themselves in the ways I discuss below, works of contemporary fiction are tapping into what they sense to be a shared lineage with a long history.

The trust-building and market-soliciting capacity that imaginative writ-ing shares with monetary writing – what we might call its "fiduciary circulability" or "fiduciary exchangeability" – is one of those forms of "secular enchantment" that has survived (or rather, drawn strength from) the processes of modernization.[50] As historians of reading and of the book have shown, however, in the eighteenth and nineteenth centuries an absorptive reading experience was only one (albeit important) motivation for the consumption of fiction; so too were other things that one might "do" with books, from communal reading to commonplacing to decorat-ing to conspicuous display. The model of book consumption that is now so familiar to us that it is liable to appear as a transhistorical norm – that of gaining access to a solitary experience of absorption in a narrative world – is of relatively recent vintage (dating roughly to the achievement of near-universal literacy in Britain and other industrially advanced nations around the end of the nineteenth century).[51]

As Kuijpers et al. suggest, narrative "absorption" is a metaphor (an imperfect one, but probably the best we have) for "an experiential state . . . characterized by a reader's focused attention on the story world presented in the text," in which it's possible (even as one remains latently conscious of one's surroundings) to feel "transported to the world of the story," a feeling "supported by strong emotional reactions to what happens in the story world."[52] The market dominance of texts able to elicit this kind of state over the past century is abundantly confirmed by studies of twentieth- and twenty-first-century bestsellers, which, whether they simply submit their corpura to close critical scrutiny, or run them through the latest text mining software, stress that the novels that have achieved the greatest commercial success invariably do so by establishing and upholding "fictional contracts" that sustain readers' envelopment within their imaginative universes.[53]

As I argued in the Introduction, the present escalation of tensions inherent to a post-Romantic literary culture – tensions between art and commerce, between autonomy and incorporation, and between a *"critical relation"*[54] to the market and willing capitulation to it – has seen these tensions (which have consistently shaped literature's forms and structures) burst to the surface of many texts, appearing as explicit, and overtly self-reflexive, content. In the context of the novel, this is the phenomenon I identified in the Introduction and Chapter 1 as "market metafiction."

Many works of market metafiction perform this self-interrogation by foregrounding their kinship with the monetary and financial instruments that dominate a present-day credit economy of unprecedented scale. Contemporary British and American novelists are preoccupied by the market-imposed obligation to elicit tacit belief that their writing shares with contemporary money and finance, and it is no wonder that, in tracing the convergence of literary and financial forms of credit, they turn consistently to genres marked by the presence of the magical, the fantastic, the supernatural, or the futuristic. To be sure, such "speculative" genres are well suited to exploring an age of "Frankenstein finance," with its exotic array of synthetically engineered derivatives products and algorithmic trading bots. Yet, as we saw in the Introduction, these very generic inclinations themselves bespeak an acute sensitivity to market trends and pressures: such genres have a long-established popularity, and have proven themselves especially bankable in recent decades in a cycle of overlapping "booms" in public enthusiasm for particular branches of supernatural lore (aliens, vampires, zombies, wizards, werewolves, and so on). At the same time, though, the adoption of these genres provides contemporary authors with opportunities to test precisely how "speculative" – how outlandish, estranging, or counterfactual – financial and fictional objects may become before some limit is reached and the confidence of investor or reader begins to break down, shattering a shared state of fiduciary exchangeability.

The economic sociologist Jens Beckert has made the case forcefully that "the functioning of money and credit … depends on" "confidence," which is "created and maintained" through "discursive processes," "means of interpretation," and "narrative construction." Investigating the "processes through which confidence in financial markets is created or shaken," he suggests, is thus "a highly consequential field of research of capitalism."[55] As one of the reviewers of Beckert's *Imagined Futures: Fictional Expectations and Capitalist Dynamics* (2016) notes, however, the book's aim of rethinking economic sociology in light of literary notions of fictionality is indifferent to works of fiction themselves; hence, there remains work to do "to deliver on these possibilities of fully realizing the connection Beckert imagines between the worlds of fiction and finance."[56] One of the further-reaching aspirations of this and the following chapter, therefore, is that an examination of actual fictional narratives – narratives that take precisely Beckert's dynamic of financial "creating" and "shaking" as their organizing principle – may offer insights into the affective structures and relations that sustain or imperil a state of fiduciarity, and hence make a distinctive contribution to the social-scientific debates with which it is in dialogue, as well as to its primary field of contemporary literary studies.

Do You Buy It? Market Metafiction's Credit Limits

Each of the examples of market metafiction that I consider in this section (novels by Bret Easton Ellis, Anne Billson, Stephen Marche, and Jonathan Coe) is representative of one of the genre-inclined forms of contemporary fiction that, if not always unmistakably postmodernist in style or technique, are all products (as I argued in the previous chapter) of a postmodernist cultural dominant in which a direct engagement with the market is unavoidable. By overtly foregrounding or allegorizing their ambivalent internalization of the dynamics of fiduciary exchangeability, these texts make explicitly visible the market logic that, I've suggested, informs a wider contemporary will to genre, as well as a renewed investment in readerly belief and absorption in contemporary writing more generally.

Bret Easton Ellis is perhaps the best-known novelist associated with the Avant-Pop style of postmodernism, and his most notorious book exemplifies the conflictedness with which contemporary authors treat the phenomenon of fiduciary exchangeability, and the self-consciousness of what I have called market metafiction. In *American Psycho* (1991), Ellis draws heavily on Gothic and occult horror modes in pointing to grisly affinities between Wall Street (half of which is said to be owned by the family of the serial-killing investment banker Patrick Bateman) and supernatural rites.[57] We learn, for example, of a "young stockbroker" linked to "occultism or Satan worship," who has been charged with "performing voodoo rituals" with the "body parts" of a young girl, and of Halloween parties at which guests dress as notorious financial criminals, if not, as in Bateman's case, as a "mass murderer," decked out in real human blood, hair, and bone.[58]

Lost, during dinner with his fiancé, in his "own private maze" of Wall Street products – "warrants, stock offerings, ESOPs, LBOs, IPOs, finances, refinances, debentures, converts, proxy statements" – Bateman is accused of being "inhuman," "a ghoul" (341–42) (elsewhere, he is likened to a "banshee," a "demon," and a "ghost . . . something unreal, something not quite tangible" [166, 179, 349, 71]). Bateman's personality, as he acknowledges towards the end of the novel, has the qualities both of an imaginary, supernatural being and of a financial product: "there is an idea of a Patrick Bateman, some kind of abstraction, but there is no real me, only an entity, something illusory." Bateman's "self" is "fabricated": "*I simply am not there*," he confesses (376–77; italics in original). Ellis's entire narrative, meanwhile, is an exercise in testing how far it is possible to push an audience while still guarding one's bestseller status – whether by bombarding readers with repeated bouts of sickening violence or (more subtly, but no less alienatingly) by littering the text with jarring, ontologically inconsistent details (everything from reports of zombies on the streets of New York [383] to an automated teller machine that communicates in "weird messages" [395] to murders that apparently both do and do not happen), which make the narrative's own "illusory," "fabricated" status obtrusively and distractingly apparent. Late on in the novel, Bateman notes that an acquaintance – a character suggestively named "Price," who introduces himself on the first page of the novel as "an *asset*" (3; emphasis in original) – has a "smudge" on his forehead; at the very moment of observing this strange mark, though, Bateman acknowledges a "feeling that if I asked someone else if it was truly there, he (or she) would just say no" (384). The effect of this peculiar moment is both to heighten the novel's impression of ontological disjunction and to point to the rubbing away of the novel's own exchange value that is an inherent risk of such diegetic incoherence (even if this was a risk ultimately curbed in this case when *American Psycho*'s publication turned out to be one of those rare cultural events in which sheer media obsession with a text's sensational content virtually guarantees sales, almost irrespective of its formal features).

These concerns are all the more pronounced, if – in important ways – reconfigured, in Ellis's quasi-sequel to *American Psycho*, *Lunar Park* (2005), a novel that even more fully inhabits a Stephen King-esque horror style than its predecessor. In the world of *Lunar Park*, suburban buildings are wrapped with "gigantic liquid-crystal display screens, and zip strips quoting stock prices";[59] a "possessed" accountant, exorcized in his condominium, "[speaks] backwards in Latin" and "[bleeds] from his eyes" (260); and the ashes of a man who made his fortune from "highly speculative real estate deals . . . during the Reagan years" communicate with his son via email "in the middle of the night" from their resting place in a safe deposit box at a Los Angeles branch of Bank of America (5, 67–68). The narrator of *Lunar Park* is a writer named Bret Easton Ellis, whose body of work and (to a certain extent) biography correspond to those of the novel's actual author. "Ellis" – the character – is acutely conscious of financial concerns: that "people [are] making so much money" from his books; of the need "to appease [his] fan base" and keep his work on "every best seller list"; and of the risk, if he does not meet consumer demand, that his publisher will "suffer huge financial losses." "Everything about my career was now measured in economics," he laments (21).

The novel's first chapter, a sort of prelude to the main narrative, refers, in closing, to the contract with Knopf for the publication of the book itself, immediately before offering a kind of contract (implicitly "signed," of course, in the actual, real-life author's own name) to the reader: "Regardless of how horrible the events described here might seem, there's one thing you must remember as you hold this book in your hands: all of it really happened, every word is true" (30). These "horrible events" consist of seemingly supernatural attacks on "Ellis" and his family and community, most disturbingly by what appears to be the author's own most notorious creation, Patrick Bateman – a "ghost" or "monster" "escaped from a novel" (124, 147). Richard Godden suggests that Ellis decides "to turn Bret Easton Ellis . . . into a fiction in order to maximize his credit,"[60] and indeed the novel seems designed to interpellate readers into crediting still more overtly fictional entities: "Ellis" recalls that his best-known novel wasn't so much written as "wrote itself and didn't care how I felt about it" (13). As if drafting another contract, but not quite authorizing it in his own hand, "I would fearfully watch . . . as the pen swept across the yellow legal pads I did the first draft on. I was repulsed by this creation and wanted to take no credit for it – Patrick Bateman wanted the credit" (13).

By the end of the narrative, there are suggestions (though far from conclusive ones) that the assailant is a real person, who has merely adopted the persona of Bateman, but "Ellis" still wants to believe "that the killer was fictional. That his name was Patrick Bateman . . . and for a brief time over the course of a year he [became] real, as so many fictional characters ultimately are for their creators – and for their readers as well" (301). If, in *American Psycho*, Patrick Bateman and the world he inhabits are progressively derealized, in *Lunar Park* the emphasis is on the reality and credibility of character and narrative – on how even "highly speculative . . . deals" (between author and reader as much as investor and realtor) can be turned to account. Many readers have applauded Ellis's efforts in this regard, praising a novel that, while on the face of it wildly implausible or excessively self-indulgent, quickly becomes immersive, believable, or indeed (to quote one reader) "realistic and credible."[61]

* * *

An alternate strategy for testing the limits of the "fiduciary contract," in both financial and fictional contexts, features in another novel of the early 1990s, to which *American Psycho* has been frequently compared, and which also displays the kind of fascination with consumption and mass-market cultural forms characteristic of the Avant-Pop style. The English author Anne Billson's 1993 novel *Suckers* portrays the takeover of Britain by a vampire-led venture capital firm based in the new financial stronghold of London's Docklands (also, as we'll see, a major site in Sinclair's mapping of the city's occult financial force field). Billson's novel riffs on the long-established links between vampirism and capitalism understood as a relentless, all-encompassing, and undying force: a glimpse inside the mind of the chief vampire – for whom humans are mere "objects and shadows" – discloses a "vision" that is "vast and boundless," and promises an existence that will endure *"for ever."*[62] *Suckers* cannily latches onto and draws on both the perennial popular appeal of vampire narratives (there are numerous references to the *Dracula* mythology in its novelistic and filmic guises [e.g. 233, 241, 297]) and a particular late-1980s/early-1990s vogue for the genre (*Lost Boys* [1987], *Near Dark* [1987], *Bram Stoker's Dracula* [1992], Poppy Z. Brite's *Lost Souls* [1992], Kim Newman's *Anno Dracula* [1992]). "I'm going through one of my neo-Gothic phases" (190) remarks *Suckers'* protagonist, Dora Vale, and so too was the wider culture (the vampire had been "the bogeyman of the decade" according to Billson, writing in 1992).[63]

A veteran of the style and listings press when she wrote *Suckers*, Billson flaunts her novel's breezy, readily consumable qualities. She has "a real attachment," she has said, to telling "a good story": "I don't want to impress people with my writing, I want them to think, 'Hey, this is a really good read.' I want you to keep reading to the end."[64] One reviewer spoke of *Suckers'* "enjoyable weightlessness" and of ideas that bob "jauntily on the sheeny meniscus of the prose."[65] Billson's announcement as one of *Granta's* twenty Best of Young British Novelists in 1993 was widely read as a concession to mass-market taste.[66] At the same time, via her protagonist's role as a "Creative Consultant," Billson self-consciously signals her own courting of popular success. It is Dora's job "to keep publishers informed about their target market of upwardly mobile young adults with disposable incomes." She takes "the Creative' part of [her] job description literally": "most of the information I provided was completely fictitious" (4). Dora is adamant, however, that her "fictions" are perfectly calibrated to the market because of her own total identification with it:

> I looked upon these things as conceptual art. They may have been made up, but they seemed no less accurate than any other form of market research . . . My attitude was that I *was* the market. I told everyone my readership profiles . . . were constantly having to be updated in order to reflect the minutest fluctuations in the state of the economy. (71; emphasis in original)

If there's a "concept" to Billson's own "art," it is the desire to offer a parodic embodiment – complete with "racy title and foil encrust[ed]" cover[67] – of what the novel as a pure product of market research might look like – a work that so slavishly observes the conventions of a market-tested generic formula that it renders that conventionality glaringly apparent, paradoxically threatening readerly absorption precisely through its over-ingratiating soliciting of it. The demands – to be eager-to-please, attractive, instantly appealing – to which both narrator and novelist evidently feel themselves to be subject have, of course, a strongly gendered inflection – one from which the novel's self-parodying excesses also register a certain critical distance and which they cast into revealingly sharp relief. As we'll see, an awareness that women are under particular pressure to "make nice" in displaying themselves and their wares to the market (and at the same time liable to be accused precisely of an unseemly over-eagerness in cultivating market approval) is felt acutely by other women writers (primarily Nell Zink and Sheila Heti) discussed later in this book.

* * *

For the "Bret Easton Ellis" of *Lunar Park*, Patrick Bateman is a "monster," and in *American Psycho*, this monstrousness is stressed via repeated invocations of zoanthropy: in one gruesome scene, Bateman – with his "virtual absence of humanity" – "leap[s]" at his victim "jackal-like, literally foaming at the mouth" (327); in another he "grunt[s] and moan[s] like some kind of animal" (395). An acquaintance's offhand description of Bateman as "an animal. A total animal" (384) is truer than he knows. This kind of animalistic rhetoric (so common in discussions of financial excess)[68] is fully literalized in Stephen Marche's widely admired 2015 novel *The Hunger of the Wolf*, which tracks the ascendance, over the arc of the twentieth century, of a wealthy American dynasty, the Wylies, whose men seemingly carry a hereditary strain of lycanthropy. In an essay published around the time of the novel's release, Marche explicitly positions his narrative within the contemporary "turn to genre" on the part of ostensibly "literary" authors that we considered in the Introduction, citing Colson Whitehead's *Zone One* alongside texts by Kazuo Ishiguro, Emily St. John Mandel, and Chang-rae Lee. Marche primarily attributes this turn to a consensus that "the forms of genre" – including science fiction and fantasy novels, as well as "horror, vampire, and werewolf stories" – "have become the natural homes for the most serious literary questions."[69] In his own werewolf story, Marche uses genre modes to explore the insatiable appetites that drive markets and economies – "the desire for growth, the hunger for more"[70] – as well as the more overtly "*literary* question" of how imaginative writing can successfully enter into these same circuits of exchange.

"All money is a matter of belief" declares the novel's epigraph, from Adam Smith, and for the protagonist, a New York journalist named Jamie Cabot, fully to countenance the Wylie tycoons' inexplicable transformation into wolves is to be vouchsafed an insight into the mysterious inner processes of capitalism itself: "a glance into the hidden workings of the machinery," initiation into "the secret history of how money became everything" (20, 21). The idea that money is now "everything" would seem to be implicated when, in the essay mentioned above, Marche notes that "resistance to genre, among literary writers, has given way to eagerness to exploit its riches." The "riches" here are primarily intellectual and aesthetic, but also implicitly monetary. Whereas, "for most of the 20th century, literary art dreamed of an escape from genre . . . and, above all, the market," in the present an embrace (or "exploitation") of genre offers a means of securing a new dream: writing a book (he offers the exemplary case of Whitehead's *Zone One*) that is both a "critical darling" and a "bestseller."

If, in this essay, Marche is slightly coy about the economic imperatives that might drive a writer to adopt a particular generic mode, in his novel he is disarmingly upfront about them. After losing his newspaper job following the 2008 crash, the protagonist, Jamie, finds his "home . . . among the freelancers" of the Manhattan literary scene, obliged to second-guess the shifting currents of the book trade – "to figure out which genre the publishers won't hate two years from now" (12). (In another essay, Marche remarks that in the years after 2008, "I did not meet a single artist, in any field, who was not, when you got right to the bottom of their lives, pursuing the crudest form of personal material security. The principal question of the life of the mind was how to make a living at the life of the mind.")[71] Ostensibly a novel about the horror of lycanthropy, *The Hunger of the Wolf* is arguably more animated by the horror, for the naturalized New Yorker, of having to move back to Toronto (Marche's own place of residence, and a city described in the novel as possessing "a tremendous capacity to endure boredom" [10]). Weaving matter-of-fact descriptions of wolfish shape-shifting into a family saga-style narrative, the account of the Wylie clan that Jamie writes (and that we read) places a premium on establishing readers' trust in its "lurid" (76) sequence of events. The Wylies are Jamie's "unspoken fascination," and "the job of a writer," as he sees it, "is to monetize fascination." "If I could uncover their story," he continues, "I could sell their story ... Every story is a little miracle. You make it out of nothing and you sell it for money" (21). Created *ex nihilo*, stories are like money (as Smith would have it) – and can also make money (as Jamie asserts) – insofar as they're able to secure the subjective attachments, the "belief" or "fascination," of the public. When he has his character describe himself as "blowing delicately but furiously on the embers of the financial hope a big story might bring" (69), Marche invites us to recognize some of the pressures and aspirations shaping his own story, *The Hunger of the Wolf* itself, as well as the wider contemporary genre turn in which the novel so squarely locates itself.

* * *

Money, magic, and the self-reflexivity of market metafiction are similarly intertwined in English author Jonathan Coe's work of "crunch lit," *The Terrible Privacy of Maxwell Sim* (2010). Coe's narrative initially appears entirely consistent with the verisimilar conventions of the "credit-crisis realist novel." Like other texts of this kind, it is subject to the pull of supernatural rhetoric in its description of the crisis; but unlike virtually every other example, it follows through on this rhetoric at the levels both of plot and of form – so much so in fact that by the end of the novel its carefully constructed narrative world has thoroughly disintegrated.

The book tracks the progress of an ill-fated Everyman named Max as he makes a meandering trip across a Britain beset by "financial uncertainty."[72] According to an acquaintance, "the banks [are] about to crumble" (106) because the financialized economy lacks any solid grounding:

> The value of any object [is] entirely abstract, entirely immaterial. And yet these completely non-existent entities – we call them prices – are what we

base our whole society upon. An entire civilization built on . . . well, on air, really. That's all it is. Air . . .

Most people have gone about their daily business on the comfortable assumption that something real and solid underpins everything we do. Now, it's no longer possible to assume that. And as that realization sinks in, we're going to have to adjust our whole way of thinking. (110)

In another strand of the novel, Coe directly relates the foundation-lessness of the financial system to a specific genre of contemporary writing: the brand of speculative antiquarianism most closely asso-ciated with Iain Sinclair, but also practised by other mage-like chan-nellers of London's arcane histories, such as Alan Moore, Michael Moorcock, Peter Ackroyd, Patrick Keiller, and W.G. Sebald. Here, the narrative describes Max's father, Harold's, 1950s friendship with a man named Roger, who works at the London Stock Exchange and is the very embodiment of the occultishly inclined London *flâneur*. Roger owns a "library of volumes on witchcraft and paganism" and relishes walking "through the mazy, empty backstreets of London," pointing "out strange architectural features, quirky buildings, forgot-ten landmarks with some recondite fragment of London history attached to them" (263, 250). His world is an "alluring" place "of shadows, portents, symbols, riddles and coincidences" (267). Coe here invokes a tradition (dating back to the Financial Revolution itself) of portrayals of the City of London's "labyrinth of ancient, history-laden streets dedicated to the single-minded accumulation of money" (280) as a mysterious and enchanted environment (a tradition to which Sinclair, as we'll see, is obsessively drawn).

Ultimately, Roger attempts to build a "flawless" wager, a "phenomenally complex spread of bets" combined "into one financial instrument" (263, 264), and when Harold questions this attempt to make "money out of nothing," "out of air," Roger insists that while "lesser mortals . . . inhabit the material world," the "world of objects," "making "things and then buying and selling and using and consuming them," he and Harold are "above all that. We're alchemists" (264–65). When this supposedly infall-ible bet goes disastrously awry, however, it's implied that Roger's display of esoteric learning is as prone to embarrassing revelations of its own essential emptiness as are the equities whose trade he facilitates at the Stock Exchange. Coe thus satirizes what he elsewhere calls "the modish discipline of psychogeography"[73] as in effect the literary analogue to the contempor-ary speculative economy: both are overblown, fundamentally fraudulent, and successful only insofar as people are willing to buy into their flimsy claims. As we'll see, however, even as the arch-contemporary psychogeo-grapher, Iain Sinclair, is in the process of practising this style (as well as allied speculative genres like magical realism), he himself also subjects it to sceptical scrutiny that is likewise bound up with a critique of the financial world of the City of London.

In *The Terrible Privacy of Maxwell Sim*, Coe is similarly prepared not simply to point to the bankruptcy of other writers' favoured genres, but to undermine the narrative mode in which his own text is ostensibly situated. His interest in the "abstract and ethereal" (62) extends, to a destabilizing degree, that is, to the protagonist and his wider narrative world, whose initial believability, consistency, and three-dimensionality are gradually worn away, before being entirely cancelled. Increasingly illogical and phantasmagoric in its closing stages, Max's journey peters out in a blank, snowy no-man's land, while his sat-nav (reminiscent of *American Psycho*'s automated teller machine) converses volubly with him. True to form – as B.S. Johnson's (highly self-reflexive) biographer, and as an author whose realism (like that of a number of other contemporary writers) invariably displays full cognisance of the lessons of high postmodernism – Coe ends the novel in overtly frame-breaking fashion. Here, in another instance of authorial intrusion, Max encounters his creator, an unnamed but thor-oughly Coe-like writer, who, with a click of his fingers, brings the novel to an end by making his "imaginary friend" (339) disappear. Before being destroyed – just as he was created – by an act of fiat, however, Max is able to get in a dig at the novelist, asking "Don't you think it's rather an undigni-fied thing to do . . . making up stories for a living? . . . What about writing something more serious? History, or science, something like that?" (338–39). The author acknowledges that, "from a literal point of view," what he writes "is not objectively 'true,'" but asserts his view that fiction offers "another kind of truth – a more universal" one (339). In having Max point to the inextricable connection, for a writer, between imagination and remuneration ("making up stories for a living"), however, Coe appears wryly to acknowledge that, having "made up" a believable and empathetic character compatible with received notions of "universal" human experi-ence, his decision to erase him, and sever the bonds of attachment between character and reader is, from a commercial point of view, a wilfully perverse one. Certainly, the novel's ending has proven to be highly contentious among many of its readers.[74] Yet Coe seems to take a certain pleasure in wiping out his character, and in the consequent downgrading of his novel's credit-worthiness, as much as in the writing off of the "completely non-existent entities" traded by the "financial wizard[s]" (110, 229) of the City.

The Terrible Privacy of Maxwell Sim is typical, then, of recent novels, by major authors on both sides of the Atlantic, in which magic and the supernatural are used to explore, and bring into question, the fiduciary exchangeability of financial instruments and fictional narratives alike. In these "market metafictions," the narratives' pecuniary designs on readers are foregrounded, ironized, and undermined, at the same time as the texts' kinship with the circuits of financial exchange are acknowledged and made the basis of an anti-market critique. As such, these texts help us to gain a clearer understanding of what is at stake in the incorporations of genre forms and appeals to readers' credulity that are such prevalent features of the contemporary literary scene more generally. Nowhere have these intersecting concerns been more prominently asserted, sustainedly pursued, and subtly negotiated than in the work of the South Wales-born, London-based novelist, poet, and essayist Iain Sinclair, to which I now turn.

CHAPTER 3

"The Occult Logic of 'Market Forces'"
Iain Sinclair's Post-Big Bang London

Described by reviewers as "contemporary London's foremost chronicler" and "the capital's premier magus," akin to a "presiding London spirit,"[1] Iain Sinclair has spent more than forty years exploring the arcane historical byways of the metropolis that is his adopted home. Central to his attempt to understand the mythic forces that shape contemporary London is his exploration of the city's powerful but cloistered financial operations. Not coincidentally (for complex, ambivalent reasons, which I'll examine), an intensifying concern with London finance in Sinclair's work from the late 1980s through to the late 1990s was accompanied by his migration from the avant-garde peripheries of English literary culture to a position among the nation's most celebrated writers.

Sinclair is an especially significant author for this project because his work exemplifies postmodernism, as I've defined it, in its full breadth and diversity, blending extravagant and acutely self-conscious experimental strategies with remarkably earnest and faithful reproductions of market-approved speculative genres. As such, Sinclair's work of the 1990s, which I focus upon here, gives an early indication of a sea change in the relations between experimental "high" postmodernism and mass-market writing that has become more and more evident on both sides of the Atlantic over the past two decades. Sinclair is also notable for his determination to make the shifting relations between avant-gardism and commercialism the overt subject matter of much of his writing. Central to these strategies is Sinclair's abiding interest in London's financial bastions as charged nodes in the city's networks of power. This interest is evident from the triangulation between the Stock Exchange and other "sources of occult power" in his first major publication, the poem in verse and prose, *Lud Heat* (1975), right through to recent attacks on the speculative investment structures underpinning various overblown urban development projects – what, in *Ghost Milk: Calling Time on the Grand Project* (2011), he calls a "new economics," consisting of "multiverses of insecure investment" or "a wilderness of counterfactual theology."[2]

Sinclair's writing frequently locates itself within a longer history of "enchanted" rhetoric in literary responses to London's financial domains. In his first novel, *White Chappell, Scarlet Tracings* (1987), for example, an authorial proxy (named "Sinclair") visits the insane asylum run as an extension of Guy's Hospital by Queen Victoria's personal physician Sir William Gull, the perpetrator, so the novel (following Stephen Knight's *Jack the Ripper: The Final Solution* [1976]) has it, of the Whitechapel murders of 1888. "Sinclair" muses on the Hospital's origins in a bequest from Thomas Guy, a bookseller as well as a beneficiary of the South Sea stock bubble of the early 1720s. Guy's, with its shadowy, gothic atmosphere, is seen as a fitting product of a fortune amassed in the arcane and mysterious world of financial speculation:

> The hospital, that theatre, contains its secret history in its bland outward architecture. The forecourts, quadrangles, iron gates and chapels disguising frenzy and fear. You know that it was founded by a bookseller who made his money speculating in South Sea stocks? The nervous occultism of the merchant again: trading in invisibles.[3]

The "invisibles" traded by Guy were not only stocks, of course, but also the intangible contents of books, and it is significant that he specialized in selling cheap editions of the Bible, the primary example of what the book historian William St Clair terms the "official supernatural" print matter of the period – works that not merely invited but demanded the faith and emotional attachments of readers.[4]

The language of occultism and invisibility also echoes early eighteenth-century characterizations of finance and fiction, both then emerging (in the English context at least) in something resembling their modern form, with the proliferation of forms of "public credit" on the back of the recently established Bank of England and the new joint stock companies, and the (closely related) professionalization of authorship and emergence of new forms of prose narrative that would quickly establish the novel as a fixture of the literary marketplace. These trends converge nowhere more clearly than in the figure of Daniel Defoe. A totemic personality in Sinclair's work, whose resting place – Bunhill Fields – features as a site of vatic power in *White Chappell, Scarlet Tracings* (89), Defoe deployed a vivid supernatural rhetoric in his treatises on the "Financial Revolution" of public credit and South Sea speculation, which also resonated across his disquisitions on fiction – a rhetoric of "Air-Money," "invisible Phantoms," "substantial Non-Entities," "Alchymists," and "Philosopher's Stones."[5]

Financial enchantment – and its long-standing connections to literary enchantment – are, then, abiding preoccupations for Sinclair. They receive their most complex and extensive treatment in two texts of the 1990s: one, *Downriver* (1991), categorized as a novel and the other, *Lights Out for the Territory* (1997), designated as a work of non-fiction (for reasons that, I'll argue, are tightly bound up with Sinclair's financial concerns, the distinction in his oeuvre between fiction and what he calls "documentary" is far from clear-cut). This was the decade that saw the consolidation of Margaret Thatcher's Conservative government's radical liberalization of London's financial services sector, which began with the package of deregulatory reforms known as "Big Bang," introduced in 1986. Among Big Bang's major measures were the relaxation of restrictions on foreign ownership of British financial institutions and the expansion of market volume through a move from traditional, face-to-face "open-outcry" exchange to electronic, screen-based trading. Big Bang's overall effect of opening the City to global competition dramatically expanded the size of London's financial services industry. Trade at the London International Financial Futures and Options Exchange (LIFFE), for example, increased nearly twenty-fold in the decade after Big Bang, making it the world's third-largest derivatives exchange.[6]

Across *Downriver* and *Lights Out*, Sinclair directs his abiding fascination with the paranormal and occult towards an exploration of the explosive growth of London's financial economy initiated by the Big Bang reforms. At the same time, he reflects on how the same logic of obeisance to the market that was the rationale for Big Bang increasingly prevails in the literary field (and indeed on how processes of financialization in the wider economy directly impinge upon the business of publishing and the working life of the writer). In these texts, then, obligations to uphold various forms of fidelity – trust in seemingly flimsy monetary and financial assets; belief in wildly supernatural narratives; subservience to the demands of the market – converge and are subjected to critical scrutiny.

Downriver and *Lights Out* bring to the fore the crucial question of the politics that lies behind attempts to conjure up enchanted visions of the financial markets. Sinclair's mystical and occult interests go back to his formative involvement, as a kind of participant-observer, in the city's late 1960s and early 1970s countercultural scene, a world of squats, communes, radical bookshops, and anarchist cells. Drawn to a resurgent British pastoralism steeped in stone circles and myths of Albion, Sinclair was also receptive to experimental forms of cultural consciousness emanating from across the Atlantic, ranging from the work of the Black Mountain poets to the Beat movement to more overtly political groups like the Diggers and the Black Panthers. Sinclair's American interests and affiliations directly relate him to major points of confluence between the counterculture and the New Left in the United States, which, through the 1960s and into the 1970s, were increasingly defined, as Sean McCann and Michael Szalay have argued, by "the appeal of the spontaneous, the symbolic, and ultimately, the magical."[7] Initially evident in the emergence of new forms of public intervention – happenings, gatherings, performances, be-ins, and so on – this sensibility would find growing expression, McCann and Szalay suggest, in American novelists' attraction to ritualistic ceremonies, paranormal visitations, and mystical epiphanies – counterweights to the deadening routines of official, "administered" culture.

Rather similarly, Roger Luckhurst has shown how contemporary London novelists (including Sinclair) have increasingly adopted a Gothic iconography of revenants and haunting that is strongly redolent of (if not necessarily directly informed by) a Derridean "spectropoetics." Both for McCann and Szalay and for Luckhurst, these magical or spectral turns – for all that they claim a counter-hegemonic force – are politically ineffectual, because cut off from concrete struggles over power, wealth, and resources. As Luckhurst notes, Sinclair presents his own invocation of magic as a "necessary counter-conjuration, a protective hex" against neoliberalism's necromancy.[8] Yet, for Luckhurst, "an occultism that conjures counter-spells is itself intrinsically anti-democratic in its love of the arcane," and tends to reinforce "the hierarchies it ostensibly opposes."[9] In a similar way, critics have suggested that figuring finance capitalism through supernatural imagery and storytelling merely lends further mystification to the already mystified, inadvertently colluding in the financial industry's own desire to render itself opaque and immune to public understanding and scrutiny, rather than dispelling it.[10]

Indeed, in Sinclair's case, we might take this charge of complicity a step further, and note that, at times, his stance seems to be more than merely a critical position whose duplication of the logic of its object of critique robs it of its criticality, and more like an active expression of awe, wonder, and excitement at a spectacle – the chimerical operation of the financial markets – which realizes (albeit in a distorted form) some of the more mind-bending aspirations of what Sinclair's friend and inspiration, J.G. Ballard, called the "craze years" of the 1960s and early 1970s (one thinks here of Sinclair's description of contemporary money, in *Ghost Milk*, as a "dopey, psychedelic soap bubble").[11] McCann and Szalay argue that in its emphasis on creativity and spontaneity, and commitment to the supremacy of the symbolic and imaginative, the "magical thinking" of the convergent counterculture and New Left ended up attached to many of the more "cherished" aspects of the "folklore of the late capitalist economy" itself.[12] And in Sinclair's depiction of London finance as given over to magic (albeit of a decidedly malign, evil-eyed kind), one likewise senses something of the aging hippie's affinity for the weird or far out, an exhilarating rush at the prospect of a transformative – even, in its way, revolutionary – warping of the "straight" world by the imagined-made-real.

And the screw of complicity has a further turn because, in portraying the trust-eliciting instruments of contemporary finance via supernatural means, Sinclair (like other authors discussed above) attempts, quite openly, to cash in on the trust-eliciting generic forms – and hence market appeal – of Gothic and magical fictions. Sinclair's work thus demonstrates a double fealty to market logics that are themselves defined by faith, trust, or (suspended) (dis)belief: a veneration of financial markets' dazzling legerdemain, and a desire to secure the commercial rewards to be had by performing similar feats of narrative conjuration for his readers. As in texts discussed throughout this book, however, fidelity co-exists with an impulse towards dissent, and, in *Downriver* and *Lights Out for the Territory*, Sinclair constructs compelling, vivid, immersive visions of finance as a wondrous phantasmagoria, only to tear them down, posing the question of what happens to the marketability of financial and literary assets when disbelief ceases to be suspended, and crashes back to earth.

What is ultimately most significant about these texts is the way in which they place under the microscope, and make sharply visible, the shifting structures of attachment and disavowal, faith and doubt, adoration and loathing that define subjectivity under advanced conditions of financialization. These forms of subjective response are not only evident among Sinclair's characters, nor even merely on his own part or on the part of his various narrative proxies, but are also staged in ways that deeply implicate the reader: the texts make us want to believe – in imaginary forms of financial value, in imaginative literature – only to make us feel the disorientating collapse of that belief. In *Downriver*, this anatomization of financial feeling relates primarily to the "dematerialized" forms of contemporary finance, while in *Lights Out for the Territory* that peculiar and stubbornly persistent form of faith masquerading as materialism known as the "gold standard mentality" is laid bare in all its quirks, eccentricities, and contradictions. Across these texts, I'll argue, Sinclair provides us with something like a narrative modelling of the affective and imaginative conditions of contemporary finance.

(Dis)Enchanting the Market: *Downriver*

In *Downriver*, Sinclair examines the relationship between fiduciarity and exchangeability in the market through an autocritique of one of the most prominent and successful brands of "enchanted" fiction to float on the literary marketplace in Britain in the 1980s: magical realism. As practiced, most liberally, by Salman Rushdie, Jeanette Winterson, and Angela Carter, as well as, on occasion, by the likes of Martin Amis, Peter Ackroyd, and Ian McEwan, magical realism (or, to use the term that Sinclair deploys inter-changeably with it in *Downriver*, "baroque realism")[13] has a strong claim to having been the period's predominant style of literary fiction. This post-"Boom," Anglophone version of magical realism can be understood as another manifestation of the desire among "serious" authors of the period minimally to estrange familiar (in this case realist) narrative forms without systematically exploding or dismantling them in the manner of an earlier wave of more militantly experimental postmodernists. At the same time, however, it provides an opportunity to incorporate some of the market-friendly pleasures of supernatural genre forms (especially fantasy and the Gothic) into the "literary" novel in ways that, as we've seen, have become increasingly prevalent in recent years. For Sinclair, magical realism's "literary" status merely conceals the extent to which it owes its prevalence not to its aesthetic qualities but to a capacity to garner sales. In his eyes, moreover, magical realism's notional "literariness" does not mean that it is any less of a conventionalized genre in its own right.

In *Downriver*, the narrator – identifiable, at this point, as a fictionalized version of the author himself – recalls a dispiriting encounter with the editor of a literary magazine renowned as a "huge market-forces success," whose imprimatur confirms a writer's "bankable status" (353, 350). The narrator is warned that the editor "chops everybody. Except Jeanette Winterson. And Martin Amis, of course" (351), and, sure enough, the story under consideration is peremptorily cut into virtual nonexistence. By deploying some "knockabout ... picaresque," the narrator has made a tepid attempt at the voguish style, but has overlooked the fact that this style has a strict, market-dictated formula: "There were sexier topics out there in the slums and shanties of magical realism. Travel was sexy. Poverty was sexy. The New Physics was sexy. Sex was *not* sexy. (Except for Martin

Amis.)" (352; emphasis in original). Far from furthering a feminist or postcolonial politics, magical realism is seen here merely to offer a vapid exoticism. (This kind of appeal to a consumer desire to "slum it" via spectacles of "otherness" is something we will encounter again in considering Teju Cole's critical approach to representations of sub-Saharan Africa in Chapter 6.) The editor of the magazine – who goes under the apt name Bull Bagman – embodies the financialization of the publishing industry: "The wilder his schemes, the more the bankers loved it. He couldn't ask for enough money . . . All the 1960s scoundrels were getting out of books and into publishing. The Americans had stopped buying antiquarian literature and started collected imprints, conglomerates, prestige Georgian properties" (351). For Sinclair, it's clear that this frenzied expansion will need to be fed by giving the market only and exactly what it wants: the market wants magical realism, and such work is produced, first and foremost, to meet that demand.

It's not difficult to see why this might be so if we consider the "fiduciary contract" that not only regulates the experience of reading a fictional text, but is also central to that text's exchangeability or market appeal. By the late 1980s or early 1990s, some twenty years after the Latin American "Boom" first ignited, habitual consumers of contemporary fiction know what they are getting in reading a novel identified, by its textual and paratextual markers, as a work of magical realism.[14] What might once have been the frame- or world- (or deal-) breaking intrusion of the fantastic into the quotidian is the source of a mere momentary *frisson*, or even passes as unremarkably for the reader as it typically does for the characters or narrators of such novels. Readers have come to understand, and approve, the coherence, consistency, and reliability of the genre, whose very defining convention is the undifferentiated – normalized, familiarized – blending of enchanted and mundane elements. It is this central source of magical realism's integrity and hence marketability as a genre – its solicitation to credit unreal things, to take their matter-of-fact appearance at face value, to treat them as commonplace aspects of everyday life – which makes its congruence with the medium of market exchange itself – that is, with money, in its multiple forms – as close as that of any contemporary literary style. In *Downriver*, Sinclair exploits this congruence in order to interrogate the fiduciary basis for traffic in magical realist writing, narrative fiction in general, and, ultimately, units of exchange value as such. He does so, however, *within* the very market-driven logics of genre, fictionality, and value that he wishes to scrutinize, acknowledging the lack of an autonomous, external position from which an all-out critique might be mounted.

Indeed, the text internalizes an acute conflict over whether such autonomy is even worth pursuing any longer, or whether it is preferable simply to capitulate to the demands of the market.

This ambivalence is foregrounded in what is the closest thing to a main plotline running through *Downriver's* twelve disparate "tales": an account of the abortive production of a TV film, written by the narrator, "Sinclair," for "the Corporation" (the BBC), which is intended to explore the encroachment of the forces of gentrification upon the grimy East End demimonde that the narrator and author inhabit. The projected film is a transparent and cynical attempt to exploit the magical realist (or "baroque realist") aesthetic in pursuit of the lucrative "fees" offered by the Corporation "in its perpetual and never satisfied search for 'The New'" (92):

> Spitalfields was, currently, a battleground of some interest; a zone of "disappearances," mysteries, conflicts, and "baroque realism." Nominated champions of good and evil were locking horns in a picaresque contest to nail the ultimate definition of "the deal." We had to get it on . . . If we didn't move fast, any halfway-sharp surrealist could blunder in and pick up the whole pot. (93)

"Spitalfields," the narrator claims, means "Development Schemes," "Property Sharks," "ball-and-chain demolitions," and refrains of "*Sold!*" (93); it would be folly, he suggests, for a writer not to get in on the action, by penning a screenplay that will, in classic magical realist style, be a "a re-enchantment of that which was never previously enchanted," as the prospective director puts it in formulating his "pitch" (236).

Precisely in accordance with the logic of market metafiction identified above, Sinclair's portrayal of his fictional counterpart as a pen for hire, touting a magical-realism-by-numbers film script, appears to be a rueful acknowledgement of some of the imperatives driving his own project, the writing of *Downriver* itself, which, like the composition of all of Sinclair's work of the 1980s and 1990s, was pursued under conditions of considerable financial exigency. The novel not only gives clear indications of having been conceived in the magical realist mould, but inhabits that style convincingly, as the critic Sara Upstone, for example, testifies: "the form Sinclair employs in the novel, with its fantastic re-creations of history . . . and mythical reconstructions of place . . . has much in common with magical-realist modes of representation."[15] Sinclair's depiction of the Grub Street lifestyle and other down-at-heel milieus on the fringes of the modern metropolis seamlessly incorporates an array of marvellous scenarios: a horde of drowned souls rising out of the Thames Estuary; an encounter with a monstrous hound born without eyes; the transmigration of a woman's spirit through a succession of personae, and eventually into a ghostly afterlife; a testimony posthumously dictated by one of Jack the Ripper's victims. While *Downriver* has much of the feel of magical realism, however, it contains elements that invite us to read its narrative as a kind of counterfeit version of the real thing, or to understand magical realism itself as something like a debased currency, or an overinflated bubble. As this terminology suggests, Sinclair achieves this effect by overtly linking magical realist styles of representation to the forms of market exchange and value in which they are enmeshed.

This linkage becomes apparent via Sinclair's insistent association of the novel's more fantastical elements not only with the commercial concerns of the culture industry, but also with the transformations wrought on London by the economic policies of Margaret Thatcher's Conservative government, especially its privatization of the railways and other public utilities and deregulation of the financial services sector via the "Big Bang" reforms of 1986. One of the novel's many eccentric subplots, for example, concerns the apparent return to the streets of the Victorian penny-dreadful bogeyman Spring-heeled Jack. Spoken of in "rumours" and "whispers" (153) as the possible culprit of a spate of murders in the East End, this phantom figure is quickly identified by various cultural workers as a potential source of profit. The rumours of Jack's return are first put abroad by "some ambitious nerd on the East London Advertiser, scenting a future 'paperback original'" (153). A publisher who believes that he has had a late-night encounter with Jack likewise comes to understand the experience as a socially and commercially exploitable opportunity: "the publisher . . . dined out so often on this fable that he began, in the end, to think of it affectionately as another over-seductive synopsis; a blockbuster, commissioned but never delivered. The one that got away" (155). While the narrator of *Downriver* has more highbrow aspirations than to pen either a pulp "true crime" cash-in or a mass-market "blockbuster," his motivation in tracing sightings of Jack is no less pecuniary. Again, Sinclair appears ruefully to acknowledge some of the pressures that led him to interlace his own tales of East End lowlife with an array of colourful local lore when he has his namesake protagonist, suffering from "critical" "cash-flow" (157) and desperately in need of material for his stalled film project, obsessively follow "gnomic hints" and "clues" (153) in pursuit of "spring-heeled weirdness" (155).

The ghoulish figure of Spring-heeled Jack is not only presented as a money-making opportunity for wily hacks, however, but also as an embodiment of the tumultuous financial forces unleashed by Thatcherite policy, one of the "demons" that has "slipped the leash" amid "unchallenged social changes" that make "anything possible" (158). As the narrator interprets them, "the sightings of Spring-heeled Jack [are] no more than the first exhibitionist raid on the warp, a showy example – a mild preview of the horrors to come, clubbed from the tree by the sightless charge of capital" (171–72). The folkloric monster at large in the contemporary city – the kind of device that is the stock in trade of the magical realist – is here expressly figured as a manifestation of the new forms of speculative investment vehicle flooding the financial markets. Just as readers will pay to consume such tall tales, spliced into the everyday, so investors will jostle to accrue certificates for the "voting shares" that offer "mediumistic" control over the nation's industrial assets (171). But – the novel prompts us to ask – how can we be sure that either purchase is really worth the paper it is printed on?

The text continues to invite this question as it draws progressively more insistent connections between its magical realist mode and the Thatcherite transformation of British financial capitalism. One of the major consequences of the Thatcher government's "Big Bang" reforms, as we saw earlier, was the huge expansion of derivatives trading (centred on the London International Financial Futures and Options Exchange). The cultural theorists of finance Randy Martin and Max Haiven argue that at work within the multiple connotations of "derivative" is a common "social logic," which draws economic and cultural domains into an unexpected contiguity: in Martin's words, the "derivative" is at base "a transmission of some value from a source to something else, an attribute of that original expression that can be combined with like characteristics, a variable factor that can move in harmony or dissonance with others."[16] Sinclair mobilizes a similarly polysemic "derivative logic" in *Downriver*, and reveals how it must eventually exhaust itself. According to the narrator, for example, the "crash of markets" in the form of "screen-glitch" and "runaway numbers" is the sound of "futures" – financial derivatives, but also imagined scenarios – "that [are] all used up" (142): exhausted, no longer capable of delivering a return.

A central feature of the novel is Sinclair's imagining of one of the Thatcher government's flagship initiatives: the transformation, begun in 1988, of the dilapidated docklands area, the Isle of Dogs, into a new business district for the capital's rapidly expanding financial services industry, an area now known as Canary Wharf. Sinclair mounts his most concerted interrogation of the magical realist aesthetic in a chapter (or "tale") set in this emergent centre of financial power. This section, "The Isle of Doges (*Vat City plc*)," describes an incursion by the narrator, "Sinclair," and a band of companions into the strange new cityscape rising downriver of London's historical financial core. An exploration of the "new geography" of London dictated by "the occult logic of market forces" (265), this chapter is, by some margin, the most overtly "magical" part of the novel.

Sinclair is attuned to the surprisingly arcane resonances of what he calls "post-modern docklands" (297). According to experts in these matters, the development is propitiously situated at the intersection of powerful ley lines,[17] while the iconic tower at One Canada Square, built as a home for international banks and other financial institutions, was, as Sinclair's fellow London seer Peter Ackroyd has noted, explicitly modelled by its architect, César Pelli, on the energy-channelling form of the Egyptian obelisk.[18] Sinclair draws heavily on these mystical associations in his phantasmagoric portrayal of Canary Wharf. What would become One Canada Square is depicted as "Magnum Tower," "London's tallest man-made structure . . . the nearest point to the hand of God," whose peak is a "heavenly pyramid" or materialization of "pyramid alchemy" (278, 287, 283). As Niall Martin remarks, Sinclair's portrayal of the Isle of Dogs suggests "the sacred role of high finance within a supposedly secular world."[19] One of the narrator's companions insists on the diabolical tinge to the site's numinous enchantments: the authoritarian financial powers that command the territory have, he claims, "laid down an apparently impenetrable mental grid. They've protected themselves with an *actively* malign geometry of earth and water: formal canals, fire-towers, black glass temples" (269; emphasis in original).

Magic in this part of Sinclair's "grimoire" (as he calls *Downriver*) (407, 408) is, then, very much the magic of finance capital, its capacity to reshape the world according to its own will. Magic also, here, predominates over realism – so much so, in fact, that the "magical" element of magical realism is pushed to, and beyond, its limits, in the process pointing to what Sinclair sees as the vacuity of the magical realist aesthetic. And this exaggeration of the magical to the point of collapse is achieved through a portrayal of financial overreach and panic. These strategies converge on the rulers of Canary Wharf in Sinclair's lurid vision, who, bizarrely enough, are cardinals from the Vatican. Outlandish inventions themselves, these holy-man capitalists – or "fiscal cardinals" (263) – have powers such that "whatever they imagine" is "made instantly visible" – "cinema-generated plagues," "new rat species," "white growths," "orange bile" (288). This ability evokes the capacity of financiers to dream up "exotic" new derivatives instruments and make them "real." As the narrator puts it, in the buildings of Canary Wharf – "towering tributes to the service industries" – "anything could happen, as long as it happened *fast*. Nothing was made – except the deal. Immaculate telephone consummations" (284; emphasis in original). As Tony Norfield wryly remarks in *The City: London and the Global Power of Finance* (2016), which draws on his experiences at an investment bank in the 1980s and 1990s, "creating assets with a telephone call is how the magic of the financial markets can make you 'productive'!"[20] This ability to create things *ex nihilo* mirrors Sinclair's own power as an author, the power to "give form" to whatever "nightmares" (288) he can conceive of – a power to which he gives full vent in this chapter.

As "Sinclair" and his band of ne'er-do-wells pick their way through the desolate terrain of Canary Wharf, they witness an abundance of weird phenomena, including priests and zealous flagellants in penitential procession (279, 291); telekinetic Swiss Guards (280); ghostly doubles and disembodied voices (287–88, 289–90); a papal throne set on a carpet of human skulls (289); a pontiff who feasts on blood (292); and a woman with a face without features, "blank" and "uncontoured" (296). This stream of paranormality – a "phantasmagoric adventure," as it's later called (375) – is orchestrated around the novel's strangest, and most elaborately drawn, scene, which finds "Sinclair" and co inside the pyramid at the summit of Magnum Tower, witnessing a "secret ceremony" (283) combining an incantatory lecture by the physicist Stephen Hawking and a gruesome sacrificial rite presided over by the Haitian spirit Baron Samedi. Intended to "halt time, wound its membrane," and give the tower's occupants "access to unimagined powers" (283), this ceremony both gestures towards the cosmological origins of the expression "Big Bang" (283) and, as Roger Luckhurst notes, "literalizes the voodoo economics at work in the City."[21]

While this sequence satirizes the elaborate sham that is so much contemporary "financial engineering," then, it also parodies the magical realist style, suggesting that it, too, is fundamentally bogus. Just as the accumulation of supernatural incident, within this space of high finance, points to the acts of pure, out-of-thin-air invention that underlie the more exotic financial products, so too – through its sheer relentless profusion – does it hint at the ultimate emptiness of the magical realist enterprise. By apparently piling up whatever passing flights of fancy, baroque to the point of absurdity, popped into his head – by seemingly, that is, "making it up as he goes along" – Sinclair indicts the casual deployment of supernatural content in magical realist fiction with being an essentially facile, vacuous exercise. Magical realism works by weaving that supernatural content – content in which no one could *really* believe – into narrative worlds that, nonetheless (or, perhaps, precisely for this reason), feel substantial or "three-dimensional," and can attract the imaginative and emotional investments on which the author's ability to realize monetary reward (advances, royalties) rests.

Oneiric scenes – often of the "nightmarish" kind "given form" (288) in *Downriver* – are central to magical realism, but if "bad dreams [are] the accepted currency" (267) of the genre (as they are of Sinclair's contemporary London), then this is a currency that (in the famous phrase attributed to Lenin) may be readily "debauched" – through the over-exuberant clatter not of the mint, but of the writer's keyboard. When the author wilfully ramps up the magic, in gleeful abandon, the narrative world begins to lose its consistency, the genre's mechanisms are laid bare, and the whole house of cards trembles on the verge of collapse. ("The world beyond these concrete walls had lost all credibility," comments Sinclair's narrator in pondering his expedition into the badlands of the Isle of Dogs [267].) At this point, the magical realist text risks losing its value, both as a source of narrative engagement and as an object of market exchange. In the Canary Wharf chapter, the narrator refers to "cheques" as "folded promises" (286); Sinclair refuses to honour ("folds" on) the implicit "promise" – the "fiduciary contract" – of the novel's ostensible genre, and in so doing actively courts the indifference or aversion of the market. Later in the novel, the reader will be asked – in reference to the figure designated as "I" in the text, "'the Narrator' or 'Sinclair'" – "can we (you) trust him?" (352). The answer would appear to be *no*.

Potential readers of the novel in the United States were duly warned by a review accompanying the book's publication there in 1993 that the "futuristic scenarios of satanic rites enacted on the Isle of Dogs by papal and corporate conspirators" are typical of a text "lavishly phrased to a point of self-indulgence" and of "a troubling lack of cohesion in such diverse, unfettered flights of fancy," a lack "ultimately admitted by the narrator himself," who gives up on the attempt "to tie [the story] together." Such "restless," "wild," "frenetic" elements, the reviewer cautioned, "unfortunately ... [leave] one coolly appreciative at best." In other words, they might have some artistic interest, but they repel readerly absorption.[22]

The narrative crisis into which the text descends thus raises the possibility of a market crisis *for* the novel (an inability to circulate profitably); and it also coincides with a crisis of the financial markets *in* the novel. As noted above, the lurid magical elements of the Canary Wharf chapter reach a near-comical pitch in the Hawking/Samedi ceremony, performed to grant the "fiscal cardinals" "access to unimagined powers." As it turns out, the unearthly forces conjured up by this ritual spiral out of control, laying waste to the very sphere of luminous, electronic exchange over which its instigators had hoped to gain mastery. This reversal is depicted in terms that call to mind the Great Crash (or "Black Monday") of October 1987 (mentioned earlier in the novel [74]), which, in the United Kingdom, closely followed an equally iconic Great Storm:

> [T]he red wind was angry. An irreversible prediction. The deck of limey birdsnot screens warned of falling markets, collapse, disaster; and the markets obeyed this failsafe logic. Sell, sell, sell! The wind screamed out of a tumbling fiscal vortex. Unload wheat. Get out of coffee. Dump rubber. Shaft property. Hailstorms of alphabet glitch. The spook tornado swept up everything in the world that was not chained to the ground. (292)

In this vision of markets in free fall, we see the consequences of the withdrawal of the fiduciary ethos – the shared state of tacit trust and belief – that ordinarily helps to sustain the financial system. Shortly after depicting this failure of financial sorcery, Sinclair overtly dramatizes the disintegration of the magical narrative world itself. Having sought to dispel this magic by pushing the supernatural content past all limits of credibility, he now has his fictional proxy summon up the power of active disbelief to break the enchantment completely. Recognizing that he himself has "willed" "this labyrinth of mirrors" into existence, "Sinclair" grasps that *he* "must break it," for "only the imagination itself can rescue you" (293). Resolving to *"strengthen my disbelief"* and "believe more strongly in some other reality, a place beyond this place" (295; emphasis in original), "Sinclair" and his friends are spun free of the tower as it rips itself apart, and find themselves in the comparatively pastoral surroundings of Mudchute Park and Farm, located on the other side of the Isle of Dogs from Canary Wharf.

In Sinclair, however, escape is never total, and the end of this "tale" acknowledges the inescapability of the market for the contemporary writer. In the penultimate paragraph, "Sinclair" exults over the prospect of "escape. Flight. Careering across an alien landscape ... Running, and putting the world behind you" (298). This fantasy is echoed a moment later when he quotes that classic declaration of modernist autonomy pronounced by Stephen Dedalus in James Joyce's *A Portrait of the Artist as a Young Man* (1916): will I – "Sinclair" asks – "enjoy the luxury of silence, exile, cunning?" The answer is emphatic: "Forget it." (298). If not "escape" from "the world," will "Sinclair's" fate instead, he wonders, be total, and willing, incorporation: "letting it swallow you whole?" (298). *Downriver* – and indeed Sinclair's career in general – can be understood as resourceful attempts to fend off the latter possibility, in a full awareness that the former is no longer viable, if in fact it ever was.[23]

In its verbal inventiveness, imaginative excess, and willingness to explode its own representational frames, *Downriver* might well be read as an attempt to break out of its apparent genre of magical realism and embrace something much closer to a modernist – or more specifically Joycean – aesthetic. Among various references and allusions to Joyce, Sinclair draws one of his chapter epigraphs from *Finnegans Wake* (369), and *Downriver* is marked by an evident envy over the ways in which modernist experiments in the defiance of readerly confidence and expectation, such as the *Wake*, were enabled by, and themselves helped to carve out, semi-autonomous spaces in the cultural field, structured by alternative economies of production, circulation, and value to purely market-based ones. As Sinclair self-consciously dramatizes, however, with the contraction of such spaces amid the neoliberal restructuring of the literary field, writers face barely resistible pressures to tailor their work to the market, even where they are deeply sceptical – aesthetically, intellectually, and politically – about the market-approved styles. For Kirsten Searle, "Sinclair's texts deny easy, uncritical consumption and subsequently cause a blockage in the process of commodification. In this manner, Sinclair contends the logos of capitalist alchemy."[24] As I've tried to show, however, Sinclair's position is in fact a good deal more ambivalent than this.

Equally, and at the same time, Sinclair is aware that the relentless expansion of market dynamics entails the recuperation and commodification of modernism itself. This awareness is evident, for example, when "Sinclair" comes upon a scene on a London street in which the works of Joyce and other representatives of modernism and the avant-garde are reduced to mere sources of marketing copy:

> the fences were plastered with fly-pitched posters for rock groups whose names had all been lifted from the canon of modernist literature. A hyperactive collage of quotations; many from William Burroughs, some

from Joyce, some even from Jean Rhys. Authors whose works would finally
exist only as names on hoardings ... (237)

If "canonical" modernist works now carry a distinct marketable cachet,
then so too, the novel suggests, do contemporary exercises in a modernist
style: they are, as one of "Sinclair's" friends contemptuously remarks of
a new building in the East End, examples of "chequebook modernism"
(135). As *Downriver* presents them, then, the aesthetic options available to
the writer who wishes to avoid being "swallowed whole" by the dominant
dispensation are tightly circumscribed indeed; at the very least, however,
the novel displays restlessness, versatility, and inventiveness in probing the
economic status both of its own literary forms and of the forms of
contemporary capital themselves.

City of Gold: *Lights Out for the Territory*

Sinclair's early publication record as a prose writer was chequered. Having
been turned down by one of the United Kingdom's most prominent
presses, Jonathan Cape, *White Chappell, Scarlet Tracings* became the first
book to be published by the eccentric and entrepreneurial gallerist and
bookseller Mike Goldmark, described by Sinclair as a "one man Arts
Council" whose "name ... works like alchemy."[25] After two more major
publishers (Sinclair-Stevenson and Hodder & Stoughton) passed on them,
paperback rights were sold to Paladin, an imprint of one of the largest and
oldest British publishers, William Collins & Sons. Despite initially appearing with a micro-press with minimal marketing muscle, the book gained
a notable reputation in the British literary media (Goldmark recalls being
told at the *Guardian* Fiction Prize ceremony, where *White Chappell* was
named runner-up, that the book would have won had it not been so
"difficult").[26] Encouraged by this promising critical reception, Paladin –
by then part of the publishing giant HarperCollins, formed when Rupert
Murdoch's News Corp acquired William Collins in 1989 and merged it
with Harper & Row – went on to publish *Downriver* in 1991. Sinclair was
also at the time the editor of the Paladin Poetry series, which published
a wide range of experimental and avant-garde poetry – what Sinclair would
later describe as "the antimatter" to "the Thatcherite free-market night-
mare" (*LO* 134). Notoriously, Paladin Poetry was viewed as an insuffi-
ciently commercial proposition under its new ownership and in 1992 the
entire series was pulped. As Sinclair put it, "Rupert Murdoch's accountants
saw no reason to tolerate low-turnover cultural loss leaders" (*LO* 159). As

we've seen, in *Downriver* it was precisely with such dynamics in the publishing industry that Sinclair had been centrally concerned, as well as the wider neoliberal restructuring of the British economy of which Murdoch was already in many ways a figurehead.

In commercial terms, Sinclair's own early prose work fared only marginally better than his poetry series. Neither *Downriver* nor *White Chappell, Scarlet Tracings* was a sales success. "People found [the fiction of the 1980s and 1990s] unreadable," Sinclair has recalled; "none of these books made any money – a pittance." For reasons explained above, this reception might be considered a triumph – of sorts. But – for all-too-obvious reasons – it also confronted Sinclair with a major problem. Tempting as it might be to produce writing that "reel[s] off in any direction" – as he put it to some-time collaborator Kevin Jackson in 2002 – "it's got to have some possibility of being punted in the market-place." His reaction to his work's lack of market penetration was to transpose "very much the same material" from (nominal) fiction into (nominal) non-fiction, or what he often refers to as a "documentary" mode. While readers tended to be resistant to his material in "fictional form," Sinclair explained, "if it's put into an apparently real landscape, they're quite happy to review it and discuss it . . . That seemed to be the switch that turned things round for me, and gained me some kind of audience: shifting out of fiction into non-fiction – or calling it non-fiction." His first major volume of (nominal) non-fiction, *Lights Out for the Territory: 9 Excursions in the Secret History of London*, which was published by the mid-sized British independent Granta in 1997, "hit some note, and started to sell quite rapidly."[27] As Robert Sheppard describes, *Lights Out* "was an instant bestseller and its first edition was out of print within weeks."[28]

In Sinclair's assessment, then, whereas his work struggled to be accepted when bearing the stamp of fiction, it began to circulate more freely when it could claim, at least, to correspond to a tangible reality. That is, if Sinclair's early prose works proved to be less than readily exchangeable under the purely "fiduciary" regime of fiction, his writing turned out to be considerably more viable on this front once it carried a guarantee of "backing" by something understood to be real. This supposition of Sinclair's (apparently borne out in practice – his shift to non-fiction did indeed mark a step change in his commercial and media profile) is thus a literary equivalent of the "gold standard mentality,"[29] the conviction that for monetary instruments to have value and credibility they must be at least nominally convertible into the tangible form of precious metal, specifically gold. It's no coincidence, therefore, that, as we will see, in Sinclair's first extended foray into non-fiction, and still most celebrated work, *Lights Out for the Territory*, the desire for documentary fact becomes bound up with the iconography of gold, vaults, and buried treasure.

Relevant here is the philosopher of money Ole Bjerg's suggestion that trust in fiat money may rely to some extent on an archaic memory-trace of the "gold residing in the treasury of the state or the basement of the central bank."[30] Although the Bretton Woods "gold window" has long since closed, "metallism may serve as a component in the ideology that functions to make state-proclaimed money work as money." On this account, then, a residual feeling "that the money issued by the state is somehow backed by 'real value'" assists in allowing that money to "circulate as if it were actually backed by 'real value.'"[31]

Viewed in these terms, *Lights Out for the Territory* would seem to lend itself to a style of reading that has become standard in work informed by the New Economic Criticism, whereby gold, as an embodiment of "intrinsic value," epitomizes all that is real, tangible, and authentic, and a text that seeks to ground itself in the real may be said to aspire towards what Jean-Joseph Goux calls "gold-language" – "a full, adequate language" in and through which "the real would be conveyed without mediation," the "world . . . fully signified," and truth "formulate[d] . . . immediately."[32] As we'll see, however, in *Lights Out* Sinclair implies, with characteristic reflexivity, that what passes for "truth" or "fact" and what is esteemed as uniquely and inherently "precious" may themselves be subject to constitutive leaps of faith. In this way, Sinclair's work demands a deconstruction of the residual "metallism" that remains an underlying methodological assumption of much New Economic Criticism (for all the field's deconstructive inflections). As Bjerg notes, Marx acclaimed gold as the "natural material" of "abundance and wealth" – a statement endorsed by Goux in his major work *Symbolic Economies*; what's required, in contrast, is a critical method able to take account of how even the seemingly "inherent, real qualities" in which gold's "special" status is assumed to reside are themselves "nothing but the reflections of our own fantasmatic projections."[33]

* * *

As its subtitle suggests, *Lights Out for the Territory* consists of accounts of nine "excursions" into more-or-less obscure aspects of the metropolis (excursions that are both literal journeys – undertaken with the photographer Marc Atkins – and metaphorical explorations of history, art, literature, and myth). The strategy of recycling material from the earlier, fictional work, which Sinclair candidly acknowledges in conversation with

Kevin Jackson, is much in evidence in this first avowedly non-fictional text. *Lights Out for the Territory* is particularly reliant on *Downriver*, both for its broad thematic preoccupations and for particular images and descriptions. The close connection between the two works points, however, to an obvious difficulty with the transition initiated with *Lights Out*: how is it possible to transpose into the key of non-fiction work that, as we've seen, is often so flagrantly, extravagantly fictional? I'll argue that Sinclair's prevailing strategy is to try to persuade the reader that even some of his more outlandish and eccentric fixations might have some factual basis, albeit alloyed with a certain fictional or imaginative element. More specifically, I'll suggest that in his speculative engagements with finance in *Lights Out*, Sinclair attempts to ground his provocative claims in external sources of authority, sources that he finds in the material fabric of London, and that he identifies – implicitly at first, and then more and more explicitly – with gold. This authority to validate what would otherwise appear as pure speculation or conjecture is not of the order of the empirically self-evident, the straightforwardly factual, however, but itself rests on a foundational commitment of trust, just as gold, as Sinclair figures it, can only be *gold* – basis and totem of economy – insofar as it is on some level inherently magical or "alchemical."

In its self-conscious appeal not so much to the true as such, as to things whose "truth" relies on the degree of trust placed in them, *Lights Out for the Territory* is a distinctly unconventional work of "non-fiction." This tension between the subjective or imagined, on the one hand, and the objective or concrete, on the other, is implicit in the compound term with which Sinclair's work is most commonly associated: psychogeography. So commonly has this appellation been applied to Sinclair's writing that it has assumed a taken-for-granted quality, which obscures the idiosyncratic roots of his psychogeographic strategies. Examining these roots will help us to understand where psychogeography, as Sinclair practices it, stands in relation to the categories of fiction and non-fiction; and it will allow us to see more clearly what is at stake in his psychogeographic explorations of London finance.

Sinclair confesses to having been "distantly" aware of the original Lettrist and Situationist theories of psychogeography in the 1960s. But this tradition – with its celebration of the aleatory and resistant *dérive* through urban space – was not a formative influence on what he would come to refer to as his own psychogeographic method.[34] Instead, Sinclair's understanding of space and place was decisively shaped, in the same period, by the so-called "Earth Mysteries" school of archaeology.[35] Generally regarded more as pseudoarchaeological than archaeological proper, this is the tradition that gives us theories of ley lines and the Old Straight Track – sacred geometries supposedly built upon or inscribed into the landscape in prehistoric times. Sinclair's "deep involvement"[36] in reading such work is part of a wider immersion in that strand of literature – obsessed with arcane knowledge, lost artefacts, conspiracies, and the occult – which has been dubbed "pseudohistory" or "cryptohistory."[37] In the British context, the figure of Colin Wilson – author of a slew of inexhaustibly credulous studies of occult traditions and an acquaintance of Sinclair's in the 1970s – looms especially large.[38] Wilson is a frequent reference point in Sinclair's work, not least for his suitably conspiratorial contribution to one of Sinclair's favoured fields of arcana – the body of lore surrounding the Jack the Ripper murders, widely known as "Ripperology" (a term Wilson coined).

The pre-eminent example of pseudohistory, one that "employs all the techniques of [the mode] to symphonic effect,"[39] however, is undoubtedly Michael Baigent, Richard Leigh, and Henry Lincoln's *The Holy Blood and the Holy Grail* (1982). One of the major publishing phenomenons of the 1980s, the book thrilled readers with its claims for the existence of a labyrinthine conspiracy surrounding a royal bloodline descended from the union of Mary Magdalene and Jesus Christ. Though it didn't take long for its sensational claims to be comprehensively debunked, *The Holy Blood and the Holy Grail* was an international bestseller on its release, and has reportedly sold in excess of two million copies in its various editions, meanwhile spawning various sequels, spin-offs, and imitations.[40]

While its influence has gone wholly unremarked by Sinclair's critics, the work of Baigent, Leigh, and Lincoln is one of the major tributaries feeding his brand of psychogeography, nowhere more so than in *Lights Out for the Territory*, and especially (strange as it may seem) in its reckoning with contemporary finance. Sinclair met Richard Leigh in London in the 1970s and through this connection "got in on the ground floor of the *Holy Blood* story."[41] Sinclair has commended the "originality" of the *Holy Blood* authors' material (against the derivativeness of Dan Brown's 2003 blockbuster appropriation, *The Da Vinci Code*).[42] For Sinclair, *The Holy Blood and the Holy Grail* offers a kind of compendium of mystery and conspiracy material, and a model of how a fictive or mythic past might be made to resonate in the present – hallmarks of the psychogeographic style that he would fully realize with 1997's *Lights Out for the Territory*. The influence of *The Holy Blood* and its authors' wider work is hiding in plain sight in *Lights Out*, with their oeuvre being invoked or directly referenced at a number of points (355, 370, 371), as well as cited in Sinclair's bibliography (385, 386).

The Holy Blood was also an evident influence on the avant-gardist provocateurs of the London Psychogeographical Association (LPA), whose yoking of esoteric tradition to the spatial theories of the Lettrists and Situationists prompted Sinclair's assumption of the express mantle of "psychogeographer" in *Lights Out for the Territory*.[43] Sinclair sensed at this point that the psychogeography label could help in securing the commercial success that had earlier eluded him. Looking back in 2002, he remarked: "I thought psychogeography could be adapted quite conveniently to forge a franchise – which is what happened, more than I could have imagined. [Laughs] It took off!"[44] And in 2004 he confessed to "just exploiting [the idea of psychogeography] because I think it's a canny way to write about London." Pondering his elevation to a Hamish Hamilton list featuring household names like Zadie Smith and Alain de Botton, he noted a "sense that I must have some weird brand image as the London psychogeographer," adding "in a way I've allowed myself to become this London brand. I've become a hack on my own mythology."[45]

If Sinclair is almost single-handedly "responsible for the current popularity that psychogeography enjoys," then this is a situation about which he feels no small degree of ambivalence ("There's this awful sense that you've created a monster").[46] Having become a "hack," he says in 2004, "you can either go with it or subvert it."[47] Just as an ambivalence about, and a desire to subvert, magical realism was embedded in *Downriver*, so a similar uneasiness and resistance concerning psychogeography is already present in *Lights Out for the Territory*, Sinclair's first outing under that banner. Also as in *Downriver*, this partial sabotaging of the text's capacity to appeal to, and circulate within, the market is tightly bound up with an interrogation of the monetary forms that mediate market exchange. And in this regard, one of the major influences on Sinclair's psychogeographic method in *Lights Out* – *The Holy Blood and the Holy Grail* – is a model to be both emulated and resisted.

One of the most striking features of Baigent, Leigh, and Lincoln's long, strange, and occasionally fascinating book is an overriding conceptual and argumentative logic whereby something that appears, on the face of it, to be a material object of inherent value and beauty, turns out, under the author's investigation, to be merely a stand-in for a powerful array of symbolic meanings and beliefs. More striking still, in the present context, is the fact that the most important such objects are invariably composed of gold. Thus, the mystery that starts the investigation in motion – how, in the 1890s, an obscure French priest suddenly came into a large fortune – initially appears most likely to be "essentially a treasure story," involving the discovery of one of the caches of "hidden gold or jewels" rumoured to lie buried in the vicinity of his village. The authors come to suspect, however, that the priest's windfall derived not from "anything of intrinsic financial value," but from his having uncovered some religious "knowl-edge" or "secret" of "immense import."[48]

The supposed nature of this secret – that Jesus married and founded a dynasty, safeguarded when Mary Magdalene and her offspring were smuggled to France following the crucifixion – prompts the book's most momentous reinterpretation of the Grail legend: conventionally depicted as an object "made of gold and encrusted with gems,"[49] the Holy Grail, they propose, is in fact not an object at all, but rather nothing other than this sacred royal lineage itself. This pattern of substitution of the symbolic and mythic for the merely material is replicated in the book's numerous descriptions of actual finds of gold and other treasure: these hoards are presented as remarkable not so much for their physical splendour as for their intimations of "magic, sorcery, and divination," as the authors put it in describing the unearthing of medieval artefacts including a "bull's head made of gold."[50] As with modern money under a metallic standard, then, the significance of gold in *The Holy Blood* ultimately resides not in some given or self-sufficient property of the substance itself, or of the objects into which it is shaped, but in the forms of symbolic value that gather around those objects.

The book's authors seem on some level to grasp this connection, for their work is evidently purpose-designed to establish a singularly powerful "fiduciary contract" with its readers, and thereby maximize its circulability in the market (a circulability that would turn out to be formidable indeed). This "contract" is based on the same relationship between the material and the mythic as in the examples above. Late on in the book, Baigent, Leigh, and Lincoln step back from the details of their investigation to give an account of their method. "Since the so-called 'Enlightenment' of the eighteenth century," they claim, "the orientation of Western culture and consciousness" has been away from what they call "synthesis." A "synthetic" approach is often "discouraged as being . . . too speculative," but "one must synthesise for only by such synthesis can one discern the underlying continuity, the unified and coherent fabric, which lies at the core of any historical problem." Crucially, in this effort "it is not sufficient to confine oneself exclusively to facts" (which they liken to "pebbles dropped into the pool of history"). "One must also discern the repercussions and ramifications of facts, as those repercussions and ramifications radiate through the centuries often in the form of myth and legend."[51]

The authors' ostensible claim here is that, however "distorted" they may be, myths and legends are nonetheless able to point the way towards otherwise "irrevocable" truths about the past (a reasonably uncontroversial position).[52] These remarks also, though, hint at the proposition that all of *The Holy Blood*'s structural and rhetorical resources are mobilized towards demonstrating: that certain kinds of truth are to be found only in the realm of myth and legend itself. Insofar as it is understood to be based on established, verifiable facts, conventional or mainstream history writing has a clear power to command and bind the assent of its readers (and indeed *The Holy Blood* is replete with well-documented and widely accepted facts about, for example, the Knights Templar, the Merovingian dynasty, and the history of the early Church). But the book's wager – again, one that would turn out to be spectacularly successful – is that "pseudohistory" (the authors would, of course, prefer a term like "synthetic history" or "mythic history") has the capacity to exert an even greater attraction than its more reputable cousin: that an appeal to belief and the imagination may prove far more compelling than mere factual evidence, no matter how rock solid. Just as gold has little significance outside of its symbolic meanings, so fact, the authors imply, cannot sustain a work of history without a profound appeal to the imagination. In this regard, *The Holy Blood and the Holy Grail* inadvertently points to a truth of history writing as such: that its achievement of readerly absorption and acquiescence relies at least as much upon the deployment of meaning-making narrative structures associated with imaginative literature as upon the sheer presentation of accumulated empirical data (a point demonstrated long ago by Hayden White, among others, but still scandalous in some quarters).[53]

Sinclair's attraction to Baigent, Leigh, and Lincoln's highly imaginative and speculative brand of historiography is at once philosophical and opportunistic. In the long conversation published as *The Verbals* (2003), Kevin Jackson asks Sinclair about the extent of his investment in "unconventional or counter-cultural beliefs – the whole spiritual, metaphysical side of the sixties, from geomancy to shamanism or what have you." Sinclair responds: "All those things are absolutes in my life ... At root I'm a big believer ... I just believe in the absolute life of the imagination." Pushed to confirm whether, ultimately, he is "a materialist or not," he replies: "Not. Not at all, no. Far from it ... By nature and temperament I'm absolutely one of those mad Welsh preachers who believes that ... deliver the speech and you'll change someone's life. Or kill them. I really believe all that."[54] At the same time, his comments on *The Holy Blood and the Holy Grail* reveal a professional author's grudging admiration for peers whose canny formula hit the publishing jackpot. The evident commercial appeal of narratives that purport to unravel recondite conspiracies, coded messages, and obscure historical mysteries undoubtedly plays into the prominence of such elements in Sinclair's designedly market-friendly *Lights Out for the Territory*.

Conversely, though, Sinclair also displays a sharp resistance to the very things that draw him to a project like *The Holy Blood*. Co-existing, in "Jekyll and Hyde" fashion, with the inveterate believer, he admits, is another "side of me, which is cynical, rational and cynical, and I believe in that as well." This is the side of himself that "stands back," "comments," and "looks slightly suspiciously at all this [mystical thinking]" – the side that is happy to dismiss "the *Holy Blood* story" as "preposterous".[55] Alongside this streak of philosophical scepticism is a residual affiliation to a modernist ideal of aesthetic autonomy and withdrawal from market circulation, which makes him uneasy about his own eagerness to court the market's demands.

Thus, if the commercial success of *The Holy Blood* is reliant in no small part on the earnestness with which the authors mount their case – the unflagging sincerity of their appeal to their readers – then Sinclair's determination to ironize, mock, and undermine the various "quests" that he undertakes in his psychogeographic exploration of London in *Lights Out for the Territory* bespeaks a reluctance to establish and maintain the fiduciary relationship on which the likelihood of being embraced by a truly mass audience depends. Again, these divergent positions are figured in the two texts in terms of differing attitudes to a metallic standard of value. Though both imply that gold is not sufficient, in and of itself, to found a system of values, but instead requires a symbolic supplement in order to assume that role, one (*The Holy Blood*) is given over to a logic fully committed to forging such a bond, while the other (*Lights Out*) is drawn to a sceptical attitude that works, corrosively, against the "gold standard mentality" (a mindset that believes itself to be a materialism – insistent on the primacy of that which can be seen and touched – but is in fact a species of magical thinking). Sinclair's disruption of his own text's fiduciary circulability is allied again, then, to an attempt to probe and question the fiduciary structures that undergird market exchange more generally.

* * *

A concern with London's financial power is a recurrent feature of *Lights Out for the Territory*, and here the "big believer" side of Sinclair's temperament is frequently to the fore, formulating connections that seem to be born of the purest mysticism. "Congenitally incapable," as he puts it, "of accepting the notion of 'accident'" (104), he "meditat[es] on the relationship" (4), for example, between a near-fatal boxing match fought in the Docklands development ("where else?" [64]) in 1995 and the coincident collapse of the venerable British merchant bank Barings after the activities of its Singapore-based "rogue trader," Nick Leeson, came to light (4, 64–65). Similarly, returning to the near-simultaneous Great Storm and Crash of October 1987 evoked in *Downriver*, Sinclair posits not the common claim that the hurricane contributed to the financial collapse because it caused the closure of London's markets at a critical moment, but rather the far more outlandish idea that it was the gathering nervous tension in the markets that unleashed a "sympathetic storm" (98, 328). Sinclair likewise seems to wish to be taken at face value – to be fully credited – when he describes the activities of the City of London as "high capitalist black magic"; the financiers who work there as "hierophants," "cult" members, or "businessmen/adepts"; or its bankers as "the most baroque crooks in the kingdom. Black magicians" (1, 100, 104, 105) (rather as when, in a 2004 interview looking back on the political climate of the 1980s, he insists – "quite literally," as far as his interviewer can tell – that "You can't understand Thatcher except in terms of bad magic. This wicked witch who focuses all the ill will in society. I can't understand her except as demonically possessed by the evil forces of world politics … The fact remains that she introduced occultism into British politics").[56] *Lights Out*, then, might be considered a promising candidate for the seemingly oxymoronic category that Tobias Carroll has called "magical realist nonfiction."[57]

The logic that might underlie such seemingly logic-defying claims and conjectures begins to become apparent in *Lights Out*'s centrepiece, a long essay entitled "Bulls & Bears & Mithraic Misalignments: Weather in the City." While *Lights Out* revisits *Downriver*'s interest in the capitalist sorcery of contemporary Docklands, the later text devotes more attention to the occult vibrations of London's original financial centre, the City or "Square Mile," which forms the historical core of what is now Greater

London and has functioned as the hub of trade and commerce in the British Isles since time immemorial. The venerable financial bastions of the City exude a more overtly gothic aura than the skyscrapers of Canary Wharf: as Robert Bond remarks, in *Lights Out* Sinclair finds a "condensation of occult signifiers within the financial heart of the city" (e.g. *LO* 89–90, 100–1, 104).[58]

As I've suggested, the eccentricity of some of the characterizations of the City's financial sector in this nominally "documentary" text virtually obligates Sinclair to offer some manner of external grounding or rationale for his provocative claims. This he finds literally on, or in, the ground of the City, in the form of neglected and buried relics, ruins, and remains, which are the objects of resonant mythic and folkloric traditions. It is this network of mythically charged artefacts, Sinclair suggests, which is the source of the financiers' power, a power that they have both appropriated and corrupted. Of course, this is merely to defer the "explanation" of Sinclair's mystical claims about finance to phenomena that, while having some tangible material embodiment, seem themselves distinctly mystical, and thus – far from solidly anchoring his account – to demand their own rationale in turn. If the magic of London finance derives from the magic of the city's antique remnants, then where does *this* magic come from? And in what sense could any explanatory or evidentiary trail mounted on the order of the magical have a satisfactory conclusion? "It's magic!" would hardly seem to be an adequate assertion with which to close any inquiry. But Sinclair's point will be that propositions akin to this one are in fact widely, if tacitly, accepted: that cultural forms that make an appeal to the "real" – whether they be historical investigations or monetary philosophies – cannot, ultimately, rely on that empirical reality to "speak for itself" or command assent purely on its own basis. At a certain point, the audience or populace must be persuaded to take things on faith, to accept that particular facets of the real – *these* facts, *these* objects, *this* substance – are endowed with a special significance that marks them out and at the same time validates the meaning of the whole. Insofar as Sinclair encourages his readers to buy into the mythic lore that surrounds London's ancient relics, and that underpins his speculations about City finance, he offers an example of this process writ large; but insofar as he also sceptically unravels his own mythmaking, he contests the very paradoxical "naturalness" of this "supernatural" way of thinking.

Sinclair's antiquarian interests in *Lights Out for the Territory* focus on a series of sites and objects that he sees as material carriers of London's ancient traditions. These include Tower Hill, where, according to the

"Earth Mysteries" school of speculative archaeology, the severed head of a mythic early British king is buried (107–11); the rough-hewn block of limestone, likely of Roman origin, known as London Stone, around which a wealth of folklore has grown over the centuries (103);[59] the Elizabethan-era statues of London's legendary founder King Lud and his sons that once stood upon Ludgate to the west of the City (124); the few remaining fragments of the City's Roman Wall (104); and the Temple of Mithras, the Roman site dedicated to the Mithraic mystery cult of ritual bull sacrifice, which was unearthed in the 1950s on Walbrook, and crudely relocated some hundred metres away in the following decade (116–17).[60] For Sinclair, the deep connection to myth and folk memory embodied in barrow, stone, statue, wall, or temple has been lost as these sites and objects have been built over, demolished, displaced, or neglected in the City's headlong rush to expand its commercial operations, or – worse yet – swallowed up by and absorbed into the premises of transnational financial corporations themselves (103, 108, 117):

> Unprepared to let the past go, the off-shore investors and short-term profit takers have deliberately enslaved every artefact they can claw out of the ground … A policy of deliberate misalignment (the Temple of Mithras, London Stone, the surviving effigies from Ludgate) has violated the integrity of the City's sacred geometry; leaving … a climate in which corruption thrives. (117)

It's striking that, in decrying the esotericism of City finance for its betrayal of these venerable objects, Sinclair sounds like nothing so much as one of those "metallists" or "goldbugs" who rage at how the decoupling of money from precious metal (with the end of the "gold window" at the beginning of the 1970s) has corrupted the financial system, permitting the fevered "engineering" of newly "opaque" or "exotic" products that lack any connection to real value. That a "gold standard mentality" is at play in Sinclair's account becomes all the clearer when, in attempting to reconnect the City's energy grid – scrambled and perverted by the "black magicians" of high finance – to its sacred relics, he begins to associate those relics precisely with gold. He does so, however, in ways that, rather than affirming the gold standard mentality, in fact critique and subvert it.

This impulse is evident in Sinclair's account of one of several excursions that he styles, self-consciously, as "quests." In this case, his "researches" (116) relate to the Temple of Mithras, whose careless relocation he so deplores. He is intrigued by a suggestion, arising from the original archaeological study, that the Walbrook Mithraeum may in fact have been the satellite of a larger and more important site of worship, which remains hidden beneath the City. The ability to locate such an ur-site – "one of the crucial icons in any understanding of the psychogeography of the City" – is essential, he suggests, "if we want to uncover the subterranean mechanisms by which the contemporary City functions" (116).

Mithraism is a singularly resonant tradition for a psychogeographic odyssey devoted to understanding the role of finance in the City, for Mithraism's central icon – the bull – is of course also (along with the bear) the emblematic animal of financial trade (107). "Perhaps" therefore, Sinclair proposes, "the energy grid of the Square Mile could be graphed by the scatter" of these "totemic animals" (108, 107) in the form of statues, inn signs, and stone tablets. His conjecture is that bulls may have been "used to map the City," their "distribution" forming a kind of code that, if correctly retraced, will unlock the City's deep history (108, 107). Sinclair sets out, then, to track the traces of bull sacrifice still evident in the City in the hope of identifying the location of the original Temple of Mithras itself.

That this undertaking has an association with gold becomes evident as Sinclair describes approaching the site of the 1950s excavation on Walbrook and seeing a sign enjoining passersby to "HONOUR GOD." "Was there a missing L?" he asks, linking one nominal source of foundational value to another (115). The sign is in the immediate vicinity of "the bulk of the Bank of England" (115) and it is striking that, some 300 metres north-northeast of where the London Mithraeum was uncovered, lies the Bank's gold vault, home to one of the largest stockpiles of gold bullion in the world. Sinclair's highlighting of the proximity of Bank and Temple, and juxtaposition of both with a conflation of "God" and "gold," would seem to imply that there is a kinship between these various terms in his project: that his attempt to re-embed a City mythos corrupted by speculative finance – and to prove the validity of his own speculative theories – rests on a search for a deeply buried embodiment of the real and true that is an expression of the profound pull of gold. This disposition would be in line with the ethos that, according to Jean-Joseph Goux, is inculcated by the United States one-dollar bill, even in a post-gold standard world:

> The State (and its Treasury), God (and our faith in Him) . . . these powerful, central signifiers converge, combine, and intensify each other so as to provide the bank note with its force . . . The American bill . . . remains strongly marked by the emblems of civil religion: that is, by the imaginary realm of guaranteed value and fixed standards. The value of the bill still

refers to a certain depth, a certain verticality. Somewhere, a treasure is present, a reserve, a fund, upon which this bill is staked.[61]

As Goux remarks elsewhere, to this way of thinking it is in "the chthonian vaults . . . that originary values must be sought."[62]

In fact, though, *Lights Out for the Territory* resists a Goux-style reading couched in terms of appeals to the veridical and authentic, because it flaunts the ways in which a text (whether monetary or literary) may *fail* to accrue to itself the legitimating aura of a foundational authority, and how such an authority may itself fail to shore up its own status. Thus, Sinclair intersperses his earnest account of his "researches" into the roots of ritual bull-worship in the City with wry asides, which imply that the whole exercise is a kind of elaborate charade – that he has no real expectation that his conjectures will be confirmed by an actual discovery, and that even if, by some wildly improbable fluke, they were, the discovery would hardly bear the sacred significance that he elsewhere calls upon it to assume. He confesses, for example, that his theories about the symbolic importance of bulls to the folklife of the City are "dubious" (109), and acknowledges that the site in which he finds himself after tracing the remains of the Roman Wall and viewing the head of Mithras in the Museum of London could be called "a kind of solution" only if one were "being generous" (112). In truth, he ruefully admits, the investigation is little more than an elaborate excuse for an outing, a means of "inflat[ing] a day's wandering . . . into something that could be described as a 'quest'" (114).

When Sinclair finally confronts the excavated and relocated Temple, he is acutely conscious of its all-too-prosaic objecthood. It is revealed as a mere heap of stones: "Londoners, workers with somewhere to go, simply don't notice the rump of the Temple. It looks like an unfilled paddling pool, a parking space. Roofless, exposed to the gaze of the office block, it is a shamed structure, an approximation" (117). Like the City's populace in Sinclair's estimation, readers of *Lights Out* ultimately have little encouragement to endow these uninspiring ruins with the reverence that would be necessary for their elevation to the status of a "sacred site in the mapping of London" (116); if readers have little reason even to countenance such an extension of belief, then *Lights Out*'s speculations about the presence of the occult in the social and economic life of the City lack all warrant. Similarly, Sinclair is resigned to the impossibility not only of locating the putative larger Mithraic site, but also of finding any stable grounding for his interpretations of contemporary London. In place of solid bedrock, there is an endless, unfathomable recursion: "The hunt was over, let it drift; we'd never reach the bottom of the City's obfuscations" (117).

Insofar as Sinclair identifies the Temple – and the City's other ancient monuments and artefacts – with gold, then, he does so only, in the end, to imply that in each case one is merely confronted with an undistinguished, workaday object: a lump of stone, a block of metal. Faith and imagination may have the capacity to bestow transcendent meaning, power, and significance upon such mundane objects, but in stressing their mundanity, Sinclair poses the question of why individuals and societies should be willing to offer up such commitments, and exerts some pressure in prying apart the gold standard mentality that still, even long after the demise of a formal gold standard, plays an implicit role in underwriting the monetary and financial systems. At the same time, by poking holes in his own theories and demythologizing the relics to which they refer, Sinclair discredits the "backing" that a work such as his would require in order to cultivate readers' credulity – credulity that is itself a precondition for truly mass-market circulation. Earnestly told, internally consistent, relentlessly affirmative narratives of arcane research have an evident market appeal; less so those that acknowledge the whole escapade to be little more than a wild goose chase.

In the Temple of Mithras sequence, Sinclair sets up the terms of his psychogeographic "researches" broadly in line with the "pseudohistorical" formula perfected by the authors of *The Holy Blood and the Holy Grail*; and his own treasure hunt, for all its shaggy-dog-story qualities, no doubt yields some of the satisfactions delivered by such works. No doubt, too, he is tempted by the commercial success that sustained fidelity to that formula might allow. As he has since remarked, there is "always a slot, as Dan Brown knows, for another good conspiracy. If you want fame and fortune go for Xerox occultism."[63] Indeed, while *Lights Out* was a relative sales success (at least by Sinclair's earlier standards), a text blending his overtly "literary" stylistic abilities with a fully faithful and committed take on the antiquarian quest narrative (somewhat in the manner of Colson Whitehead's later approach to the zombie apocalypse novel) might well have been an all-the-more appealing commercial proposition. But by ultimately exposing and picking apart the conventions of the genre, Sinclair wilfully sabotages his own book's fiduciary circulability – tries, that is, via the deliberate short-circuiting of a generic formula, to resist to some minimal degree the profit-maximizing demands of the market.[64]

After the Mithras expedition peters out, Sinclair declares that the theme of his next "investigation" will be alchemy (118). The choice is fitting indeed, bringing together, as it does, the quest for gold with an esoteric tradition of mysticism and myth. The investigation is to be guided by a dossier passed to Sinclair by an antiquarian bookseller named John Hudson, which offers a "psychogeography of the City" based on the life and works of Elias Ashmole, the seventeenth-century antiquarian and alchemist (119). Sinclair at once acknowledges and ironizes the appeal of such mélanges of myth, fact, and speculation when he remarks: "Irresistible. The full monty: Invisible College, [John] Dee, Ashmole, Masonry, maps, graveyards, cosmic conspiracies" (121).

Hudson's papers instruct Sinclair to trace an alchemical symbol onto a map of the City of London, thereby revealing a line linking churches and other sites associated with St Dunstan (himself, according to earlier "researches" carried out by Sinclair, an alchemist and "bearer of west country grail-force") (130, 121). Again, though, Sinclair freely admits to the degree of fudging that is necessary to make the theory appear even vaguely credible. Tiring of the elaborate geometry involved, he "fiddle[s] the evidence to 'prove' what I had already guessed Hudson was suggesting" (121). Even then, the "demonstration" is "wobbly" at best (121).

Sinclair carries forward his concern with historical theories and financial structures that are built alike upon dubious occult foundations to his account of visiting St Paul's Cathedral. The "prime site" of Hudson's "calculations" (119), St Paul's, for Sinclair, is as much a mercantile centre – akin to a bank or exchange – as a spiritual one. Both in its "Old" form, before the Great Fire of 1666, and in its present-day incarnation, St Paul's, Sinclair suggests, has always been "faithful to the free-market flag": it is a "Thatcherite Temple" given over to "hire," "trade" and "commercial introductions"; a home formally to "moneychangers" and latterly to "cash registers"; a monument to "Christ militant laying out his business plan" (127). The Cathedral is "a fitting conclusion to an occult mapping of the city" (127), but, again, Sinclair flaunts the threadbare nature of the psychogeographic principles with which he comes equipped: he describes himself as "bilious with overripe speculations," "high with . . . cod 'discoveries,'" caught in "an arrogance of vanity and delusion" (129). In this apophenic state, it is "as if seeing a pattern was creating one. As if walks linking discrete sites could manifest some miraculous whole, compete with the gears and bearings of the secret machine" (129).

As it turns out, it is only during an "interlude," when ascending a church tower for some respite from the tendentious and monomaniacal "Dunstan thesis," that Sinclair is granted such an epiphanic vision of the city's totality – permitted "to let go, to glimpse the whole pattern, the London that was and is and will be" (130). This revelation of enduring, unshakeable truth, with which Sinclair's "excursion" into the secret history of the Square Mile culminates, is also a revelation of gold; but even here, knowing coexists with unknowing and the splendour of gold is indistinguishable from its illusoriness:

> Sunlight breaking through the flocculent quilt caught the golden cross above the dome of St Paul's ... The City is revealed as a naked brain, uncapped so that all its pulsing cells are offered for exploitation. The churches are needles, driven into the clay to bend the flow of current. Electrodes can be attached to any mogul with the price of a helicopter pad in his portfolio. The past is an unreliable dream. We know now that we know nothing ...
> We begin to see the gold of alchemy spread across the scatter of domes from St Paul's to the Old Bailey; streams of sliver spurned in the gutters – as when [during the Great Fire] the lead melted from the roof of the old cathedral and "the very streets glowed with fiery redness." (131)

Here again, the deep history of the City, channelled by sites of ritual and worship, is presented as available only for exploitation by the titans of finance capital. The revelation offered to the likes of Sinclair is merely the revelation of the impossibility of accessing an authentic past. The gold-burnished cross atop the Cathedral, meanwhile, emblematizes the conjoining of matter and faith that has preoccupied Sinclair throughout his explorations of the City, its visual impact a product at once of its own physical properties and of the fleeting grace of the crepuscular ray (or "finger of God") that alights upon it. And the surge of revelation that is also a surge of incomprehension is mirrored by the vision of roofs and streets flooded by what appear to be noble metals – supposed embodiments of the real and true – but are in fact the alchemically transmuted forms of base metal, ersatz products of recondite conjuration. Is not gold itself, Sinclair implicitly asks, essentially alchemical, in the way it is elevated from the status of a mere metal (however "noble") to a position of almost cosmic power by the mystical beliefs that play upon its surface?

The essay's final lines return to the subject of buried treasure. Shortly before, Sinclair has noted how the crypt of Old St Paul's, that money-changers' temple, was "stacked with plunder, grails and robes and effigies" (127). In the concluding lines, he reflects on other "treasures" (131) stored there during the Great Fire:

> I remember how the bookdealers packed the crypt of St Paul's with the pick of their stock, with the cathedral's own library; how they sealed away all the knowledge that was worth preserving. The church would repulse the flames of the Great Fire and London's memory would be secure in the cold vaults. (131)

As events transpired, however, hot air reached the "treasures" deposited in the "vaults," and they were reduced to "a great mound of ash" (131). Again, what is imagined as a secure repository of eternal values turns out to be perishable and insubstantial. In this sense, gold is little different from "bundles of paper and parchment" (131).

* * *

In his book, *Money: Whence It Came, Where It Went* (1975), John Kenneth Galbraith famously observes: "The process by which banks create money is so simple that the mind is repelled. Where something so important is involved, a deeper mystery seems only decent." Yet, as Galbraith describes it, the emergence of fractional-reserve banking in the late medieval and early modern periods saw the first banks customarily begin the creation of money by merely transferring "coin on deposit" via "the stroke of a primitive pen." "Another stroke of the pen," in turn, "would give a borrower from the bank ... a loan from the original and idle deposit ... Money had thus been created"[65] This celebrated account is a classic piece of demystification (Galbraith earlier laments that "much discussion of money involves a heavy overlay of priestly incantation" from those who, like "witch doctor[s]," cultivate "the belief that they are in privileged association with the occult").[66] On Galbraith's description, it is not the intrinsic material properties of metal coinage that determine monetary value, but a process of sign-making; and this symbolic intervention is not the mystical acclamation of "modern society['s] ... Holy Grail," "the glittering incarnation of its innermost principle of life" (as Marx characterized reverence for gold),[67] but the mere administrative routine of financial bookkeeping.

In this chapter, I've argued that Sinclair (like a number of other contemporary authors) mobilizes various narrative and generic strategies in order to undertake a – frequently literal – "deep reading" that shows the forms of faith and credit that sustain money and finance to lack all foundation.[68] Part of what is important in these texts, then, is their critical deconstruction of what Eve Kosofsky Sedgwick would call the "artificial, self-contradictory ... phantasmatic" grounds of contemporary economy (and, it should be added, of several major contemporary literary genres).[69]

If Sinclair enacts a "hermeneutics of suspicion" – ruthlessly exposing the fraudulence of cherished beliefs – he also, however, practices what we might call a "hermeneutics of credulity" or a "hermeneutics of specula-tion," which is eager to take these same belief systems at face value, and indeed to extend their powers of pattern-building and meaning-making in ever more baroque ways.[70] A further aspect of his work's importance, then, lies in how it helps us to grasp the forms of belief that structure both financial systems and genres of imaginative literature – precisely by making the appeal of such a credulous or speculative disposition so palpable.

As we've seen, the elicitation of a sensibility of this kind from readers is a precondition of mass-market literary success – of fiction's capacity to generate significant revenue. And something similar would seem to be true of the creation of money itself. On Galbraith's account, the only mystery would be how the monetary system operates in the absence of all mystery: and perhaps this is precisely the issue. In offering this wholly "disen-chanted" view of the creation of money, Galbraith neglects how integral the play of enchantment, disenchantment, and re-enchantment is to the monetary system. In his description, there is no need to invoke an archaic "deeper mystery" to explain a "simple" process that lies exposed in plain view; but perhaps – as the writing of Sinclair and others would suggest – it is only the persistence or ongoing cultivation of a certain mystery, a certain imaginative or phantasmatic element, that permits that logic-defying leap by which something comes from nothing, and the system continues to perpetuate itself. As critically insightful as it is, then, the attempt to lay bare how the system *really* works, outside of all imaginary mystifications, may ultimately be limited in its efficacy, insofar as those very mystifications themselves animate the system's supposedly merely technical mechanisms. Nor would the mere exposure of such mystification be sufficient to dispel it, and so bring the workings of the system to a grinding halt – an objective to which Sinclair at times appears drawn, and which he also ascribes to others, such as Ezra Pound, described in *Lights Out* as driven by an animus against "the very name of Threadneedle Street" (the location of the Bank of England) (101).[71]

In Sinclair's work and that of authors discussed in the previous chapter, we see quite how far disbelief and disenchantment may co-exist with their opposites, especially when the propagation of a "fiduciary" ethos carries with it the incentive of helping the mere flimsy written text in one's possession (whether it be a bank note or a work of literature) to circulate as an object of exchange value in the market, and when, moreover, that form of value appears increasingly to be the only one that counts. As I've suggested, we should not be surprised, therefore, that appeals to readerly trust, belief, and absorption have become such hallmarks of fiction today – as much for the "advanced" contemporary novelist as for any other – and that popular genre forms have proven so appealing to even the most "literary" authorial sensibility. Such is one of the central market logics of contemporary fiction.

* * *

In literary and cultural studies today, "deep reading" tends to be treated as synonymous with suspicion, paranoia, or critique. Yet to question the idea that a text or other cultural form should simply be assumed to say what it means and mean "just what it says"[72] – and to assert instead that what such forms communicate "on the face of it" will only ever tell half the story – is not necessarily to imply that what is latent or hidden is some manner of guilty ideological secret. As we have seen in this chapter, a project of cultural "excavation" may be attuned as much towards impulses of fantasy, reverence, and wonder as towards shameful thought crimes or self-inculpatory omissions. Often taken as the very epitome of the hermeneutics of suspicion, Fredric Jameson's aim of reading for the "political unconscious" of dominant ideological formations is – as he is at pains to stress – ultimately more concerned with the utopian longings such formations harbour than with the structures of domination and exploitation they repress.[73] It is in this manner that the next part of this book attempts to plumb another domain of contemporary financial capitalism where a spirit of faith and devotion abounds: that surrounding the idea of the all-knowing, or perfectly "efficient," market. In Part II, I have explored the conditions by which literary texts circulate in the marketplace; while I return to that question in Part III, my focus there shifts to the ways in which contemporary novels absorb market structures into their very narrative forms themselves – another key market logic shaping recent fiction.

PART III

The Market Knows

The efficient-markets theory . . . holds that markets condense all knowledge relating to their constituents and are by definition "correct" or justified: if the price or index changes, it is because there has been some increment to knowledge relative to the commodity or security, such as a rise in interest, a frost in Florida, or a suicide in the executive suite.

– James Buchan

CHAPTER 4

The Price Is Right
Market Epistemology, Narrative Totality, and the "Big Novel"

In *The Ticklish Subject: The Absent Centre of Political Ontology* (1999), Slavoj Žižek argues that contemporary "'postmodern' risk society" is defined by a loss of belief in an external agent that oversees, organizes, and bears witness to our actions (what, in his Lacanian vocabulary, he calls the "big Other" or the "Subject Supposed to Know"). Echoing Walter Benjamin's image, in the "Theses on the Philosophy of History" (1950), of an all-knowing chronicler, who records every earthly event, no matter how minor, Žižek claims that, for us, there is "no Other Scene in which the accounts are properly kept, no fictional Other Place in which, from the perspective of the Last Judgement, our acts will be properly located and accounted for."[1] In an earlier, "first" modernity, Žižek suggests, two visions of a "global mechanism regulating our interactions" faced off.[2] The first was "the infamous 'invisible hand of the market,'" under whose guiding touch "each of us pursues his/her particular interests, and the ultimate result of this clash and interaction of the multiplicity of individual acts . . . is global welfare."[3] Against this "basic premiss of free-market ideology" stood the leftist idea (which Benjamin's philosophy of history was itself an attempt to articulate) that the market, as the "modern form of Fate," could be superseded by "the establishment of a self-transparent society regulated by the 'collective intellect'" – the communally shared sum of human knowledge and experience, a kind of total, democratically constituted gnosis.[4] Yet in our "second," "late," or "post" modernity, a pervasive disenchantment with these opposed master narratives has left people "desperately looking for another agency which one could legitimately elevate into the position of the Subject Supposed to Know," up to and including "the paranoiac big Other, the secret invisible Master of conspiracy theories."[5]

Žižek's diagnosis is typically compelling in its magisterial sweep, but the contemporary texts – novels, as well as works of economic theory and other cultural narratives and discourses – that I examine in this and the next chapter tell a distinctly different story. While often drawn to conspiratorial rumination (and conventionally read in terms of a "paranoid style" of political thought), the "encyclopaedic" or "systems" novels discussed here testify to a wider resurgence of faith in the market (more specifically, the financial market) as the ultimate presiding agent of history – not a behind-the-scenes strings-puller, but an absolute, impartial, and massively distributed aggregator of social life: "the greatest information processor known to humankind."[6] The reaction formation in the face of conditions of "postmodern" disorientation that I theorize in this chapter and trace in my close readings in the following chapter, then, is not a waning but rather a revival of belief in the divinatory power of the market. At the same time, I argue that contemporary narratives at once diagnose and manifest a blurring of the division between bourgeois and radical understandings of social totality in relation to the financial markets. The "anonymous," "alienated social Substance" that is the market under the sway of the invisible hand is seen, that is, to be suffused by the communitarian spirit of the "collective intellect."[7]

Žižek is surely right to claim that the leftist vision of a collectivity existing outside market relations lost much of its authority in the last decades of the twentieth century. But as a conception of the market as a total social aggregator conversely (and contra Žižek) grew in strength, communitarian- or socialist-minded writers and thinkers came increasingly to identify with – to pledge fidelity to – the market. They did so not (or not purely) in some spasm of sell-out capitulation or surrender, but because they saw in the image of the market (and the financial markets, in particular) a reflection – albeit a distorted one – of their frustrated political hopes. But this traffic has not only been in one direction. As the texts I discuss in this Part help us to see, an underlying desire for the pure collectivity of the demos – a utopian "political unconscious" – subtends even (or rather, especially) the extreme strain of free-market ideology propagated by financial economics' "efficient market hypothesis." In works of fiction – but also outside them – we encounter a back-to-front world, in which leftist thinkers and militants begin to sound like free-market zealots, while "market fundamentalists" take on the appearance of radical communitarians or Benjaminian political mystics.

Even amid these multiple ideological inversions, however, we can detect a persistent anxiety, on the part of left-identified writers, that to venerate the omniscient power of the financial markets is both to concede too much to a system that, whatever its seductions, must ultimately remain an antagonist, and to revere a form of totality that is never far from becoming outright totalitarian. This anxiety prompts writers to adopt dissenting narrative strategies that resist the totalizing knowledge claims they associate with the market, and to point out the holes (growing ever wider in the wake of the global financial crisis) in "efficient market" thinking. In carving out zones of opacity within narrative structures modelled on the notionally omniscient and transparent structures of the financial markets, moreover, such texts also (as with techniques discussed in detail in Part II) assert their refusal to be wholly assimilated to a literary marketplace that itself prizes qualities of transparency and full disclosure in the narratives that circulate within it.

In the next chapter, I focus on texts by two authors – Don DeLillo and Hari Kunzru – but my argument is that the wider phenomenon of the big, brainy, intricately structured novel – exemplified by DeLillo's and Kunzru's work, and such a prominent feature of the US literary landscape in recent decades – is shaped by an ambivalent relation to the correspondingly capacious, complex, and informationally rich sphere of the financial markets. Having laid out the historical and theoretical basis for my argument in the first two sections of this chapter, I devote the third section to surveying a range of so-called "encyclopaedic" or "systems" novels in order to demonstrate the pervasiveness of a fascination with the supposedly omniscient powers of financial markets in such writing. In order to make this case, it is necessary first to sketch a genealogy of the idea of the all-knowing market, as well as to discuss, in rather more detail, its contemporary apotheosis in the form of the efficient market hypothesis. Providing this intellectual context gives me an opportunity to highlight connections that scholars working on earlier periods have drawn between knowledge as a property of markets and knowledge as a dimension of fictional narrative, and allows me to sharpen the terms of my own argument.

Market Omniscience from Smith to Hayek

Proponents of markets as the great collators of dispersed knowledge and activity find their most distinguished antecedent in the founding father of modern economics, and in one of the discipline's most celebrated ideas. As Žižek's invocation of Adam Smith's notion of the "invisible hand" indicates, the Scottish political economist's rather modest account in *The Wealth of Nations* (1776) of a merchant who, in favouring domestic over foreign investment, pursues only his own "security" and his own "gain," but is "led by an invisible hand" to promote the interest of the nation at large,[8] has come to be read in the most far-reaching ways. In his pioneering lectures on liberal and neoliberal thought, *The Birth of Biopolitics* (1978–79), Michel Foucault notes how the notion of the invisible hand (quickly received, if not originally formulated, as the invisible hand *of the market*) would come to be understood as fixing "the empty, but nonetheless secretly occupied place of a providential god" at the heart of the economic process. On this understanding, "there is an essential transparency [to the] economic world," and if "the totality of the process eludes each economic man," there is nonetheless "a point where the whole is completely transparent to a sort of gaze of someone [who] draws together the threads of all these dispersed interests."[9]

Eleanor Courtemanche has argued persuasively that this expanded and overtly theological conception of the invisible hand metaphor provided a model for the nineteenth-century British novel. The interplay between ignorance and omniscience – the "worm's-eye view" of the characters and the "bird's-eye view" of the narrator"; a fascination with the workings of chance, contingency, and unintended consequences coupled to a providentialist understanding of human affairs; a vision of society as "unknowably complex" and yet "organized in some kind of spatial totality" – all of these hallmarks of nineteenth-century fiction reveal a "structural reliance on ways of understanding the social world that are derived implicitly from the invisible hand metaphor."[10]

If Smith was the patron economic saint of the nineteenth-century novel, then, as Jennifer Wicke and Carey James Mickalites have argued, the guru who presided over the market consciousness of early twentieth-century, modernist fiction was undoubtedly John Maynard Keynes (himself a habitué of Bloomsbury salons, and an intimate of many of the major figures of British, and international, modernism).[11] For Wicke, Keynes's rejection of "the invisible hand of a self-regulating market" and "insistence on the chaotic nature of the market" put "the modernist economic theorist" and "the modernist writer" in the same position, where "the imperative is to re-pre-sent what is acknowledged beforehand to be resistant to representation, at least by traditional (realist, rationalist) means."[12] At the same time, however, for the modernist the market is a "mode of collective consciousness," expressed in such forms as the inter-crossing, nigh-on "telepathic," streams of Woolfian consciousness.[13]

The contemporary novelists I discuss in this part of the book retain from their modernist forebears a concern with the points at which transparency – economic, narrative – lapses into cloudiness or obscurity, as well as a sense that market relations generate an enigmatic but powerful form of collectivity. At the same time, these writers gravitate away from a modernist focus on deep interiority and the minutiae of human consciousness, and hark back to the broader narrative canvases of the nineteenth-century social novel, though with an all-the-greater emphasis on the systems, structures, grids, and networks in which characters are enmeshed. Whereas Victorian authors (like their economic exemplar, Smith) were inclined to conceive of the social totality as defined by the boundaries of the nation (an inclination continually confounded by foreign wars or flows of international investment),[14] contemporary "encyclopaedic" or "systems" novelists attempt to reckon fully with the truly global scope of present-day financial markets. Crucially, too, the style of contemporary fiction I discuss here emerges alongside, and is deeply shaped by, a paradigm shift in economic thinking: a rejection of Keynesianism (itself never fully at ease with economic units greater than the nation) as the default tool kit of governments and economic advisers, and a revival and re-articulation of a free-market tradition that traces itself back to Smith.

The arch-prophet of this neoliberal turn was the Austrian School economist Friedrich Hayek. For much of his career, however, while statist and welfarist (not to mention socialist) economic models prevailed across most of the globe, Hayek was something of an isolated voice. He remained consistently committed, though, to what he saw as the momentous epistemological implications of the metaphor of the invisible hand. Smith and the invisible hand underlie the central article of faith of Hayek's economic philosophy: that market economies are necessarily more efficient than planned ones because of their superior capacity to channel and aggregate "dispersed bits of . . . knowledge not given to anyone in [their] totality," as he writes in "The Use of Knowledge in Society" (1945).[15] According to Hayek, the nature of modern economies is such that the knowledge we wish somehow to have access to is, in a very real sense, knowledge of *everything*, since "there is hardly anything that happens anywhere in the world that *might* not have an effect on the decision [the 'man on the spot'] ought to make."[16] The solution to this problem is, of course, the market, via whose catallactic dynamics individuals make manifest in "price signals" their "unique knowledge of the particular circumstances of time and place."[17] "It is more than a metaphor," Hayek insists, "to describe the price system as a kind of machinery for registering change."[18]

Out of step with prevailing wisdom in the 1940s, Hayek's ideas would come to look like bold new thinking to western governments beset by the stagflation and labour militancy of the 1970s, and had, by the end of the century, been installed as central tenets of the ubiquitous ethos of the agora-as-demos that Thomas Frank has termed "market populism."[19]

During the period, the purest expression of this ethos was found increasingly in the financial markets. This focus on finance as the site where the social becomes knowable in its totality is an under-recognized feature of the ambitious fiction of the late twentieth and early twenty-first centuries, and further distinguishes contemporary novels of the market from their nineteenth- and early twentieth-century precursors.

In the nineteenth-century novel, it is primarily the forces of industrial trade and production that stand for the interlocking workings of social systems and narrative forms (Dickens's "mighty store of wonderful chains ... for ever forging, day and night, in the cast iron-works of time and circumstance"); and in modernist fiction this role is predominantly played by the rhythms of shopping, advertising, and consumption (Clarissa Dalloway setting out to "buy the flowers herself" and in the process "making," "tumbling," "creating" "it" – "life; London; this moment of June" – around her).[20] In the novels of recent decades that I discuss in this Part, however, it is the financial sector whose markets – to quote one such text – are seen as beating out the "amplitude pulse of history."[21]

This contemporary preoccupation with the oracular power of finance relates especially closely to a theoretical paradigm – dominant in the field of financial economics over recent decades – which finds in the stock exchange or the currency markets the purest manifestation of a Hayekian market epistemology. The "efficient market hypothesis" "translates Hayek's central doctrine" of market-based information processing "into the stochastic formalism of neoclassical finance theory."[22] It is the fully formalized summation of the line of economic thinking initiated by Adam Smith and the notion of the invisible hand.

All Available Information: The Efficient Market Hypothesis

The efficient market hypothesis (EMH) emerged as a distinct school of thought over the course of the 1960s, primarily through the work of the American economists Paul Samuelson and Eugene Fama.[23] In the defining terms in which it was formulated by Fama, the theory maintains that prices always fully reflect all available information. That is: within large capital markets, numerous individuals devote themselves to identifying and acting on information that indicates a potentially profitable discrepancy between the price of a security and its underlying value (an obscure company announces a revolutionary invention, or a blue-chip corporation reveals that it is facing a multi-million dollar law suit, for example); because new information is sought so assiduously by so many people, when it emerges it is instantaneously incorporated into prices as investors, through their very attempts to exploit the opportunity, bid the price up or down, thereby erasing the discrepancy as soon as it appears. Thus, "for believers in the efficient market hypothesis," arbitrage opportunities – "moments at which assets are 'mispriced' relative to their theoretical value" – are predestined to be "instantaneous[ly] and immediately foreclosed."[24] The new price at which an asset settles – the aggregate of the various bids and transactions performed in the wake of the information's appearance – necessarily represents the appropriate adjustment or "correction." In this paradigmatic case of the "wisdom of crowds" principle, bids or offers made on the basis of subjective assessments of what the security is now worth result in an objective measure of its value.

According to the EMH, the level at which an asset price comes to rest is not only an optimal reflection of the past and present, but also of the future. The exhaustive projections that lie behind investment decisions mean that prices always incorporate an aggregated "best guess" about future conditions. Even with an optimal forecast of the future factored or "discounted" into their prices, however, financial assets are exposed to such an enormous range of variables that events not already accounted for will occur at a virtually continuous rate, prompting successive, instantaneous – but necessarily unpredictable – price corrections. Future events, that is, are either anticipated in advance, in which case they are already reflected in prices ("priced in") and cannot be exploited for profit, or they are unanticipated and unanticipatable, and represent investment opportunities no more attractive than betting on the toss of a coin. In the words of Paul Samuelson, in his classic contribution to the field, "if one could be sure that a price will rise, it would have already risen."[25]

The EMH theorists' early interventions were fortuitously timed, appearing on the cusp of the massive expansion of the financial sector that would begin in the early 1970s. The notion of markets as tending towards a state of perfect informational efficiency had an especially direct and immediate impact on currency trading, itself at the epicentre of financial innovation in the early 1970s, when, amid the unravelling of the Bretton Woods international monetary system, the then chairman of the Chicago Mercantile Exchange, Leo Melamed, developed the world's first currency futures market, the International Monetary Market. Melamed's plans were crystalized by an article concerning the economist Milton Friedman's ardent, but frustrated, desire – on efficient market grounds – to be able to short sell the beleaguered British pound.[26] Indeed, as early as 1953, Friedman, one of the

leading lights (like Eugene Fama) of the University of Chicago's
Economics and Business faculty, had made the case – effectively
a version of the EMH *avant la lettre* – that currency exchange should be
as open and flexible as possible, because only then would it allow informed
traders to exercise their information to the fullest extent.[27]

Melamed realized that gaining Friedman's endorsement of his new
currency market would be crucial in establishing its credibility, and the
future Nobel laureate's bestowal of intellectual patronage is typical of how
the idea of market efficiency has provided ideological cover for the development of increasingly complex or exotic financial products: if markets are
essentially efficient, then, so the argument goes, niche, "designer" asset
classes – far from threatening to introduce destabilizing risk and volatility
as the (likely socialized) costs of providing lucrative new opportunities for
market participants – simply help to refine that efficiency still further, by
allowing investors to act on information in ever-more precise, targeted
ways. Melamed's establishment of the International Monetary Market on
the basis of the open, transparent circulation of information is also typical
of how efficient market theory has been incorporated into markets' operational principles, structures, and practices. The EMH rapidly became
central to the new forms of financial modelling demanded to price,
trade, and hedge the derivative instruments that proliferated from the
1970s onward. As the historian of financial economics, Philip Mirowski
comments, the EMH cemented itself as "the First Commandment of
models of financial assets," and "has subsequently been built into models
that inform and conduct trading on all the world's major exchanges."[28]

Looking back over the past few decades, however, there's abundant
evidence of financial markets' tendency, contrary to the EMH, to misprice
assets (to fail, that is, to factor in crucial information) or to move – sometimes wildly – for no obvious reason at all. By the time of the 2008 crash,
though, the EMH, in Mirowski's words "had proven so rabidly tenacious
within orthodox economics, occupying pride of place for decades within
both microeconomics and finance, that economists had begun to ignore
most attempts to disprove it."[29] The crisis – which looked for all the world
like a conclusively disconfirming "natural experiment," since prices had so
catastrophically failed to reflect the true fundamentals – has begun to prise
apart the theory's hold, but it has by no means broken it (and many
proponents have in fact redoubled their grip).[30] Why, Mirowski asks,
"did the EMH become Dulcinea in the destructive love affair that the
economics profession seemed unable to shake off?"[31] The explanation, he
suggests, lies in the fact that the EMH has simply become so integral to the

prevailing theories and practices of finance that it cannot be cast aside without endangering the coherence of an entire discipline and an entire industry.[32] As persuasive as Mirowski's assessment is, the tendency of the EMH to spawn strange, logic-defying, and yet zealously proselytized claims suggests the presence of more profound – affective, libidinal, and even devotional – factors in economists' and policymakers' clinging attachment to the theory – factors that, as we'll see, works of contemporary fiction bring sharply into focus.

An especially notable phenomenon in this regard is efficient market hypothesists' ambivalent attachment to the "strong-form" of their theory. The version of the EMH that I have been elaborating up to this point is known as the "semi-strong form." It is the most widely and confidently endorsed variation, and makes the specific claim that all *publicly available* information is already fully reflected in current prices. The "strong-form" of the EMH, however, holds that *all* information, both public *and* private, is always built into prices, so that opportunities for risk-free profit are foreclosed even to insider traders. Jonathan Clarke, Tomas Jandik, and Gershon Mandelker emphasize the profoundly counter-intuitive nature of strong-form market efficiency:

> the strong form of [the EMH] states that a company's management (insiders) would not be able to systematically gain from inside information by buying the company's shares 10 minutes after they decided (but did not publicly announce) to pursue what they perceive to be a very profitable acquisition ... The rationale for strong-form market efficiency is that the market anticipates, in an unbiased manner, future developments and therefore the stock price incorporates all information and evaluates it in a much more objective and informative way than the insiders.[33]

In Burton Malkiel's words, "the 'strong' form goes flat out and says that ... everything that is known, or even knowable, has already been reflected in present prices."[34]

The economists Thomas Copeland and Daniel Friedman aptly refer to strong-form market efficiency as "telepathic rational expectations," since it assumes in effect "that traders can read each other's minds."[35] While advocates of the EMH are almost always obliged to acknowledge that the strong-form of the theory fails to stand up to empirical scrutiny – that investors can and do profit by anticipating price movements through access to privileged information – it has remained integral to endorsements of market efficiency in general, receiving respectful treatment in every defence of the theory. If it is reasonable to assume that there would be a strategic gain for efficient market theorists, in terms of the credibility of their model, in disassociating its mainstream variant from its self-evidently counter-factual (one might even say science-fictional) form, then this reluctance to cast the strong-form version adrift suggests that its assumption of the world's absolute knowability and transparency – at least to the gaze of the market – holds some special appeal.

The notion of market omniscience appears as an absolute and inviolable article of faith elsewhere in the EMH literature. At stake here is what appears, on the face of it, to be a maddening paradox: under the EMH, the streaming letters and numbers on the stock ticker are assumed to incorporate information about world events; yet there is no reliable way of reading those events off the symbols. True, price movements, though inexpressive in themselves, can sometimes be readily correlated with identifiable events – oil futures contracts spike after a bombing in the Middle East; airline stocks plunged following the 9/11 attacks – but often no event can be identified that accounts adequately for a given price movement.

For Eugene Fama, chief formulator of efficient market doctrine proper, however, the very fact that we may not know what causes prices to move is grounds to place even greater faith in the information-processing power of the market. This element of his thinking became clear after the "Black Monday" crash of October 1987, whose effects were at least as severe in New York and Chicago as in London (the latter the focal point of Iain Sinclair's account of the crash, as discussed in Chapter 3). In the eyes of many commentators, Black Monday was a serious blow to the EMH because no piece of information of remotely sufficient magnitude to account for the collapse could be identified. When pressed on this discrepancy, however, Fama insisted that "the appropriate response to the October performance of the market is applause." As Justin Fox explains:

> Fama's reasoning was that an inefficient market would have been one in which the price decline occurred slowly. The rapid adjustment (a.k.a. crash) was evidence of how quickly the market processed new information. Left unanswered was what exactly the new information was. If your belief in efficient markets was strong enough, you didn't need to know. The omniscient market had been able to sense something that, even after the fact, individual scholars and investors were unable to pin down.[36]

For Fama, the fact that experts cannot establish why the market plummeted is not evidence against the idea that prices accurately reflect information, but, on the contrary, evidence that markets process information far better than experts ever will. The sheer fact that the market fell is sufficient to tell us that there was a reason for it to fall; we may not know what that reason was, but we can rest assured that the market does. This is an instance of what Philip Mirowski and Edward Nik-Khah describe as modern economics' tendency to characterize "The Market" as possessing a "depersonalized and deracinated supra-human" knowledge *"not 'known' by any individual human being at all."*[37] The attraction of the efficient market becomes all the stronger, then, if we imagine that the endless rows of symbols and digits register historical reverberations or "deeper truths"[38] that are beyond our ken, and to which we would otherwise remain wholly oblivious.

The EMH's central policy implication – "that regulation is largely unnecessary because markets allocate resources and risks efficiently via the 'invisible hand'"[39] – has been essential not only to the lax regulatory environment that gave banks the freedom to design ever-more risky financial products, but also to the wider ethos of "the market knows best" that has steadily infiltrated virtually every area of life in the United States, Britain, and elsewhere over recent decades – from healthcare to education to prisons to environmental protection. The EMH thus formed the leading edge of the neoliberal Weltanschauung, with its cult of the market. Thomas Frank's *One Market Under God* (2000) remains the best study of how a notion of the market as a specifically epistemological and representational technology, emerged, in the late twentieth-century United States, as a consensus position among politicians, business leaders, and large segments of the media, and eventually came to form part of the ambient "cultural wallpaper" of everyday life.[40] As Frank shows, intellectuals and other cultural figures associated with the radical movements of the 1960s were not immune to the lure of this insurgent faith; indeed, such figures seemed peculiarly attracted to the idea that markets enjoy "some mystic, organic connection to the people."[41] In recent decades, prominent left-identified or counterculturally affiliated novelists writing in the United States have been similarly drawn – albeit ambivalently and conflictedly – to such a conception of the markets.

Maximalism and the Market

This, then, is the gradually coalescing background against which a mode of fiction has emerged that by turns mimics and rejects the structures of market epistemology. I have in mind that sprawling, labyrinthinely plotted, arcanely learned narrative style that rose to prominence in the 1970s, and was initially defined, in still-influential critical studies, as the "encyclopaedic"[42] or "systems"[43] novel, or by reference to an "art of excess."[44] Later designations, which have emerged alongside the style's own development, include the "maximalist novel,"[45] the "Mega-Novel"[46] or "megafiction,"[47] "technomodernism,"[48] "Translit,"[49] and "hysterical realism."[50]

While these terms are not wholly interchangeable – with each pointing, with a greater or lesser degree of specificity, towards particular authors, styles, and preoccupations – they nonetheless mark out roughly the same portion of the literary field, whose identifying markers are proper names such as Pynchon, DeLillo, and Wallace, and terms such as technology, power, paranoia, structure, connection, and control, and whose landmark texts' defining characteristic can be summed up in one word: big. Though predominantly emanating from and concerned with the United States, novels of this kind are strongly international in outlook in their attempts to grasp the full extent and complexity of contemporary systems – if not of The System as such. In Don DeLillo's words, these are "those massive novels of information and intense experience" that provide us with a "map" of "planetary consciousness."[51] As I noted in the Introduction, the encyclopaedic or systems novel is of course another of the key forms of postmodern fiction. While the focus of Part III is the market logic whereby authors absorb the ambitions and contradictions of the EMH into the narrative form of the novel itself, I return in this chapter (in my discussion of David Foster Wallace's *The Pale King* [2011]) – and more extensively in the final section of the following chapter – to the question of how such forms respond to the closely related logics of the literary marketplace.

The critic James Wood was being uncomplimentary, but not inaccurate, when, in an essay of 2000, he identified the "hysterical realism" of the contemporary "big, ambitious novel" with its commitment to "bringing us the information" – especially "the latest information" – even to the point of turning information into "the new character."[52] My argument is that a hitherto unrecognized factor in such writing's omnivorous hunger for new information is a desire to emulate and outdo the prodigious information-gathering capacities of the financial markets, whose growth and ideological entrenchment, as we've seen, track the style's development. Contemporary novelists are deeply attracted to the markets' apparently seer-like ability to apprehend and illuminate the gestalt; indeed, they wish to (re)claim that prerogative for themselves, even as they also at times recoil from such a totalitarian, panoptic ambition.

That an advanced understanding of the economic system makes up a significant part of the "information" that encyclopaedic or systems

novelists wish to "bring" us is evident enough. But what has gone unrecognized is the extent to which that system – more specifically, a constituent
part of it, the financial sector – provides these novelists with a model for the
structuring and processing of narrative information in general. In differ-
ently historicizing the encyclopaedic or systems novel, that is, my argument equally challenges prevailing understandings of the mode's forms and
preoccupations: in particular, my account suggests that we might read such
narratives as attuned less to the intent, deterministic patterning typical of
paranoid or conspiratorial thought (however "decentred" or "overdetermined" the putative conspiracy may be),[53] and more to the rudderless,
anonymous, and contingent – yet communally synchronized – dynamics
that characterize the quintessentially "efficient" market.

I develop the central argument of Part III in two main ways. In the next
chapter, I do so on a micro level via sustained readings of two case study
texts located at either end of what we might think of as the efficient market
era: DeLillo's *Players* (1977) and Hari Kunzru's *Gods Without Men* (2011).
In the remainder of this chapter, though, I identify evidence for the wider
validity of my thesis in the striking propensity of other major examples of
the encyclopaedic or systems mode to correlate the epistemological and
organizational structures of the financial markets with their own narrative
forms. In this way, I argue, such texts self-consciously signal their ambivalent attachment to efficient market thinking.

* * *

This tendency is clearly apparent in the archetypal work of recent encyclopaedic fiction – the central late-twentieth-century exemplar in Edward
Mendelson's foundational categorization of the form: Thomas Pynchon's
Gravity's Rainbow (1973). The organizing social phenomenon of Pynchon's
novel is ostensibly war – most obviously the Second World War, in whose
closing stages the narrative is largely set, but also the omnipresent fact of
military conflict more generally. In an oft-quoted passage, however, the
narrator insists that "the real business of the War is buying and selling."[54]
While "the murdering and the violence are self-policing, and can be
entrusted to non-professionals," and "the mass nature of wartime death
is useful," serving as "spectacle, as diversion from the real movements of the
War," the "true War is a celebration of markets" (124–25). "Organic
markets, carefully styled "black" by the professionals, spring up everywhere," the narrator adds (125). While this characterization of markets as
more fundamental forms of warfare sounds an obviously jaundiced or
oppositional note, the text also betrays a certain affinity with market

systems – with their awesome scale and with their capacity to weave together (as Pynchon's narrative itself also attempts to) a vast social totality, as when the narrator contemplates "fluctuations in currencies, the establishment and disestablishment of an astonishing network of market operations winking on, winking off across the embattled continent" (133). We find a similar suggestion that markets – more specifically financial markets – might (like the novel itself) somehow seek to capture the pulse of entire populations when a character wonders whether "fluctuations in the sexual market, in pornography or prostitutes," could perhaps be tied in to "prices on the Stock Exchange itself" (101).

Gravity's Rainbow's broad concern with markets includes a particular focus on "fluctuations in currencies" (133). Even as conflict rages, we're told, "Scrip, Sterling, Reichsmarks continue to move, severe as classical ballet, inside their antiseptic marble chambers" (125). Pynchon's notion of currency exchange as an intricately ordered and synchronized dance is very much of its moment – that is, of the late 1960s and early 1970s, when calls to reform an international monetary system seen as hopelessly imbalanced were loud and widespread, and plans to institute a foreign exchange market founded on efficient market principles were, as we saw above, coming to fruition. Indeed, the chief developer of those plans, Leo Melamed, drew the same connection as Pynchon between the monetary conditions of World War II–era Europe and those of the Bretton Woods world in its twilight. A Polish Jew who was seven in 1939, Melamed fled his homeland with his family following the Nazi occupation, making his way across wartorn Central and Eastern Europe – Pynchon's "Zone" – to Lithuania, before obtaining passage, via Russia, to Japan, and finally to the United States.[55] Melamed describes how, in pioneering Chicago's International Monetary Market, he was informed by "layers of past experience." As a "child transported from one border to another," he had, before the age of nine, "lived with the Polish zloty, the Lithuanian lit, the Russian ruble, the Japanese yen, and the American dollar," giving him a "peek into the mysterious realm of changing faces and values of foreign exchange," later to be a central preoccupation for him, as it is in *Gravity's Rainbow*.[56] For both Melamed and Pynchon, currency markets stand for commensurability across difference, the capacity to assemble diverse units into a single – complex but meticulously choreographed – structure.[57]

Not surprisingly, given this concern and the narrative's setting, Pynchon's novel pays special attention to one of the great outbreaks of disorder in currency values – the German hyperinflation of the 1920s, a disaster precipitated by financiers like Hugo Stinnes "speculating in currency, buying foreign money [and] driving the mark down" (339). A Russian black market fixer named Semyavin, whom the novel's protagonist, Tyrone Slothrop, encounters in Zürich, complains that, "before the first war," currency "was no more than a sideline, and the term 'industrial espionage' was unknown" (307). But following "the German inflation" – "zeros strung end to end from here to Berlin" – "information" has "come to be the only real medium of exchange" (307). Anticipating a "wave of the future" that was swelling as Pynchon worked on *Gravity's Rainbow* (and is now cresting, as we'll see, in our own present), he remarks that the process of gathering information for the purpose of trading in the markets will "someday . . . all be done by machine. Information machines" (307).

This convergence of markets, information, and machines assumes a wholly constitutive role in one of the few novels of the 1970s whose stature rivals that of Pynchon's opus: William Gaddis's *J R* (1975). If *Gravity's Rainbow* epitomizes the contemporary encyclopaedic novel, then few if any texts occupy the overlapping category of the systems novel more fully than *J R* (coined by the critic Tom LeClair in a book on DeLillo, the term "systems novel" is at least as applicable, as LeClair himself makes clear, to Gaddis, and especially *J R*).[58] Financial markets do not simply provide a model for the organization of narrative material across *J R*'s 700 pages, but actually constitute long stretches of that narrative, made up simply of telephone exchanges between the eponymous protagonist, an eleven-year-old entrepreneurial prodigy, and an array of brokers, traders, and other financial operatives. J R gets his start in the business world through a classic attempt to exploit or "arbitrage" an inefficiency in commodities markets (specifically, and rather bathetically, a discrepancy in the pricing of picnic forks). Far from being consistent with principles of informational efficiency and transparency, however, the fluctuations that J R goes on to incite across a range of markets are based on deceit and misrepresentation. There's euphemistic talk of "technical readjustments taking place in our present dynamic market situation,"[59] but J R's precocious foray into financial trade is an old-fashioned, EMH-defying, boom and bust. Similarly, the information that makes up the narrative itself is consistently difficult to source and authenticate, consisting almost entirely of unattributed, and frequently fragmentary, dialogue.

At the same time, however, this undifferentiated mass of voices, though Babelic to be sure, suggests the possibility of what, in his reading of the novel, Michael Clune calls "a collective market subjectivity."[60] Clune is thinking of the way in which J R himself, in particular, seems wholly plugged into what Hayek calls the "price system," but the frequent indistinguishability of any single character's voice from that of any other augurs a still more radical merger of the individual into the collective within the space of the market. The tangle of crisscrossing dialogue seems to hold the potential somehow to cohere into a pure, transparent flow of communication – a prospect detectable amid the clamour of the financial markets, in ways that seem, for Gaddis, to be precluded elsewhere. Likewise, the multiple investment concerns of a conglomerate – Typhon International – with which J R's own market activities become entangled allow Gaddis to draw into his narrative a kaleidoscopic array of fields and discourses: as Nicky Marsh puts it, "Typhon International's appetite for investment is insatiable and its interests range from politics, foreign affairs, defence, health, and education to telecommunications, sport, and literature."[61] J R, then, sits beside his "Quotron" (which provides "the latest information on any stock" by "pressing a button or two") at the centre of a "Paper Empire" – a credit-based business operation, a 700-page novel – that contains multitudes (85, 651).

If, in James Wood's words, the ability to perform "great displays" of "obscure and far-flung social knowledge" has "become one of the qualifications of the contemporary novelist," then, as Wood suggests, no writer today is better qualified than Richard Powers, the author of a succession of intimidatingly learned and cerebral novels.[62] Nowhere is Powers' encyclopaedic ambition more evident than in his debut, *Three Farmers on Their Way to a Dance* (1985). Described by one reviewer as a "whale of a book about nothing less than the 20th century,"[63] Powers' novel branches out from August Sander's famous, titular photograph of three doomed young men on the eve of World War I to assemble a dazzling gallery of many of the century's most celebrated – and also more obscure – events, personages, and technological developments: exhibits drawn from "the vast warehouse of cultural quintessence."[64] One of the novel's central characters, Peter Mays, a technology journalist, spends much of his time "gazing into the data stream ... of the ticker" (104), and, via Mays, Powers makes it clear that the ultimate comparator for the novel's attempt to survey the contours of twentieth-century history is the stock market. As Mays reflects, the first news of the sinking of the Lusitania will be preserved there, in the price record, in Sea Board Shipping's stock falling "a handful of points" a few hours later (104). Powers here echoes early twentieth-century responses to the spread of the stock ticker, which, as Peter Knight has shown, understood the device as a minutely sensitive "seismograph" or "barometer" on which historical events indexically imprinted themselves.[65]

In the novel's 1980s present day the inscription of history in market prices is understood to occur almost instantaneously. As Mays sees it, "moving and shaking [in] various parts of the globe" – "something, however inconsequential, happen[ing]" – is conveyed immediately "through the electronic moving finger" of the "teletype news wire" as it "spit[s] out data" (103). This "news" – "the real current of history" – is then "sent . . . violently into the hands of the thousands of information brokers on the receiving ends of world events," and rapidly finds its way into the financial "data stream (the only natural resource left to contemporary life)" generated by the "prolific chatter of the ticker" (104). While Mays can "see" the output of the ticker, however, he is "unable to comprehend" it (104): what the market's recording of history gains in comprehensiveness it loses in intelligibility. The novel attempts to alter this equation, making a virtue of the necessity of selectiveness in its treatment of history (while retaining that panoramic view that it associates with the market), and striving to make the deeper significance of the restless play of events visible. In pursuing this project of historical reconstruction – at once aligned with and distinguished from the market's role as universal chronicler – Powers draws heavily on the redemptive historiography of Walter Benjamin – a connection that, intriguingly, also presents itself to Slavoj Žižek and, as we'll see, to Hari Kunzru.

Market epistemology has an even more prominent role, and functions all the more clearly as a structuring principle, in Powers' *Plowing the Dark* (2000). The novel's global scope is immediately apparent in its juxtaposition of two seemingly worlds-apart narrative strands: one located in a virtual reality lab on the shores of Puget Sound, and the other in the cell of an American hostage in Beirut. Set in the "miracle year" of 1989–1990, the narrative is also saturated with images – from Berlin, Beijing, and elsewhere – which convey a planet-wide "igniting" of "collective life," a "great awakening" that is almost sufficient, as one character puts it, to make one "believe in a Zeitgeist."[66] The novel's own world-spanning ambitions are closely mirrored by the work of the VR programmers it depicts, who are designing a "market model" (75) capable of generating an informationally dense, three-dimensional visualization of the entire global economy. The "room of economics," as this virtual space is termed, is based in a rudimentary form of market exchange, which gradually scales up to form "markets as complex as those run by the world at large" (75). In total fulfilment of efficient market aspiration, the exchanges performed by these markets "cull the factual wheat from its fallacious chaff" (82) to

produce a meticulously precise simulation of the economic world-system
in all its vast expanse. The narrator figures this visualization as a text that –
like Powers' own novel – invites careful and sustained scrutiny: the
"simulation means to render mystery visible. To throw open the global
portfolios ... for close reading" (82).

This "global economic simulator" (82) goes beyond even the most
fervent fantasies of the EMH enthusiast, however, in making accurate
forecasts of future economic and political events. As the narrator notes,
"predictive economics" in the tradition of the "classical economist" (the
lineage, beginning with Smith, in which the "neoclassical" EMH is
located) have tended to "crash and burn" (73). "Prediction markets"
predicated on the EMH can, at best, claim to identify the most likely
future outcome, based on all presently available information. The "economics room's" "market model," however, is able to factor in precisely the
"random," "unknown" future scenarios – "political upheavals. Crazy heads
of state. Grassroots revolutions. Technological breakthroughs" (335) – that
the efficient market, by definition, cannot.

A notable rhetorical feature of the novel – which we'll also see elsewhere – is Powers' enumeration of the kinds of data represented in the
"informational fantasia" (83) of this simulated market system: "protective
tariffs, striking shipbuilders, the G7, Paraguay, Kabul"; "last season's cod
haul off Georges Bank, this week's top box-office grossers, four centuries of
Lycian olive pressing"; "Who will swap salt for ocher? How goes the
southern coffee bean harvest? Will the scares in Johannesburg tip the
Frankfurt Börse?" (81–83). Such lists always carry an implicit ellipsis at
their end – an acknowledgement that they might well trail off into infinity,
and a tacit admission of the inability of narrative fiction, no matter how
great its ambition, to match the market when it comes to sheer data-
processing power.

This rivalry also has a crucial role in the fiction of Jonathan Franzen.
Designed to emulate the preceding generation of systems novels,[67]
Franzen's early work *Strong Motion* (1992) surveys the interlocking
social systems (economic, scientific, religious) that structure the
American city in the late twentieth century. Set in the Boston area,
its plot centres around efforts by a young Harvard seismologist named
Renee to determine the cause of a succession of mysterious earthquakes. The novel's shaping conceit is an understanding of financial
markets and works of social fiction as themselves forms of "seismograph," whose function it is to pick up "tremors" in the wider world.
Fittingly, what the text describes as the "rippled" line of a "digital

seismograph" appears indistinguishable – in its presentation on the cover and title page of the original Picador edition – from the fluctuating profile of a stock chart.[68]

Deeply versed in geological literature, the novel also makes clear its awareness of economic theory (not least through the inclusion of a pet gerbil named Milton Friedman). These concerns most clearly converge when Renee is approached by a wealthy heiress, Melanie, who "want[s] information" (271) for the purposes of managing her extensive stock holdings. Melanie's investments are declining in value because of the threat of earthquakes, and she needs to know whether to "cut [her] losses" (274). For Renee, "destructive earthquakes" are "full of information" (81), but Melanie, fully conversant with efficient market orthodoxy, derides the abundance of information about the quakes already written up "in the paper" because "everyone can read it," and so "it's automatically worthless as investment information" (275). In response, Renee closes the loop between the seismograph and the stock chart by agreeing to sell "secret" data "behind her employer's [i.e. Harvard's] back," and tell Melanie "what this particular stock is going to do in the next three months or six months" (296, 295). Eventually, Renee learns that the company in which Melanie is heavily invested is in fact the source of the earthquakes, which it has caused through its illegal practice of injecting toxic waste into wells. A final, devastating quake makes itself felt on Renee's instruments, in the collapse of the company's stock price, and in the narrative's reconfigured social relationships.

The relative capacities of narratives and markets as information systems is likewise a central question of Franzen's friend David Foster Wallace's posthumously published *The Pale King* (2011).[69] Incomplete at the time of Wallace's death in 2008, and pieced together from drafts by his long-time editor Michael Pietsch, the published volume (subtitled "An Unfinished Novel") is a remarkably sprawling and discontinuous thing. Heterogeneity, superfluity, and digression are hallmarks of Wallace's fiction, however, and the text's unwieldy shape is evidently a product as much of design as of the exceptional circumstances of its publication. As Pietsch remarks: "It became apparent as I read that David planned for the novel to have a structure akin to that of *Infinite Jest* [1996], with large portions of apparently unconnected information presented to the reader before a main story line begins to make sense."[70] By the narrator's own admission, the novel reads at times like a "data-dump" (70, 71); and well it might if, as a life-changing lecture witnessed by one of the main characters suggests, the key challenge of

contemporary life is nothing other than "herding, corralling, and organizing" the "torrential flow" of "the real world's constituent info" (242).

The lecture's primary concern is the examination of tax returns, an
occupation that involves "riding herd on the unending torrent of financial
data" (235). According to one IRS worker, "the Service" wishes the public
to "see it as nothing but a completely efficient, all-knowing instrument"
(112), and the main narrative drift of the novel, set in the mid-1980s,
concerns attempts to achieve this goal by reforming the Service's operations in line with "the market model, efficiency, and a maximum return
[on] investment" (85). These reforms – known collectively as the
"Spackman Initiative" – reject the idea of "tax and its administration as
an arena of social justice and civic virtue" and aim at the neoliberal
transformation of the IRS into "a for-profit business" (84–85). According
to Wallace's notes, the "Big Q" of his work in progress "is whether [the]
IRS is to be essentially a corporate entity or a *moral* one" (545; emphasis in
original).

The spearhead of the corporatizing agenda is a top administrator in the
IRS's "Systems Division," a "Systems icon" named Merrill Errol Lehrl (8).
Lehrl's axiom is that "the definitive test of the efficiency of any organization
structure [is] information and the filtering and dissemination of information" (14). The measures he aims to implement are not only market-
orientated but also conjoin "technology and efficiency" (150) in moves to
automate the examination of tax returns on a "digital Fornix network"
running "a high-powered statistical … algorithm" (70). Appropriately,
Lehrl's chief outrider, Claude Sylvanshine, arrives at the Regional
Examination Center in Peoria, Illinois (the novel's main location) from
Chicago, fount of theories of market-based informational efficiency that,
in the mid-1980s, were being readily absorbed by what Wallace calls the
"motivated, focused kids at U of Chicago" (166).

Sylvanshine is part of Lehrl's "strange team of intuitives and occult
ephebes" (82). His particular peculiarity is his status as a "fact psychic" or
"data mystic" – an individual whose consciousness is inundated by the
world's "fractious, boiling minutiae" (120, 122). Cue multiple examples of
what we might think of as the contemporary systems novel's "infinity lists."
We're told, for instance, that Sylvanshine is spontaneously aware of

> The population of Brunei. The difference between mucus and sputum.
> How long a piece of gum has resided on the underside of the third-row
> fourth-from-left seat of the Virginia Theater, Cranston RI … The amount
> of undigested red meat in the colon of the average forty-three-year-old adult

male resident of Ghent, Belgium, in grams. The relation between the Turkish lira and the Yugoslavian dinar. The year of death for undersea explorer William Beebe. (122–23)

"Sometimes . . . queerly backlit, as by an infinitely bright light an infinite distance away" (123), the "data" keep coming, as if there will eventually be no "fact" that Sylvanshine the Memorious – a kind of walking "market model" – has not known.

For his own part, Wallace seems uncertain as to whether his project should be dedicated to standards of pure comprehensiveness and transparency, or whether its material should receive the qualitative differentiation that might permit some form of "moral" significance to emerge. Crucially, just as the demand for total knowability is shown in the novel to be bound to "the market model," so the impulse towards narrative transparency is identified as related to "market forces" (83). This connection becomes clear in the "Author's Foreword" (Chapter 9 in the volume assembled by Pietsch), where readers find themselves addressed by a voice – announcing itself as that of "David Wallace" – that confidently asserts "All of this is true. This book is really true" (68–69). Operating on a kind of literary wisdom of crowds principle, "Wallace," we're assured, has "aggregated" numerous sources of information in order to arrive at the closest possible approximation of the truth: as "an aggregate, [these sources] have provided reminiscences and concrete details that . . . have yielded scenes of immense authority and realism, regardless of whether this author was actually corporeally right there on the scene at the time or not" (74).[71]

This claim to accuracy is part of "a kind of unspoken contract between a book's author and its reader" (74). "The subliminal contract for nonfiction," "Wallace" notes, "is very different from the one for fiction," and on the basis of "Wallace's" insistence that the book we're reading is "not fiction at all, but substantially true and accurate," "our mutual contract" – "our doing business together . . . in today's commercial climate" – must be "based on the presumption of . . . my veracity" (75). "Wallace" admits to being swayed by "the dramatically increased popularity of the memoir as a literary genre," and since "popularity is . . . a synonym for profitability," "that fact alone should suffice, personal-motivation-wise" (82–83). He would, he says, "be a rank hypocrite if I pretended that I was less attuned and receptive to market forces than anyone else" (83). For all its information-density, however, the actual form of *The Pale King* (both as we have it today and, it would seem, as Wallace envisaged it), is shot through with the kind of veracity-shattering literary devices – "shifting p.o.v.s, structural fragmentation, willed incongruities" – that "Wallace" aligns decisively with fiction (74). The fissures that Wallace purposefully opens up in the narrative stand as formal ripostes – "moral" ones, and arguably political ones as well – both to a market-driven neoliberal demand for total informational disclosure and efficiency and to the perceived market dominance of writing branded as reliably veridical and authentic. "Wallace" insists in the "Author's Forward" that "the very last thing this book is is some kind of clever metafictional titty-pincher" (69); maybe so, but the text practices the strategies of what I have called "market metafiction" with uncommon assertiveness.

Paying tribute to Wallace after his death in 2008, the critic and then-aspiring novelist Garth Risk Hallberg saluted an author whose "work has mattered more to me, and for longer, than any other writer's." The signature feature of Wallace's oeuvre, Hallberg observed, was his ability "somehow ... to pay attention to everything."[72] Self-consciously conceived in the systems novel vein, and readily compared to the form's landmark works by reviewers when it arrived in 2015, Hallberg's debut novel, *City on Fire*, revealed a similar all-encompassing intent. While flaunting the influence of Wallace and other American maximalists, *City on Fire* – in its depiction of a crumbling 1970s New York crisscrossed by downtown artists, Wall Street executives, and guerrilla insurgents – is perhaps most redolent of DeLillo's genre-defining systems novels of the period – the likes of *Great Jones Street* (1973), *Running Dog* (1978), and, especially, *Players* (1977). Like *Players* (as we'll see), *City on Fire* aligns its widescreen narrative ambitions with the recording and visualizing powers of the markets – what the narrator describes as "the tremendous data machine that [is] taking over finance" in the 1970s.[73]

This aspect of the novel becomes most evident via the figure of Keith Lamplighter. A Manhattan stockbroker, Lamplighter's name evokes the capacities for illumination that he ascribes to the stock prices he negotiates. In a key moment, Lamplighter ponders the dismal state of the economy implied by the prices displayed on the stock ticker: "the smug numbers of the ticker machine," he notes, say "real estate [is] depressed" (266). Lamplighter, however, is convinced that financial assets are undervalued: it's 1973, and with the Vietnam War winding down and a huge cohort of young men set to "return to rent apartments, look for jobs, [and] consume durable goods," it's only a matter of time, he reasons, until the economy comes "roaring back" (266). Lamplighter's bullishness makes him "want to take the ticker machine up to the top" of the office tower in which he works "and show it the ... landmass of Manhattan" (266), where all of this pent up potential for growth lies ready to be actualized. For Lamplighter, ticker numbers sent "skyward" reflect the swarming activity – "the animal business, the getting and spending" – of the streets (661). As for many financial professionals and economists in recent decades, financial prices in his view are – or should be – mimetic reflections of a vast socio-economic panorama.

A stock ticker being held aloft at the top of a skyscraper: this latter-day variant on Stendhal's famous characterization of the novel ("a mirror being carried along a road") is echoed in *City on Fire*'s depictions of a number of real or imagined artworks. The stock ticker's function is similar, for example, to that of a painting by a reclusive artist, which tries "to re-create the face of the entire city" (667) in the conviction "that American art should be Big" (555). And it resembles the opus – the "Great American Novel" (5) – envisaged by an author manqué as a continuation of the "old idea" that the novel might "teach us . . . about everything" (354) in "a book . . . as big as life" (867). It stands, that is, as a proxy for Hallberg's own attempt to portray the teeming social totality that is New York City at its dropping-dead, mid-1970s fiscal nadir-cum-pop-cultural zenith.

Another writer is described as wanting his works "to be, not infinite exactly, but big enough to suggest infinitude" (183). For Hallberg's frustrated novelist, a character named Mercer, the problem is precisely his reluctance to settle for the mere suggestion of infinitude in place of the impossible dream of its actuality: he begins avoiding his manuscript because of "the swelling contradiction between the world and the novel as he imagine[s] it" (867). In his head, the book keeps "growing and growing in length and complexity, almost as if it ha[s] taken on the burden of supplanting real life, rather than evoking it" (867). In a nicely absurd moment, Mercer calculates that at a rate of "30-odd pages for each hour spent living," it "would take . . . 2.4 million months to finish" or "2,500 lifetimes, all consumed by writing" (867). In my reading of Hari Kunzru's *Gods Without Men* later in the next chapter, I argue that the rhetorical device I have been calling the "infinity list" is a compromise solution to this problem of reality's inassimilability to narrative totalization – one that there, again, is modelled on "the tremendous data machine" that contemporary finance is frequently imagined to be.

* * *

In examining an array of ambitious contemporary novels in this section, I have been developing my argument that such "big books" find a key model for their own encyclopaedism – their will to encompass and synthesize the multiplicity of social reality – in the financial markets' information-crunching price mechanisms. As my readings have already suggested, however, this encyclopaedic impulse tends to coexist with a desire to escape or resist the totalizing drives of market data-processing and narrative incorporation – drives towards omniscience that are seen to augur an oppressive and ominous omnipotence. That a distinct anti-encyclopaedism is a recurrent – perhaps even constituent – feature of the "encyclopaedic" novel is well established in the criticism,[74] but, again, what has gone largely unnoticed is that this dissenting strategy – just as much as the affirmative one – is so frequently entangled with the epistemological structures of the financial markets.

The signal statement of how forms of organization modelled on market mechanisms must ultimately undermine themselves would be the one that Pynchon, in *Gravity's Rainbow*, gives to a character named Roland Feldspath, a deceased "expert on control systems" (283) who is contacted in a séance. Speaking from "the other side" (36), Feldspath contemplates the idea (as found in Hayek and efficient market theory) that understandings of the market no longer require a vestige – however "invisible" – of an external guiding force, but should be framed instead in terms of spontaneous self-organization. On this account, "a market need no longer be run by the Invisible Hand, but now could *create itself* – its own logic, momentum, style, from *inside*. Putting the control inside was ratifying what de facto had happened – that you had dispensed with God" (35–36; emphases in original). However, to do away with what Foucault, in his reading of Adam Smith, calls the "secretly occupied place of a providential god" is, according to Feldspath, merely to take on "a greater, and more harmful, illusion. The illusion of control" (36). For this oracular voice from the beyond, the malfunctioning of "economic systems" is "a given condition of being," and incidents such as the "humiliating" "fail[ure]" of "the feedback system expected to maintain the value of the mark" during the German hyperinflation frustrate a "Schwärmerei for Control" – as do the many strategic obliquities, ellipses, and dead ends of the novel's own narrative (283).

In the following chapter, I examine the distinctive and inventive ways in which Don DeLillo and Hari Kunzru, in their novels *Players* and *Gods Without Men*, register dissent from a paradigm of market efficiency and unerring "price discovery" towards which they also at times exhibit remarkable fidelity. The resistance to mastery and closure on display in these novels is typical of a more general tendency in the encyclopaedic or systems mode in its possession of a distinctly gendered freighting. It has not escaped critics' attention[75] that the encyclopaedic/systems novel fraternity is just that – an overwhelmingly male (more specifically white male – Kunzru, of mixed British and Indian heritage, is in the minority) grouping, though one whose admission criteria women writers, and especially women writers of colour, such as Leslie Marmon Silko, Karen Tei Yamashita, and Zadie Smith, have made important steps towards redrafting.[76]

Among the male authors of such texts, there is, I would argue, a certain awareness of the way in which their obscure technical preoccupations place them in uncomfortable proximity to a stereotype of the developmentally arrested hobbyist, obsessing over his machines and gadgets. Moreover, these authors exhibit an anxiety that the will to knowledge – of which their own texts liberally partake – is inextricable from an aggressively masculine will to power ("phallic meganovels" is Hallberg's wry designation).[77] The result is a tendency to overcompensate, by aligning that which eludes the mastery of dominant systems of knowledge – especially "irrational" domains of feeling and experience – with women. This valorization of femininity as a privileged site of resistance to a panoptic state of surveillance (frequently associated, as we've seen, with the financial markets), however, merely re-inscribes the binary between masculinity-knowledge and femininity-non-knowledge that generations of feminist critics have been at pains to deconstruct.

Typical here would be a character like Adie Klarpol in Powers' *Plowing the Dark*. A rare woman and lone artist in a community of econometricians and software engineers, Adie's propensity for logic-defying intuitive leaps is coded as the necessary corrective to the technocratic, hyper-rational – and overbearingly masculine – culture of her employer. Discovering that the scenario-mapping capabilities of the company's market modelling system will be put to military use, she deletes her contributions to the project and plays the lead role in a mysterious closing sequence that defies rational explanation, before "disappear[ing]" into "negative space" (403). Such links between women and acts of erasure – and such portrayals of women as sites of erasure themselves – play a similar role, as we'll see, in DeLillo's *Players* and Kunzru's *Gods Without Men*. It is to these novels that I now turn.

CHAPTER 5

Fully Reflecting
Knowing the Mind of the Market in DeLillo and Kunzru

Building on the previous chapter's theorization of efficient market utopianism and its relation to what James Wood calls the "big, ambitious novel," this chapter engages closely with two exemplary texts in this tradition. First, I analyse how Don DeLillo's *Players* (1977) registers fascination and excitement, but also disquiet, at the new understandings of financial markets' epistemological capacities that were filtering into public consciousness in the mid-1970s. In developing my reading of the novel, I diverge from the two main tendencies in its critical reception. First, I argue that, rather than merely testifying to the unmasterability of postmodernity's labyr- inthine power networks,[1] the manifest drift and inconclusiveness of the novel's ostensible conspiracy plotline more specifically model an efficient market world where omniscience and randomness co-exist in alarming conjunctions. And second, I argue that while part of the novel's critical project may be to decry evidence of "finance capital's self-referential nature,"[2] the text has deep affective and ideological investments in the idea of financial markets as intensely and capa- ciously *referential* systems, albeit ones whose referential claims are eluded by that always indeterminable referent that is the future.

Moving from the period of efficient market theory's emergence into the public sphere to that of its greatest crisis of legitimacy, the second section of this chapter reads Hari Kunzru's *Gods Without Men* (2011) as entranced by the new digital trading technologies that seemed, for a while, to bring the most far-flung efficient market fantasies within reach, and appalled by the ways in which those same technologies exacerbated the flaws in the efficient market paradigm in the run up to the crisis of 2007–8. At the end of the chapter, I argue that the novel's formal enactment of these flaws also stages a critical engagement with the logics of the literary marketplace.

Far-From-Equilibrium States: Don DeLillo's *Players*

Players bears the clear imprint of a moment when efficient market theory was migrating from academic finance journals into the strategies of portfolio managers, the pages of mainstream newspapers, and the bestseller lists (in the form of Burton Malkiel's Efficient Market Hypothesis [EMH]-based guide for the layperson, *A Random Walk Down Wall Street*, which appeared in 1973, and quickly established itself as an amateur investors' bible).

Players' protagonist, Lyle Wynant, works "in a roar of money" on the "floor of floors" on the "street of streets" – that is, as a broker at the New York Stock Exchange (or "Eleven Wall" as it's repeatedly termed).[3] A description of trading at the Exchange early in the novel, focalized via Lyle, precisely captures the spontaneous emergence of objectivity from subjectivity and equilibrium from chaos that is so central to the theory of efficient markets:

> There was sanity here, even at the wildest times. It was all worked out. There were rules, standards, and customs. In the electronic clatter it was possible to feel you were part of a breathtakingly intricate quest for order and elucidation, for identity among the constituents of a system. Everyone reconnoitered toward a balance. After the cries of the floor brokers, the quotes, the bids, the cadence and peal of an auction market, there was always a final price, good or bad, a leveling out of the world's creaturely desires. (28)

While the "final price" may be "good" or "bad" from the point of view of individual dealers, concerned only with their own profit or loss, it possesses an ungainsayable authority as the aggregate outcome of multiple signals emanating both from the trading floor itself and from "the world" beyond. The Stock Exchange, from this point of view, is an environment subject to "the strict rationalities of volume and price" (157).

In a similar vein, Lyle imagines himself and his colleagues to be "clerks of history" (83), and from his point of view comes the suggestion that the brokers' deepest responsibility is somehow to preserve historical time itself as it streams by. New York's Financial District is imagined as structured around a sacred inner sanctum that channels the very rhythm of history, transcending the inevitably inadequate content of individual human experience: "The district grew repeatedly inward, more secret, an occult theology of money, extending ever deeper into its own veined marble . . . At the inmost crypt might be heard the amplitude pulse of history, a system and rite to outshadow the evidence of men's senses" (132).

This notion of finance as plugged into the machinery of history itself, and animated by its beat and throb, also enthuses characters far removed from the ostensible ideological position of a financial professional like Lyle. Indeed, such a conception is articulated by members of a far-left cell, who plan a bombing at the New York Stock Exchange. While this attack is very overtly envisaged as a strike against the power of finance capital, the terrorists' rage at that power seems to be a function of their own intoxication by it. The sister of the lead conspirator explains the group's guiding philosophy after her brother's arrest following a shooting on the floor of the Exchange:

> Rafael wanted to disrupt their system, the idea of worldwide money. It's this *system* that we believe is their secret power. It all goes floating across that floor. Currents of invisible life. This is the center of their existence. The electronic system. The waves and charges. The green numbers on the board. This is what my brother calls their way of continuing on through rotting flesh, their closest taste of immortality. Not the bulk of all that money. The system itself, the current ... "Financiers are more spiritually advanced than monks on an island." Rafael. It was this secret of theirs that we wanted to destroy, this invisible power. It's all in that system, bip-bip-bip-bip, the flow of electric current that unites moneys, plural, from all over the world. Their greatest strength, no doubt of that. (107; emphasis in original)

In the vision of the stock market relayed here we find the conception – familiar from Part II – of financial workers as constituting a kind of insular religious sect. Here, it is particularly significant that this characterization is bound up with the idea that the financial marketplace draws into itself the totality – the "all," the "existence," the "life" (albeit in "invisible" form) – of the economic system. It is notable, moreover, that this community of financial mystics is imagined as seeking an "immortality" that lies, if it lies anywhere, in the "green numbers on the board." For Rafael, the "secret" fantasies that underlie efficient market thinking – that the market absorbs everything that happens; that our lives and experiences are preserved in the lists of prices – lend a grandiosity and sublimity to capitalist profit-making that he finds repellent; yet even as he aspires to "disrupt" or "destroy" these fantasies, he is evidently drawn to their "power," "strength," and "spirituality." Rafael, his sister, Marina, who recounts his ideas, and – I would contend – DeLillo himself testify here to the ambivalent impulses that efficient market ideology is liable to arouse in leftist consciousness: an object of acute, even violent, antipathy, the idea of the efficient market also awakens desires for a paradisiacal state of communal existence. In a much quoted statement from the early 1990s, DeLillo aligns his work with that of "the writer in opposition, the novelist who writes against power, who writes against the corporation or the state or the whole apparatus of assimilation";[4] but here, in this key early novel, a far more ambivalent set of commitments is evident.

A simultaneous loathing of and reverence for the "secret power" of the financial markets pervades DeLillo's novel, nowhere more so than in the depiction of the protagonist, Lyle. Lyle becomes entangled in the bombing plot, eventually avowing a desire to render "the system" "less inviolable," to "set loose every kind of demon" and "announce terrible possibilities" (183). His motivations and allegiances remain difficult to read, however, as he moves between the floor of the Stock Exchange, terrorist safe houses, and assignations with representatives of the intelligence services. As undecidable as his true commitments may be, we catch a glimpse of his worldview that stands as perhaps the purest expression in the novel of the redemptive and transcendent ethos that shimmers through efficient market thinking. This moment comes as Lyle contemplates one of the "yellow teleprinter slips," which he "sometimes carrie[s] . . . with him for days" (70). Lyle's response to market information of this kind is complex. He experiences exhilaration at figures that seem at once to be indexical imprints of "the world" and abstractions of that world to a point of total invisibility and intangibility – to be charged with a total plenitude of being and at the same time drained of it:

> He saw in the numbers and stock symbols an artful reduction of the external world to printed output, the machine's coded model of exactitude. One second of study, a glance was all it took to return to him an impression of reality disconnected from the resonance of his own senses. Aggression was refined away, the instinct to possess. He saw fractions, decimal points, plus and minus signs. A picture of the competitive mechanism of the world, of greasy teeth engaging on the rim of a wheel, was nowhere in evidence. The paper contained nerve impulses: a synaptic digit, a phoneme, a dimensionless point . . . On the slip of paper in his hand there was no intimation of lives defined by the objects around them, morbid tiers of immortality. Inked figures were all he saw. This was property in its own right, tucked away, his particular share (once removed) of the animal body breathing in the night. (70)

Here, what McKenzie Wark (following Georg Lukács and Antonio Negri) calls "second nature" – the realm of "labor, capital, [and] commodities," "production, existence, and survival" – is imagined as ascending onto the plane of "third nature" – the weightless domain of financial data.[5] Even as one would want to decry the occlusion of labouring, suffering bodies that

Lyle relishes, one can also respond to the utopian sparks that flare out from this vision, bespeaking a world in which the toil and pain of the productive economy would be acknowledged and preserved and at the same time bathed in a redemptive light.

In his characterization of Lyle, DeLillo pinpoints the kind of mentality that it would be necessary to have if one were to be at ease with an apparent contradiction in efficient market thought. In the last chapter, I noted the odd conjunction, in this body of theory, between strident assertions that financial markets encode the world, and an apparent sanguinity about, even enthusiasm for, the idea that we need not, or cannot, know *what*, specifically, they encode. I gave the example of Eugene Fama's response to the seemingly acausal "Black Monday" crash of October 1987. Fama's field-defining study of 1970, "Efficient Capital Markets: A Review of Theory and Empirical Work," is highly suggestive here too.

In this piece, Fama (who would win the Nobel Economics Prize for his work on the EMH in 2013) formulates the notion of market efficiency in terms that have been repeated innumerable times: an efficient market is one "in which prices always 'fully reflect' all available information."[6] The central metaphor here – whose status as metaphor Fama's scare quotes serve to bring back into focus – is at once apt and misleading, for while prices may "reflect" information in the sense of "to take account of," "incorporate," or "register," they do not do so in the sense (as the *OED* has it) of "to display as if in a mirror; to reproduce, esp. faithfully or accurately; to depict . . . to reveal (an underlying reality or cause); to make manifest, express." On the contrary, we might even say that, with respect to access to those underlying realities or causes, prices tend (in an obsolete sense of "reflect") to "direct . . . away from a course, to divert; to turn aside, deflect." In this foundational text of the EMH literature, then, the key notion of a full and direct mirroring of the world carries with it the implication of its opposite – of the way, that is, in which market data is in fact typically received, not as an image of the world but as a wall of blank, abstract, impenetrable code.

Yet, as we have seen, the difficulty of "getting behind" the numbers, of using the Rosetta Stone of economic and political events to decode the hieroglyphs of the price record (as in the economic subdiscipline of "event studies"), is far from dispiriting for proponents of the EMH. Rather, it serves, if anything, as a reinforcement of faith. Here DeLillo's portrayal of Lyle Wynant is telling, for it suggests that for devotees of market efficiency, the very abstraction of "numbers and stock symbols" – their simultaneous drawing in and filtering out of "the external world," "reality," "the resonance of [the] senses," and so on – may be precisely a source of their utopian attraction: one wants at once to know that the world is encoded within the numbers and symbols, but to be able to encounter it in transcendent, immaculate, purified forms.

Lyle has a counterpart in this respect in the figure of J. Kinnear, an elusive, chameleonic individual who has "dropped out of sight" and "resurfaced" (132) in various radical and criminal milieus over a period of decades, and mirrors Lyle in becoming an agent for the CIA even as he orchestrates the terrorist bombing at the Stock Exchange. Less a character than a site where "points of confluence" (145) intersect, Kinnear, Lyle surmises, has "been an agent, in spirit, for twenty years," functioning "simultaneously on two levels." "Counterpoise" has characterized his existence: "his life was based on forces tending to produce equilibrium ... He could not act without considering entire sets of implications" (145). Like the optimally efficient market, then, Kinnear has maintained a minutely calibrated position, adjusted only in full cognizance of the relevant information. Kinnear's career also, though, highlights how such a finely poised state may be abruptly and devastatingly disrupted. After the terrorists learn of his links to "the agency" (101), his equilibrium is "ended," "collapsed inward." "Possibly," Lyle reflects, "he'd worked it that close to the edge intentionally" (145).

Lyle's and Kinnear's affinities with the efficient market are evident, too, in the ways in which they hoover up information. Kinnear is notorious in espionage circles for harbouring "information somebody wanted" (154), and seems to have accumulated inside knowledge of some of the murkiest episodes in recent American history: "enormous improbable intrigues," "mazes, covert procedures," "strange, strange, strange relationships and links" (104, 181). In the figure of Lyle, mean-while, the good financial professional's commitment to keeping tabs on incoming data in order to maintain market efficiency seems to have turned pathological, or to have assumed outsize proportions akin to those of the stock market itself. Possessing the "annoying faculty" of "compulsive information-gathering," he has an irresistible urge to "enumerat[e] [the] facts" and "physical description[s]" of the men and women he encounters in the city, or to memorize "the numbers on license plates of certain cars" and "hours later ... repeat the number[s] to make sure he still" knows them (129, 45, 46). Lyle's objective, then, is precisely that which, according to the EMH, drives the financial markets: to observe, and record, everything.

If one of Lyle's psychopathologies is that he is an obsessive accumulator of "publicly available" information – information visibly displayed on the streets of New York – then another is his perception that, as in the strong form of market efficiency, even the fragments of experience enclosed in his own mind are liable to show up in lists of stock prices. Here, Lyle stands for those numerous elements of the economic field hopelessly exposed to the efficient market's implacable, penetrating gaze. Moving back and forth across the floor of the Exchange, he is gripped by the suspicion that the market is literally telepathic and that the traders can genuinely read each other's minds:

> It was the feeling that everyone knew his thoughts ... An electric cross-potential was in the air, a nearly headlong sense of revel and woe. On the board an occasional price brought noise from the floor brokers, the specialists, the clerks. Lyle watched the stock codes and the stilted figures below them, the computer spew ... If everyone here knew his present thoughts, if that message in greenish cipher that moved across the board represented the read-outs of Lyle Wynant, it would be mental debris ... that caused him humiliation, all the unwordable rubble, the glass, rags, and paper of his tiny indefinable manias. The conversations he had with himself, straphanging in a tunnel. All the ceremonial patterns, the soul's household chores. (22)

This passage suggests ways in which the theory of market efficiency might encode dystopian anxieties as well as utopian fantasies. In its limit form, the EMH extends the benign promise that a thing need only exist in the world – silently, obscurely, remotely – for it to be recognized and accounted for in some world-historical record. However, during a period (well underway in the 1970s) in which state and corporate surveillance of everyday life has relentlessly expanded, there cannot but be something nightmarish about the idea that, through the existence of the financial markets, the social field would be rendered obscenely transparent, and any vestige of secrecy, privacy, anonymity, or forgetting erased. Jean Baudrillard refers to such an x-ray-like vision, which penetrates the social body to its core, as the "ecstasy of communication" – a state of obscenity that is "no longer the obscenity of the hidden, the repressed, the obscure," but rather "the obscenity of that which no longer contains a secret and is entirely soluble in information and communication."[7]

Hence, in the texts I'm analysing in this chapter, an attraction to the mapping of social and economic totality promised by the idea of the efficient market coexists with a fear that such a mapping risks being oppressively totalizing – even totalitarian – in nature. This anxiety, in turn, instils a desire to foreground factors that disrupt or elude the epistemological mastery of the market. In Hari Kunzru's *Gods Without Men*, discussed in detail later in this chapter, we find a mounting formal commitment to the frustration of narrative closure, which parallels the novel's emphasis on the affront to financial knowledge claims posed by the "credit crunch." In *Players*, DeLillo calls our attention both to the rogue elements that the market cannot incorporate, or which disturb its smooth running, and to the temporal limitations of even the most "efficient" market – its inability to imagine a future that is anything other than a steady continuation of the present.

A kind of grit in the cogs of the market's epistemological machinery is found, in DeLillo's novel, in the indigent figures who drift daily into New York's Financial District. These "outcasts" or "living rags" – "women with junk carts," "a man dragging a mattress," "ordinary drunks," "people without shoes," "amputees and freaks" – are incongruous presences amid the financial strongholds of Broad Street (27). Lyle thinks of these people as "infiltrators in the district. Elements filtering in. Nameless arrays of existence" (27). The lowest of the *Lumpenproletariat* (from the German *Lumpen* – "rag") are excluded from the circuits of economic production, and even from the economy as such, and hence inassimilable to the financial system's calculations. If the Financial District is a "test environment for extreme states of mind" (27), it lacks the measuring equipment to register such abject poverty and dysfunction. The depersonalizing, homogenizing, and reifying language here ("living rags," "nameless arrays") very much corresponds to Lyle's distanced, uncomprehending, unsympathetic point of view, but the very abjection of these figures seems to embody a certain, albeit minimal, resistance, if only to the financial markets' drive to anatomize, codify, and catalogue everything that falls within their dominion.

This image of infiltration by foreign bodies is echoed shortly after by an incident on the floor of the Stock Exchange itself. As we've seen, the trading floor and the market that is enacted into being there are experienced by Lyle as sites of order, regularity, and coordination. It is immediately after Lyle has reflected on the "lucid view" of "the world" and disinclination to "drift beyond the margins of things" that he shares with the other "floor members," however, that "something happen[s]" at the Exchange, with devastating effect (28). This occurrence is initially presented as an unaccountable disturbance in the perceptual field: "To Lyle it seemed at first an indistinct warp, a collapse in pattern. He perceived a rush, unusual turbulence, people crowding" (28). The disturbance, it transpires, is the fatal shooting of one of Lyle's colleagues by Rafael Vilar, the leader of the terrorist cell with which Lyle will soon become embroiled. The killing is a shattering blow to the usual order of the trading floor, and

DeLillo's rhetoric – a rhetoric of skewing and falling, panic and stampede – also suggests the vulnerability of the stock market itself – that less tangible but no less real presence – to similar upheavals, or what, in the parlance of the EMH, are termed "external shocks."

"The outside world" that lies beyond the activities of the brokers at the Exchange is repeatedly invoked in the novel (23, 65, 66, 157). Lyle is disconcerted by his colleague McKechnie's gloomy view of "the outside world" as placing those "inside" at the mercy of a succession of unpredictable disruptions: "Things that happen and you're helpless. All you can do is wait for how bad" (65). In these conversations, Lyle and his interlocutor articulate an idea central to the theory of efficient markets. As noted in the previous chapter, according to the theory financial markets reflect not only all available information about the past and present, but also everything that can be foreseen about the future. The only certainty, however, is that events will transpire that prove this "best guess" wrong. All you can do is wait for how bad (or good) these events will turn out to be. In this sense, the EMH is a theory both of omniscience and of acute uncertainty and contingency: it assumes that markets know everything there is to know about what has happened before and what is happening now, but operate with only the most heuristic picture of what will happen next. Their knowledge of the future, that is, is valid only to the extent that the future follows its most probable trajectory. Of course, in reality, deviations from the markets' aggregated prediction of the future occur all the time, prompting continual price fluctuations or "corrections." Because such new information is, by definition, unknown until it appears, it is in statistical terms random, as are the price movements that result from it. It is for this reason that the EMH insists on the impossibility of profiting by anticipating in advance how prices will move: they move only because of occurrences that precisely cannot be predicted.

The basic pattern posited by the EMH is of minor units of information prompting minor price movements – now up, now down. As Ivan Ascher puts it, in the view of the pioneering efficient market theorists, "from one moment to the next, the price of a stock could go up or down, it could change a lot or a little, but more likely than not, the price of a stock at one moment would be roughly the same as it had been the moment prior."[8] This is the "random walk" made famous by Burton Malkiel's *A Random Walk Down Wall Street* – a meandering path around and about an initial point (as with a chart of successive coin tosses). But there are also the "external shocks" – the events that seem, at least, to come from nowhere, blindsiding the markets, and carrying with them massive implications for asset prices (the terrorist attacks of 11 September 2001 – so eerily prefigured in *Players* – are especially stark examples). If the market, as described by the EMH, sometimes sounds like God,[9] then this is a God that *does* play dice. In the EMH universe, things are always on a knife edge: at any given moment, they can go either way, and by a tiny increment or a vaulting leap. Time is not a steady progression, but quantized into a series of discrete, disjunctive units; no long-term trends and trajectories – just one damned thing after another. In the economic argot, the EMH posits a state of "dynamic stochastic equilibrium": the market is consistently at a point of balance, but also always only an interval away from a random shock that will necessitate a – perhaps drastic – rebalancing. In *Players*, such a state of openness and contingency is a source of anxiety, but also offers a kind of refuge from the oppressive panopticism associated with the financial markets.

Towards the end of the novel, Lyle registers the unsettling impact of abrupt, unexpected interruption when, alone in his bedroom, his methodical domestic rituals are disturbed by the buzz of the telephone:

> When the phone rang he didn't want to answer it. He'd already fixed in his mind certain time spans. There were boundaries to observe, demarcating shades of behavior. Some faint static could disturb the delicate schedule he'd established, a closed structure of leave-taking and destination. (179)

Again, Lyle's disposition towards the world here is exactly that of the efficient market, which, like him, would remain entirely undisturbed if the future simply proceeded along predictable tracks, rather than being jolted off course by external intrusions.

In fact, something close to the state of equipoise that Lyle desires here defines the prevailing tone of the novel as a whole. As I've suggested, the main plotline, involving Lyle and the terrorists, hangs in the balance throughout: we do not know whether his loyalties lie with them, and their plan to blow up the Stock Exchange, or with the intelligence services, for whom he acts as an informant. Similarly, the narrative proceeds not by dramatic twists and turns, but by minor adjustments, recalibrations. Lyle and the other parties involved in the conspiracy seem curiously unsurprised by the passage of events – the revelations, betrayals, and clandestine encounters – as if content simply to drift as things play out (they are, after all, merely "players"). The prospect, and reality, of violence elicits barely a flicker from DeLillo's impassive creations; even the slaying on the floor of the Exchange leaves its witnesses oddly unmoved once the initial hubbub has subsided, its main function being merely to nudge Lyle gently in the direction of the terrorist cell.

Indeed, grief itself, in the world DeLillo portrays, is something simply to be regulated, managed, and administered. Lyle's wife Pammy works for the Grief Management Council, which bills itself as "serv[ing] the community in its efforts to understand and assimilate grief" (18). The firm has anticipated the demand for a "clerical structure" through which people may "codify their emotions" (19). Successive modifications to the floor plan of the firm's headquarters (situated among the many financial firms occupying the north tower of the World Trade Center) are imagined as if they were fluctuations on a stock index, "directed to adjust the amount of furniture to levels of national grief" (19) (Pammy later likens the firm to the Dow Jones [54]).

Like fluctuating stock prices on the random walk model, then, *Players* is governed by a kind of Brownian motion, in which one character collides randomly with another and then another. My argument, in other words, is that DeLillo's narrative – driven, on the face of it, by the epitome of the paranoid-style conspiracy plot that is often taken to define the "systems" mode in general – aligns itself more closely, instead, with the non-deterministic, stochastic patterning of the stock market. On the one hand, this style creates an impression of matters placidly working themselves out, with the minimum of alarm or upheaval. On the other hand, however, precisely this unmotivated quality to the movement of the plot (why does Lyle conspire with the terrorists to blow up his own workplace? why does he also go to the CIA? why does he agree to help the double agent J. Kinnear when he absconds?) lends the novel an arbitrary, aleatory effect, a disquieting sense that *anything* might happen next.

This potential for the radically unforeseen to intrude is most obviously realized when, towards the end of the novel, Pammy's friend, Jack, inexplicably and seemingly without warning commits suicide by self-immolation. In one sense, it is perhaps ironic – given her employment in "grief management" – that Pammy turns out to be the one character in the novel who displays a full-scale emotional response. But in another – that is, in view of the gendered dimensions of the "systems" novel that I highlighted in the previous chapter – it is wholly logical. Pammy's femininity is figured as inseparable from her capacity to register the full incomprehensibility of the self-destructive *acte gratuit* perpetrated by her friend. Her awareness of Jack's death is tellingly subcognitive – a ferocious "oceanic" "roar" within her skull (199). The shock, she senses, is "driving in on her," "massing," as if "something irrevocable, something irrevocable and lunatic, something irrevocable, totally mad, [will] happen" (199). Similarly, Jack's ambiguous sexuality (he is in a relationship with a man but claims that he is "not really gay" [136]) is presented as inextricable from a more general association with the obscure or ineffable evident in everything from the "patch of pure white at the back of an otherwise dark head of hair" that is "the mark, the label, the stamp, the sign, the emblem of something mysterious" (19) to his utterance of "sentences [that] never quite [end]" but instead "[open] out into a sustained noise" (175) to his apparent observation of UFO activity in the night sky (171) to – of course – his baffling act of self-destruction. Both femininity and queerness, then, figure in the novel as sites that are withdrawn or withheld from intelligibility, sites that – as Pammy exemplifies in "grasping" for the "meaning" of a street sign at the end of the novel – "mysteriously [evade] the responsibilities of content" (208).

If Pammy's terrifying sensation of a yawning gap in the world's meaning after Jack's death is a delayed reaction to the "irrevocable," "lunatic" thing that has *just* happened, it also – in the problematically gendered terms I've highlighted – captures an intimation of imminent rupture that pervades the novel (ever more intensely as it approaches its end). Jack's death is such a rupture itself, and makes all the more acute the question of when, or if, the "impossible to anticipate" "calculated madness" (108) of Marina and the other terrorists will erupt.

As the bomb plot gathers pace, Kinnear – a disembodied voice on the telephone now, having gone to ground following the terrorists' discovery of his betrayal – warns Lyle not to let his involvement in the conspiracy "reach the point where either way you turn there's pure void, there's sheer drop-off" (179). More and more, then, as the novel approaches its conclusion, the prospect is not of another minor redirection, but of a devastating convulsion that will tear at the heart of the financial markets, and of the narrative whose style so closely mirrors their ordinarily stately, composed movements. While the decisive moment – the crisis – always seems just on the verge of arriving, however, it never quite does.

The final chapter finds Lyle in a motel room somewhere outside Toronto with a woman named Rosemary, his initial contact in the terrorist underworld and an associate of Kinnear's. The invasive, disruptive influence of "the outside world" is again embodied here by the telephone. Lyle is expecting a call that will send him "somewhere" with "detailed instructions" (210), but it is unclear whether the caller will be a member of the terrorist cell actioning the attack, or one of Lyle's other contacts: Kinnear; his CIA handler, Burks; or some other party entirely. While the novel's earlier chapters are narrated in the past tense, this final chapter shifts into the present, bringing the character's and the reader's anticipation of what will come next into precise alignment. Here, more than anywhere, the novel gives us a formal means of grasping the disjunctive temporality posited by the efficient market hypothesis.

Even in his precarious situation, Lyle still clings to "rationality, analysis," and the ability to "pull things into a systematic pattern" (or at least the "illusion" of such a pattern) (210, 211). "Instinct" leads him to sense that the phone "will shortly ring," and, as if performing a market time series analysis, he "decides to count to one hundred" (211); "if the phone doesn't ring at one hundred," he tells himself, it will be because "his instinct has deceived him" and "the pattern has cracked (211). He cannot bear the prospect that "his waiting" should prove of indeterminate duration, "open[ing] out to magnitudes of gray space" (211–12). He would rather "pack and leave" (212). In fact, however, when "nothing happens," he simply lowers the count, first to fifty, and then to twenty-five (212).

Lyle's Beckettian predicament – resolute in his determination to depart, but remaining inert as he contemplates an expanse of greyish indistinction – is a moment both of stalemate and of maximum possibility. Something – anything – may be coming to break the deadlock, but it will not arrive before the end. In the narrative declension that forms the novel's final lines, information – even about what is right in front of us – dwindles into insufficiency, to the point where virtually nothing can be known. Tellingly, one of the things to go in this lapse into obscurity is Lyle's identifiable maleness, heightening the "uncertain masculinity" (as Anne Longmuir puts it) already evident in the "near-effeteness" (26) of his appearance earlier in the novel and the reversal of heteronormative roles apparent when his companion and sexual partner, Rosemary, wears "a plastic phallus harnessed to her body" (197).[10] At the end of the novel, Rosemary is naked and asleep, absorbed into the "tidal life of the unconscious, a state beyond dreaming" (209). "To watch a woman at this stage of sleep, throbbing, obviously in touch with mysteries, never fails to worry [Lyle] a little" (209), we're told, and the closing lines suggest his own reduction to a similar state of remoteness and obscurity that is also a state of emasculation:

> Spaces and what they contain no longer account for, mean, serve as examples of, or represent. The propped figure, for instance, is barely recognizable as male. Shedding capabilities and traits by the second, he can still be described (but quickly) as well-formed, sentient and fair. We know nothing else about him. (212)

What will happen next? The novel, like even the most optimally efficient, informationally rich market, does not know. The phone call may come the moment after the narrative ends; or the moment after that; or it may not come at all. If the call is received, it may augur destruction – of people, property, and market value; or it may signal the aversion of such destruction; or it may announce some other, altogether unimagined, occurrence. There is anxiety, terror even, in this radical openness – and something troubling, too, in the suggestion that to become unknowable is to become female, or at least indeterminately gendered. But the novel finds a certain fugitive freedom here, in this moment of erasure, to the extent that the horizon of the future, at least, exceeds the market's logic of epistemological enclosure.

Magic and Positivism: Hari Kunzru's *Gods Without Men*

A similar nexus of concerns, anxieties, and hopes animates Hari Kunzru's 2011 novel *Gods Without Men*, a text from what may turn out to be the late age of efficient market thought, and probably the most interesting novel to emerge as a response to the global financial crisis of 2008, which posed such stark questions for EMH orthodoxy. Kunzru's narrative displays clear lines of continuity with novels of earlier decades discussed above – not least perhaps because (like Hallberg's *City of Fire*) *Gods Without Men* is a recent systems-style novel that works over the countercultural milieus with which early examples of that form were directly engaged. We can measure the distance between *Gods Without Men* and the "EMH novel" of the 1970s in a number of ways, though. First (as I'll discuss in a moment), there's the novel's engagement – at the levels both of plot and (as I'll argue) of form – with computerized market trading technologies barely imaginable even a few decades ago. Then there's the extent to which Kunzru can take it for granted that "market efficiency" as defined by the EMH is a familiar concept, which can be casually deployed (in ways we'll see below). And, above all, there's the novel's quintessentially post-credit crisis apprehension that while the EMH still retains vestiges of its utopian appeal, its epistemological claims for the financial markets are flawed in ways that even authors like Pynchon, Gaddis, or DeLillo, writing in the 1970s, had not fully reckoned with.

Kunzru's narrative, however, confronts a financial industry that had been emboldened in its belief in the perfectibility of market-based information processing by a technological revolution that unfolded over the opening decade of the twenty-first century. This revolution was the rise of algorithmic trading, and especially its major variant, "High-Frequency Trading" (HFT), in which computers run algorithms programmed to initiate orders in split-second response to changing conditions. By 2009, HFT accounted for around 70 per cent of US stock trading volume. A key use of HFT systems involves coupling trading algorithms to programmes that scour news feeds, social media platforms, and the wider web "for textual clues that might indicate how investors should feel about a stock";[11] these trawls prompt algo-traders' instantaneous adjustments of market positions.

Such systems promise to process information and incorporate it into asset prices at a speed and on a scale that would have been unthinkable for the codifiers of efficient market theory in the 1960s and 1970s, much less for Hayek in the 1940s. The vision that underpins this computerized approach to the translation of information into investment is vividly captured by Scott Patterson in his account of the rise of the hedge fund Kinetic Global Markets, one of the pioneers of "AI trading" (note again in this passage the use of the "infinity list" – evidently *the* rhetorical means by which the totalizing ambitions of contemporary finance are conveyed; note also Patterson's overt acknowledgement of the list's inevitable endlessness):

> As computers spread across the world, more and more information was available about . . . well, *everything*. Shipping trends in the Persian Gulf. The amount of wheat grown in Kazakhstan. Rainfall in British Columbia. Birth rates in Latin America. Oil shipments in the Strait of Hormuz. The list was endless. One fact was clear: The human mind could never process the Big Data. But a computer, perhaps? And, perhaps, a Big Data trading machine could troll the Web and other data systems and discover patterns . . . Those patterns, if all worked as planned, could provide signals that a machine could use to buy and sell stocks for a massive profit.[12]

Several recent fictional narratives explore the imaginative possibilities presented by such technologies: novels including Teddy Wayne's culture-clash tale *Kapitoil* (2010) and Robert Harris's *Frankenstein* homage *The Fear Index* (2011); and films like Darren Aronofsky's debut feature, the cyberpunk thriller π (1998), and the Australian drama *The Bank* (2001), directed by Robert Connolly. Kunzru's *Gods Without Men*, however, is by far the most subtle and revealing narrative exploration of the new financial technologies.

As with other novels discussed in this book, much of the interest and significance of Kunzru's novel lies in the way in which it troubles a critical tendency to think of texts as either diagnoses or symptoms of a given ideological formation. Emanating from a demonstrably (and avowedly) leftist position,[13] *Gods Without Men* both critically anatomizes the utopian logic of the efficient market paradigm and finds itself intoxicated by that same logic; and it does so, I argue, precisely because the all-knowing, world-embracing efficient market seems to answer to that deep need of the contemporary left for a means of envisioning the global totality (what Fredric Jameson famously identifies as the imperative of "cognitive mapping").[14]

Kunzru has admitted to finding the "suprahuman" domain of the financial markets "fascinating, beautiful, and scary all at once." The genesis of *Gods Without Men*, he says, lay in approaching the "esoteric" work of financial analysts and traders "as a sort of research into the nature of existence." It struck him "that someone interacting all the time with these extraordinarily complex, changing, very beautiful abstract systems might come to believe they were in some way getting glimpses of the face of God."[15] In the novel, this person is Cy Bachman, the designer of a hyper-advanced algorithmic trading system used by a New York hedge fund. The radiant, celestial plane on which Kunzru imagines the markets operating is first envisioned, however, via a group even more fervently devoted to arcane theories than the "quants" of contemporary finance.

This group is the Ashtar Galactic Command, a "UFO religion" that establishes itself on the mythically-charged patch of the Mojave Desert around which all of the novel's action revolves. The movement's founder, Schmidt, claims that the alien beings who make up the Galactic Command are able to "absorb and transmit huge bodies of information in the blink of an eye. All human history [can] be transferred from one entity to another in as little time as it takes to listen to an episode of a radio serial."[16] This channelling of information suggests to Schmidt the potential for entry into a condition of radical collectivity – "a kind of mind-melding, a total communion with each other and with the cosmos" (76). By the late 1960s, following Schmidt's death, the movement has come to imagine this future state in a thoroughly utopian form – perfectly keyed to the tenor of the times – in which every human "soul" has a place reserved for it, both as an individual entity with its own singular identity and as part of a unified, synchronized whole. Two of Schmidt's deputies, who have assumed his mantle as spiritual "guides," convey this message in an incantatory "invocation": "*Forty million are with us, forty million souls!*" they intone. "*Do not fear, Children of Light! Each of your names is punched into record cards held in the brains of our giant computers! We know exactly where you are! We know exactly where you are! . . . All is in the plan*" (172–73; italics in original).

The group asserts its opposition to the "negative energy vibrations" emanating from various conventional manifestations of the authoritarian power of "the Man," including "the financial markets" (161). It's ironic and intriguing, then, that in the narrative's present day a representative of those markets should imagine a role for the financial system that so strongly evokes the utopian longings of these harbingers of the Age of Aquarius. This is the path pursued by Kunzru's hedge fund computer genius Cy Bachman.

While this utopian vision of finance is initially Bachman's, it assumes centre stage in the narrative because it also captures the imagination of the protagonist, Jaswinder "Jaz" Matharu, an Indian American MIT physicist, who follows the well-trodden path from academia to Wall Street to take a job in quantitative finance. As a junior analyst at Bachman's hedge fund, Jaz is responsible for the day-to-day running of a computerized trading system known as Walter, which has a "voracious thirst for data" (134). As we will see shortly, Jaz is charged with feeding the programme with every conceivable form of information. Introduced by Bachman as "a new global quant model," Walter is hailed by the more ebullient CEO of the fund as a "goddamn theory of everything" (133). Bachman wryly demurs – "Everything would be kind of a large dataset" – but Jaz later reflects that "it was as if Bachman were trying to fit the whole world into his model. What was external to Walter? Was there anything it didn't aim to comprehend?" (133, 135). Walter, then, is Schmidt's cosmic "transmitter," or one of the "high gods" themselves, incarnated in code and silicon.

Among Bachman's many "mystical" and "esoteric" (139) interests, a privileged place is occupied by the Jewish Kabbalah, especially the work of the great sixteenth-century Kabbalist Isaac Luria (148). It is in light of this interest that the significance of the name "Walter" becomes apparent – an allusion to Walter Benjamin, and in particular to the late, messianic and Kabbalistic Benjamin of the *Theses on the Philosophy of History*. Paraphrasing the account of Luria's teachings offered by Gershom Scholem – Benjamin's main source of Kabbalistic knowledge – Bachman conveys to Jaz his vision of the world as *zerstreut* (scattered, divided) and in need of the Kabbalist's divinatory powers to restore its former unity:

> There's a tradition that says the world has shattered, that what once was whole and beautiful is now just scattered fragments. Much is irreparable, but a few of these fragments contain faint traces of the former state of things, and if you find them and uncover the sparks hidden inside, perhaps at last you'll piece together the fallen world. (138)

Ultimately, the goal of the "Walter" project, as Bachman imagines it, is to "discover" the "face of God." "What else would we be looking for?" he asks (139). Later, Bachman confides in Jaz's wife, Lisa, his hope that Walter will contribute to this process of what Kabbalists call *tikkun* – "rectification" or "repair":

> You know we work with data . . . For a Kabbalist, the world is made of signs . . . The Torah existed before the creation of the world, and all creation emanates from its mystical letters. Of course the modern world is terribly broken. Its perfection has been dispersed. But I like to think that in our small way, by finding connections between all these different kinds of phenomena, Jaz and I and the rest of our team are reading those signs, doing our part to restore what was shattered. (149–50)

For Bachman, then, the text that is the world has become corrupted, but he believes in its continued legibility, and in the possibility of its ultimate reconstruction. He is both a close reader – attentive to the "presence" (138) possessed by particular incidents and artefacts – and (in Franco Moretti's terms) a "distant reader,"[17] with Walter the computational means via which he will parse this endlessly unfurling text. If these passages embed a certain conception of reading, their overtly religious and mystical language points also to the presence of an always implicitly religious and mystical impulse in the imaginative life of the efficient market hypothesis. It is precisely by (as Bachman puts it) "contributing to market efficiency" (156) – identifying, exploiting, and closing arbitrage opportunities – that Walter promises to ensure that "nothing that has ever happened should be regarded as lost for history," as Benjamin writes in the *Theses*, envisaging a divine chronicler who would be minutely attentive to the myriad shards of daily experience.[18] Bachman partakes of what the economic anthropologist Hirokazu Miyazaki refers to as "a recursive dimension" to the faith in efficient markets – recursive because, in acting upon this faith through actions in the market, "the arbitrageur helps the market to realize its inherent orientation toward efficiency." What is at stake here, then, "is a particular self-image, of the arbitrageur as both swept up in the 'invisible hand' and *part of* its agency."[19]

It is striking, and unsettling, that Kunzru should depict Bachman, this embodiment of advanced capitalism, as finding inspiration in the redeemed future envisaged by Benjamin, a Marxist (albeit of a highly idiosyncratic kind) and icon of the intellectual left. The novel should not, however, be read here merely as portraying a crude and cynical appropriation of communitarian spiritual tradition by the power of finance capital. Instead, this meeting of seemingly incompatible perspectives answers, again, to a utopian logic that cuts across ideological divides. Kunzru's apparent attraction to the financial markets as extending the possibility of a kind of Benjaminian preservation and redemption of history is no doubt disconcerting, but if the leftist commits a "betrayal" by identifying with the market, then so too do market ideologues themselves, by identifying with what is – in the pure form in which such adherents articulate it – a vision of mass collective coordination. That a kind of answer to the radical hopes both of a Benjamin and a Bachman should be found in the financial markets is not, then, as incongruous as it might seem. Complicity and critique, in other words, are here totally imbricated; indeed, it is in the very act of complicity that an unexpected criticality arises – an understanding of the ways in which market ideology, pursued to its limits, reveals its otherness from its own ostensible principles of atomism and self-interest.

That Kunzru is inspired – artistically and intellectually, affectively and politically – by a vision of financial markets as quasi-divine recorders of everyday history is abundantly apparent from the numinous Benjaminian rhetoric in which he has his character, Bachman, expound upon the capacity of his programme to gather together the splinters of a fragmented world. The strong investments that Kunzru has in such a vision are evident, too, in the way in which he constructs his own narrative as a kind of capacious information-absorbing machine – like Walter or like the stock market itself. Kunzru acknowledges the applicability of the term "systems novel" to his attempt to incorporate into his narrative as broad a sweep of contemporary (and historical) reality as possible. He prefers, though, to think in terms of the "network" – "the figure that defines our period" and "a really powerful mediator of our lives."[20]

On a geospatial level, the networked structure of *Gods Without Men* is highly expansive, linking together – via the itinerancies of migration and memory – locations as disparate as LA, Seattle, New York, London, Baghdad, Punjab, Guam, and the Pyrenees. Like other contemporary authors of "big" novels, Kunzru reckons with the task of providing a cognitive mapping of our present. The task is, ultimately and necessarily, an impossible one, but by embracing an array of diverse but tightly interconnected locales, his form goes a significant way towards capturing the "action at a distance" characteristic of what Jameson calls the "decentered global network" of contemporary capitalism.[21] Also notable in this regard is the level of research – abundantly apparent in the finished novel –

that Kunzru undertook during its composition, both on the ground ("eight journeys connected with the book," amounting to "five months of travel") and via secondary sources scoured from the internet ("everything from UFO and spiritualist tracts to anthropological texts").[22] For one reviewer, the resulting profusion of detail – a "rampant Franzenism," "almost documentary in its extent" – is "the novel's principal flaw."[23] While a reluctance to crank the filtering mechanism up to full power does hamper the forward thrust of Kunzru's narrative, it also confirms the importance for his project of a principle of inclusiveness – of putting *everything* (or as close to it as possible) in. The narrative has as much breadth along its historical axis as along its spatial one, shifting back and forth between the present and multiple points extending back as far as the 1770s (and conjuring up a sense of mythic time whose roots lie much deeper still, in some archetypal state of prehistory).

If Kunzru's narrative is centrifugal, spinning out in space and time, however, it is also centripetal, drawing everything back to a single, central point. This pivot point is the spot in the Mojave Desert – a distinctive "three-fingered" rock formation known as Trinity or Pinnacle Rocks – where Schmidt has his initial alien encounter and establishes his UFO cult, and where, in one of the narrative's critical moments, Jaz's son, Raj, goes missing. Raj's disappearance – and eventual, equally mysterious, reappearance nearby – is just the latest strange occurrence in a place that, we come to suspect, is a kind of portal, an entry point for otherworldly beings – angels, aliens, gods, spirits – and, perhaps, a cosmic gateway into which unsuspecting wanderers may be absorbed. It is on this site of visitation, revelation, and ascension that all of the novel's myriad plotlines converge. Similarly, the recurrence of uncannily similar paranormal encounters in the same place over centuries, as well as the disruption and flattening out of temporal progression effected by the novel's chapter-by-chapter transitions (from 2008 to 1778, back to 2008, then to 1958, and so on), implies that all of the narrative's events somehow simultaneously occupy a single timeless moment. The space-time of the narrative is defined, then, by the way in which the multiple characters and events gravitate towards the same site, and seem to coexist on an immortal, atemporal plane. The narrative, that is, is structured on the same model as Walter, and by the extension the idealized capital market, whose "efficiency" Walter helps to guarantee via an endless process of information gathering.

The purest manifestation of this convergence between the logic of the Walter project and Kunzru's own formal strategies comes in the form of several extended lists, which enumerate the data – of every conceivable

kind – with which Jaz feeds Walter's "voracious thirst." In order to convey
the effect of these passages, it is necessary to quote from them at some
length; as I'll explain in a moment, however, it is part of my argument that
it may not be necessary to *read* them – at least not in anything more than
a cursory manner:

> There was . . . data . . . on shopping-mall construction, retail-sales figures,
> drug-patent applications, car ownership; on the incidence of birth defects,
> industrial injuries, suicides, controlled-substance seizures, cellphone-tower
> construction. Walter consumed the most esoteric numbers: small-arms sales
> in the Horn of Africa, the population of Gary, Indiana, between 1940 and
> 2008, the population of Magnitogorsk, Siberia, for the same years, prostitu-
> tion arrests in major American cities, data traffic over the TPE trans-Pacific
> cable, the height of the water table in various subregions of the Maghreb. (135)

> The stream of data continued. Gas volumes pumped through the BTC and
> Druzhba pipelines, racial assaults in Australia, coltan mining yields in the
> DRC free-zones, incidence of Marburg hemorraghic fever in those same
> zones, hourly volume of technology stocks traded on the Nikkei . . . The net
> worth of retirees in Boca Raton, Florida, oscillating in harmony with the
> volume of cargo arriving at the port of Long Beach, Southwestern home
> repossessions tracking the number of avatars in the most popular online
> gameworlds in Asia. (141)

Here, we are very clearly in the domain of what the art critic Julian
Stallabrass, writing about contemporary digital media visualizations of
financial markets, has called the "data sublime."[24] These passages cumula-
tively perform a kind of synecdochal function – a singular one in which the
"parts" stand for a "whole" that is actually *the* whole, something like "the
global" or "the totality" or "history" or "reality" or simply, as the text itself
has it, "everything." Interestingly, moreover, this is a rhetorical strategy in
which metonymy – contrary to prevailing definitions – is necessarily
subsumed under synecdoche, since when the thing signified is *everything*,
anything linked to or associated with it must be a *part* of it.

   What is the effect of this strategy? Discussing the realist aesthetic of
Gustave Flaubert, Roland Barthes famously identified a "reality effect," in
which small textual details simply say "*we are the real*," their purpose being
simply to signify "the category of 'the real' (and not its contingent
contents)."[25] In a similar way, Kunzru, like other writers of contemporary
"big novels" seeks a kind of "infinity," "totality," or "globality" effect. In
these "infinity list" passages, we find that effect in something like its pure,
essential form: we might, it is true, revealingly ponder the content of the

lists Kunzru provides – notably the references to the nations of the "developing world" and the "Global South" and to the condition of subaltern groups in general, references that hint at a latent political consciousness – but the primary purpose of the data he enumerates, in their disparateness, diversity, and idiosyncrasy, is simply to signify the sprawling nature of "the global" as such. Any single element might be replaced by a different one without this primary signification being substantially altered.

The very means, however, by which Kunzru signifies "the category of 'the global'" (to paraphrase Barthes) immediately reveals its absolute inadequacy in the face of the actual conditions of globalization. The more data he presents (and the more apparent it becomes that each unit is readily replaceable by another), the more keenly we feel the absence of the infinite number of things that *aren't* listed, not to mention the lack of a qualitative texture to the events and experiences that *are* invoked but only in the most reductively quantitative terms. What Kunzru's text indirectly signals is the impossibility of enumerating even a tiny fraction of the factors that bear materially on the conjuncture that is contemporary global history, even if one were to devote an entire novel to the task – or an entire life, like the Tibetan monks who set out to list "The Nine Billion Names of God" in Arthur C. Clarke's 1953 story of that name.

Kunzru's solution to the problem of parsing the informational plenum is akin to that of the hedge fund managers he depicts (and the monks in Clarke's tale): he gets a computer to do it – or rather, he imagines into being a computer programme capable of comprehensively scanning the vast expanse of global data, an expanse that the text itself may then merely denote in the gestural, shorthand way I have been describing. The critically minded, oppositional contemporary novelist wishes to survey this expanse but cannot navigate the "waves of ungraspable data";[26] recent advances in the hardware and software of financial trading platforms, however, mean that it is plausible to posit the existence of technological systems that *can* chart this territory, turning defeat into partial victory via a kind of cognitive mapping by proxy. *Gods Without Men* may give us no more than the most fleeting glimpses into the workings of such a system, but we are to understand that Walter is whirring away in the background, "mapping and remapping" the world, as Alberto Toscano says of such programmes, so that the narrative discourse itself does not have to.[27]

There remains a problem of synthesis, however. We may imagine that, like the *Arcades Project* as Benjamin envisaged it, Walter has the capacity to fuse together the disparate fragments it collects, so that the totality of which they are parts will prove recoverable. This is Bachman's aspiration:

that his programme will cultivate "relationships," "rhymes," "echoes," "links," and "connections" between "disparate things," and so "restore what was shattered" (134, 138, 149). But no such synthesis emerges into visibility, for the reader, from the lists that Kunzru provides: instead, they remain inert on the page, a mere jumble of incongruous and incommensurable data points.

Theodor Adorno's famous critique of Benjamin's method in the *Arcades Project* – a method founded on the conviction that a sheer accumulation of documentary material will prove sufficient to speak for itself – is apposite here. For Adorno, writing to Benjamin after seeing work on the project in the late 1930s, his friend's approach was flawed because "the mediation through the entire social process is missing" and because of a "superstitious tendency" to attribute a "power of illumination" to "mere material enumeration." Adorno feared that a "theological" (more specifically Kabbalistic) belief in the Adamic power of "calling things by their names" tended to "switch into the wide-eyed presentation of mere facts." "If one wanted to put it rather drastically," he continued, "one could say your study is located at the crossroads of magic and positivism. This spot is bewitched."[28] One thinks here of Bachman's "signs" and "mystical letters," which are supposed to become legible once more through Walter's amassing and combining of "all these different kinds of phenomena" (149). If, like his intellectual inspiration, Benjamin, and like his character, Bachman, Kunzru too is drawn here to "material enumeration" as a means of conjuring up an apprehension of an "entire social process," then Adorno's words would seem to sound an apt note of scepticism with respect to the viability of such a project.

For Adorno, the missing ingredient in Benjamin's work in progress was dialectal materialism: only a properly Marxist methodology offered a theory of mediation adequate to articulate the relation between individual facts and the social field at large. In Kunzru's case, pure enumeration is not, of course, the prevailing strategy across the text as a whole; for him, the mediating element is novelistic narrative itself. The novel, and especially the "networked" novel, he has said, is peculiarly well equipped to synthesize the stuff of globalized life into a coherent, integrated whole: to "show the way places and times have an impact on one another"; to "do abstract explanations, and very close work about an individual's subjective experience and affect, and link it to social forces."[29] To subordinate a strategy of pure, unadulterated "info-dumping" to the imperatives of narrative patterning (the need to select from an infinity of possible material; to draw the bounds, however capacious, *somewhere*) is necessarily, however, to set about constructing *a* whole at the cost of surrendering the possibility – however notional – of encompassing *the* whole. Selection and synthesis or infinite, indiscriminate enumeration: as I've argued, Kunzru tries, as far as he can, to have it both ways – to foreground narrative while "delegating" data accumulation to Walter's implicit background rumblings. But the problem of how an adequate representation of totality might be mounted remains (no doubt necessarily) unresolved.

Nevertheless, a desire for knowledge, and indeed omniscience, is very clearly both a thematic preoccupation and a shaping formal principle of *Gods Without Men*, even if it remains inevitably unrealized. This impulse, however, exists in tension with – and is ultimately displaced by – a conviction that some aspects of the world simply defy our drive to know – are fundamentally incompatible with epistemological processing. Towards the end of the novel, Kunzru offers a telling set of reflections from the point of view of Jaz's wife, Lisa. Observing her fellow citizens going about their daily business, she ponders the prevalence of an assumed entitlement to total knowledge – or at least to an assurance that responsibility for assembling such knowledge has been assigned to an appropriate delegate or surrogate:

> They were the inheritors of certain rights, among them the right to know the world in its totality, or if they chose not to know (for they had other claims on their time, such as working and being entertained), then for others to know on their behalf, so that an explanation could potentially be made to them, or if not to them, then to an expert who would receive it and act in their best interests. (358)

If, as I've been arguing, Kunzru earlier – with his invocations of Walter's data-scanning abilities – pursues a strategy that precisely corresponds to this tendency to defer to a "surrogate knower," then Lisa's subsequent meditations cast further doubt on the efficacy of this strategy. The hysterical public response to the inexplicable disappearance – and miraculous return – of Lisa and Jaz's son, Raj, points, she believes, to the "flipside" of the prevailing "self-assurance":

> the outrage when something unknowable reared up before them, not just unknown for now, because they or their designated expert had yet to enquire into the matter ... but unknowable in principle, inaccessible to human comprehension ... In their blind panic they'd turn on whoever they could find as a scapegoat, would tear them into pieces to preserve this cherished fiction, the fiction of the essential comprehensibility of the world. (358)

Lisa has come to "the understanding that at the heart of the world, behind or beyond or above or below, is a mystery into which we are not meant to penetrate" (359). Her characterization is redolent, then, of Alice Jardine's account – in her classic work of feminist theory, *Gynesis* (1985) – of Western "master narratives' ... non-knowledge," that which has "eluded them [and] engulfed them": an "other-than-themselves" that 'is almost always a 'space' of some kind (over which the narrative has lost control)," a space "coded as feminine, as woman."[30] Jardine wishes to join the male theorists she discusses (the likes of Derrida and Lacan) in a "valorization of the feminine" understood as the site of the "unknown," the "unconscious," and the "non-sensical"[31] – a valorization that, as we've seen, male authors of the epistemologically obsessed encyclopaedic or systems novel are likewise inclined to assert. Yet as another major feminist critic, Mary Ann Doane, notes in examining the work of these same theorists, the "non-knowledge or even anti-knowledge" that the female subject is said to inhabit "is linked to the realm of the mystics and hence, at the very least, divorces the register of knowledge from the register of discourse. The woman cannot say what she knows ... The woman here becomes emblematic of the subject who is duped by the unconscious, of the non-knowledge of the subject."[32] To be clear, my critique (like Doane's) is aimed not at the possibility of *alternative* forms of feminine knowledge (or of indigenous knowledge, which the novel's portrayal of the Mojave Desert implicitly invokes) but of a tendency to reduce such epistemological alternatives to outright *absences* of knowledge (as well as reason, logic, order, etc.) – even (or especially) in the process of seeming to celebrate them.

Lisa, *Gods Without Men*'s main female character, is problematically marked, then, by what the narrator calls her "reverence for the unknowable, impenetrable beyond" (359). As the narrative unfolds, various elements come to function as embodiments of that which she imagines to lie outside the "limits" (359) of human knowledge. There is the vast brooding vacancy of the desert itself, where, in the words of Honoré de Balzac, there is "everything and nothing," "*Dieu sans les hommes.*" There are also the strange visitations witnessed by a succession of characters – encounters whose precise status (true union with the numinous? psychotic break?) the text resolutely refuses to confirm. And there is a procession of lost children, swallowed up by the desert and then disengorged, apparently anointed with some unearthly aura (they seem, eerily, to "glow" [67, 215–16, 308–9]). Each of these manifestations of unknowability refracts perhaps the greatest challenge to epistemological "self-assurance" – and to the assumed authority of expert knowers – to have occurred in recent times: the global financial crisis or "credit crunch."

For mainstream financial economists, as well as the analysts and traders who incorporated their models into their strategies, the crisis was, in a very real sense, unknowable: structurally inassimilable to their frames of knowledge. Many models simply excluded the possibility of a large-scale, synchronized decline in the real estate values that underpinned the boom in financial securitization.[33] And, driven by the prevailing belief in the essential efficiency of markets, it was assumed that any possibility of widespread default that might exist was "priced in": if the prices of mortgage-backed securities and other assets correlated with them were riding high, then it could be safely assumed that this rosy picture reflected the underlying robustness of the housing market itself. As Randy Martin remarks:

> It is possible to see in that crisis moment of September 2008 a whole array of knowledge failures ... A knowledge failure in the price mechanism; a collapse of prediction and theory; an evacuation of expert authority; an unmaking of what contains or bounds the economy as a distinct domain; and a shift in the relation between knowledge and its presumed opposite, nonknowledge.[34]

Jaz, Bachman, and the other members of the hedge fund – as well as the trading model that they have come to rely upon to "know" on their behalf – are as oblivious to the impending crunch as any of their real-life counterparts. For all its supposed omniscience, Walter cannot detect the vast object hovering just over the horizon. After leaving his job, following Raj's disappearance, Jaz learns that "the Walter fund had been leveraged to an unprecedented degree, borrowing to take long positions on the mortgage market. When the crash came and their line of credit dried up, the business unraveled" (338). The "giant abstractions" in which Walter was trading were "gambles on thin air" (338), without any foundation in the world outside themselves.

This, it seems, is the realization to which Cy Bachman comes in the closing sequence of the novel, as he re-enacts the final journey of his philosophical exemplar, Walter Benjamin, and dies – apparently from suicide – near the Pyrenean town of Portbou (347). Bachman's death, in very similar circumstances to Benjamin's, signifies the ultimate unsustainability – for all its utopian appeal – of his Benjaminian vision of the financial markets as universal historical chronicles. Bachman's model and the markets at large – both organized around assumptions of seamless informational efficiency – excluded from their aggregations the very things to which they should have been most attuned.

Whereas earlier in *Gods Without Men*, and especially in the sequences featuring Jaz, Bachman, and Walter, there is an evident attraction to formal and stylistic principles of comprehensiveness, unity, and consistency, as the narrative approaches its conclusion, it is increasingly guided by a logic of incompletion, a desire to foreground how the world confounds the will to know, how events like the credit crunch may register only as gaps or blanks in established systems of knowledge.

This strategy focuses, in particular, on the character of Raj, Jaz and Lisa's son. Raj is a source of bewilderment throughout the novel, and his incomprehensibility is repeatedly figured in terms of an affront to a specifically financial form of knowledge. This is true even before his baffling disappearance in the desert. We learn early on in the narrative that Raj is autistic, and when Jaz recalls receiving this diagnosis, he does so with the mind-set of the professional risk analyst: "What were the odds? He knew exactly. One in ten thousand in the seventies. Now down to one in a hundred and sixty-six" (51). While Jaz makes his living "building mathematical models to predict and trade on every kind of catastrophe," this is "an event for which he ha[s] no charts, no time series" (51). Like the trading strategy that Walter will adopt, disastrously, later in the novel, Jaz's situation is "an entirely unhedged position" (51). After Raj vanishes during a family excursion to Pinnacle/Trinity Rocks, Jaz's only certainty is that there exists a chain of associations linking his missing son, financial trade, and the strangeness of the Mojave: "All he could say for sure was that everything was connected – Raj, Walter, the desert" (331). Raj's disappearance and eventual recovery – when he is found walking in the desert, unharmed but apparently emitting a strange glow – coincide with the onset and escalation of the financial crisis: "the collapse of Lehman Brothers, the plummeting Dow" (338). What Jaz thinks of as two parallel "realities," the reality of his family's ordeal and the "alternate reality" (338) of the markets, are, again, rhetorically paired. Raj's baffling disappearance – so insistently associated with the unthinkable crisis in the financial markets – is a "lesson" for his mother, Lisa, in the core of unknowability "at the heart of the world" (359), and it opens up an unfillable gap, too, at the centre of the narrative. Questions – "What happened to you?" "Where did you go?" (342) – resound throughout the latter part of the novel, but Kunzru insists on keeping open every conceivable explanation, including the idea that Raj has been harboured by some form of paranormal, if seemingly benign, agency.

Increasingly desperate for answers, and increasingly estranged from Lisa, Jaz absconds with Raj and flies back to California. Lisa follows, and the three of them make a frenzied, stumbling return visit to the Rocks where Raj vanished, and where a hubbub of unanswered questions has gathered over the centuries. The scene that awaits them – as described in what turn out to be the last sentences of the present-day narrative – offers anything but the longed-for revelation, however: "The air was blue. Ahead of them lay only a vast emptiness, an absence. There was nothing out there at all" (381). One final, brief chapter follows. It returns us to 1775 and provides another testimony to the strange power of this site, this time in the words of a Spanish missionary. As the Padre describes it, his experience is, precisely, a moment of revelation – an angel descends, "revealing certain mysteries concerning life and death" – but this knowledge is uncontainable "in the mind of man" and immediately "recede[s] into forgetfulness" (384). "I received all this in silence and stillness," he writes in the novel's final line, "and then the creature retreated into the sky and I was once again alone in this desert place" (384).

Gods Without Men closes, then, by underscoring its insistence on the fundamental unavailability of certain kinds of knowledge or explanation – or their incommensurability, at least, with human ways of knowing – and returns, in pushing home this apophatic vision, to the emblematic vacancy of the desert, a space triangulated, as we have seen, with Raj's mysterious fate, which transpires there, and with the credit crisis – so shattering to the confident knowledge claims of economists, financiers, and technologists. Moreover, by refusing – emphatically, in the end – to disclose the momentous secrets that dwell in the desert – by leaving them as blank patches in the textual "network" – Kunzru provides a telling narrative figuration for the structures of exclusion that shape the epistemologies of financial markets and models, structures liable to screen out precisely those elements that it is most critical to factor in if a complex scenario is to be accurately and reliably mapped.

Thus, just as the work of Iain Sinclair and other contemporary novelists discussed in Part II by turns imbibes and refuses the "fiduciary" structures of financial exchange in its formal and generic arrangements, so Kunzru, in *Gods Without Men*, is drawn to install the informational efficiency of the idealized financial market as a narrative principle, only ultimately to leave zones of opacity in the text that frustrate such a totalizing logic. For Kunzru, Sinclair, and others, too, this pattern of formal alignment with and divergence from the processes and mentalities of financial markets also enacts anxieties over the contemporary author's identification with the literary marketplace (itself a sector subject – as we've seen – to multiple, intensifying forms of financialization). Kunzru makes this connection between narrative structure and market positioning most explicit in an interview, when (like other commentators on the novel form, as we've seen) he invokes the language of contract to characterize the relationship between author and reader. Reflecting on the "gaps and deliberate unknowns" in *Gods Without Men*, Kunzru acknowledges that

> I sort of break that primary "contract" between the reader and the writer, which is that if I tell you something, you're going to get it explained in the end, and I very deliberately don't do that. At the heart of that book there's something that doesn't add up: what happens to that kid that is in some ways the same child and at other times not ... There's kind of an impossibility in it, something that drains meaning away.[35]

Kunzru's deployment of the idea of the "fictional contract" here invites comparison with the uses made of that notion by one of his most prominent contemporaries: Jonathan Franzen. Both noted for their broad, densely patterned narratives (recall the characterization of *Gods Without Men* as practicing a "rampant Franzenism"), Kunzru and Franzen also share an equivocal affiliation with the American systems novelists who rose to attention in the 1960s and 1970s – the likes of DeLillo, Pynchon, and (centrally for Franzen) Gaddis. If Kunzru has distanced himself somewhat from the "systems" label, it is because, for him, a particular *type* of system – the network – "defines our period" and provides a more apt tag for the kind of fiction he wishes to write.[36] For Franzen, however, this relationship is more fraught and conflicted: having allied himself to the systems camp with his first two novels (*The Twenty-Seventh City* [1988] and its follow-up *Strong Motion* [1992], which I discussed above), he staged an equally self-conscious departure with his breakthrough, *The Corrections* (2001), a no less wide-angled, but more accessible and humanistically warmed-through, offering. Among ambitious contemporary novelists, no writer embodies the widespread turn against experimental postmodernism, the rapprochement with realism, and the renewal of relations of trust and belief between author and reader more clearly than Franzen.

In 2002, he openly declared his apostasy in an essay entitled "Mr Difficult," which lambasted Gaddis's later work, in particular, as well as much of the wider systems novel canon. For Franzen, in this essay, the systems novel was based on the premise that "closure was the enemy," and in its resistance to formal or narrative (as much as political or social) closure "breached" the "Contract model" of text–reader exchange, in which "the deepest purpose of reading and writing fiction is to sustain a sense of connectedness," so that "a novel deserves a reader's attention only as long as the author sustains the reader's trust."[37] As Rachel Greenwald Smith notes in a commentary on Franzen's essay, "for a novel to follow through on its promises, in this context, it has to offer means for ... connection: through identification, a sense of alliance, and emotional enrichment."[38] In "Mr Difficult," Franzen declares himself a "Contract kind of person," and one can readily detect his fidelity to the Contract model in his work from *The Corrections* onwards, with its determination to tie up loose ends and render its social world full and transparent (he has spoken more recently of a mounting desire to press language "more completely into the service of providing transparent access to the stories I was telling and to the characters in those stories").[39] It's equally clear that Kunzru's *Gods Without Men* breaks its implicit "contract" with the reader on Franzen's model (as it does, indeed, on Kunzru's own). This strategy has evidently troubled many of the novel's actual readers: while the text has relatively positive Amazon ratings overall, the majority of negative comments emphasize the narrative's inconclusiveness – one reader, for example, complaining that "the hope that there would be some point to all of the struggling/searching/seeking [is] simply discarded in the end."[40]

As we saw in Part II, the idea of a "fictional contract" has a tendency to become more than merely metaphorical. So it is in Franzen's essay, which implies that the Contract model is both superior to and culturally dominant over its rival – the "Status model," with its fetishization of "art-historical importance" – because it answers to an irresistible economic imperative. "Fiction is ... conservative and conventional," Franzen explains, because of a market structure in which novelists, if they are to "make a living," must do so "one book at a time, bringing pleasure to large audiences." "Closure," "connectedness," a sustained sense of "trust" between text and reader: these are undoubtedly the hallmarks of market-friendly contemporary fiction (Franzen's own post-1990s work again being a case in point).

Kunzru is also acutely conscious of the economic position of the contemporary writer. A generation younger than a product of the 1960s counterculture like Iain Sinclair, he too laments "the demise of a sort of quasi-bohemian intellectual class." Writers, he has said, "occupy a precarious place in the current social order," tending "to be freelancers, with variable incomes and little security," and therefore – "despite our education and privilege" – caught in a predicament shared "with other workers who are forced to operate 'paycheck to paycheck.'"[41] To forsake the market's approved model of narrative closure, completion, and transparency is thus to risk a less-than-optimal return on one's writing and an entrenchment of one's position among the ranks of the "precariat." Of course, such a literary strategy might be understood as an attempt to cultivate an alternate, niche market – for the "experimental" or "art novel" – where artistic "status" generates its own economic value, and incompatibility with the "mainstream" market is itself a source of marketability (the contemporary fate of modernism as Sinclair depicts it in *Downriver*).

But, as we saw in the Introduction, in the face of converging ideological and material pressures militating towards the absolute *maximization* of market appeal, the relative autonomy involved in pursuing strategies liable to find a receptive readership only on the fringes of the mainstream, if at all, has a meaningful status. Insofar as *Gods Without Men* makes such an assertion of autonomy, it is striking that the lingering perplexities (Raj, the desert) that militate against narrative closure and mass-market circulation – the novel's unidentified narrative objects, if you will – also, as I've argued, figure the unidentified economic object – the real estate crisis – that fell outside the field of vision of the financial markets. Those elements liable to throw a little grit into the literary market's cycles of consumption also, that is, stand for that which confounds the knowledge-building assemblages that make up the much vaster markets of the contemporary financial system.

PART IV

The Moment of Market Metafiction

A commodity is something that is exchanged in the market for money or other commodities ... It seems clearer than ever that art is one form of commodity production in a wider field of cultural commodity production. What remains open to debate, however, is the extent to which the meanings generated by the resulting products can accrue added value. That is, the extent to which they can retain and articulate critical distance from the commodity system at large; or whether the "drag" of embeddedness at the economic level in the circuits of production, exchange, and consumption vitiates the possibility of distance at the level of the imaginative-symbolic.

– Paul Wood

CHAPTER 6

Putting Everything on the Table
Markets and Material Conditions in Twenty-First-Century Fiction

I began this book by considering Tao Lin's signal decision in 2008 to sell shares in an in-progress novel – part of a self-promotion campaign that helped him to secure a contract with a major New York press for his subsequent book, *Taipei*, published in 2013. One of the most striking features of the latter novel is the extent to which it rolls together what one character refers to as "work on writing" and "promotion things."[1] Written in Lin's signature "concrete/literal" style,[2] much of *Taipei*'s narrative is concerned with the various ways in which one might go about achieving the "specific goal [of] selling books," as the protagonist, Paul (Lin himself in virtually all but name), puts it (83). Paul is referring most directly to the selling of other people's books (from an impromptu sidewalk stall he and a friend set up to try to remedy the friend's "'fucked' . . . financial situation" [84–86]), but – a writer himself like many of his acquaintances – the remark encapsulates a more general life objective. This much is evident from the sheer quantity of the narrative devoted to various forms of literary promotion, from pitches, jacket designs, release parties, readings, book tours, panel discussions, signings, author interviews, and writers' fundraisers to newspaper cover stories, online profile articles, Twitter, Facebook, and blog posts, and the MFAs in fiction or poetry that are increasingly required credentials for would-be professional writers. Towards the end of the novel, while visiting his parents in Taiwan, Paul and his new wife Erin gravitate to "a bookstore near Taipei 101" (formerly the Taipei World Financial Center), one of Asia's leading financial services hubs and at the time "the third-tallest building in the world," where they sit "holding each other on the floor in the fiction section" – as if having come to rest at the very nexus of literature and capital that the novel has been tracing (204).

Ian Sansom observes suggestively that Lin's novel demands a "kind of contractual bond . . . with the reader" that entails an element of "collusion."[3] To buy and read *Taipei*, I'd suggest, is to participate in the cycle of marketing, publicity, and promotion that is the narrative's major topic and without which the novel itself would not have appeared, at least in its glossily packaged, major press-backed form – and it is to do so without ever being sure whether the text is unapologetically flaunting this cycle, self-critically satirizing it, or (as all of its surface effects suggest) observing it with the strictest neutrality. Indeed, there is a recurrent suggestion that, for all the narrative's concretism and literalism, the experiences of which it is composed are not determinate phenomena in their own right, but instead inhabit a kind of promissory dimension, their true meaning, significance, and value only to be apprehended from a future vantage point. This future is repeatedly presented as both virtual and actual, at once yet-to-come and already-at-hand: we're told, for example, that "the nothingness of the future ha[s] gained a framework-y somethingness ... like ... the beginning elaborations of a science-fiction conceit" (not unlike that of *Back to the Future* [1985], a poster for which Paul photographs) or that "one seem[s] simply to be here, less an accumulation of moments than a single arrangement continuously gifted from some inaccessible future" (8, 108, 12).[4] Most strikingly, Paul has the peculiar feeling when drifting into sleep that "the information of his existence, the etching of which into space-time [is] his experience of life" (and the stuff of the novel) is "being studied by millions of entities, billions of years from now, who [know] him better than he [will] ever know himself." These entities seem to know "everything about him, even his current thoughts, in their exact vagueness, as he move[s] distractedly toward sleep"; "maybe" they will "study" him "in their equivalent of middle school" thinks "some fleeting aspect of Paul's consciousness, unaware what it [is] referencing" (124). Given Lin's manifest concern with finance capital both in *Taipei* and in his wider activities, it's no coincidence, I'd suggest, that this strange projection into the future is so redolent of the uncanny temporality of the financial derivative, as described by Richard Doyle:

> The derivative can only have an anticipated value ... [S]omething other than contemporary human subjectivity ... underwrites or advances the derivative, perhaps a human that becomes the financial subject only retroactively, perhaps only after its death; the derivative casts its shadow from the future ... Thus the distance of the derivative from a "price" is cast as a loss of knowledge and of vision, a shadow cast from a lurking presence in the future, a presence that, "for now," projects an unclear specter.[5]

Lin is not alone among contemporary writers, I'll argue in this chapter, in imagining a future for his writing that partakes of the complex logic of the derivative. Lin's stock issue scheme, as well as the novel, *Taipei*, whose breakthrough was enabled in part by it, also emblematize various other concerns of this book – and of this final Part in particular: the ways in which the machinations of professional authorship and publishing may become important elements of the marketing of a writer's public persona; an attendant slippage between the various "epitextual" factors (media reports, interviews, publicity campaigns, and so on) that surround a text and the content of the text itself;[6] the positioning of a barely fictionalized version of the author at the centre of the narrative; and an appeal to the text's future reception as the only meaningful determinant of its value.

In this chapter and the next, I argue that the centrality of such concerns to what looks to many critics like the vanguard of twenty-first-century fiction (especially in the United States) marks the coalescence of market metafiction – long an important element of the novel under neoliberalism – as a distinct and highly visible mode in literary culture. In addition to Lin's writing, I argue that this mode is paradigmatically at work in texts by five other prominent contemporary authors: Lin's fellow New Yorkers, Ben Lerner, Teju Cole, and Joshua Cohen; the German-domiciled American Nell Zink; and the Torontonian Sheila Heti. If not quite forming a fully constituted "school," it is no surprise that critics have frequently made connections between these authors: their strong affinities are manifest not only in their fiction itself, but also on acknowledgments pages, in their public references to one another's work, and in the numerous instances of one interviewing, reviewing, or blurbing another. Elements of the features I examine in these authors' texts are also evident in works by a wider (again, in some cases personally affiliated) group of authors who similarly blend memoir with novelistic techniques and other prose forms, such as criticism, history, theory, and philosophy. In the United States, such authors include Maggie Nelson, Jarett Kobek, Benjamin Kunkel, Kate Zambreno, Eugene Lim, Ben Marcus, and Helen DeWitt. In the United Kingdom, work by Tom McCarthy, Rachel Cusk, Lars Iyer, Olivia Laing, and Adam Thirlwell would also fit into this category, while the recent prominence of the Italian Elena Ferrante and the Norwegian Karl Ove Knausgård in Anglophone literary culture has reinforced a consensus that it is in such hybrid forms that prose narrative's "advanced" form currently lies.

The authors upon whom I focus in this Part (as well as a number of those I have just mentioned) are often described as writers of "autofiction" – that is, prose writing in which the protagonist shares a name (or at least a set of key identifiers) with the author, but has experiences that are to some extent fictional.[7] The term was first used in the late 1970s by the French novelist and critic Serge Doubrovsky as a means of designating his own work as well as a long tradition in French literature. In the context of this book, Iain Sinclair's novels (with their author/bookseller figures named "Sinclair" – or sometimes "Norton") could be readily located in this category, as might texts associated with the "reality hunger" of postirony or New Sincerity, such as *The Pale King* (with its "author here" interjections) or even *A Heartbreaking Work of Staggering Genius* (which strives to generate and sustain readers' belief even while acknowledging the fictionality of elements of its "memoir" narrative). A number of other texts discussed above (including novels by Gilbert Sorrentino, Kathy Acker, Martin Amis, and Bret Easton Ellis) also display clear autofictional tendencies. Of the novels I consider across this chapter and the next, three (Lerner's *10:04* [2014], Cohen's *Book of Numbers* [2015], and Heti's *How Should a Person Be?* [2010]) conform to even the strictest definition of autofiction (first-person, author-name narrator), while two others (*Taipei*, discussed above, and Cole's *Open City* [2011]) fit slightly looser definitions (third-person and first-person narratives respectively, in which the protagonists bear demonstrably close resemblances to their authors, despite having different names). While the term has been applied to Zink, it fits her work less comfortably, especially the novel I focus upon in Chapter 7, *Nicotine* (2016), a third-person narrative in which no single character is an obvious authorial proxy (even though, as I'll suggest, self-consciousness about authorship is central to its strategies).

The term "autofiction" has some use as a means of grasping what unites these authors, then, but in what follows I largely set it aside – not primarily because of the definitional complexities it throws up, however, but because, in the texts I analyse, the self-reflexivity concerning the relationship between art and life characteristic of autofiction centres on one question in particular: how – or if – the text can fulfil the author's simultaneous goals of being an expression of artistic, intellectual, and political autonomy *and* a marketable literary commodity. I define these texts, then, as works not (or not simply) of autofiction but of market metafiction. Again, as in narratives discussed earlier in this book, these novels work out their positionings in the cultural field in and through dialogues with aspects of contemporary financial capitalism.

A text which now seems to have anticipated much of the present appetite for self-exposure in fiction-writing, and which is an acknowledged influence on a number of the authors mentioned above, is also notable for the centrality of its concern with the material conditions of authorship and their relation to wider economic forces. Chris Kraus's *I Love Dick* (1997) appears "on the surface of it," as the author has remarked, to offer a "kind of gender romantic comedy" (in the depiction of the protagonist, Chris's, obsession with her husband's academic colleague), but ultimately, she suggests, positions gender and sexuality as crucial axes of social relations that are structural before they are personal: "when I wrote *I Love Dick*, very early on I felt like my goal was to put everything on the table that was transacted under the table ... Really it's about power. And not even personal dynamic power; more like economic power and cultural-politics power, and how things are transacted."[8]

A repeated assertion in the narrative is that writers and artists who "forget [that] you live by compromise and contradiction ... just die like dogs" (the point is quite literal, with Kraus relating a series of harrowing stories of artists in the Downtown literary scene who perished through some combination of poverty, homelessness, or illness during the 1980s and early 1990s).[9] We see this obligation to live out "the internalized contradictions of late capitalism" (218) especially clearly in the way in which Chris and her husband Sylvère (based on the theorist Sylvère Lotringer, to whom Kraus was then married) monetize his scholarly expertise in "the more 'transgressive' elements of modernism" (such as Georges Bataille's "heroic sciences of human sacrifice and torture," as well as figures like Antonin Artaud, covered in Sylvère's in-progress opus *Modernism & the Holocaust*) (17, 19, 22). Asking whether "in late capitalism ... anyone [is] truly free," Chris describes how the spectacle of the "mostly young white men" who are "Sylvère's fans" "going out to Exchange Ideas with [him] in bars after his lectures" prompts her to respond "by milking money from Sylvère's growing reputation, setting ever-higher fees" (16, 17). There's a certain inevitability, then, to the moment, later in the novel, when a poststructuralist semiotician "marshal[s] a gang of little men, the banker, the Lacanian and Sylvère, to the cardroom to drink scotch and talk about the Holocaust" (167). Chris's assertion that "Sylvère and I are Marxists ... He takes money from the people who won't give me money and gives it to me," redressing "our culture's distribution of it ... based on values I reject," is not so much straightforwardly ironic as a sign of the extent to which Chris is, as she puts it, "suffering from the dizziness of contradictions" (71).

We saw a similar conflicted awareness of the potential commercial exploitability of forms of aesthetic transgression inherited from modernism in Iain Sinclair's work, and in the next chapter we will consider related concerns in Joshua Cohen's fiction. Kraus's *I Love Dick* (as well as her more recent, similarly autobiographically-infused novels) also anticipate the texts I discuss in these two chapters in the remarkable permeability they establish between life and text – between the things that Chris Kraus says and does in the world, and the things "Chris Kraus" says and does in the novel. One of the authors I discuss here, Ben Lerner (speaking in an interview with Tao Lin), has noted the increasing prevalence of such permeability in contemporary literature:

> Maybe it's just that for a lot of people – sometimes in interesting ways, some-times in stupid ways – there's no division between the art object and what surrounds it. So your interviews or blog posts or whatever are less supplements to your novel than part of it. I'm not private, but I believe in literary form – I'll use my life as material for art (I don't know how not to do this) and I'll use art as a way of exploring that passage of life into art and vice versa.[10]

The writers I consider in this Part share Lerner's sense that, while the literary form of the novel continues to play an important mediating role, when the author's selfhood is as central to the narrative as it is in these texts, other forms of public self-presentation are necessarily inseparable from the novelistic project proper. Thus my corpus for these chapters consists not only of novels but also of interviews, profiles, news stories, columns, and essays in which the authors I study discuss their lives and careers. These latter texts are useful sources of biographical detail, but they also function as extensions of the novels' own attempts at once to expose the machinations of marketing and to market themselves.

Lerner mentions blogging as a mode of self-expression that seems increasingly proximate to autobiographically-based forms of contemporary literature. Hywel Dix has argued that the key context for the present prominence of autofictions of various kinds is "the growth of so-called 'reality television' over the past two decades," as well as the prevalence of "the related confessional genres of magazine journalism, televised soap opera, and certain kinds of online narratives, especially blogs."[11] These are certainly credible factors in accounting for a general contemporary vogue for self-revelation-via-fiction; the rise of online writing platforms, in particular, undoubtedly informs the work of the authors I discuss here (several of whom – Lin, Heti, Cole – have, at least for a time, maintained visible online presences themselves). The fully fledged coalescence of the mode I call market metafiction over the past decade, however, is attribu-table, first and foremost, to the global financial crisis and "Great Recession," which – as I detailed in the Introduction – have made the fragility of twenty-first-century authorship's material conditions newly palpable, and entrenched a neoliberal ideology of the market in practice, even as they have discredited it in theory.

How do twenty-first-century authors attached to the conjunction of left politics and experimental aesthetics, but concerned to achieve cultural visibility for their work and (far from incidentally) make a living as a professional writer, negotiate the resulting pressures, tensions, and contradictions in their literary practice? In the remainder of Part IV, I examine novels published since 2010 by five high-profile authors, analysing how their strategies not only seek viable means of reconciling competing political, aesthetic, and economic demands, but also, in the process, foreground and reflect upon this very challenge.

Each of the texts I discuss in Part IV demonstrably harbours (to a greater or lesser extent) what Mark Banks refers to as a "belief in the utopian possibilities of artistic and cultural labour, in its capacity to act as an incubator" of "radical social transformation" – a belief that remains "vital and enduring." Yet they also acknowledge that in the daily practice of the contemporary cultural worker (very much including the contemporary writer), the most that one can hope for is often "subsistence, survival and 'making the best' of the conditions" under which one works. None of the texts I discuss "solves" this tension: rather they each in their different ways exhibit what Banks calls a "socially embedded, compromised or 'negotiated' autonomy," drawing attention to the "routine conditions of cultural production where workers find themselves engaged in a quotidian 'struggle within' to try to mediate, manage or reconcile the varied opportunities and constraints of the art-commerce relation." In some cases (Lerner, Cohen, Heti), this drawing of attention to the complex factors shaping the text's own production – what I call market metafiction – could hardly be more overt, while in others (Cole, Zink) it takes less direct – more figurative or allegorical – forms. While their specific strategies differ, then, these texts all revealingly dramatize the interplay between a desire to escape the logics of neoliberal capitalism and a search for "opportunities for meaningful self-expression within [capitalism's] limits."[12]

In the next chapter, I argue that, examined together, novels by Zink, Cohen, and Heti triangulate a set of key options open to the formally ambitious novelist in the contemporary moment. In the remainder of this chapter, I focus on conjunctions of finance capital and conditions of contemporary authorship in novels by Lerner and Cole. Lerner's key strategies in *10:04* revolve around the phenomenon of "hedging" –

a practice central to both the publishing industry and the financial sector. Cole's *Open City* strives to extricate itself from a trade in crude narrative portrayals of Africa and Africans that reproduce the depredations of global finance capital, while at the same time acknowledging the relative privilege that permits such a project.

Hedging on the Future: Ben Lerner's *10:04*

Speaking in 2013, Ben Lerner describes the political and economic conditions bequeathed by the global financial crisis as forming a confounding paradox:

> Neo-liberalism, the latest incarnation of capitalism, has been a total failure economically. Many of us have this sense that it can't possibly go on and yet it has been a total triumph ideologically because so many people have difficulty imagining any alternatives. So there is the strange sense that it is both doomed and the only option.[13]

Lerner's *10:04*, I'll argue here, understands itself as exhibiting what a novel that simultaneously cannot and must conform to a neoliberal logic of the market might look like. Lerner moved to novel-writing having established a reputation on the "innovative" wing of contemporary poetry in collections marked by a scrutiny of their own procedures that he has attributed to the influence of John Ashbery. Ashbery is also the tutelary spirit of Lerner's first novel, *Leaving the Atocha Station* (2011), a study in the political and artistic ambivalence of a callow American abroad that was an unexpected critical and commercial success for its Minneapolis nonprofit publisher Coffee House Press. *10:04* marked Lerner's entry into the publishing mainstream, appearing in 2014 from Faber & Faber (at the time separate from the London-based company and affiliated to Farrar, Straus, and Giroux, part of the Macmillan Group). The novel is deeply shaped by Lerner's thinking about the power, and limits, of markets.

In the interview with Tao Lin referenced above, Lerner remarks that "many of the left thinkers . . . that formed a big part of my thinking about politics and art" (one of whom is evidently Fredric Jameson)[14] "emphasize how capitalism is a totality, how there's no escape from it, no outside." While acknowledging that "every relationship can feel saturated by market logic," Lerner describes himself as increasingly inclined to question "this notion of totality" and explore "how there are all kinds of moments in our daily lives that break – or at least could break – from the logic of profit and the modes of domination it entails." For Lerner, these moments represent "zones of freedom, even if it's never pure," and he is drawn to the idea – while recognizing it as "an enabling fiction" – that they constitute "fragments from a world to come, a world where price isn't the only measure of value."[15]

In *10:04*, Lerner's narrator and protagonist, Ben, insistently draws attention to the ways in which the narrative is shaped by a ubiquitous market logic even as it strives to hold open spaces for other forms of value. This continual use of "self-reference," as Lerner puts it, clearly marks *10:04* as a work of metafiction, but he is at pains to distinguish his method from conventional understandings of that style (familiar from accounts of the now-canonical exponents of the 1960s and 1970s) according to which metafictions are "works that draw attention to their own devices, their own artificiality, in order to mock novelistic convention and show the impossibility of capturing a reality external to the text."[16] Lerner is "really interested in the way a work can acknowledge its constructedness," but "not to show in some post-structuralist way how you can never access reality." Rather, his goal is "to totally acknowledge the specific material conditions of the book." On the one hand, this means highlighting the forms of "privilege" that allow such a novel to be constructed at all, such as the narrator's – and Lerner's – (relatively) affluent Brooklyn lifestyle, college teaching post, literary world contacts, and so on. And on the other, it means making clear the often incompatible pressures – from fellow writers, from critics, from publishers, and above all from the market itself – that cause the novel to be constructed in the way it is. As Lerner says, "I want all that in the book": "the self-reference is a way of acknowledging honestly the ground for the social experiment the book is," of "inhabit[ing] the contradictions and possibilities of my position in the world" and "acknowledg[ing] and respond[ing] to those pressures."[17]

We see one of many instances of these competing pressures when Ben and some fellow writers transition from a panel discussion at the Columbia School of the Arts to an "elegant dinner," and the discussion shifts abruptly from "the usual exhortations to purity – think of the novel not as your opportunity to get rich or famous but to wrestle, in your own way, with the titans of the form" to "small talk" "all ... about money: had you heard about X's advance, how much money Y received when her aggressively mediocre book was optioned for film, and so on."[18] Ben similarly finds himself subject to sharply diverging conceptions of how literature should be evaluated when *The New Yorker* shows interest in his writing after the "unexpected critical success of [his] first novel" (unnamed, but bearing a close resemblance to *Leaving the Atocha Station*, itself a meditation on contradiction and inauthenticity – the universal experience of "squatting in one of the handful of subject positions proffered by capital" or existing as "a bit player in a looped infomercial for the damaged life").[19] The magazine accepts one of Ben's stories, but wants a "major cut," excising the section he considers "the story's core" (56). Ben perceives this response as an attempt to "standardize his work," its "primary motivation" being "on some level … the story's marketability" (56). Torn between the appeal of "approximately eight thousand dollars," on one side, a reluctance to "violate the integrity of my writing" and an attraction to the "vanguard credibility" of having turned down *The New Yorker*, on another, and the views of friends, family, and fellow writers – all of whom think the cuts improve the story – on yet another, Ben first withdraws the piece and then sheepishly backtracks, publishing it – cuts duly made – in what he later thinks of as an "exchange" of "a modernist valorization of difficulty as a mode of resistance to the market" for "the fantasy of coeval readership" (56–57, 93).[20] The story that is presented in *10:04* as the product of these complex and competing pressures – "The Golden Vanity" – appears as the second section of the novel, having earlier been published, under Lerner's own name, in the 18 June 2012 issue of *The New Yorker*. As such references to the novel's own construction make clear, *10:04* is not metafiction as conventionally understood, then, but an especially well-elaborated example of what I call market metafiction.

Lerner makes clear just how complex the pressures shaping his writing are when he affirms the view that fiction must be more than a commodity produced merely to assuage market demand, but does so in distinctly equivocal terms. "I do," he says, "believe in works that resist a certain kind of smooth consumption," as in the case of "work that's designed to pacify [the reader] or be consumed in advance, like 'I buy this kind of book because I know what kind of ending it's going to have and it requires as little of me as possible.'" He distinguishes this pre-digested style of narrative from "a work of literary art that actively enlists the participation of the reader," but goes on to stress that "that's not to say one of those works can be pure pleasure and the other has to be a difficult moral lesson. I think you can still have an exciting or entertaining book or whatever."[21] What Lerner endorses here, then, is fiction that is both a pleasure and a challenge to read; both readily accessible and abstruse; market-friendly and market-resistant (elsewhere, he remarks that while "the arts" constitute "a space where we try to imagine forms of value that aren't dictated by price," that "doesn't mean it's totally pure and not caught up in the market, or the market is only bad").[22]

As Theodore Martin suggests, this tension plays out in *10:04* in the narrative's continual hovering between two polarized positions: between asserting a claim to having overcome "literature's enmeshment in the market," on the one hand, and admitting that it was "written only because the market solicited it," on the other. Martin makes the case that the novel's most pervasive feature – its formal and thematic "commitment to contradiction" – is a necessarily "unsuccessful but not necessarily unhopeful" response to "the ambivalence it can't escape."[23] What I want to argue here, however, is that the novel's version of "compromise aesthetics" (to borrow Rachel Greenwald Smith's term) follows a very particular logic: the logic of hedging.

In *10:04*, Ben is accused of "hedging" by a female friend, Alex, when, in the short story ("The Golden Vanity"), based in part on their relationship, he seemingly uses the protagonist's drunkenness during an intimate moment as a means of (to quote the *OED*) "avoid[ing] committing oneself irrevocably" or "leav[ing] open a way of retreat or escape." "What about the part about smoothing my hair in the cab?" Alex, asks; "the alcohol is a way of hedging. So that whatever happens only kind of happened" (136). We see a similarly hesitant, non-committal disposition in Ben's engagements with everything from the ethics of his local food cooperative (95–96) to the politics of Occupy Wall Street (46–47). This sense of hedging as the extension of a commitment that one at the same time in some way withholds or offsets is of course closely related to a further meaning: "to secure oneself against loss on (a bet or other speculation) by making transactions on the other side so as to compensate more or less for possible loss on the first" (*OED*). Hedging of this kind is essential to the operations of today's financial markets: the practice gives its name to one of the major forms of contemporary financial institution – the hedge fund – and many of the High-Frequency Trading systems we considered in the previous chapter are devoted to constructing and maintaining portfolios that optimally hedge a firm's exposure to risk.

As Randy Martin describes, financial hedging amounts in effect to buying "an insurance policy on the total or underlying value of some bundle of goods ... to hedge or protect against the volatilities of the marketplace." This is typically achieved via "financial derivatives [that] manage risks of unwanted or unexpected variations in price ... The same collection of goods could have all manner of derivative contracts taken out on them – some anticipating that prices would rise, others that the prices would fall short of expectation."[24] Among the types of derivatives most commonly used for this purpose are futures contracts – which "lock in" the price at which one will in due course buy or sell an asset so as to guard against unpredictable fluctuations – and options, which allow investors to insure against price falls, taking out an option to sell an asset they hold at a fixed price, so that if the asset in questions performs more poorly than they expect and falls below that price, they can exercise the option and limit their losses.

As John Thompson shows in his study of the twenty-first-century book business, *Merchants of Culture* (2012), hedging strategies closely akin to those used in the financial sector are widely deployed in the editorial departments of the leading publishers. Mainstream publishing houses' ubiquitous practice of "thinking by analogy" – that is, evaluating prospective acquisitions on the basis of their resemblance to proven sales successes – is a means of "hedging the indeterminacy of the new" by "attach[ing] some value to the new book in advance of knowing what the real value is." With a similar intent to the taking out of a derivatives contract (albeit with considerably less precision), this practice aims to lock in future value, backing a variant on a proven formula in order to offset "the intrinsic indeterminacy of the not-yet-published book."[25]

Books that lend themselves most readily to this form of hedging are, unsurprisingly, ones that occupy the more-or-less formulaic fields of what Thompson refers to as "commercial fiction and popular non-fiction." To the extent that publishing corporations "seek to develop a balanced list," by acquiring "books of a more serious kind" to complement their more overtly commercial offerings, it is often less possible to make immediate, direct, or compelling comparisons with titles already on the market. Yet acquiring books of this kind is itself a form of hedging, and in two ways. Firstly, the symbolic capital that a publisher stands to accrue by publishing books liable to be admiringly reviewed, shortlisted for prizes, or (less importantly but not irrelevantly) incorporated into university curricula acts as a hedge in the event that the book performs poorly in sales terms. As Thompson notes, for a mainstream press it would take a considerable quantity of symbolic capital to compensate for negligible sales, but one does go some way towards offsetting the other. Moreover (and this is the second point), with the help of critical garlands, even seemingly uncommercial propositions may, on occasion, break through to a mass-market readership. Given that, by the same token, even apparently sure-fire hits may ultimately disappoint, "it makes sense to hedge your bets" by "creating a diversified portfolio of risk."[26]

10:04, I want to argue, enacts – and self-consciously acknowledges itself as enacting – these various forms of hedging within a single book. That is, the novel shows signs of attempting to annex the conventional narrative templates that are (relatively) predictable bases for market success, and at the same time exercises sufficient formal innovation that it can hope to fall back on alternate, non-market forms of evaluation (while holding open the possibility that this very appeal to symbolic or aesthetic value may itself have an indirect economic dividend). In the process, the novel explicitly relates its literary strategies to techniques of financial hedging.

These converging strategies are made most overt in what is probably the novel's centrepiece scene, a meeting between Ben and his agent to celebrate the sale of his book (presumably the book we're now reading) to a major publisher. This scene is previewed at the opening of the novel: Ben recalls that "a few months before, the agent ... e-mailed me that she believed I could get a 'strong six-figure' advance" for a novel based on his *New Yorker* story; Ben's "earnest if indefinite proposal" has led to "a competitive auction among the major New York houses" and eventually to him and the agent enjoying a celebratory dinner "eating cephalopods" at a Japanese restaurant in what, we're told, will "become the opening scene" (4). A much fuller account of this dinner appears later in the narrative. Here, Ben expresses his incredulity that "anybody would pay such a sum for a book of mine, especially an unwritten one, given that my previous novel, despite an alarming level of critical acclaim, had only sold around ten thousand copies."[27] His agent replies that part of what publishers pay for is "prestige": "even if I wrote a book that didn't sell, these presses wanted a potential darling of the critics or someone who might win prizes." The resulting "symbolic capital ... help[s] maintain the reputation of the house even if most of their money [is] being made by teen vampire sagas or one of the handful of mainstream 'literary novelists' who actually [sells] a ton of books" (154).

On this account, then, the symbolic capital likely to accrue to a novel by an already-admired writer is a hedge against the possibility (or even likelihood) that it will not be a market success. As noted above, however, few mainstream houses would be so sanguine about the idea that any book they published "wouldn't sell," no matter how acclaimed it might turn out to be. Ben suggests as much, remarking that the idea of publishers investing funds purely for the purpose of generating symbolic capital "would have made sense to me in the eighties or nineties, when the novel was more or less still a viable commodity form"; but he cannot understand "why ... publishers, all of whom seemed to be perpetually reorganizing, downsizing, scrambling to survive in the postcodex world, [would] be willing to convert real capital into the merely symbolic" (154).

Ben is surely right to question his agent's explanation, for while, as we've seen, publishers do still place some value on texts that are not obviously geared towards existing markets, the kind of structural factors that Ben points to mean that the overriding imperatives in the industry, if they encourage experimentation at all, tend only to encourage heavily moderated forms. Indeed, Ben's agent concedes that the publisher who has bought his book in fact envisages a slightly different hedging strategy, in which it will benefit from Ben's critical reputation while at the same time acquiring a text that curbs the risks inherent in innovation by assuming a more familiar and hence more predictably marketable form: "your first book was unconventional but really well received. What they're buying when they buy the proposal is in part the idea that your next book is going to be a little more ... mainstream" (155).

As discussed above, conventionality or comparability – the capacity to place a book in a recognizable, market-tested category – is one of the key ways in which the industry "determine[s] the value of something which, at the time when it is being offered by agents and considered by editors and publishers, is a mere hypothetical asset whose value is strictly unknown."[28] Paradoxically, the very insubstantiality of the book at this point – its merely promissory status – can enhance the value assigned to it: as Thompson describes, while a book still exists only "in the space of the possible" it can be nourished to a virtually limitless extent "by hope and expectation," caught up in a "web of collective belief" composed of the "performative utterance" that is "buzz" and the "contagion effect" of phenomena like the auction.[29]

Ben's agent thus cautions him that "your book proposal might generate more excitement among the houses than the book itself ... It may have been easier to auction the idea of your next book than whatever you actually draft" (155). Ben has been a beneficiary of the fact that "an auction has its own momentum," driven by "imitative desire": "consensus emerges regarding your importance"; "competition produces its own object of desire" (155). Ben loves the idea that "my virtual novel was worth more than my actual novel" (155). Lerner draws explicit attention here to the remarkable commonalities between the logics of publishing (and other cultural industries) and the core dynamics of the financial markets – so profoundly shaped by collective belief and mimetic desire – as well as the specific forms of derivatives instruments involved in financial hedging. Ben is conscious of "the rise and fall of art commodities and tradable futures in the dark galleries outside the restaurant" (156) (they are in Chelsea, surrounded by numerous art dealers, and close to the cavernous trading floors of the Midtown financial district), and finds himself unsettled by the presence at the next table of "investment bankers or market analysts in their twenties," since "I was crossing my art with money more explicitly than ever, trading on my future" (156–57). As with the expiration time of many futures contracts, Ben's "first draft [is] due in a year" (157). He alludes to Wallace Stevens – "money was a kind of poetry" (158) – and later reflects that he has "monetized the future of my fiction" (170).

As Daniel Katz suggests in his reading of *10:04*, "just as futures traders, by their very activity, create the future towards which they trade," "so the advance on the novel will in many ways create the story which the (sold) novel is to tell."[30] It will do so, however, in complex and multivalent ways. Randy Martin argues that

> derivatives work through the agency ... of small interventions that make significant difference, of a generative risk in the face of generalized failure but on behalf of desired ends that treat the future not simply as contingent, uncertain, or indeterminate but also as actionable in the present, as a tangible wager on what is to come.[31]

Lerner insistently relates the temporality arising from this "derivative logic" to a messianic temporality in which in "the world to come ... everything will be as it is now, just a little different" (2) as well as to the temporality of his own novel. When Ben asks his agent, "What happens if I give them a totally different book than the one described in the proposal?" she replies, "Depends. If they like it, fine. But you need to keep the *New Yorker* story in there, I think" (156–57). As we've seen, the finished novel does indeed retain this story. As Theodore Martin remarks, "what choice does he have, really?" – after all, if the publisher rejects it, Ben will "have to give the money back. And yet I planned to spend my advance in advance" (155).[32] It also contains considerable material elaborating on the scenario – concerning the counterfeiting of literary archives – that Ben outlined in his proposal and which generated such "excitement among the houses" and secured him the advance.

Despite these concessions to pecuniary imperatives, however, the novel more generally, as Martin puts it, refuses "to conform to the expectations of popular literary fiction."[33] Ben's agent reminds him that his prospective book is his "opportunity to reach a much wider audience," which he takes to imply that he should "develop a clear, geometrical plot; describe faces, even those at the next table; make sure the protagonist undergoes a dramatic transformation" (156). Yet the novel "scrupulously ignores"[34] this advice to reproduce what Ben refers to as "the realistic fiction the world appears to be" (7). When, in the previous paragraph, the narrative does "describe faces" – those of the women at the adjacent table – it pointedly does so only in terms ("eyes lined with shadow") that imply obscurity or inaccessibility as much as distinctiveness or relatability (156). Similarly, it could quite fairly be said (as Ben himself does) that – at least as compared to the dramatic character transformation that the agent seems to envisage – the only thing about the protagonist that "undergoes change" is "his aorta" (156) (which he discovers to be "dilated" – a condition whose likely outcomes still remain to be determined at the end of the novel).

Moreover, "in decid[ing] to replace the book I'd proposed with the book you're reading now," Ben dispenses with a single, consistent narrative world, in favour of a "present alive with multiple futures" (194). Ben will, that is, "expand the story" by "project[ing] myself into several futures simultaneously" (4). Some of these narrative strands will "lock in" elements whose economic value has already been partially established (the *New Yorker* story; the proposed examination of "literary fraudulence" [194]), hedging against those that are far riskier elements of a "mainstream" novel: not only the refusals of literary fiction's realist descriptive and narrative norms in favour of something closer to a "scrapbook of provisional notes for a novel,"[35] but also the frequent digressions on such topics as advanced poetry, avant-garde art, and the more mystical fringes of political philosophy.

We should be wary of taking *10:04*'s account of its own genesis too literally (Lerner has said, for example, that though he was taken out for a dinner similar to the one in the novel, it was "not by an agent," while his advance was "much less" than the "two hundred and seventy thousand dollars" after tax [155] his narrator receives).[36] Instead, what scenes like that with the agent dramatize are the kinds of pressures that demonstrably shape the processes of literary production when an author accustomed to an experimental poetry scene in which readers are counted in the hundreds writes a novel for a major mainstream press. Where the novel is absolutely accurate is in casting these competing pressures in terms of the logic of the hedge, where elements amenable to consumption are continually offset by something much closer to what Ben calls "a modernist valorization of difficulty as a mode of resistance to the market." As I've argued, such resistance has real political meaning and significance, but it would be naïve to imagine that it does not have the capacity to produce its own forms of capital – symbolic, certainly, and even potentially economic. Thus any failure of the text to circulate as a mass-market commodity stands to be (partially) compensated for by an appeal to an alternate sphere of valuation.

As John Guillory has written, there is "no formula for . . . conversions" between symbolic and economic or "material" capital, "nor can there be," and hence no direct way of comparing one quantitatively with the other.[37] Nevertheless, it seems fair to conclude that *10:04*'s success so far lies more on the symbolic than on the material side of the ledger. The novel has certainly registered in the marketplace (spending a week in the *Los Angeles Times* top 20 bestseller list in the month of its publication, September 2014, for example), but the critical attention and acclaim it has received is of a different order of magnitude to such relatively modest evidence of its sales track record. The novel was shortlisted for, and won, prestigious prizes; was named a book of the year by numerous prominent newspapers and magazines; and has quickly assumed the status of a (even *the*) key text in scholarly discussions of contemporary fiction.[38] In the wake of its appearance, Lerner was named a Distinguished Professor of English at Brooklyn College and recipient of a MacArthur Foundation Fellowship (the so-called "Genius Grant," whose symbolic value may be inestimable, but whose cash value – $625,000 over five years – is well-publicized). If *10:04* has not (yet) set the world alight in sales terms, the appeal to alternate forms of value that is its hedge against its riskiness as a pure market proposition appears to have been remarkably successful. Lerner, then, is an especially striking example of a twenty-first-century writer who has benefited from the persistence of residual institutions that co-exist with and to an extent mitigate the dominance of the market.

Of course, the very capacity to garner rewards in the literary field (both symbolic and material) rests on privilege of multiple kinds – privilege that, as we saw earlier, Lerner is also intent on acknowledging in his fiction. *10:04* does this perhaps most obviously when, in what Ben De Bruyn describes as "a picture of the global network,"[39] Lerner's narrator draws attention to inequalities in light of which he cannot but appear a figure of nigh-on grotesque privilege (his advance is equivalent to "about twenty-five years of a Mexican migrant's labor, seven of Alex's in her current job" [155]) and to the kinds of asymmetric, globally dispersed social relations ("the rhythm of artisanal Portuguese octopus fisheries coordinated with the rhythm of laborers' migration," themselves "coordinated . . . by money" [156]) of which he is a (troubled) beneficiary.

The "lines of the capitalist system"[40] whose "majesty and murderous stupidity" Ben feels "coursing through him" at this moment (156) are also evoked at the end of *10:04*. During the blackout of large parts of New York caused by Hurricane Sandy, which hit the Eastern Seaboard in October 2012, Ben and Alex, picking their way through the streets of

Lower Manhattan, see "a bright glow ... among the dark towers of the Financial District, like the eyeshine of some animal" (236) Later, Ben tells us, they will learn that it was "Goldman Sachs, see photographs in which one of the few illuminated buildings in the skyline was the investment banking firm, an image I'd use for the cover of my book" (237) (as indeed Lerner did for the first edition). When Ben wonders whether the bank building has "access to a secret grid" (237), the implication is that this putative hidden network is not simply a literal source of electricity, but an occluded system of economic power – one to which Ben may not have direct access, but in which (as earlier scenes have suggested) he is unavoidably implicated. We find a similarly eerie portrayal of New York's Financial District, and a similar understanding of this space as plugged into global networks of accumulation and exploitation that place character and author in an uneasy position of simultaneous critique and complicity, in Teju Cole's 2011 novel *Open City*.

Plunder, Profits, and Privilege: Teju Cole's *Open City*

The narrator of *Open City* is an intellectually omnivorous half-Nigerian, half-German resident in the Psychiatry programme at New York's Columbia Presbyterian Hospital named Julius. The novel's episodic narrative consists of a series of descriptions of Julius's urban wanderings – mainly around his adopted home city – in which he muses on the palimpsestic histories underlying the contemporary metropolis. Four of the novel's most historically charged set pieces consist of visits by Julius to Lower Manhattan's Financial District, where he contemplates the deep interconnections between the area's commercial operations and the ongoing histories of slavery and colonialism. On the first such occasion, early in the novel, Julius is on his evening commute when he finds himself rendered strangely immobile in a southbound subway car, at once intent on, and unaware of, his destination. In this fugue-like state, Julius gazes, tellingly, at a scene of readers and reading matter:

> To my right sat a man whose full attention was on Octavia Butler's *Kindred*, and to his right, a ... man leaned forward in his seat and read *The Wall Street Journal*. His natural expression was delirious, which gave him the aspect of a gargoyle ... At Forty-second Street, a man in a pin-striped suit entered holding a volume with the title *You've GOT to Read This Book!* [41]

Here, the presence of Butler's narrative of an African American woman transported to a plantation in the antebellum South meshes with Cole's own concertinaing of Black history, while *Kindred*'s conjunction with the other two titles suggests both the interweaving of slavery and a rapacious financial capitalism that will be another of Cole's key concerns, and the liability of even a novel as resistant to the commodification of Black experience and identity as Butler's to find itself packaged by a heavily financialized publishing industry as a compulsory purchase "must-read" (released in 2004, the current trade paperback of *Kindred* – very likely the one the man on the train is reading – is billed as "a whole new look for the classic novel that has sold over 450,000 copies").

The gargoyle-like man's newspaper of choice also prefigures the destination to which Julius will turn out to have been irresistibly, if unconsciously, drawn: "At Wall Street, more people, all of them probably workers in the financial world, got on the train, but no one got off. Just as the doors were closing at this station, I stood up and slipped out of the car" (45). Like the City of London in the work of another latter-day *flâneur*, Iain Sinclair, Cole's Wall Street is a phantasmagoric environment where the sacred (in the form of Trinity Church, the imposing neo-Gothic presence at the west end of the Street [48–51]) and the profane (in the shape of the "big buildings of the trading district," such as the World Financial Center,[42] whose tallest tower anticipates the obeliskoid silhouette of another of its architect, César Pelli's, creations, One Canada Square in Canary Wharf), co-exist and seem to reinforce one another: the New York Stock Exchange itself, with its "six massive Corinthian columns . . . illuminated from below with a row of yellow lamps," appears, eerily, "to levitate" (57, 55, 57, 48). Looking back on his peculiar, automaton-like visit to the Financial District later in the novel, Julius will recall "the street's ominous character" and a "Dantesque vision of huddled and faceless bodies" passing like shades through the "deep clefts formed by the sides of skyscrapers" (161).

The particular freighting that Cole's spectral portrayal of the Financial District carries begins to become apparent when, during this same nocturnal sojourn, he stands on the Battery Park City Esplanade, sensing "out ahead of me, in the Hudson . . . just the faintest echo of . . . the generations of New Yorkers who had come to the promenade to watch wealth and sorrow flow into the city . . . Each of those past moments was present now as a trace" (54). In his monumental *Specters of the Atlantic: Finance Capital, Slavery, and the Philosophy of History* (2005), Ian Baucom explores how wealth and sorrow eddied across the "circum-Atlantic archipelago of flows" that constituted the eighteenth- and nineteenth-century slave trade.[43] For Baucom, the spectres lapping the shores of lower Manhattan take multiple forms: the unquiet dead of the Middle Passage; the "speculative, abstract, money-into-money trades" that "enabled and secured" this traffic in "human property"; and earlier phases of capitalism's phylogenesis, which recapitulate themselves, at a higher level, in "the hyperfinancialized late twentieth century and early twenty-first."[44] The "specters of value" that define this hyperfinancialized present are thus "both the imaginary, disembodied value forms trading on the floor (or across the digital circuitry) of the globe's money markets and stock exchanges and the ghostly reappearances of such exchangeable abstractions, haunting reminders and revenants of this present's what-has-been." In this way, for Baucom, as for Cole, a present formed in the image of an "extranational, circum-Atlantic geography of exchange" is "not singular but plural, not present to itself alone but to a cycle of 'times' it accommodates within itself. Time does not pass, it accumulates."[45]

Describing himself as, among other things, "a part of the Black Atlantic," Cole remarks that he feels a strong link to "the historical network that connects New York, New Orleans, Rio de Janeiro, and Lagos" – all cities that have functioned as what Baucom (echoing Giovanni Arrighi) calls "'spaces-of-flows' for an Atlantic cycle of accumulation," "commodity entrepôts and finance zones of the long twentieth century's oscillating regimes of accumulation."[46] As "important nodes in the transatlantic slave trade and in black life in the century following," these cities are, Cole says, "the vertices of a sinister quadrilateral."[47] These and other hubs of the Atlantic rim were (and are) shaped (as Walter Johnson puts it in his recent *River of Dark Dreams: Slavery and Empire in the Cotton Kingdom* [2013]) "at the juncture of ecology, agriculture, mastery, and economy: weather patterns, crop cycles, work routines, market cycles, financial obligations."[48]

The ways in which "insurance, stocks, bills, and . . . the variant forms of 'paper money' derived from the establishment of a modern, credit-issuing system of banking"[49] radiated across, permeated, and facilitated the brute material violence and exploitation of "the Atlantic trade" come to the fore during Julius's next visit to Wall Street. Julius is unimpressed by the "brightly colored advertisements" for the "tourist site" (58) that is the Museum of American Finance at 48 Wall Street, an institution that boasts of being "the nation's only independent public museum dedicated to celebrating the spirit of entrepreneurship and the democratic free market tradition which have made New York City the financial capital of the world,"[50] and his own exploration of the area provides Cole with an opportunity to offer something like a counter-archive that belies such upbeat rhetoric, revealing the extent of the city's financial institutions' involvement in perpetuating the historical violence done to Black bodies.

The apparent precondition for this act of historical recovery, however, is Julius's amnesia concerning his own personal finances: going "down to Wall Street to meet ... the accountant who was doing my taxes," he unaccountably forgets both his checkbook and the pin for his ATM card (160–61). It is as if Julius must become untethered from the kinds of "nagging, prosaic tasks" that are how most of us engage with financial systems most of the time – what Leigh Claire La Berge calls "low finance" – precisely in order to envisage the "high finance of global capital flows" and their relations to the history of slavery.[51]

After an embarrassing meeting with his accountant, Julius walks the short distance to Battery Park, occasioning one of the novel's Sebald-esque historical meditations. "This," he tells us "had been a busy mercantile part of the city in the middle of the nineteenth century," with New York still "the most important port for the building, outfitting, insuring, and launching of slavers' ships" (163). The City Bank of New York (the forerunner of Julius's own bank, Citibank [166]) was "not unlike ... other companies founded by merchants and bankers in the same period," he says, in "profiting from slavery" (163). Julius refers to Moses Taylor, "one of the world's wealthiest men" and a board member and eventual president of the City Bank, who

> made massive profits from brokering the sale of Cuban sugar in the port of New York, investing the profits of the sugar planters, facilitating the processing of the cargo at the New York City Customs House, and helping finance the acquisition of a "labor force." He had made it possible, in other words, for plantation owners to pay for the purchase of slaves. (163)

Stressing the tightness of the interrelations between the processing, financing, and conveyance of the products of slavery, as well as the disciplinary regime that enforced that system, Julius notes that "the circuit from the old Customs House to Wall Street, and then down to South Street Seaport, was a distance of less than a mile," while "the Customs House faced Bowling Green, which had been used in the seventeenth century for the executions of paupers and slaves" (164).

Later, Julius will find it hard to dispel the "strange feeling ... of standing alone, standing in Wall Street, my memory gone ... while all around me the smart set made deals, talked on cellphones, and adjusted their cufflinks ... I imagined I had forgotten not just that number but all numbers, as well as all names, and why I was even there on Wall Street in the first place" (166). Again, though, this state of vacancy is the corollary of the novel's recovery of, precisely, names (individuals like Taylor; companies like the City Bank, AT&T, and Con Edison [163]) and numbers ($13,000 for "a fully outfitted slaving ship"; $200,000 for the "human cargo" it "could be expected to deliver" [163]) that draw connections between the slick whirl of Wall Street today and its past as the linchpin of the Atlantic slave trade.

In her extraordinary recent blend of theory, criticism, and memoir, *In the Wake: On Blackness and Being* (2016), Christina Sharpe reflects on the inextricability of "the history of capital . . . from the history of Atlantic chattel slavery," and the perpetual presence in Black lives of "the precarities of the ongoing disaster of the ruptures" of the slave trade.[52] Against the background of this condition, Sharpe draws on the multiple meanings of "wake" ("keeping watch with the dead, the path of a ship, a consequence of something, in the line of flight and/or sight, awakening, and consciousness") in order to develop a method of confronting a past that is not past: what she calls "wake work." Sharpe thinks of this "new analytic" as a means of "plotting, mapping, and collecting the archives of the everyday of Black immanent and imminent death, and . . . tracking the ways we resist, rupture, and disrupt that immanence and imminence aesthetically and materially."[53] *Open City*, I'd suggest, performs something very much akin to Sharpe's wake work – nowhere more clearly than in its third account of an excursion around lower Manhattan.

During this walk, Julius contemplates the AT&T Long Lines telephone exchange building on Church Street, the property of a company in whose forebear (as alluded to earlier in the novel [163]) the banker and slave trade abettor Moses Taylor had a significant interest.[54] This "giant concrete slab," which "mimic[s] the form of a castle's keep flanked by gatehouse towers," granting it a "military aspect," seems to Julius "like nothing so much as a monument or a stele" (218–19). What this "windowless tower" (218) might conceivably be a monument *to* is suggested a little further into this section, when Julius describes coming across an actual monument: the African Burial Ground National Monument on Duane Street, a stone memorial whose design itself echoes an armed stronghold, namely one of the forts of the West African coast whose "doors of no return" (which give the monument's entranceway its name) symbolize, as Sharpe puts it, "the moment of historical and ongoing rupture" that was consignment to the Middle Passage.[55]

As Julius describes, the "patch of grass" on which the memorial sits, "surrounded by . . . huge office buildings" (220), was, in the seventeenth

and eighteenth centuries, part of a much larger site, where, "on the out-
skirts of the city at the time, north of Wall Street and so outside civilization
as it was then defined . . . blacks were allowed to bury their dead" (220).
"Into this earth," he says, "had been interred the bodies of some fifteen to
twenty thousand blacks, most of them slaves, but then the land had been
built over and the people of the city had forgotten that it was a burial
ground" (220). Even today, most of the gravesite is "under office buildings,
shops, streets" and the other features of the urban environment that make
up "the endless hum of quotidian commerce and government" (220). At
least some of "the dead returned" (220), however, when human remains
were unearthed in 1991 during the construction of the Ted Weiss Federal
Building (which houses the IRS and the General Accounting Office among
other federal agencies). In describing the burial ground as literally "in the
shadow of government and the marketplace" (220) as they operate today,
Cole suggests that the ultimate significance of the presence of "the mass
grave site of . . . African-American slaves" within "lower Manhattan, with
its financialisation of the world markets" – as Madhu Krishnan writes – is
its signalling of "the violence, not just of colonialism and imperialism," but
of neoliberalism and contemporary finance capital, which derive from, and
in crucial ways perpetuate, those earlier forms of domination.[56]

Describing how he found himself "steeped," at this moment, "in the
echo across centuries, of slavery in New York," Julius remarks that many
"excavated bodies bore traces of suffering: blunt trauma, grievous bodily
harm" (221), but also notes evidence of attempts to assert some degree of
agency and identity on behalf of the dead: "each body had been buried
singly according to whichever rite it was that, outside the city walls, the
blacks had been at liberty to practice" (222). Rebekah Cumpsty suggests
that Julius here performs a "communion with the dead," fulfilling an
obligation to "create a narrative of their history, and in doing so reinvest
the city with its dead with whom he identifies as part of the Black
Atlantic."[57] Yet what Julius stresses is precisely his acute difficulty in
establishing an identificatory relation to the unknown dead: "I had no
purchase on who these people were whose corpses, between the 1690s and
1795, had been laid to rest beneath my feet" (220). In a telling detail, Julius
notes that some bodies were "found with coins over their eyes" (221): likely
an attempt to secure safe passage for the departed soul,[58] the image also
suggests, more malignly, the ways in which, as Baucom puts it, the slave
trade "treat[ed] human beings not only as if they were a type of commodity
but as a flexible, negotiable, transactable form of money."[59] Via Julius,
Cole grapples with the simultaneous challenge and necessity of

reattributing depth and individuality to people reduced to the status of mere abstract units both by the passage of time and by the economic system that defined their existence while they still lived: "How difficult it was . . . to fully believe that these people, with the difficult lives they were forced to live, were truly people, complex in all their dimensions as we are, fond of pleasures, shy of suffering, attached to their families" (221–22). Sharpe's notion of "wake work" is highly apposite here, suggesting a commitment to abide, dwell, or "sit with"[60] the dead, without presuming to "commune" with them directly.

Other connotations of "wake" (to which Sharpe is also closely attuned) come to the fore in the novel's final scene, in which Julius once again visits the southern tip of Manhattan, this time not by land but on the water that, for all his *flâneury*, has preoccupied him throughout the narrative. Unexpectedly invited aboard a cruise boat, Julius soon passes the spot on the bank of the Hudson, close to the World Financial Center, where he first caught "echo[es]" of the city's doleful maritime history; indeed, he and the vessel in which he sails here become material embodiments of the "past moments" whose "trace[s]" he sensed during that earlier wander, as if (as Julius thinks of two old men he passes during his walk by the Hudson) "visiting from the other side of time" (55):

> We traced a fast arc south, and the taller buildings of the Wall Street area soon loomed into view on our left. Closest to the water was the World Financial Center, with its two towers linked by the translucent atrium and lit blue by night lights. The boat rode the river swells. Sitting on deck, watching the frothy, white wake on the black water, I felt myself pulled aloft and down again, as if by the travel of an invisible bell rope. (258)

The line scored in the water in this climactic moment suggests the starkly racialized violence that has tainted this seemingly pristine, resplendent hub of global finance, while the rise and fall of the boat capture how moments of uplift are always subject to a countervailing pull in what Sharpe calls the "continuous and changing present of slavery's as yet unresolved unfolding."[61]

* * *

As I've been arguing, *Open City* configures its exploration of the history of slavery in such ways as to suggest that the power emanating from New York and other financial centres during the age of European colonialism has morphed into new forms of capitalist domination in the present. Elsewhere, Cole could hardly be more explicit on this point. In an essay on Conrad, for example, he remarks that *Heart of*

Darkness (1899) "was written when rapacious extraction of African resources" was "gospel truth – as it still is."[62] In another piece, he describes the relations between rich and poor nations today as "a system developed on pillage," and points, in particular, to the neoliberal "structural adjustment" programmes imposed on developing economies, including the country where he grew up, Nigeria, by global financial institutions – principally the International Monetary Fund and the World Bank – during the 1980s and 1990s.[63]

In *A Brief History of Neoliberalism* (2005), David Harvey locates the preconditions for structural adjustment interventions in the mid-1970s, when Saudi petrodollars, swelled by the oil embargo and OPEC price hike of 1973, began to be recycled through New York investment banks, which identified credit-starved governments in the developing world as the most profitable outlets for the massive funds newly under their command. Harvey quotes the famous remark of Walter Wriston, head of Citibank, that this strategy seemed the safest bet because "governments can't move or disappear." Large-scale lending of this kind, however, "required the liberalization of international credit and financial markets," and the US government "began actively to promote and support" this agenda "globally during the 1970s."[64] As Wriston had predicted, the fixedness and answerability of governments would eventually prove to be an advantage for the New York banks when, in the wake of the "Volcker shock" (US Federal Reserve Chairman Paul Volcker's precipitous lifting of interest rates, with the aim of curbing inflation, between 1979 and 1981), debtor nations began to face the prospect of default. The IMF and World Bank – centres, by the early 1980s, "for the propagation and enforcement of 'free market fundamentalism' and neoliberal orthodoxy" – undertook to arrange debt rescheduling, "but did so in return for neoliberal reforms": "indebted countries were required to implement institutional reforms, such as cuts in welfare expenditures, more flexible labour market laws, and privatization."[65]

Under this structural adjustment model, borrowers were "forced by state and international powers to take on board the cost of debt repayment no matter what the consequences for the livelihood and well-being of the local population. If this required the surrender of assets to foreign companies at fire-sale prices, then so be it."[66] What Harvey calls "the Wall Street–IMF–Treasury complex" that dominated US economic policy by the 1990s allowed "owners of capital . . . in the US and elsewhere in the advanced capitalist countries" to reap "surpluses extracted from the rest of the world through international flows and structural adjustment practices."[67] Structural adjustment programmes, that is, worked to prise open developing economies and exact a "flow of tribute" from "impoverished Third World populations in order to pay off the international bankers."[68]

It's easy to see why, in Christina Sharpe's words, "living the disastrous time and effects" of "continue[d] imperialisms/colonialisms" in the form of "structural adjustment" imposed across sub-Saharan Africa is part of what it means to "liv[e] in the wake on a global level."[69] What I now want to argue is that, for Cole, the exploitative relations exemplified by structural adjustment programmes are replicated in the ways in which the cultures – very much including the literary cultures – of the Global North appropriate and commodify images of a supposedly dysfunctional, backward, poverty-stricken South – particularly sub-Saharan Africa. Structural adjustment is by no means the only way in which the Global North exploits the Global South, but it is for Cole the epitome of a wider system of exploitation that also plays out at the level of image, discourse, and representation. For a global publishing industry centred on New York City as much as for a global financial sector also headquartered there, that is, immiseration at the peripheries translates into profit at the core. In this way, Africans within a global culture and African Americans within their particular national culture are subject to the same logic, whereby, as Cole puts it, the "erasure" of black bodies goes hand in hand with "the unending collection of profit from black labor and black innovation," in the form of pervasive imitation of "the black body" – a "vampiric ... co-option of black life" that extends "throughout the culture."[70] We have of course encountered a scathing critique of exactly such processes in the form of Percival Everett's aptly titled *Erasure*, which I discussed in Part I.

In recent years, scholars in postcolonial studies have increasingly addressed the tendency of North American and European publishers (as well as reviewers and readers) to evaluate literary texts from formerly colonized regions and other areas outside the advanced capitalist core on the basis of how successfully they trade in stereotypes of cultural alterity.[71] Inquiring into "the laws of supply and demand that govern the global cultural marketplace," Graham Huggan notes the "remarkable discrepancy [that] exists between the progressiveness of postcolonial thinking and the rearguard myths and stereotypes that are used to promote and sell 'non-Western' cultural products in the West" – that is, "texts ... that emanate, or are perceived as emanating, from cultures considered to be different, strange, 'exotic.'" Against the background of "the mainstream demand for an 'authentic,' but readily translatable, marginal voice," postcolonial writers, Huggan argues, are liable to be seen as "translators and exemplars of their own 'authentically' exotic cultures," and to find themselves cast as "*culture brokers* mediating the global trade in exotic – culturally 'othered' – goods."[72]

This is a role that Cole decisively sets himself against. In an essay considering the relation of his "generation of post-colonial writers" to its forebears, for example, he discusses the Nigerian author Amos Tutuola – in the 1950s, the first Anglophone African writer to gain significant attention outside the continent – and describes finding the work "odd, minor. There was something in Tutuola's ghosts and forests and unidiomatic English that confirmed the prejudices of a European audience."[73] As he explains in his widely discussed essay "The White Savior Industrial Complex" (2012) (where he addresses the phenomenon of structural adjustment), Cole reserves particular disdain for narratives – "from the colonial project to *Out of Africa* to *The Constant Gardener* and *Kony 2012*" – in which Africa appears as an abject, benighted space, stricken by the twin plagues of "evil" and "helplessness," and "a backdrop for white fantasies of conquest and heroism." The presence of "bridge characters" or "white saviors" in "Third World narratives" serves, he suggests, to "make the story more palatable to American" consumers.[74] The flipside of these narratives, meanwhile, is a bromide like the one Cole offers in "In Place of Thought," an homage to Flaubert's *Dictionary of Received Ideas*: "AFRICA. A country. Poor but happy. Rising."[75]

Open City displays a recurrent concern with how stereotyped images of Africa are marketed and consumed in metropolitan centres like the two in which the narrative is predominantly set, New York and Brussels. Directly anticipating his "White Savior Industrial Complex" critique, for example, Cole has Julius recall watching a film (evidently Fernando Meirelles' 2005 adaptation of John le Carré's *The Constant Gardener*) about "the crimes of large pharmaceutical companies in East Africa," which left him "feeling frustrated" because of its "fidelity to the convention" whereby "Africa [is] always waiting, a substrate for the white man's will, a backdrop for his activities" (29). Later, the novel stages a debate around marketability and exoticism in relation to a major contemporary North African writer, the Moroccan Tahar Ben Jelloun. During a trip to Brussels, Julius befriends a compatriot of Ben Jelloun, a frustrated intellectual named Farouq, and mentions that he has been reading the celebrated novelist's work. Referring "disapprov[ingly]" to Ben Jelloun's "big reputation" (102), however, Farouq (an avowed devotee of Edward Said [104, 128]) suggests that the books are written "out of a certain idea of Morocco"; Ben Jelloun "writes ... stories that have an oriental element in them. His writing is mythmaking." (103). In response, Julius remarks:

> It is always a difficult thing, isn't it? I mean resisting the orientalizing impulse. For those who don't, who will publish them? Which Western publisher wants a Moroccan or Indian writer who isn't into oriental fantasy, or who doesn't satisfy the longing for fantasy? That's what Morocco and India are there for, after all, to be oriental. (104)

Open City is purposefully designed, I'd argue, to resist the demand for a mingling of exoticism and abjection that the global literary industry makes of the postcolonial novel. In his insightful reading, Pieter Vermeulen argues that Cole's novel "invite[s] consumption" as a "moving [tale] of migration and exile," only to refuse "to offer the kind of gratifying and cathartic emotive transports that circumscribe the niche of literary migrant fiction in the global marketplace" – categorically so at the end of the narrative, when it emerges that, as a teenager, Julius raped the sister of a friend (244), a revelation that renders him "conclusively ... unavailable for readerly empathy."[76] In a similar way, I want to suggest, *Open City* deliberately evades what Cole views as a dominant and clichéd set of cultural representations of contemporary Africa and Africans – stock spectacles of "primitive" folk belief or obscene violence, poverty, and degradation offered up for easy metropolitan consumption. In making his narrator and protagonist a product of a conspicuously middle-class, "westernized," and highly educated African milieu, who is conversant with Yoruba cosmology (25, 34) and who encounters acute poverty on the streets of Lagos (223), but exists at a decisive remove from them, Cole refuses to perpetuate what he sees as the exploitative, nigh-on pornographic traffic in images of this kind. Instead, he explores a range of other narrative avenues, even as, via this very positioning of his narrator, he acknowledges the privilege that gives him access to such a comparatively rarefied vantage point and that makes the sidestepping of standard, market-approved representations an economically feasible option.

Open City contemplates atrocities past and present, both in Africa and beyond (most obviously, as we've seen, the ocean-spanning brutalities of the slave trade), but, rather than wallowing voyeuristically in their lurid and grotesque details, sets them within longer histories, and against an array of intellectual contexts that testify to Julius's (and Cole's) formidable stores of cultural capital (as Lily Saint notes, Julius displays "an intimidating range of esoteric knowledge from fields as disparate as biology, art history, literature, classical music, psychology, and colonial history").[77]

The novel makes a point of highlighting Julius's (relative) affluence: the son of a successful engineer (226), he appears to the inhabitants of a Lagos "slum" to represent "unimaginable wealth and privilege" (223), and his family are themselves, albeit in modest ways, beneficiaries of flows of investment capital, as indicated by "the annual reports of the Nigerian companies in which my parents held stock" that Julius remembers seeing as a child (134). The text also stresses the educational experiences (a renowned, if discipline-heavy, school in Nigeria, followed by a series of prestigious US colleges) that have fostered the highly cultivated, literary persona, possessed of a stately and ornately formal narrative voice, who is our guide through the novel.

The novel's emphasis on Julius's privileged social status, which simultaneously places the narrative in a register at odds with prevailing expectations of representations of African life and acknowledges the capital (of various kinds) permitting one the liberty to make precisely such a move, is of a piece with Cole's more general tendency (like other authors I've discussed) to draw attention to the question of the author's positioning in relation to market and prestige economies. In an interview, for example, he refers to his keen awareness of "various indelible realities":

> the sordid processes of publishing and marketing, the difficulty of writing well, the unfairness about who gets celebrated and who gets ignored, the difficulty of getting properly paid for any of it. To the extent that I'm in the public eye, I do like to speak to those realities. I speak not as someone who's above it all, but as someone who tries to be aware of labor, systems of rewards, canon formation, and all the various problems of prejudice that just won't go away. I try to stay awake.[78]

This self-critique extends beyond the literary field to Cole's social and economic position more generally. As he puts it in "The White Savior Industrial Complex":

> I write all this from multiple positions. I write as an African, a black man living in America. I am everyday subject to the many microaggressions of American racism. I also write this as an American, enjoying the many privileges that the American passport affords and that residence in this country makes possible. I involve myself in this critique of privilege: my own privileges of class, gender, and sexuality are insufficiently examined. My cell phone was likely manufactured by poorly treated workers in a Chinese factory. The coltan in the phone can probably be traced to the conflict-riven Congo. I don't fool myself that I am not implicated in these transnational networks of oppressive practices.[79]

What Cole wants to signal, then, is that while, as a person of colour raised in Africa, he is subject to structures of inequality that have centuries-long histories and exist on a global scale, he is also, as a moderately affluent resident of a rich country (and as a heterosexual man), a "beneficiary" of those same structures in the way in which Bruce Robbins has recently defined that term: "the relatively privileged person in the metropolitan center who contemplates her or his unequal relations with persons at the less-prosperous periphery and feels or fears that in some way their fates are linked." As Robbins pithily, and aptly, summarizes, "when you say rue-fully, to yourself or to others, that our beautiful iPhones and iPads wouldn't exist without low-paid and overworked Chinese workers, you are speaking the discourse of the beneficiary."[80] Precisely as in Cole's reference to the production of such devices, the iPhone or iPad stands, then, as a metonym for an affluent western lifestyle that is underpinned by forms of exploitation elsewhere.

It's in this context that Cole takes up the notion of "Afropolitanism." He has no interest in indulging in bland celebrations of the affluence and mobility of a narrow segment of African society, as if one should stop discussing the continent's problems because a strata of its youth can afford to pursue hip urban lifestyles in glamorous global cities (the general tenor of the concept in the view of its critics); rather, "the discourse around Afropolitanism" is valuable, for him, precisely because it "foregrounds questions of class" in ways that "the 'I'm not Afropolitan' crowd don't want to deal with and in ways the 'I'm Afropolitan' crowd are often too blithe about."[81] Accordingly, Cole is consistently upfront about his own class position. Of leaving Nigeria to go to college in Michigan, for example, he remarks, "I certainly did not arrive in the US as a desperate and eager immigrant"; while his family "had very little money" (at least by US standards), "the privilege of choice was there."[82]

The "privilege of choice" (another term for which might be "auton-omy") is also something Cole describes enjoying in writing his two novels, *Open City* and its predecessor, the Lagos-set *Everyday is for the Thief* (2007). He recalls the luxury of shaping these novels to his own priorities while enjoying a degree of insulation from strictly economic demands on his writing having capitalized on his earlier educational advantages in order to gain a place as a graduate student at Columbia University (in the doctoral programme in Art History rather than – as in the case of Julius, whose CV parallels, without quite matching, his authors' – the psychiatric residency programme). Here again, then, we see how the shelter offered by particular kinds of semi-autonomous institutions can be used to deflect straightforwardly commercial pressures (and in this regard it is worth noting Cole's subsequent appointment to a writer's residency at Bard College and – in 2018 – to the Gore Vidal Professorship in the Practice of Creative Writing at Harvard). Tellingly, Cole describes *Every Day Is for the Thief* as a "limited-edition experiment" undertaken almost entirely for his own satisfaction: "I wrote one chapter each day. In effect, I was blogging on this weird project eight hours a day for an entire month." The project only later attracted the interest of a Nigerian publisher, Cassava Republic Press, and "was edited and found a second life as a book."[83]

Recognizing that his writing wasn't overtly commercial, he wrote both novels, he says, "without thinking how they were going to be received in the marketplace as works of fiction. So that allowed me to be difficult. I do have an experimental instinct and I thought that meant I was condemned to writing for completely obscure publishers. And I was fine with that." As such, the "fact that those books then became interesting to publishers" has, for Cole, a fortuitousness akin to "winning the lottery" (Random House and Faber & Faber brought out *Open City* in the United States and United Kingdom respectively, and also both subsequently published editions of *Everyday is for the Thief*, following its initial publication by Cassava Republic, a major force on the African literary scene, and increasingly in North America and Europe).[84]

What I've been arguing, then, is that Cole's "experimental" approach in his breakthrough novel, *Open City*, deliberately departs from market-endorsed conventions of African and, more broadly, postcolonial fiction that reproduces larger structures and histories of financial and economic exploitation. I've also made the case, however, that Cole embeds in the novel a recognition of the privilege that underwrites such departures – privilege that is ultimately inextricable from the very forms of domination against which his writing sets itself. In this way, *Open City* offers an exceptionally searching, self-critical, and far-reaching interrogation of the material conditions of contemporary authorship and their imbrication with globally extensive networks of financial and economic power. The difficulties – for authors as much as activists – of dissociating an anti-capitalist politics from the logics of capitalism themselves are central concerns for other contemporary novelists to whose work I turn in the following chapter.

CHAPTER 7

Between Autonomy and Heteronomy
Exchanging Capital in Zink, Cohen, and Heti

In this chapter, I analyse three prominent works of market metafiction that, together, mark out a triangle of positions that the formally ambitious novelist might adopt within today's heavily marketized literary field. In *Nicotine* (2016), I argue, Nell Zink gravitates towards an accommodation with market-approved narrative forms, while registering market forces (whether bearing on books, financial assets, or real estate) as phenomena that tend to maim the very things they at the same time enable. Joshua Cohen, in contrast, takes a leaf both from the radical literary experiments of modernism and from the stock market-defying projects of the contemporary tech sector in *Book of Numbers* (2015), seeking not so much to satisfy an existing market as to create a new one. Finally, Sheila Heti attempts in *How Should a Person Be?* (2010) to step out of the vexed relation between economic and symbolic capital, in order to reconceive the novel as defined not merely by market success and/or critical recognition, but by its potential effectivity in the lives of its readers. The strategies I examine in this chapter not only further demonstrate the centrality of market metafiction to major currents in the twenty-first-century novel, but also indicate the diversity of techniques and positionings still open to novelists today, even in an increasingly circumscribed literary field. They also highlight the variety and multivalence of the market logics to which that field remains subject, and the potential to open up pockets of dissent or autonomy that continues to exist within twenty-first-century literary culture. The texts I discuss, then, present tactics for negotiating the conditions of contemporary literary production that are not straightforwardly reducible to either pole of the resistance/complicity or critique/postcritique binaries.

Fixing Up and Making Do: Nell Zink's *Nicotine*

Nell Zink's appearance on the contemporary American literary scene has been widely hailed. Indeed, her unlikely rise from obscurity to celebrity is one of literary culture's most irresistible stories of recent years. The "Zink Phenomenon" displays the tensions I have been tracing throughout Part IV (and indeed throughout this book) especially vividly. As a media phenomenon as well as a strictly literary one, I pay especially close attention in this section to a corpus of media texts in which Zink and others chart and reflect upon her rise to prominence.

In a varied and colourful career that has provided rich material for profile writers, one experience stands out: Zink's correspondence with, and eventual promotion by, Jonathan Franzen. As discussed at the end of Chapter 5, Franzen, probably the best known "serious" novelist at work today, has over the past two decades pursued success via a concerted effort to write fiction that satisfies the prevailing expectations and desires of readers: in other words, he has very deliberately tailored his work to dominant consumer preferences in the marketplace. Franzen's patronage of Zink, and encouragement of her to reshape her own writing along more marketable lines, has come to stand for her, I'll argue here, as the exemplar of a paradigm that recurs in her reflections on her career and plays a central role in her third novel, *Nicotine*. This is a paradigm in which the imposition of market logics on spheres previously at least partially external to them is experienced as at once a form of salvation or rescue and a form of destruction. As we'll see, in *Nicotine* this logic is especially evident in the phenomenon of "gentrification," in which "saving" or "resurrecting" a neighbourhood (from one point of view) is accomplished by processes that only (from another) serve to destroy or efface it.

Zink's life has been famously itinerant (born in California, she grew up in Virginia and spent spells in Washington, DC, New Jersey, Philadelphia, and Tel Aviv, before moving, in 2000, to Germany, where she currently resides outside Berlin). The eclecticism of her career has also been much commented upon (she has worked, variously, as a bricklayer, restaurant server, secretary, zine publisher, musician, technical writer, translator, and media studies doctoral student). She has spoken often, however, of fiction-writing as a lifelong vocation that has persisted amid this diversity. Yet she insists that it was not until she was in her late forties that she began to form ambitions towards publication, and then only under very contingent circumstances. Prior to that, she explains, she usually showed her attempts at fiction to no more than one person, and often to no one at all; she admits to having, on a number of occasions, thrown away or deleted all copies of a piece of writing.[1] It was clear to her, she says, that "there was no market" for the strange, fabular stories she was writing, "and never would be, because there's never a market for true art."[2] "For years," she remarks elsewhere, "I had only the sensation of making something I loved, and having the privilege of being my own favorite writer."[3]

Zink has spoken of the impact on her thinking of Pierre Bourdieu's *The Rules of Art*, his study of the literary field of late nineteenth- and early twentieth-century France, and her reflections on the appeals of obscurity and self-sufficiency for the writer often echo Bourdieu's terms.[4] In an interview, for example, she acknowledges her deep-rooted affiliation to "the avant-garde ideal from the 19th century" that "self-respecting artists" should eschew "popular mass appeal": this is the avant-gardism of "the French symbolists Verlaine and Rimbaud, the feeling that art is supposed to appeal initially to only ten people and then twenty years later maybe to fifteen, and then maybe you're famous after you're dead."[5] As she describes it, then, the writing practice that Zink pursued for many years would seem to take to its limit the "independence . . . with respect to the demands of the 'general public' and the constraints of the market" that Bourdieu attributes to the Symbolists and other avant-garde groups:[6] not only written with no intent towards publication, her work was often not even intended to be read by others (certainly not beyond the tightest of inner circles), and in some cases was absolutely excluded from the possibility of public circulation by being disposed of or erased. In my discussion of *Book of Numbers* in the next section of this chapter, I argue that Joshua Cohen places his fictional alter ego in a condition of absolute heteronomy as he struggles to eke out the most abject of Grub Street existences. In contrast, Zink presents the large part of her writing life as having existed in something like a state of pure autonomy: virtually unbeholden to any external demand, obligation, or expectation whatsoever.

While Zink is insistent on the satisfactions of producing art only for oneself, she also points to the psychic costs of writing in a near vacuum, with very little access to recognition, affirmation, or encouragement. She describes, for example, the pleasure of "tweak[ing]" a text and being able to "say, okay: It's good now," but also the additional pleasure that comes from discovering "that there are people who agree with you – *yes, it's good now.*" "Of course," she adds, "that came late in life for me, and was a very cheering experience."[7] As already discussed earlier, the first voice in the chorus of approval that provided Zink with this belated external validation was one of the most influential that any author could hope to attract. As the now near-legendary story goes, Zink initially wrote to Jonathan Franzen in 2011 to seek his advocacy in a shared area of environmental concern – the protection of migratory birds – but so impressed him with the liveliness of her voice that he began to solicit fiction from her and eventually offered to use his influence to find a publisher for her work.[8] Zink's numerous reflections on this serendipitous course of events (unsurprisingly, the Franzen connection is near the top of interviewers' lists) are marked by a striking dividedness: on the one hand, expressions of gratitude for a bestowal of patronage that affirmed her belief in herself as a writer and opened a route to a viable (indeed, lucrative) authorial career; and, on the other, sharp expressions of resentment at injunctions to bend her writing to market-oriented criteria that struck her as betraying the artistic priorities that obscurity had left her free to pursue.

Zink is frank, for example, about her reluctance to accept her famous mentor's work as a model to be emulated. She hadn't read Franzen's fiction when she initially wrote to him, and describes finding the first book she picked up (*Freedom* [2010]) to be "very stodgy, square conservative work."[9] Recalling Franzen's admonition that her "backlog of finished manuscripts" was "probably that arty crap that nobody wants to publish," and that she should instead "write something sellable," Zink remarks that while she would end up being "so grateful to him," there "was a real conflict between us."[10] Zink considered *The Wallcreeper* (2014) – the manuscript she wrote in three weeks in response to Franzen's exhortations – to be "trash,"[11] but nonetheless pursued publication, placing the book with the St Louis-based, micropress Dorothy, a specialist in books by and about women, and earning an advance of $300 – "my lifetime income from writing books" at that point.[12]

At the same time, Franzen had been touting around one of Zink's older manuscripts, *Sailing Towards the Sunset by Avner Shats*, judging it to be a more commercial proposition than *The Wallcreeper*.[13] Yet, as Zink remarks, he was "trying to sell [a] really weird novel"[14] – a madcap mélange of spy thriller, fantasy, and metafiction featuring Mossad agents, half-human sea creatures, and a supposed descendant of King David (the novel began as a private joke between Zink and the Israeli writer Avner Shats – the non-Hebrew-reading Zink's attempt to "translate" Shats' 1998 novel *Lashut El Hashkia* ["Sailing Towards the Sunset"] into English; it would eventually be published in 2016, following Zink's rise to fame, in a collection wryly titled *Private Novelist*). Zink describes feeling an obligation, after Franzen's futile efforts on her behalf, to "write something with a little bit more commercial potential,"[15] and she quickly drafted *Mislaid* (2015), which, with its provocative and zeitgeisty reverse racial "passing" plotline and Dickensian adeptness with the mechanisms of fate, coincidence, and long-delayed reunion, was, as she puts it, deliberate "agent bait."[16] With the representation of Franzen's own agent, Susan

Golomb, the book was quickly acquired by Ecco, an imprint of HarperCollins, for a six-figure advance.[17] By the time *Mislaid* appeared in May 2015, *The Wallcreeper*, published the previous October, had already far surpassed the expectations of its small publisher, requiring two reprints in its first three months and the assistance of a specialist distribution company to meet demand, its sales fuelled by widespread critical acclaim.[18]

The *New Yorker* profile of Zink that appeared just before the release of *Mislaid*, and took her public presence to a new level, thus had an extraordinary tale to tell. That tale – retold in numerous interviews, profiles, and reviews since – has been central to the promotion of Zink's work and persona: the improbable story of transition from "private novelist" to marketable literary sensation, that is, has served as a key factor in further extending that marketability. Zink has acknowledged as much herself, responding to the observation that "you've had one of the most interesting literary careers in recent memory" by remarking, "I'm glad to be interesting because it's my job to sell some books. Being interesting is one of the ways I can do that because other avenues, such as extreme beauty, are closed to me."[19]

While Zink evidently views "interesting" as something of a consolation prize, the cultural theorist Sianne Ngai has argued that the category of the interesting, as a form of aesthetic judgement-cum-social evaluation, tends, if anything, to be privileged over "beauty" in the contemporary moment. Indeed, Zink's varied, itinerant, and at times improbable career (like much of her work) is "interesting" in precisely the ways that Ngai theorizes in her major study *Our Aesthetic Categories: Zany, Cute, Interesting* (2012): marked, that is, by "eclectic difference and novelty," "irregular[ity]," "diversity," and "hybridity."[20] For Ngai, the interesting, along with the zany and the cute, are the aesthetic categories "in our current repertoire best suited for grasping how aesthetic experience has been transformed by the hypercommodified, information-saturated, performance-driven conditions of late capitalism." United by "some kind of relation to change and/or indeterminacy," the "informal forms" of the zany, cute, and interesting are, more specifically, tied "to late capitalist modernity['s] ... culture of informalized, casualized work," Ngai argues.[21]

If Zink's work history and writing practice are *interesting*, then they are also, and to an even greater extent, *zany*. Tracing this term to commedia dell'arte's stock figure of the *zanni*, "an itinerant servant modeled after peasants seeking temporary work" in early modern Venice, Ngai suggests that "zaniness is at the deepest level about work."[22] The prevalence of the term "zany" in media coverage of Zink ("the zany world of Zink"; "the new zany-brainy novel from Nell Zink"; "[Zink's] unique brand of zany"; etc.) is of a piece with fascination over her eclectic CV – a zany litany indeed, insofar as the zany, as Ngai puts it, is "unusually flexible or capable of fluidly switching from task to task" and taking on "virtually any job at any moment in an incessant flow or stream of activity," exhibiting a "despecified relation to working" that is an exaggerated form of "the growing informality of late twentieth-century postindustrial work" in general.[23] The work that has become increasingly central for Zink over recent years – novel writing – meanwhile exhibits the speed, intensity, productivity, and time sensitivity that are the corollaries of the "zany" flexibility of contemporary work.

The exceptionally tight time frame – reportedly a mere three weeks – in which Zink set about drafting "something sellable" (resulting in the 200-page *The Wallcreeper*, the novel that would establish her profile) forms another important plank of her public reputation.[24] Striking a very different note to her celebrations of a carefully preserved autonomy, quoted above, Zink at times seems quite content to flaunt her capacity for "on demand" or "just-in-time" production to meet the commercial pressures of the moment – her ability to write "to order," as she puts it.[25] She recalls, for example, receiving advice from her agent to the effect that there would be "a brief window of time" after the appearance of the *New Yorker* profile in May 2015 and before the publication of her first book with a major press, *Mislaid*, when, amid considerable buzz, but "before there [were] any sales figures," her "market value" would be likely to "reach an all-time high," providing a uniquely lucrative opportunity if she had a new manuscript to offer to publishers.[26] Following a logic that she also, as we'll see, explores in her fiction, Zink here casts her personal brand as akin to an exciting new start up, whose frenetic work practices and surrounding buzz gift its stock price a "market value spike" or "market cap[italization] peak" (as she puts it in similar discussions elsewhere) precisely because it has not yet posted concrete results, and investors can therefore imagine the sky to be the limit.[27] Sure enough, after Zink, confident in her ability to "write fast," drafted a version of what would become *Nicotine* in "a few weeks," she was duly rewarded with a $425,000 advance, again from Ecco (her agent apparently only disappointed that it was not the million dollars she had sought).[28]

Employing a suitably zany image (that is, whacky and offbeat, but also suggestive of the becoming mechanical of the labouring mind and body), Zink compares her hyper-efficient writing process to "a cuckoo clock . . . The wheels turn in silence, and then everything lines up and the cuckoo comes out and says its piece."[29] If the mechanisms of the cuckoo clock (the archetypal Rube Goldberg machine)[30] typify the qualities of the zany, then their end result – the appearance of the diminutive, stylized bird-on -a-spring, whose chirruping "little trill" Zink imitates in this interview – is a conspicuously cute object. For Ngai, the relationship between zaniness and cuteness indexes precisely that between work and the commodity thereby produced – the cute commodity exemplifying the commodity as such by virtue of its especially strong capacity to activate a desire to touch, hold, and consume (a desire, as Ngai puts it, for "an ever more intimate, ever more sensuous relation to objects").[31]

It's perfectly logical, therefore, that Zink should describe the manuscript she rushed to produce in order to capitalize on a peak in her marketability as having been designed with the hallmarks of cuteness very much in mind. Her avowed intention in producing this initial, publisher-enticing draft, that is, was to populate *Nicotine* with the kind of compulsively consumable "adorable cast of characters" typical of a "binge-watch"-inducing television show (Zink's initial subtitle was apparently "a series," rather than a novel, while the manuscript owed much to the "script" or "storyboard"), and to infuse the narrative with the "breathless quality" of the "popular genre [of] young adult fiction."[32] YA fiction not only operates in a quasi-infantile zone inhabited by beings not quite fully mature, formed, or defined – the very condition of cuteness – but is also a model to "emulate" for Zink because its common use of the present tense is, she believes, one of the "ways you can draw [readers] in," since "you're seeing it unfold as it happens. It is in realtime. You're observing the events," so "you can't figure out when" to stop consuming the narrative.[33]

On this account, then, the origins of *Nicotine* would appear to lie in what Zink openly admits is a "cynical-sounding idea."[34] Her acute attunement to the ways in which particular genre conventions may be deployed to elicit particular effects means, she says, that one "really can legitimately call me a post-modernist."[35] Yet this would seem to be very much Hal Foster's "postmodernism of reaction" – an all-too-easy embrace of the conventionalized, normative, and market-approved – and a far cry from the "deconstructive" formal interventions that, for Foster, characterize a "postmodernism of resistance."[36] (As Zink herself puts it in describing her style of "post-modernism": "I'm not very often playing games with the medium itself in a way that has to do with form and words like a language poet. That's not what I'm up to.")[37]

When describing her work in these terms, then, Zink gives the impression of having quite strategically and deliberately sacrificed artistic integrity to commercial exigency. Elsewhere, however, she offers a much more troubled account of her accommodation to the diktats of the market, which suggests a critical dimension to *Nicotine* at odds with descriptions of the novel as a mere exercise in infectious, page-turning storytelling, and an understanding of the cultivation of market approval as at once necessary to the very possibility of making a life from writing and antithetical to that which, for Zink, makes such a life valuable in the first place.

As Ngai argues, the very hyperactive intensity of zany spectacles of production and the very cloyingness of cute commodities mean that such phenomena are always at risk of pushing positive affective states (fascination, exhilaration, care, desire) too far so that they morph into negative states (unease, anxiety, hostility, revulsion). In her words, "there is something strained, desperate, and precarious about the zany that . . . activates the spectator's desire for distance," while perceptions of cuteness are never far from flipping into feelings of "aggression," "phobia," and "disgust."[38] Zink, I want to argue, shows signs of harbouring such "ugly feelings" towards her own recent work: a sense of unease at the "extreme lengths" to which she was willing to "exert herself . . . to perform a job" (to quote Ngai) in drafting *Nicotine* in mere weeks to capitalize on a brief window of commercial opportunity, as well as an aversion to the perky, ingratiating product of that labour.[39]

Zink's discontent in this regard evidently registers a sense that she and her work are subject to demands – to be on point, agreeable, eager to please – that have a distinctly gendered valence. This awareness is apparent in *Nicotine* itself, which returns repeatedly to the idea that capitalism has made a reality of the wholly transactional model of human social relations envisaged by neoliberal "human capital" theorists like Gary Becker – a world where, as the novel has it, "everything's for sale" and "love" is to be understood in terms of a "heterosexual market economy."[40] In the words of one character, under such an economy everyone is "working . . . to make a product to sell to people," and for women, in particular, that product is simply themselves – "*them*. The women" – with a conventionally dutiful, nurturing self-presentation – the "good homemaker," the crafter of "birthday cakes and homemade socks" – commanding the highest market value (107; emphasis in original). A sense that the woman writer may be under particular pressure to rein in her intellectual and artistic ambitions in ways akin to the self-effacing and placatory "labour of love" demanded of women in a market-like sexual economy[41] is thus registered within the novel itself, and this resistance factors into the aesthetic and political auto-critique that Zink offers elsewhere.

Most notably, in an essay for *n+1* published soon after the release of *Nicotine* and reflecting on its writing, Zink expresses her dissatisfaction with the tendency of "'realistic' novels" (a category within which her own recent book comfortably sits) to want merely "to 'work,' to be 'good reads,' by manipulating emblems of meaning smoothly in a framework of familiar myth."[42] "Many," she continues, invoking precisely the kinds of cutesy effects that she elsewhere describes dabbling in herself, "work contemptibly, steering sentimental nodules of canned subjectivity into the cheesiest myths imaginable." Authors' overriding hope, she argues (echoing the Frankfurt School critique she imbibed as a media studies doctoral candidate in Germany),[43] is "to inhibit readers' critical urges entirely for as long as a given book lasts." "In essays [and] interviews, we hint" (precisely as we've seen Zink herself hint) "at the tricks we use to facilitate total audience immersion in our shared dream." She adds:

> Where we do intend readers to exercise critical faculties, those should be directed at something other than the work. They want a trance state, and we want to give it to them. But in that transaction, something vital is lost . . . You can't communicate with people you're trying to hypnotize!

Zink goes on to describe how she has long felt "a certain antagonism toward the pure-storytelling model of fiction," and refers to *Nicotine* (using distinctly more resistant terms than we've seen elsewhere) as "a way of dealing with the constant pressure to consume TV and film, storytelling's leading vehicles for nearly a century." While nodding to "earlier critically-minded authors," such as Brecht, who "battled the hypnotic imperative with work designed to be super boring and make the suspension of disbelief impossible," she wryly admits that pecuniary considerations militated against her adopting such a flagrantly anti-commercial strategy herself: "I knew my bank balance couldn't handle that." And she also acknowledges the difficulty, if not impossibility, of trying to "outgun film's hypnotic arsenal with the written word alone." The final, published version of *Nicotine*, moreover, retains clear traces – in its present tense narration, its goofy characters, and its soapy plot developments – of the initial draft that Zink recalls rush-producing to incite publishers into a bidding frenzy, features that, as she puts it in her *n+1* piece, appear to have "worked": "the *New York Times* [reviewer] said he couldn't put it down . . . It was a Book-of-the-Month Club selection." Nevertheless, the version of the novel that eventually reached the market, I'd argue, incorporates precisely into its market-friendly, realist texture narrative elements that not only point to the profound conflicts that stem from the demand to shape storytelling to commercial priorities, but also dramatize a wider dynamic whereby market forces inevitably mar the very activities they at the same time enable. In these ways, what Zink describes as her enduring "fear of the mass audience" and of the "banal[ity]" that seems to her to go with it is internalized within a novel that might otherwise appear to be an exercise in ticking the boxes of mass-market appeal.[44]

* * *

Nicotine centres around a squatted house in a rundown neighbourhood of Jersey City. The house is dubbed "Nicotine" because it is the one residence in a local network of activist-run squats where smoking is permitted (the spectacle of cigarette-puffing environmentalists announcing the novel's concern with compromised idealism). The house was the boyhood home, and is still the legal property, of a New Age guru and celebrated operator of a shamanic healing centre named Norm Baker. When Norm dies early in the novel, the house is inherited by his wife, daughter, and two sons from an earlier marriage. Recently graduated and adrift after her father's death, the daughter Penny decides to fix up the house, only to find it occupied, leading her to take on something of a double-agent role, loyal both to her mother and older half-brother, who want to protect the value of their asset, and the community of squatters into which she becomes increasingly integrated.

Penny's endearingly klutzy persona (one of the more obvious indicators of Zink's indebtedness to YA fiction) co-exists – as her name ("'money-Penny.' Get it?" [275]) suggests – with a peculiar intimacy with financial matters. As her half-brother acknowledges, "Penny's a flake, but she knows about finance" (146). Early in the novel, we're told that Penny "isn't worried about money," or rather that she just wants the things – "a job and a place to stay" – that will allow her not to "end up worrying about money" (37). In view of these pressures, "she doesn't feel guilty for thinking about money":

> It's the foundation of material existence, at least until the revolution comes and sweeps it away. Until then, we need to find our place in the money ecosystem, our niche in the money chain. You can't understand the modern world if you can't imagine selling what you love best. You're under no obligation to take part, but you have to understand it. (37–38)

This is what her father – who turned his reverence for shamanic healing practices into a lucrative profession – "taught her," and "it's why she majored in business" (38).

If the echoes of the predicament that Zink herself has navigated over recent years are clearly detectable here, then that connection becomes all the clearer when we learn that, like the author of the novel in which she appears, Penny has realised that the commodity that she is best able to offer is storytelling. It was her parents' own "manipulat[ive] ... tales of the financial and intellectual independence I'd be having" that, she says, "shanghaied" her "into getting a business degree," from which she, in turn, "only learned one thing": "how to make things up"; how to be someone who "tells a story" in such a way that "people will believe anything" (130). There's a degree of inevitability, then, to Penny's appointment to a job writing reports for the finance industry as a "global commodities market analyst trainee" (233) at the Manhattan investment bank where her mother Amalia works as an HR manager. Penny has by this time developed a strong sympathy for her squatter friends' anti-capitalist ethos, and her acceptance of a job at "Big Bad Bank" (276) – "sullen and rebellious" (218) and sardonic ("I have to go occupy Wall Street now" [275]) as that acceptance may be – is evidence, she says, of the "amaz[ing] ... things people will do for money" (223). Zink is at pains to suggest, however, that there is a more dialectical dynamic at work here than in the straightforward phenomenon of "selling out." Penny, for example, takes quite seriously her mother's remark – in laying out the advantages of coming to work for the bank – that "nothing in the world is more expensive than your anarchist revolution" (209), and the idea that some form of accommodation to capitalist market forces is not simply a betrayal of an anti-capitalist politics but – paradoxically, regrettably, yet necessarily – its precondition resounds throughout the text.

In contrast to the prevalence of caricatures of the hypocritical, cynically self-serving leftist, it is, as Keith Gessen says in an interview with Zink, "pretty rare in American fiction that someone is sympathetic to anarchists, or leftists in general."[45] In another interview, responding to the suggestion that "*Nicotine* satirises a group of young political activists," Zink replies: "I don't think of it as satire because I like those people. I think of politically active, politically involved people as the salt of the earth. They're my favourite people."[46] (She has spoken affectionately of her connection to figures in the Philadelphia anarchist scene, dating from her time living in the city in the 1990s.)[47] The problem as she sees it, however, is that "they can't achieve a lot, we know that, so they're trapped in an eternal structural irony." Hence, "if you talk about [that] reality it sounds like satire."[48]

This "structural irony" is especially evident when Penny and her activist friends visit lower Manhattan for a rally against TTIP (the Transatlantic Trade and Investment Partnership – a proposed ultra-neoliberal trade agreement between the United States and European Union whose measures, if enacted, would significantly curtail the scope of sovereign governments to regulate or otherwise act against the interests of transnational corporations). The cohort's presence is depicted as at once vital – since "opposition to secret trade negotiations" is exactly the kind of action in which "activist groups" (110) should be visibly involved – and futile, for while the impacts of TTIP would be very real, it remains too remote and inscrutable in the public consciousness – a mere "news item. Another bad omen in the sky" (112), as one of Penny's group puts it – for the protestors to hope "to change hearts and minds" (110), let alone materially impact the talks themselves (as the same member of the group, with a strong sense of the structural irony in which he is caught, wryly remarks, "It's nice to know" – following the day's speeches and placard-waving – that "TTIP is dead and buried" [113]). The novel points, then, to the inevitable gulf between the activists' immediate ambitions – which, in the words of one, "are trivial as all get-out" in the scheme of things – and their loftier avowed goals, which Penny, with knowing glibness, sums up as "bring[ing] down the WTO and put[ting] an end to globalization" (115).

As I've already intimated, a further aspect of the "structural irony" Zink describes is the extent to which, precisely in order to pursue work that, while limited in impact, is valuable and important, the activists are obligated to mimic key elements of the very system they oppose. As Rob, one of the residents of Nicotine, explains when Penny first visits, the house is "one of a group of properties administered by Community Housing Action" (CHA), an "umbrella organization for housing co-ops" across North Jersey where "political activists" from "all over the political spectrum" are permitted to live, provided they meet the "requirement" that "activism be your main occupation" (52–53). The suggestion here that, rather than being a cause, vocation, or mission, activism is merely another form of job or profession is reinforced when (during the anti-TTIP rally) Penny observes that the Nicotine house-mates are "all pseudo-self-employed"; she further notes that, while they are squatters, they are also – in quintessentially bourgeois fashion – "paying off a home improvement loan from CHA" (114).

As one of the residents acknowledges, anarchism, from this perspective, can begin to look like "the poor man's B-school" (115). Penny replies by comparing CHA to a "case" she studied as part of her own (more conventional) business school education: "the dot-com boom." CHA, she says, is

> like an overcapitalized start-up, having to adjust its goals upward to justify the faith placed in it by its investors. You know that saying "Think Globally, Act locally"? That's what start-ups do. You have to tell the VCs you're going to change the world, even when what you've got is an app that tells you when to refill the dog dish. To get liberal seed money for a free house . . . you have to say you're achieving way more than cheap rent. (115)

Penny's characterization of CHA as caught up in a market logic that it cannot escape but also cannot ultimately fulfil is a counterpoint to a remark a moment earlier from her friend Rob, who, in typically self-critical spirit, speculates that "CHA is probably bankrolled by the Koch brothers" (the billionaire American industrialists Charles and David Koch who are notorious for their conservative and libertarian political activities). While of course fanciful, the idea is also, Rob suggests, logical, since even the "liberal" funding that does in fact (presumably) support the housing organization is liable, through the very left-wing political action it enables, to redound to the advantage of the likes of the Kochs. "You want to control the left, offer it cheap rent," Rob explains; "we get to live for free" and indeed, with this basic material condition in place, to "work in a way that's potentially effective," but the Kochs (or their ilk) benefit because "we stick to specific issues" while the "effectiveness" of this work tends to amount in practice to "join[ing] the service economy," with "the service we're providing" being to act as a mere "sop to people's conscience. Make them think there's somebody out there fighting TTIP" (114). The activist community emerges from Rob's account as multiply compromised, then: not only obliged – in order to do the political work that is its raison d'être – to secure "bankroll[ing]" like any other entrepreneurial venture, while limiting its activities to tolerated areas, but committed to interventions that risk becoming indistinguishable from the wider "service sector" as they pacify, rather than enflame, dissent. Read with a knowledge of Zink's own conflicted feelings about her writing in mind, the allegorization here is impossible to ignore, with the activists' predicament refracting a situation in which the freedom to devote one's life to writing comes at the expense of commoditizing that writing, forcing it into approved forms, and sending it out into the world in an awareness that its function may merely be to intensify the culture's lulling, trance-inducing spell.

A further way in which the squatter characters in *Nicotine* are shown to be entangled with capitalist dynamics they ostensibly oppose is via what would appear, on the face of it, to be their most radical form of intervention: that is, squatting itself. Squatting is an overtly ant-capitalist activity insofar as it transgresses private property rights, refuses to recognize the commodity status of housing, and unilaterally withdraws a unit of real estate, with at least some potential market value, from the market where that value pertains. Yet in areas where squatting is common (such as the Jersey City neighbourhood of Zink's novel), the maintenance and improvement of residences while they are in the hands of the commons, as well as the bohemian cachet attached to the squatter lifestyle, may significantly boost that value when those residences eventually return to the market, at the same time enhancing the desirability of the area more generally, and putting upward pressure on real estate values across the board. Thus, as Freia Anders and Alexander Sedlmaier observe, "under the conditions of neoliberal real estate valorization and its concomitant displacement of less affluent social groups, squatters have been facing an intensifying debate concerning their own role in processes of gentrification."[49]

Appealing to exactly this logic, in Zink's novel Penny attempts to persuade her mother Amalia to hold off from evicting the squatters and immediately realizing the value in her newly inherited property because "they might be squatters, but they're making improvements all the time. They're maintaining that house. Enhancing its value while the market picks up. You ought to pay them a bonus" (139). While Penny is being disingenuous (she wants the squatters to stay because she considers them her friends, and has fallen in love with one of them, Rob), the older of her two half-brothers, Matt, who places great emphasis on his credentials as a hardheaded "businessman" (45) is persuaded that Penny's argument makes sound "financ[ial]" sense, telling Amalia: "I don't know why you're in such a rush . . . They're not hurting that house. And the neighborhood is on the brink. Those left-wingers are making it safe for democracy. You really want to be first in, first out? The sticker price could double in two years" (146).

Eventually, after a violent altercation with the squatters, which leads them to vacate the property, Matt attempts to capitalize on *Nicotine*'s countercultural aura by redeveloping the building as a conspicuously bourgeois-bohemian "community center" – "a 501(c)(4) charitable institution" that will boast, as Matt puts it, "an anarchist café bookstore . . . yoga classes, baby massage, all that shit" (218). Matt's building contractor comments approvingly, "That could work out pretty nice for you … It's going to revitalize this neighborhood right up" (218). This is indeed "Matt's plan": he names the building "the Norman Baker Center," after his father, in the hope of attracting "donations or other support from his father's cult, reducing his time to break even while freeing up cash for real estate speculation" (218); later, we hear of his "new hobby of buying up houses near the Baker Center" (278). "Ultimately," Matt admits to himself, "some neighbors may face rent hikes" (218), but the publicity for the Center speaks only of the site "anchor[ing] political empowerment and economic development in the whole neighborhood" (223). While Penny has by this point departed decisively from her assigned role of acting as "gentrification shock troops" (48), it appears virtually inevitable that the objective of her initial mission will nonetheless be realized.

Gentrification – "the transformation of a working-class or vacant area of the central city into middle-class residential and/or commercial use," which today constitutes "the leading edge of neoliberal urbanism"[50] – is another of the Janus-faced economic and cultural processes that fascinate Zink, trailing with it developments that give new leases of life to urban areas whose built environment and infrastructure have lapsed into disrepair, dysfunction, or disuse, but in the process tending to price out or otherwise exclude residents who have long worked to make lives there. It's fitting that a key flashpoint for tensions around Matt's gentrification drive is the bookstore at the Baker Center – which Matt himself views purely in terms of "commerce" (275) and "serious business" (263), but which the local anarchists who work there envisage as a "collective" (276) with a much wider mission – since gentrification is another phenomenon via which Zink explores logics to which her own books have been subject, another way of reckoning the gains and losses involved in a writerly project of fixing up; making smart, tidy, and respectable; and readying for market.

As things turn out, *Nicotine* has a distinctly upbeat ending, as Matt abandons the store to the Baker Books Collective and "gift[s]" (albeit with ill grace) the "whole house" (288) to Penny and Rob, who're now a couple. While this conclusion optimistically suggests the possibility of redemption even for the vicious Matt, there remains something troubling about the way in which the novel's upholders of some notion of the commons gain a reprieve from the full force of the market – and a glimpse of an alternate form of exchange economy – only because a wealthy "businessman" and "real estate speculat[or]" has it in his gift. Yet as we have seen, in Zink's world one takes what one can get, and tries as best one can, in always compromised circumstances, to do (as Rob does when pictured in his bicycle workshop in a moment of unalienated labour at the end of the novel) the work that one values, finds meaningful, and, more than anything, "like[s] doing" (287). If Zink's *Nicotine* enacts and thematizes an uneasy accommodation with market logics militating towards conformity, domestication, and presentability – in which experiences of autonomy are to be grasped fugitively and piecemeal – then the novel to which I turn next, Joshua Cohen's *Book of Numbers* (2015), performs a full-spectrum assertion of autonomy, while, in so doing, finding itself entangled with an alternate set of market logics.

"The Art Section Is for *Art Business*": Joshua Cohen's *Book of Numbers*

Elsewhere in this book, we've considered novels that perform some manner of trade-off between appeals to critical endorsement and consecration (which may yield indirect economic rewards – though rarely substantial ones) and direct targeting of mainstream consumer preferences (where the potential for remuneration is typically much greater). In this section, however, we encounter a text that stakes everything on being one of those era-defining novels so acclaimed for its innovations within the form that it creates a perpetual market for itself. Such an effort is necessarily a long shot, but the potential rewards (of every kind) are correspondingly large. In undertaking this task, Joshua Cohen's *Book of Numbers* is every bit as self-conscious about its narrative and marketing strategies as the other novels discussed so far in Part IV.

On today's cultural scene, Cohen has argued, "the story behind the story has become the only tale to tell."[51] Rather than focusing on novels and other artworks themselves, that is, cultural commentators increasingly fixate on the deal-making, promotional campaigns, and revenue generation surrounding them. While he is critical of this tendency, Cohen's own interviews and writings are evidence of its prevalence. Speaking in 2015, for example, he complains of having "spent a decade entirely broke, published by small presses, read by no one"; he recalls receiving advances of "$50 and ... beer" (from the tiny Czech publisher that brought out his first book in 2005) and a comparatively healthy, but hardly livelihood sustaining, $1,200 (for his first major novel, *Witz* [2010]).[52] A grimly comic 800-page slab of postmodern picaresque tracing the wanderings of the last Jew on the Earth, *Witz* was turned down by at least eight major New York publishers.[53] Cohen recalls apologetic editors explaining the market-focused considerations that rendered the book unviable: that "they would publish it if it was 200 pages" or that "10 years ago they would have done it, back when people read novels."[54] The book was eventually picked up by Dalkey Archive Press, a nonprofit, university-affiliated house that specializes in keeping twentieth-century avant-garde literature in print and publishing emerging authors working in a similar experimental vein.

Cohen's career entered a new phase, however, when his next novel *Book of Numbers* was acquired by Random House, the flagship imprint of the world's largest publishing company Penguin Random House. In an essay that appeared at the time of the book's publication, Cohen reflects on the challenges to a writer's artistic project posed by just such a step into the industry's mainstream:

> Say you're an American novelist, published by the largest publishing house in the world. Their goal is to make as much money from you as possible, to have as many people read your book in as many formats as possible. How can you hope to speak intimately to the numbers of people that represent the book sales required? But also how can you not?[55]

I read *Book of Numbers* as an attempt to slip this double bind: the novel, I argue, actively rejects the conventional hallmarks of mass-market appeal and the establishment of intimate bonds with its readers; but its wager is that this very departure from market-sanctified forms will prove revelatory and compelling enough in the long run to open up a new market segment for itself and other books like it. I argue further that this strategy has an uneasy affinity with the business practices of the contemporary tech sector, which the novel criticizes, but also implicitly venerates for an uncompromising singularity of vision that in the short term defies prevailing stock market wisdom only ultimately to win investors' fervent approval. Cohen thus aspires to the status of what Mukti Khaire calls a "pioneer entrepreneur" – an individual who *creates a new market for a radically innovative good, which is . . . not understood and thus not valued by consumers.*" For such a strategy to be successful, consumers must come to "understand the value of new and original – even potentially subversive – ideas and goods so that consumers buy them – literally and figuratively." In this process, what Khaire calls "intermediaries" – those who produce "the discourse that educates consumers about the good" – are "as essential to the market as the good itself," since "they are involved in the 'production of belief' in the value of the product."[56]

In the literary field, such an undertaking clearly partakes of Pierre Bourdieu's logic of "loser wins," whereby the Symbolist poet, say, had to be content with the "win" of gaining his peers' respect as compensation for the "loss" of having a product of negligible value in the market.[57]As Bourdieu argues, it has long been possible for a scenario of loser who wins eventually to become a case of win-win, as one artistic and critical generation gives way to the next, and academic canons and public taste are reshaped to accommodate the once-outré artwork (intermediaries – or what Bourdieu calls "symbolic bankers" – here playing a crucial role).[58] Today, however, any mainstream publisher backing a novel that attempts to defy the market with such authority and conviction that it forces the market to reshape itself to make space for the distinctive new style would want to see this process unfold at accelerated speed – for there, that is, to be an overtly entrepreneurial strategy in place.

I've noted Cohen's dissatisfaction with cultural journalism's shift into an extension of the business pages ("the art section" is increasingly "for *art business*," he has said).[59] Rather than try to ignore this phenomenon in his fiction, however, he felt obliged, in *Book of Numbers*, to address it directly: "If I was going to write another book," he remarked in 2015, "I was going to have to deal with how all this chatter about the death of the book, or the death of fiction, was in fact about money": about the fact that "sales, especially print sales, were low," or at least "lower than the publishers required."[60] Thus, for example, in a scene late in the novel set at the Frankfurt Book Fair, the protagonist, a writer named Joshua Cohen, meets a reporter with whom he recalls briefly overlapping at *The New York Times*: he thinks of his former colleague as "my successor" and as emblematic of a sea change in the media sector, for "while [Josh[61] had] written criticism," the new hire was charged with covering

> the publishing beat … whose "news" about how much culture was being bought or sold for, how much it grossed, and the business behind its production, was now unequivocally established as the apotheosis of culture and criticism both: the dramas and appraisals of boardroom and backstage, in one convenient package.[62]

Under this regime, "cultural" journalism means headlines like "Slicing, Dicing, Ebook Pricing" (1.521), and "the biggest story" (the most important news item; the most significant new work of literature) is merely the one associated with "the biggest advance" (1.524). Meanwhile, the primary audience is made up of "the shareholders," who "can't read" (1.524).

This encounter is just one instance of Cohen's determination in *Book of Numbers* to install what he calls "the story behind the story" as a core *part of* the story: to incorporate an account of the economic pressures that shape literary production into the end product itself – the signature gesture of what I call market metafiction. Fittingly, given the intimate if often conflictual relationship between literary and financial value that the novel traces, *Book of Numbers'* protagonist Josh cultivates his writerly ambitions while working in a bookstore close to Wall Street – a "messy swamp on the groundfloor of a lowrise" where "literature [is] cornered, condescended to, by the high finance surrounding" and the proprietor aims to purvey "fiction and non-fiction of general interest to the Financial District's lunch rush," a "business plan" whose prospects are perennially "bleak" (1.19–20).

In contrast, the owner's brother Aaron ("Aar") is a literary agent who successfully straddles the world of finance and the precincts of intellectual history and rare "Judaica" (1.19) that form the bookstore's core stock: "Aar ... knew everything," Josh recalls, "stocks and bonds and realestate [*sic*], Freud and Reich, the fate of the vowels in Yiddish orthography" (1.121). It's Aar who talks Josh out of pouring his energies into "a long poem conflating the Inquisitions and Crusades," dismissing the project as "not commercial," and instead "talk[s] only profitability," which, after a trip to Central Europe, he identifies with "Mauthausen, Dachau, family history" (1.20) (it's 1996, and, following the success of Spielberg's *Schindler's List* [1993], an awareness of the commercial exploitability of the Holocaust is at its height). This is the moment for Josh "to mention [his] mother" (1.20) – a Polish survivor – and he will go on to write a book tracing her flight from Nazi persecution to the United States. The multiple maternal debts that Josh has incurred become painfully apparent at the book's launch party, when he is obliged to thank "my mother ... who fled Poland, for giving me the money to travel to Poland, only so I could write a book about her life" (1.14).

Josh's book clearly invites comparison with his namesake and author's novel *Witz*: both centre on the Holocaust and feature lengthy retracings of *Mitteleuropean* Jewish ancestry, for which their writers undertook extensive on-the-ground research. But the differences are also instructive: while *Witz* wilfully eschews obvious commercial trappings in favour of a deranged display of fabulism, digression, and word play, Josh's book is meticulously crafted to tap into the 1990s "Holocaust Industry" and a wider boom in family history-cum-memoir.[63] And while Cohen's novel, as noted earlier, was eventually only taken on by a small Midwestern nonprofit, Josh's book is published by a leading New York press (one whose history mirrors that of Random House: formerly "operated as if a charity by sentimental Jews," the house has been "bought out by technocrats from Germany" and now forms part of a "Verlagsgruppe" within a larger "multinational . . . media conglomerate" [1.46]). Here, then, Cohen seems intent on signalling the distance between himself and his protagonist: while they share a name, some obvious biographical details, and certain historical interests, we are to recognize a sharp divide in their literary ambitions, even as we read a text that marks Cohen's own entry into publishing's big league.

As it turns out, however, all of Josh's "writing [and] rewriting" and "all [his] investments" of money left by his father and loaned by his mother (1.10) turn out to be for naught, for his book has the misfortune of being published on 11 September 2001: no sooner have copies arrived "in whatever non-chain bookstores were at that time being replaced by chain bookstores about to be replaced by your preferred online retailer" than terrorists fly planes into what Josh cannot help but think of as "the Twin Towers of my Life and Book" (1.11, 1.10). In the wake of 9/11, nobody is interested in reading, reviewing, or promoting a family chronicle concerned with a very different historical catastrophe (indeed, in one of the novels many mordant riffs, publishers' main concern turns out to be their editors' unaccountable failure to have a slew of domestic terrorism- and Islamic fundamentalism-themed texts in the pipeline, ready to feed a reading public suddenly hungry for information on one set of topics alone [1.79]).

Cohen tightens the novel's connections between literature, money, and markets in tracing Josh's post-9/11 life and career. After the death of its owner in the attacks, the bookstore where Josh was moulded as a writer is assimilated into the wider ecosystem of lower Manhattan when its premises are bought by a bank, which turns "a floor once filled with rare gallery catalogs and quartet partitur" into a site of mere "ceaseless withdrawing [and] depositing" (1.22–23); the books themselves "[go] away and [are] turned into money" (1.535). Josh, his literary ambitions crushed and the advance on his ill-fated book dwindling, becomes the very embodiment of the jobbing writer, willing to take on any and every paying gig. He finds himself churning out "catalog copy"; "falsifying résumés"; "fabricating papers for degrees, grad and undergrad"; concocting "capsule descriptions of hotels and motels in cities I'd never visited"; working for a "compliment firm" posting "fake consumer reviews of New England B&Bs I wasn't able to afford"; speechwriting for "a MetLife jr. manager"; producing ad agency copy; and consulting on product "brandings and renamings" (1.32–34).

This dispiriting litany portrays a writing practice reduced to something like a state of pure heteronomy: this is writing wholly directed by others' demands; entirely in the service of an instrumental (and directly or indirectly commercial) purpose for its commissioners, and a pecuniary end for its producer; and utterly dissociated from the writer's identity (Josh notes that his words only appear "'in print' ... anonymously, polyonymously, under every appellation but my own" [1.32]). This habituation to self-effacement makes Josh willing, in the novel's key turning point, to ghostwrite a memoir by a famed tech CEO, also named Joshua Cohen. The irony here, of course, is that in this case Josh's name will be all over the book, but also "nowhere on it, in a sense," since this is precisely not *his* name but that of the other, more celebrated, Joshua Cohen, which has "obliviated [Josh's] own" (1.8). Being accustomed to writing purely for money also makes Josh susceptible to this offer: as his agent Aaron says, "what compels ... is the money" and on this occasion "it's a lot of fucking money" (1.47) – an advance of "$440 K" (1.99). Josh is determined "to earn better money ... this time," following the failure of his first book, even "at the expense of identity" (1.9).

It's this commission to act as his namesake's "ghost" (1.8) (to which I'll return in a moment) that eventually leads Josh, in the novel's closing sequence, to Frankfurt, a location whose culminating role in an exploration of the "business behind [literature's] production" is thoroughly overdetermined. Not only does the city host the annual gathering of publishers bringing new "property to market ... to show it off, or show its price" (1.523), but the towering business district of "Bankfurt" or "Mainhattan" (a "skyline ... like apocalypse does Dallas" in Josh's estimation) is the most important financial centre in continental Europe ("your friendly neighborhood global banking headquarters") and plays a key role in the operations of the German and other European media conglomerates that increasingly dominate the global publishing industry (1.505). As the originating site of "Frankfurt School theory classes" (1.494), moreover, the city is the source of the very "culture industry" thesis that its commercial life would appear to confirm.[64]

Perhaps less obviously, *Book of Numbers* also positions Frankfurt as central to the intertwined histories of literature and money because it was to its "medieval markets" that a man from nearby Mainz brought "literally the first printed editions of the word of God" in order for them to be "bought like any other commodity" (1.492), almost overnight transforming the city's long-established *Messe* (fair) into a *Buchmesse*. This understanding of the bibles sold by "that scum capitalist Gutenberg" (1.492) as commodities imprinted with divine authority is picked up in a subsequent "speculation" (1.505) that Josh offers on the printer's father:

Friele Gensfleisch zur Laden, was employed by the ecclesiastical mint. . . . Chirography, typography, money mania. A coin is minted by mold, the metals are poured into it, and an image is stamped on the surface. Given that a nickel now is just a quarter nickel, it's strictly the image that coins the worth, glyphs of tetrarchs and portraits of feudal royalty, with time becoming kitschy graphics of livestock and wheat. Given that paper's still paper it's the scripting that authenticates the bill, the signatures of presidents or primeministers [*sic*], treasurers, reserve chiefs. Pecuniary inscription being a residuum of the regent's seal or signet ring, the guarantor of authorship and so, of authority. Sphragides, sigilia, specie and fiat currencies, movable type, all systems of writing to date, in each instance an arbitrary materiality is forcibly impressed with transitory value. Proof of identity. Colophons of self. (1.505–06)

Here, the line of descent from money coiner to bookmaker (minter to printer) is shown to be a thoroughly continuous one. Josh describes money's historical reliance on various forms of sovereign fiat, culminating in the emergence of fiat currency proper (that is, paper money validated as such by the state, rather than by convertibility into precious metal). As Joseph Vogl writes, "until the sixteenth century, the fiscal levying of monetary duties meant that the arbitrary act of sovereign power – represented as *valor impositus* impressed on the coins as the nominal value – signified the legitimation" of "sovereign statehood."[65] In Part II, we encountered various literary texts that align themselves (albeit ambivalently) with fiat money's tendency to circulate on the basis of convention, habit, and tacit agreement. Here, though, the emphasis is on the role of the state's authorizing imprint in guaranteeing the currency's validity – precisely, that is, on the act of fiat: of will, assertion, and authority. The characterization of this act as a form of "authorship" of course directly relates to Josh's commission to ghostwrite his namesake's memoir: while the resulting book will be in a certain sense counterfeit ("I'm writing the memoir of a man not me," Josh remarks [1.5]), the stamping of the legendary CEO's name on the cover (which is the same name as the actual writer's, but at the same time not) will be sufficient to endow the text with authenticity. In a similar way, as I'll argue further shortly, Cohen casts his own book (that is, *Book of Numbers* itself) as born of an assertion of pure fiat – as imperiously *demanding* to be treated as valuable, regardless of whether its readers are predisposed to do so or not.

The Joshua Cohen who commissions a ghostwriter to produce his memoir is the head of a Silicon Valley giant called Tetration. The firm is essentially Google and Apple rolled into one: in the world of the novel, one "Tetrates" where you or I would Google, while the company is also an industry leader in computers, phones, and tablets. Cohen drew on the biographies of various personal computing pioneers in researching the book, but his gnomic, Buddhist tech visionary (the very embodiment of the "Californian Ideology" of digital capitalism coupled to Eastern-inspired spiritualism)[66] bears an especially clear resemblance to Apple co-founder Steve Jobs. This guru-like savant – referred to throughout the novel as "Principal" – grants Josh a series of interviews in which he describes the rise of his company. Central to his account is a problem as familiar to the writer or artist as to the inventor or engineer: that in order to realize a creative vocation, one requires financial support, but that in practice obtaining such support invariably entails compromising the project's creative integrity.

Principal's attempted solution to this problem in Tetration's early days was, he explains, precisely a writerly one. In "writing the algy" (that is, the web search algorithm that would eventually make the company's name and fortune) and "writing the businessplan" concurrently, Principal aimed to maintain the clarity and integrity of the one while tailoring the other as closely as possible to the preferences, desires, and deficiencies of the "VCs" (venture capitalists) who were its intended readership:

> The algy used sequences of numbers to represent functions, the bplan used sequences of letters to represent the dysfunctionality of its intended readership, manipulating prospective investors according to sociocultural filters and career trajectories, levels of greed and their enabling inadequacies, significant degrees of gullibility too, or just plain unadulterated stupeyness. (0.225)

Initially, however, Principal's storytelling missed the mark: "basically no one wanted to fund us. No one even wanted to discuss our funding." While Principal (who consistently refers to himself, regally, in the first person plural) was convinced of the revolutionary significance of Tetration's nascent search engine, "we could not explain what we did, or could not explain how there was money in it . . . Every firm . . . responded firmly the same. Profitability implausible" (0.278).

This experience establishes the key theme of Principal's reminiscences: a faceoff between Silicon Valley and Wall Street, in which the former is the epicentre of the culture's most radical energies, while the latter is an unimaginative enclave populated by "rapacious [graduates] from B School" (0.279), whose narrow educations leave them hopelessly ill-equipped to understand where the value (both financial and cultural) of a phenomenon like Tetration lies. Principal remembers how the conservative mind-set that he associates with the financial sector appeared to be vindicated by the bursting of the "dot-com" tech stock bubble in the spring of 2000. With the crash, the market seemed to hand down an unimpeachable, and emphatically negative, judgement on the start-up culture of the late 1990s: having been caught up in the "irrational exuberance" of the period ("this was a time of major seeding, major sowage. Sums were being strewn to the breezes," just not in Principal's direction [0.278]), Wall Street came to its senses, and now exhorted the tech companies themselves to do the same. As Principal recalls the consensus of the time:

> 1.0, the first online generation, was over. The stocks had dissolved, if the businesses themselves were frauds shares of them were doubly fraudulent, hallucinations of hallucinations. Now that enlightenment had arrived in the form of the NASDAQ Composite in spiral, gratitude was called for, they were calling for a reevaluation of priorities. Young companies, they said, young execs like us, had to respect their elders, learn what the market was teaching. We had to put off going public, stay lean, buckle down, attain profitability through ubiquity. If we did that, they said, we might just be the ones inheriting the lineage, becoming the online manifestation of IBM, the second bodhisattva emanation of Xerox. (0.370–71)

Principal will turn out to have the last laugh, however, as his company retains faith in the transformative potential of its means of navigating the web and is eventually vindicated by the stock market that once spurned it: when we first meet Principal, in 2004, Tetration has "just gone public, at $80/share, for a market capitalization in excess of $22B" (1.27). Importantly, Principal presents Tetration's ultimate elevation to the status of investors' darling as a mere contingent outcome of its dedication to purifying its own autonomous vision. He notes that it was a refinement to the system by an employee named Moe – "an artist, an engineer" who "could never even balance his checkbook" – that pushed the company into profitability (0.279). Like the true artist, Principal's star coder feels no obligation to anything other than his project, which becomes remunerative only as a by-product of the effectiveness with which he realizes its inherent logic: he "made us profitable, but accidentally. This we have to stress, it was never his intention" (0.279).

If Moe, on Principal's account, is the genuinely autonomous "artist," then Principal himself holds to the more ambiguous form of autonomy asserted in a remark often attributed to his primary historical model, Steve Jobs: that market research is to be avoided because "consumers aren't in the business of knowing what they want." While, as Nicholas Brown has commented, "there's a certain similarity of attitude" between Jobs' purported statement and an assertion of autonomy proper, they differ in that the corollary of this claim is that Jobs "is precisely in the business of knowing what consumers want or will want" – it being his role to create products so perfectly realized on their own terms that they generate consumer desires that did not previously exist – while the truly autonomous position (closer to the one that Moe supposedly occupies) is one in which what the consumer wants is "irrelevant" to the producer.[67] As I want now to make clear, my argument is that the Jobs-esque Principal's "gamble" (0.279) in contemplating his commercial fortunes mirrors that of the novel in which he appears: the gamble, that is, that uncompromising adherence to one's own complex technical and intellectual programme – pursued in a state of indifference to *existing* market signals – will ultimately succeed in carving out a new market niche for its product.

The memoir that Principal has commissioned Josh to write on his behalf is in many ways an "I told you so!" exercise: an exhaustive articulation of the revolutionary new technical architectures and business practices via which Tetration at first defied market wisdom, and then bent it to its own will. This self-congratulatory undertaking is presented in the novel in the form of Josh's verbatim transcriptions of what are notionally interviews with Principal, but in fact consist almost entirely of monologues delivered apparently with only the barest awareness of an interlocutor's presence. A couple of typical passages of this material – which makes up much of the novel's 250-page middle section – give a good impression of its effects:

> We would begin with the concept of existing space vs. new space, proceed into talking through the entailments of each w/r/t data and electricity, racked mountables per cabinet, and cabinets per corridor, seismal dampering algidities, praxeological redundancies. (0.295–96)

> We flamed the PARCy with emails, as like other avatars, as like the same avatars but registered with other services, batchelor but now @prodigy, cuddlemaven but now @Genie. We even went trolling for him among the dossy BBSes and subscribed to leetish listservs and wrote posts or comments or whatever they were called then to autogenerate and hex all the sysops down. (0.216)

Principal's characteristic verbal tics (the use of the majestic plural; the peculiar "as like" construction) combine with the barrage of unglossed technical terms and acronyms to create an exceptionally forbidding prose style (as Adam Rivett comments, "rarely has a contemporary writer been this willing to let his prose be . . . contaminated with modern tech talk").[68] Cohen's assembly of a language that makes so few allowances for those to

whom it's presumably addressed amply fulfils his avowed intent in portraying the character of Principal. The genesis of this depiction, he has said,
lay in his observation of "techpeople," the typical example of whom struck
him as

> someone who made very few to no concessions to convention, who didn't
> care or was perhaps unaware of how he was perceived, or even if he was
> understood . . . Techpeople . . . weren't going to compromise, they weren't
> going to adapt socially, they were just going to change the world – they were
> going to impose themselves . . .
> The entire world has to learn [Principal's] language, has to learn his mind,
> or be left behind . . . This is how he thinks, and speaks.[69]

It's clear here, as indeed it is in *Book of Numbers* itself, that Principal's
absolute single-mindedness is to be viewed as monstrous – a monomania
bordering on "psychopathy" or "sociopathy," in Cohen's words.[70] And yet
in presenting how Principal "thinks, and speaks" in such a thoroughly
undigested, unforgiving form in the novel, Cohen makes much the same
intransigent and overbearing demands on his readers as his character makes
on his "family," "friends," and "company."[71] In other words, the excesses of
"Joshua Cohen" are also the excesses of Joshua Cohen. Indeed, I take
Cohen's decision to make his "techperson" character a namesake of himself
to signal an uneasy acknowledgement of the overlap between the avant-
garde ethos of defamiliarization and disorientation, with which he affiliates
himself, and the Silicon Valley cult of the paradigm-shifting "disruptor."[72]
One of the leading-edge models of contemporary capitalism, the ideology
of digital disruption partakes of what Luc Boltanski and Ève Chiapello, in
The New Spirit of Capitalism (1999), call the "artistic critique" of capitalism, which tries to break free of the "disenchantment generated by the
processes of rationalization and commodification of the world inherent in
capitalism" but is at the same time put to the service of capitalism's
renewal, finding its major expression in the rhetoric of "autonomy, spontaneity, authenticity, self-fulfilment, [and] creativity" common in neoliberal management discourses.[73] As Sarah Brouillette suggests, "literary
tradition has helped to constitute and legitimate" "conceptions of culture"
that emphasize "freedom from constraint of any kind" and the "ideal of the
autonomous artwork, expressive of individual genius and innovation, that
has proven so useful to neoliberal capital."[74] As we've seen, though, while
today's mainstream literary culture may pay lip service to notions of
aesthetic autonomy and innovation, it is increasingly inhospitable to
them in practice, while "constraints" are virtually its defining features.

Cohen's novel, then, is an attempt to challenge the publishing industry's mounting editorial conservatism, even as, in the process, it reflects a wider contemporary climate proclaiming the virtues of creative destruction.

The long sections of the novel in which Principal details the innovative elements of Tetration that stock market investors for so long undervalued are also the sections that struck many reviewers as especially likely to limit the book's immediate appeal in the literary marketplace, and indeed led them to caution would-be readers about the book's challenges. The tenor of these comments is very consistent: even a "dedicated simulation of boredom is still boring" and "still a slog to read";[75] "your interest in *Book of Numbers* will depend on your enthusiasm for passages" made up of "twitchy idiosyncrasies" and "ugly ... jargon";[76] if you think "trying to concentrate on an online article that keeps being interrupted by flashing ads ... is an interesting reading experience ... then you may well enjoy *Book of Numbers*."[77] Mark Sarvas sums up the consensus neatly in *The New York Times Book Review*: "Cohen will test the commitment of his readers." This has certainly turned out to be the case if online reader responses are any guide: as I write, the most common rating of the book on Amazon .com, by some distance, is one star out of five, and numerous reviewers complain in anguished tones of the book's unreadability and Cohen's self-indulgence and contempt for his readers.[78]

If Cohen were looking for instant reader appeal, however, he would surely have written a decidedly different book. Instead, I'm suggesting, he has learnt a lesson both from the history of modernism and the avant-garde and from the contemporary tech sector, and made the speculative wager that in standing his ground and offering something markedly distinctive he may, over time, drag the market in his direction. Significant here is Cohen's candid admission that the density and obsessive attention to detail that characterize *Book of Numbers* is born of "a version, or a travesty[,] of the Joycean hope: to keep the academy busy for a while."[79] He wanted, as he puts it elsewhere, to write a "book that dictates serious academic literary attention."[80] Cohen is of course echoing James Joyce's notorious remark that in writing *Ulysses* "I've put in so many enigmas and puzzles that it will keep the professors busy for centuries arguing over what I meant, and that's the only way of ensuring one's immortality."[81] Cohen invokes Joyce in the context of his description of Principal's dictatorial personality, discussed above, and we see a similar logic: the Master imposing his agenda and obligating others to decode it. As has been well documented, the fruition of Joyce's aspirations for his novel in the middle decades of the twentieth century – with the academic enshrinement of *Ulysses* at the core of the modernist canon, and the proliferation of scholarly approaches to the novel – played a crucial role in transforming the text from an object of coterie appreciation into a genuinely mass-marketable publishing proposition – both a fixture of university reading lists and a guaranteed bearer of cultural capital beyond the academy.[82]

Offering a self-consciously schematic, but not unwarranted, gloss on the "great divide" of twentieth-century cultural history, Cohen has observed that "Modernism was something made by and intended for a small but discerning audience; postmodernism, by contrast, had popular or populist aspirations – it wanted to be famous, *and complex!* It wanted money, *and respect!*"[83] In the "postmodernist" culture that, on Cohen's definition at least, we surely still very much inhabit, one of the key ways in which it has proven possible to hold open a space straddling the domains of coterie respect and market success is precisely, as Cohen has argued, through a strategic deployment of modernism itself – and especially the names "Joyce" and "*Ulysses*." Pondering the description of his own *Witz* as a "Jewish *Ulysses*," Cohen notes the prevalence of one version or another of this appellation. As he puts it: "Having worked as a weekly book reviewer, I came across marketese like this all the time: 'Known in its nation of origin as the Icelandic *Ulysses*' – publicity talk for 'a difficult but ultimately rewarding novel by a dead man from Reykjavik.' In other words, the *summa* of a culture."[84] "*Ulysses*" becomes a marketing tag, then, because Joyce's novel seems so neatly to model the desired transition from obscure opus to cultural touchstone, and its invocation aims, by a kind of sympathetic magic, to promote a similar outcome for the text now being marketed.

Cohen is suitably wry about this process here, but the commercial fate of his own novel, *Book of Numbers*, is necessarily staked, I'd argue, on its capacity to channel something of this logic: to parlay formal innovation into market appeal by at once identifying itself with a lineage of "difficult but ultimately rewarding" novels and distinguishing itself from them – adding, that is, the all-important modifier to the earlier masterwork. This lineage would consist not only of modernist classics like *Ulysses*, but also texts in the mode that Cohen identifies as exemplifying the "postmodernist" attempt to leverage literary experimentation into commercial success: that is, the ambitious "systems novel" associated with the likes of Thomas Pynchon, Don DeLillo, and William Gaddis, as well as "heirs" like David Foster Wallace.[85]

It's of no small significance, then, not only that *The New York Times Book Review* considers *Book of Numbers'* manifest challenges only befitting of a "digital-age *Ulysses*"[86] or that *Vice* considers its "intimidatingly brilliant" author a "cracked James Joyce computerman,"[87] but that other prominent publications acclaim a work that "succeeds at doing to the Internet what David Foster Wallace's *Infinite Jest* … attempted to do to television";[88] that is "David Foster Wallace-level audacious";[89] that "like Pynchon and Wallace," displays "tireless virtuosity about absolutely everything";[90] that "manages to bring the paranoiac energies of the maximalist systems novel – à la Pynchon, DeLillo and Wallace – to a sustained exploration of the post-Snowden era";[91] that is "a book after William Gaddis's heart";[92] or that stands as the "Great American Internet Novel,"[93] or simply "the next candidate for the Great American Novel."[94] It's Joyce and Pynchon (as well as the likes of Bolaño and Knausgård), who also come to the minds of those amateur reviewers (certainly the minority, but not insignificant in numbers) who commend Cohen's novel in online forums.

To be sure, such critical plaudits, rapturous though they are (and there are many others like them), are no guarantee of runaway commercial success (though it's notable that, despite rousing a fair amount of antipathy among readers, the novel was quickly able to boast national bestseller status).[95] Much less do they guarantee the backlist longevity that would be vouchsafed by full elevation to the canon. Yet insofar as such accolades function as illocutionary performatives – speech acts that potentially bring about what they announce – they at least open a path to the novel's being garlanded in such ways. And insofar as their perlocutionary (that is, actual) effects follow suit – that is, insofar as *Book of Numbers* does indeed come to solidify and define a major new literary mode ("the internet novel"), obligating each subsequent literary treatment of the net to nod in its direction, and functioning as one of those privileged markers by which readers' cultural literacy is measured – Cohen's high-risk strategy will have paid off handsomely. The interplay between symbolic and economic capital has been a key concern of this book, and Cohen's novel is the clearest instance we have encountered of a text whose reception is predicated on their potential convertibility. In the final section of this chapter, however, we turn to a novel that aims to inhabit a third position outside of the bipolar (if also, under certain circumstances, collapsible) relation between critical consecration and market circulation.

Neither Modernism nor the Market: Sheila Heti's *How Should a Person Be?*

Like many other novels discussed in this book, Sheila Heti's *How Should a Person Be?* (2010) depicts a literary and artistic milieu – in this case, that of a group of hipsterish writers and painters living in Toronto – that is tightly hemmed in by economic forces. The narrator, Sheila, imagines herself to be surrounded by "all the people who stand on the floor of the stock exchange with their computers and their ticker tape,"[96] while we learn that in the recent past (presumably in 2007–8), "the economy collapsed," making new undertakings of various kinds "impossible" (150). In a key scene, Sheila and her friend Margaux (based on the painter Margaux Williamson) attend the American offshoot of Art Basel, held annually in Florida. The fair "is sponsored by a bank" – "on the banners hung outside the building ... was this message: *USB* [*sic*] *welcomes you to Art Basel Miami Beach*" (107; italics in original) – and plays much the same function in the novel as another renowned cultural-cum-commercial jamboree, the Frankfurt Book Fair, in Cohen's *Book of Numbers*. Sheila experiences the art fair as a vast emporium where producers and dealers try to display their wares as enticingly as possible, in the hope of catching the eyes of passing collectors: "there were thousands of artists and so many galleries, and all of the art just laid out to speak for itself like cereal boxes on supermarket shelves, but without even the words" (103). While the elite international art fair has become one of the natural environments of contemporary "advanced" art, its "supermarket"-style layout makes it rather an alien one too, since, as Margaux reminds Sheila, such art doesn't ordinarily try to sell itself merely on the basis of its immediate visual appeal or decorative potential, but rather establishes its saleability at least as much by generating critical discourses that testify to its importance. For Margaux, it goes without saying that there are artists exhibiting at the fair that are "really truly great." One can't "see that" from a single work, though, and must instead have absorbed the "nuances" offered by "extensive articles" and other forms of "context" (103).

This discussion returns us, then, to the relationship – and degree of convertibility – between economic and symbolic capital. As Peter Wollen has described, the literary marketplace and the market for visual art differ considerably in this regard. For visual artists, "commercial success ... comes from selling, for a high unit price, to an élite of collectors and museums, who are guided in their opinions and tastes by currents they pick up from within the art world itself." In contrast, "because novels sell at a much lower price than paintings or other artworks, the market for literature is much greater and commercial success comes from volume of sales." Hence, while "rich and successful artists are often militantly avant-garde in their commitments or their general approach," "bestselling writers tend to write 'in the tradition of the realistic novel' and avant-garde writers cannot realistically hope for much commercial success."[97]

As we've seen, though, avant-garde or experimental fiction continues to occupy a space in the literary field and may even, under certain circumstances, register a significant presence in the marketplace. The art fair scene, then, highlights a relationship between different value systems that has a crucial bearing on a range of art forms. This relation is central to *How Should a Person Be?*, whose titular question continually shades into another, which directly concerns the novel itself: how should an artwork be? Heti's text, I'll argue, ponders three answers to this question. Two we have just touched on, and have recurred throughout this book: first, that the artwork should be *desired* – not really an artwork at all, that is, but a pure commodity given over to the satisfaction of consumer demand; or second, that it should be *admired*, an object of veneration by virtue of its originality and aesthetic importance. The third answer is more distinctive: that the artwork should be *used* or at least *usable* – something with the capacity to be absorbed into and strategically put to work within the lives of those to whom it's addressed.[98]

The first, market-orientated model of personal and artistic being is especially prominent in the early part of the novel. Here, Sheila asserts her conviction that she must be whatever will "make the universe love me", "as if the universe would delight in me for being a certain way," whereas, "if I did things badly, I would surely lose all its favors, all its protection" (42–43). In wondering how a person should be, then, Sheila inevitably "can't help answering like this: a celebrity" (2) – someone whose identity has received endorsement by the mass media and the mass market. Hence Sheila's only "consistent typo": the misspelling of "soul" as "sould" (5). Making a direct connection between the self and "the art impulse," Sheila describes "the attempt to make the self into an object of need and desire by tending to the image of our selves" (184). Invoking the language of marginal utility theory, in which the value of a commodity is ultimately indexed to its capacity to meet acute bodily need (such that nothing is as valuable as a glass of water in the desert), Sheila remarks that "we have wanted to be like coke to the coke addict, food to the starving person" (184) – the very pinnacle of desirability. The danger, however, is that this pursuit of desirability results merely in uniformity, all people turning themselves into identical replicas of a single bestseller: "one unit of a hundred thousand copies of a book being sold" (185).

The second model of how an artwork should be – that defined by categories of acclaim, respect, or importance – inevitably carries with it the hoary notion of "genius." If the understanding of the artwork as existing to elicit desire has an implicitly feminized inflection in Sheila's account (implying, again, that the demand to make oneself and one's work openly appealing falls especially heavily on women writers and artists), then for her (as for many feminist critics)[99] the notion of genius carries a pronounced masculine bias – one that, paradoxically, may be liberatory for women in Sheila's view: "one good thing about being a woman is we haven't too many examples yet of what a genius looks like," and therefore "it could be me" (4). "For the men," on the other hand, "it's pretty clear. That's the reason you see them trying to talk themselves up all the time. I laugh when they won't say what they mean so the academies will study them forever. I'm thinking of you, Mark Z., and you, Christian B. You just keep peddling your phony-baloney genius crap" (4). (If the book had been written a few years later, Sheila might have been thinking of you, Joshua C.) While Sheila is dismissive of an overtly masculine understanding of genius based in contrived obscurity, she nonetheless holds, for much of the novel, to a markedly traditional notion of artistic importance.

This is especially evident in her reflections on the play that she has been struggling to write for several years. The play is a commission from a feminist theatre company, and Sheila acknowledges that she took it in part because "I needed the money" (41). Yet it's evidently important to her, at this point in the novel, that these external factors not be thought to compromise the project's artistic integrity: she stresses that the conditions are minimal (it need not even be a "feminist play," but merely "about women"), and she's keen to cast the undertaking as a classically autonomous creative endeavour: "I had to . . . leave the world for my room and emerge with the moon, something upon which the reflected light of my experience and knowledge could be seen: a true work of art, a real play" (40–41). In the grandiose terms to which Sheila is prone in discussing her project, she suggests that the play's cultural significance does not in any case rely on her being its singular originator: "I could just as easily lead the people out of bondage with words that came from a commissioned play as I could writing a play that originated with me" (41).

Heti has spoken often of her inclination towards writing that is autonomous, transformative, and formally difficult. As she tells one interviewer, "my heart has always been with those artists whom you would call 'experimental.' I believe the artist should originate things from within and not be imitating other artists."[100] Elsewhere, she has described her first novel, *Ticknor* (2005), as "such a modernist book" – a "forbidding" text in which "I was thinking about Beckett and Joyce and all these people who made very dense works on the margins."[101] A dramatic monologue in novelistic form, tracing the conflicted feelings of one nineteenth-century writer for another, *Ticknor* seemed intended at once to dazzle and confound: in *The Library Journal*'s estimation it is "not really a novel at all but rather an extended prose poem [that] will appeal mainly to writers and critics interested in literary experimentation, rather than general readers looking for a satisfying yarn."[102] Reviews of the novel were indeed consistently laudatory, but sales "scant."[103]

Speaking shortly after the publication of *How Should a Person Be?*, the follow-up to *Ticknor*, Heti explained that "one of the things I wanted to kill in myself" in the writing of her latest book "was this modernist artist. To me the modernist is the one who tries to create one great monument . . . I'm not thinking that way anymore."[104] *How Should a Person Be?* dramatizes this disillusionment with modernist monumentality as Sheila's determination to write a play that will stand as an artistic landmark results only in her becoming hopelessly blocked. Eventually, she can persevere no longer and makes an exultant declaration: "I'm renouncing this play because it's not in service of my life." "If the primary thing was the work," she adds, "I'd spend all of my time on the play. But you know what? This does not serve my life!" (71–72).

Explaining her decision to "cancel" her play to her analyst, Sheila remarks that "life doesn't feel like it's in my stupid play, or with me sitting in a room *typing*"; rather, she finds "life" simply in "*talking*" with her friend Margaux, which, she argues, "is an equally sincere attempt to get somewhere, just as sincere as writing a play" (82; emphases in original). Sheila's analyst, however, is troubled both by her client's apparent lack of "concern for making a living" (Sheila's impecuniousness is repeatedly noted [41, 52, 56, 253] and the play was, after all, among other things a paying gig) and by what seems to be her abdication of the artist's responsibility to work "to the end and [wind] up with something solid" (82). Indeed, the analyst Ann (a Jungian who "studied in Zurich" [81]) is evidently something of a modernist: invoking the figure of the "great artist," she advocates "work that begins and ends in a passion, a question that is gnawing at their guts, which is not to be avoided but must be realized and lived through the hard work and suffering that inevitably comes with the process" (84, 85). Sheila, however, suggests that it might be possible to produce "something solid" – that is, a tangible art object (as opposed to the "pure act" of mere "talking") that is at once sellable and possessed of a certain "sincerity" – without having to revert to a vision of the artistic process as the heroic, agonistic realization of the masterwork (82). She might find this "solidity," she tentatively ventures, simply in "the story of what happened" – "the story of [her] talking to Margaux" (82–83).

So it is that Sheila ends up setting aside her play and channelling her energies into reconstructing conversations (many of which she has preserved on a portable tape recorder) with Margaux and other members of her circle of artist and writer friends. We're to understand that this practice forms the basis of the book we're now reading (and indeed it apparently reflects Heti's own working methods in producing *How Should a Person Be?* closely).[105] Much of the content of the novel therefore consists of an episodic series of freeform conversations about art, money, work, sex, friendship, and other topics. There is little in the way of a central plotline, though certain strands, including Sheila's difficulties with her play and the dominating, coercive, and sexually aggressive behaviour of her sometime partner, an artist notable for his "killer . . . soul-sucking eyes" (76), run through much of the text.

In transforming her mode of writing towards the recall or transcription of everyday conversations, Sheila instantly feels a sense of "naturalness," "ease," "freedom" "calm," "fluidity," "happiness," "peace," "security," "goodness," "truth," and "pride" (157–58). Subtitled "A Novel from Life," then, the text, I'm arguing, likewise asks to be measured not primarily by the extent to which it satisfies prevailing consumer preferences, nor by the critical and academic acclaim it commands (though of course as a novel written for publication it cannot escape, or afford simply to be indifferent to, either form of evaluation), but, first and foremost, by its capacity to be put into what Sheila calls the "service" of life – to make life more liveable.

The "life" in question is the author's/narrator's, but also the reader's, and here the novel intersects with what would ordinarily be a category beneath the notice of the serious literary author: that of self-help writing. The novel's Prologue, which introduces the text's intertwined concerns with art-making and self-making, closes with a discussion of this genre:

> Margaux's mother had a friend who was a bit messed up and really into self-help books and all sorts of self-improvement tapes. One day, she had been telling Margaux's mother about a technique in which, whatever problem

> you came across in your life, you were just supposed to throw up your hands
> and say, *Who cares?* (6; italics in original)

If this moment is liable to be taken as an initial jibe at a genre often
demeaned as vapid, manipulative, or narcissistic (in ways that have a great
deal to do with its predominantly female readership),[106] then the remainder of the novel belies such a reading, as Sheila repeatedly deploys the
seemingly bland mantra "*Who cares?*" to surprisingly varied, but consistently pointed, effect (38, 204, 230, 274). Heti has described how, while
writing the book, "I couldn't bring myself to read a novel" – novels at the
time striking her as "so lame" and "so fake" – but "I could read self-help
books."[107] The widely circulated description of *How Should a Person Be?* as
"a postmodern self-help book"[108] is reasonable enough insofar as the label
suggests the text's distance from the genre's typically methodical and
systematic style: as Christopher Fenwick suggests, Heti offers a "rattle
bag of aphorisms, stories[,] ideas [and] anecdotes" of "the kind ... to be
found in self-help books" – covering Sheila's sex life, her friendships, her
writing, and her money troubles – but she "deliberately avoids providing
any coherent program."[109] The application of "postmodern" to the novel's
version of self-help would be distinctly misleading, however, if it were
taken to imply a straightforwardly ironic or parodic stance. Unconcerned
with adhering to the genre's market-sanctioned conventions, *How Should
a Person Be?* is at the same time unembarrassed about pursuing self-help's
avowed goal of presenting readers with materials that might provide
insight, guidance, consolation, or – more actively – means of levering
a degree of agency in situations where it's curtailed, as Sheila's often is,
especially in her relationships with male characters.

Heti underscores her unapologetic, and unfashionable, insistence on
fiction's didactic or pedagogical function in an interview, when she compares *How Should a Person Be?* to *Girls* creator Lena Dunham's breakthrough film *Tiny Furniture* (2010). Responding to the suggestion that
Dunham's character is "unlikeable" (and again employing the versatile
exclamation "*who cares?*"), Heti remarks:

> Her character *is* likeable, and even if she isn't, *who cares?* Why do characters
> have to be likeable? Female characters especially have to be likeable, which is
> crazy. But is Achilles "likeable"? Is King Lear "likeable"? Characters aren't
> there for us to like them; they're instructional.[110]

Rejecting one of the paramount criteria by which a work of fiction's
marketability is conventionally gauged today (as well as, again, the overtly

gendered slant to this creed of "likeability"), Heti places her emphasis, once more, on such works' alternate obligation to guide, counsel, and equip: their obligation (to echo the words of the song) to give the reader not what they *want*, but what they may, perhaps unknowingly, *need*, and may be able to learn from and tactically deploy. That *How Should a Person Be?* presents characters liable to be perceived as unlikeable (many reviewers and readers complain of their self-obsession, immaturity, unexamined privilege, and so forth), but whose romantic, artistic, and professional travails may nonetheless be "instructional" is evident from the critical response to the novel. As Joanna Biggs neatly summarizes in her own assessment in the *London Review of Books*: "Reviewers described wanting to throw the book across the room or to stock up on copies to give to friends, sometimes both."[111]

For a long time, however, the difficulty of placing *How Should a Person Be?* within the publishing industry's standard categories presented a serious impediment to its publication. For many publishers, the book apparently displayed neither sufficient high-art ambition to warrant a publication strategy based on reaping the commercial rewards of strong critical acclaim, *nor* a sufficiently well-keyed grasp of mainstream convention to be an immediately marketable proposition (people in publishing "prefer what they've seen before, with a twist," Heti has remarked; "if you're not doing that, it's harder").[112] Heti's US publisher, the prestigious New York house Farrar, Straus, and Giroux, had backed the "forbidding," "modernist" *Ticknor*, but passed on what Heti viewed as its relatively "accessible" and "seemingly easy"[113] follow-up, unpersuaded by her attempts to explain her project by reference to the episodic, phatic, relationship-focused encounters of the MTV "structured reality" show *The Hills*.[114] The book was also turned down by at least five other US publishers, as well as a number of Canadian presses, and for many of them the problem evidently lay with a failure to display standard markers of mainstream fiction.[115] Like other contemporary writers to whom I've referred, Heti is remarkably forthcoming in discussing the vexed process of bringing a book to publication, and has cited editors' rejection notes that refer to her novel's lack of a sufficiently compelling storyline, the flatness of a particular character's presence in the narrative, or the difficulty of "sell[ing] a book about not being able to finish a play."[116] Heti recalls one editor counselling, "Oh sweetie. Maybe you and Margaux should get famous first and *then* publish this book."[117] In other words, how should a person be if they want to sell their book?: a celebrity.

Heti's "weird book,"[118] as she calls it, was eventually picked up by the Canadian independent press House of Anansi, which embraced its generic incoherence and casual shifts between nominally "high brow" and "low brow" forms, billing it as "part literary novel, part self-help manual, and part racy confessional."[119] Greeted with unexpected critical fanfare, especially in the United States, the novel found its elusive American publisher in another venerable firm, Henry Holt (also, like FSG, a subsidiary of Macmillan), and has gone on to enjoy an all-the-more surprising degree of commercial success.

Reflecting on the book's strong sales performance, though, Heti has insisted: "I really don't feel like something has more value because it has more readers. That's not part of how I value something. But I know other people do. I know almost everybody does. But I don't."[120] Even while her book was still without a US publisher, she declared herself to be philosophical about the situation: "Every book has its own life, and I'm sure that the people who could get something out of reading this book will end up reading it."[121] If there's arguably something naïve (or perhaps faux-naïve) about the idea that books "find their readers," outside of the mechanisms of publicity, marketing, and promotion, these remarks nonetheless make clear, once again, Heti's determination to carve out some degree of distance from a purely market-based mode of evaluation – not, however, by an appeal to "seriousness," "originality," or "importance," but rather by stressing the significance of enabling her readers to extract something – some serviceable message or tool – from her writing: hers is an ontology of the artwork orientated neither towards desire nor acclaim, but towards use. It's precisely in the apparent modesty of this ambition that its radical streak resides, indicting publishers' loss of faith in literature's entitlement to impart lessons other than those that they believe readers already want to hear. And if this undertaking still strikes us as unduly quietist – a mere attempt to ameliorate the psychic aches and pains of the bourgeois individual – then that would be to misunderstand Heti's feminism, which emphatically reasserts the political nature of personal experience, situating the most intimate dimensions of everyday life as the sites where wider asymmetries of power are most keenly felt, and where tools for living can be most tellingly deployed. If there were any lingering doubt over the political significance of such a strategy, then it has surely been laid to rest by the rise of the #MeToo movement – a reckoning with the simultaneously intimate and structural dynamics of gender, sex, and power of which *How Should a Person Be?* now reads like a crucial early document.

Hardly indifferent to a market model of evaluation, then, *How Should a Person Be?* aims at the same time to deprioritize it, and to push to the fore alternate – even opposing – ways in which a work of literature might make meaningful and significant interventions in the world. While Heti's project in this regard is distinctive and even idiosyncratic, writers discussed throughout this study have been engaged in related efforts, and in closing the book I turn to consider whether it might be possible to imagine different infrastructures of literary production capable of consolidating, nurturing, and reinforcing such efforts.

Coda
Basic Income, or, Why Barbara Browning's The Gift Is Not a Gift

> Watch in the spring sunshine the stockbroker and the great barrister going indoors to make money and more money and more money when it is a fact that five hundred pounds a year will keep one alive in the sunshine.
>
> – Virginia Woolf

In this book, I've argued that the intersecting market logics of the financial sector and the publishing industry and book trade have placed intense material and ideological pressures on the forms, techniques, and preoccupations of ambitious contemporary fiction. At the same time, I've highlighted the strategies that the authors of such fiction have adopted to reflect upon these pressures and to attempt to prise open spaces of autonomy within the literary field brought into being by the prolonged hegemony of neoliberalism and financialization.

In the spirit of a speculative thought experiment, this brief concluding Coda turns to an exemplary work of twenty-first-century market metafiction – Barbara Browning's *The Gift* (2017) – in order to contemplate ways in which contemporary authorship might be placed on alternate material groundings more conducive to the production of complex, innovative, "autonomous" works of literary art. Browning's novel, I suggest, points in this direction not ultimately by affirming the viability of its titular form of non-market economic exchange, however, but rather by indicating precisely why such works of art cannot aspire to the purity of the true gift, in which writers are able simply to give, regardless of whether or not they also receive. Such should not be the cause for despondency, however, but for fully acknowledging and thinking anew the material conditions of the literary.

The Gift makes clear the extent to which what I've been calling market metafiction has now coalesced into a distinct and recognizable mode that a text may quite knowingly and deliberately inhabit.

Browning's novel could hardly display this affiliation more explicitly, making numerous references and allusions to texts in this vein by authors discussed earlier – Chris Kraus,[1] Ben Lerner (103, 131), Sheila Heti (147–48) – as well as to closely affiliated writers like Maggie Nelson (17) and Kate Zambreno (200–201). Only minimally plotted, the novel consists of the narrator and protagonist – named Barbara *Anderson* – describing her attempts to "help jump-start a creative gift economy" (5) by giving away ukulele covers of popular songs, reflecting on her job as a university teacher and her participation in the New York performance art scene, and worrying over her collaboration with a musician based in Germany whose identity may be more complicated than it initially appears. Like many works examined in this book, *The Gift* takes it as axiomatic that following the "implosion of the global financial system … we [need] to try something else" in the "world of exchange" (5) – something other than "the so-called free market" (191) that, as we've seen, has so profoundly shaped both the careers and the imaginations of contemporary writers. Like Lerner's *10:04*, Browning's narrative intersects at various points with the Occupy Wall Street movement, and like Lerner, too, Browning is inspired by the leading Occupy intellectual David Graeber's account of "baseline communism" (37, 139)[2] – the minor, everyday forms of altruism that Graeber relates to Marcel Mauss's attempt in *The Gift* (1925) "to get at the heart of precisely what it was about the logic of the market that did such violence to ordinary people's sense of justice" (33).

In addition to its attempt to imagine "cultural practices that reject a market model of self-interest" (33), Browning's *The Gift* also shares with many other texts I've discussed an interest in "the economic issues surrounding the creation of art" and "the kinds of economic transactions that make art possible or impossible" (219, 113, 218). Barbara describes, for example, her performance artist friend's attempt "to have a moment of transparency" during one of his shows, in which he goes "over the economic terms of the performance" in considerable detail (30). Barbara's own desire to be "transparent. Or naked" (168, 236) is both literally evident (in her naked or semi-naked dances – stills from Browning's performances of which appear in the book, with videos posted online) and figuratively so in her repeated laying bare of her own economic circumstances: the relative security of a stable university teaching position (Browning herself is an Associate Professor in the Department of Performance Studies at NYU); and what we can perhaps safely call the absolute privilege of an apartment (presumably university subsidized) off Washington Square that is large enough to have two entrances and be divided into separate dwellings for her and her son (65).

A significant degree of transparency concerning the economic conditions of literary production is also a feature of *The Gift*'s framing apparatus. The novel was published by Emily Books, an imprint of the Minneapolis nonprofit Coffee House Press (which also published Lerner's debut novel, *Leaving the Atocha Station*), and the press not only makes a point of acknowledging the support of "private foundations, corporate giving programs, government programs, and generous individuals" on the book's copyright page, but also lists these bodies and many of these individuals by name at the end of the volume (238–39). Both the novel's concern with the phenomenon of gift-giving and the "transparency" of its text and peritext raise a significant issue. This point relates first of all to a seemingly banal observation: namely, that while continually insisting on its gifthood in everything from its title to its closing signoff ("I made this for you ... It comes from the heart. Love, Barbara [236]), the novel is not, by any conventional definition, a gift: rather, one will be asked to pay $13.49 (according to the listing on the publisher's website) in order to obtain it. Closely related to this fact is the presence, among the entities whose support is acknowledged at the end of the book, not only of state and federal bodies like the Minnesota State Arts Board and the National Endowment for the Arts, but also of schemes affiliated to major global corporations (such as the Amazon Literary Partnership) and leading financial institutions (including the Schwab Charitable Fund and the US Bank Foundation).

My point here is not a cheap gotcha: I don't mean to accuse Browning and her publisher of being caught in an embarrassing contradiction in casting as a gift an artwork that one is in fact required to pay for, or to suggest that they are inherently or fatally compromised in offering a celebration of Occupy Wall Street made possible in part by several of Wall Street's most prominent representatives (such incongruities between artworks' political content and the conditions of their presentation to the public hardly, in any case, being uncommon on the contemporary cultural scene). Rather, I want to suggest that the novel's highlighting of its own commodity status (precisely in idiosyncratically and provocatively presenting itself as a gift) and its publisher's foregrounding of its business model (based on the "gifts" of its donors) usefully emphasize for us that if "obscure little postmodern novel[s]" (35) and other formally innovative works of literature not geared to prevailing market norms are to continue to be produced, then they themselves cannot simply be gifts: we, or someone, will need to pay for them – whether by directly purchasing them or by providing the financial and other resources necessary to sustain and foster their writing and publication.

Browning's novel might, though, lead us to ask what the sources of such funding ought most desirably to be. As John Thompson notes, the "grants from foundations, trusts, and individuals" that not-for-profit publishers receive "cushion them to some extent from the harsh realities of the marketplace"; and as Lee Konstantinou remarks, nonprofit initiatives in the literary world "often pursue worthy goals and nurture the careers of many serious artists."[3] Yet, as Konstantinou adds, "they also institutionalize all of the . . . problems of the neoliberal nonprofit sphere, which, far from creating anything like a cultural commons, privatizes support for the arts," with "tax-exempt gifts provid[ing] quiet public subsidies to projects that private individuals choose, without subjecting that indirect public spending to political or democratic accountability."[4]

If there's a case for bringing the support of publishing outlets more fully into the sphere of public deliberation, then there's also a debate to be had about direct support for writers themselves. Several countries offer state stipends to qualifying authors, liberating them from the necessity to sell their work in large quantities or take on additional employment.[5] Yet perhaps to make such funding contingent on being "an author" in some publicly recognized sense (whether this be defined by productivity or the nature of the material produced) is already to impose unwarranted conditions. Commenting on Marx's famous hypothesis, in *The German Ideology*, that "in a communist society there are no painters but at most people who engage in painting among other activities," John Guillory suggests that "what Marx represents as the disappearance of autonomous production can also be construed . . . as its *universalization*. No one is a painter because everyone is (or can be)."[6] The ultimate goal of a left politics of culture, then, would be a situation in which no one is excluded from those activities that bourgeois society calls "art" by a lack of access to material resources, or obligated to practice those activities only in particular ways by the necessity of accruing those resources through the production of works that sufficiently appeal to buyers in the marketplace.[7]

The mid-twentieth-century Western European and North American welfare state could hardly be said to have embodied such a society. Yet in its creation of pockets of what critics like to denigrate as "state-sponsored bohemia," it left a legacy that cries out to be revived and radicalized. To take one apt example: in her recent biography of Kathy Acker, Chris Kraus comments that before the austerity policies that followed New York City's fiscal crisis of 1975 largely put paid to them, "welfare, unemployment insurance, and disability SSI [Supplemental Security Income] were the de facto grants that funded most of New York's off-the-grid artistic enterprises," providing at least a degree of "what most writers want": "time and money to read, write, think, and be left in peace."[8]

The idea of providing to "every person a guaranteed amount of money that they would receive absolutely unconditionally, irrespective of work or any other qualification" and without any of the "strings that are attached to traditional welfare plans" – a so-called Universal Basic Income (UBI) – has been much debated over recent years.[9] It's easy to overstate the utopian potential of such a plan: for every enthusiast for whom UBI paves the way to tomorrow's "fully automated luxury communism," there's a sceptic who sees only a ploy in a neoliberal bid to privatize what remains of the welfare state.[10] It's clear, though, that for such a grant to be "set high enough to allow people to live at a level of basic decency whether or not they work," and for it to be a *supplement* to the welfare state rather than a replacement of it," would entail what Robert Meister describes as a "collective demand for money – neither wages nor credit, but simply money as a redistribution of wealth – [that] could be disruptive of the financial system in the sense of making a common claim on the publicly created and guaranteed collateral that is used to secure accumulated wealth that remains in private hands."[11]

The question of how such an ambitious project might be achieved, in the face of the vast forces arrayed against it, lies well beyond the scope of this book. There is something irresistibly appealing, though, about the idea of the accumulated wealth of a financial sector whose relentless extraction of profit has done so much to constrain the activities of contemporary writers – and hardly writers alone – being redistributed in ways that might loosen the grip of the market on their everyday practice. In a book published in the United Kingdom in 2018, the former Conservative skills minister Nick Boles insists that "the main objection to the idea of a universal basic income is not practical but moral." For Boles, it is "dangerous nonsense" to imagine that "we will all dispense with the idea of earning a living and find true fulfilment in writing poetry, playing music, and nurturing plants." Rather, "mankind is hard-wired to work. We gain satisfaction from it. It gives us a sense of identity, purpose, and belonging . . . We should not be trying to create a world in which most people do not feel the need to work."[12] On the contrary, of course, the production of literature and other forms of expressive art (and indeed the cultivation of plants) is work; it is merely not (or at least not as Boles envisages it) work for the market, and it is precisely this potential to decouple work (of all kinds) from the demand that it answers only and fully to market imperatives that is one of the core attractions of something like UBI.

Of course, the implications that such a loosening of the grip of necessity would have for *literature* are hardly the most significant considerations that one might contemplate, but they are perhaps not so trivial for all that – for if nothing else the literary, as we've seen, is one of those spheres where humans strive to exercise whatever autonomy – whatever freedom from the given and necessary – they can access to the fullest possible extent. In this book, we've considered a wide range of literary texts that, even amid the acute material pressures exerted by neoliberal market logics, have offered extraordinary imaginative and formal experiments in fictional narrative. For Nick Srnicek and Alex Williams, the significance of a "non-reformist reform" like UBI is that it "not only provides the monetary resources for living under capitalism, but also makes possible an increase in free time," thereby granting "the capacity to choose our lives: we can experiment and build unconventional lives, choosing to foster our cultural, intellectual, and physical sensibilities instead of blindly working to survive."[13] If such a hypothetical world would make routine the exercise of capacities, potentialities, and pleasures barely imaginable in the cramped circumstances of the present, then how inconceivably richer and stranger still might be the fictions it dreams for itself?

Notes

Introduction

1. See Tao Lin, "I Am Offering 60% of the U.S. Royalties of My Second Novel to 'the Public,'" *Reader of Depressing Books*, 31 July 2008, http://reader-of-depressing-books.blogspot.co.uk/2008/07/i-am-offering-60-of-us-royalties-of-my.html.

2. See Frank Guan, "Nobody's Protest Novel: On Tao Lin," *n+1* 20 (2014), https://nplusonemag.com/issue-20/reviews/nobodys-protest-novel/.

3. For an account of this episode, see Alison Flood, "Taking Stock of Tao Lin," *Guardian*, 6 August 2008, www.theguardian.com/books/booksblog/2008/aug/06/takingstockoftaolin.

4. See Guan, "Nobody's"; Stephan Lee, "Tao Lin Talks his Upcoming novel *Taipei*," *Entertainment Weekly*, 1 February 2013, http://ew.com/article/2013/02/01/tao-lin-talks-his-upcoming-novel-taipei-also-see-the-cover-its-shiny-and-it-moves-exclusive/.

5. Guan, "Nobody's"; Emily Witt, "Tao Lin Announces Five-Figure Sale of *Taipei, Taiwan* to Vintage," *New York Observer*, 15 August 2011, http://observer.com/2011/08/tao-lin-announces-five-figure-sale-of-taipei-taiwan-to-vintage-tim-oconnell-prolific-tweeter-to-edit/.

6. Pierre Bourdieu, "The Essence of Neoliberalism," trans. Jeremy J. Shapiro, *Le Monde Diplomatique*, December 1998, https://mondediplo.com/1998/12/08bourdieu.

7. The classic study is Andrew Gamble, *The Free Economy and the Strong State: The Politics of Thatcherism* (Durham, NC: Duke University Press, 1988).

8. Pierre Bourdieu, *The Rules of Art: Genesis and Structure of the Literary Field*, trans. Susan Emanuel (Cambridge: Polity, 1996), 121, 220.

9. Ibid., 344, 345, 347.

10. The key contributions are: Arne De Boever, *Finance Fictions: Realism and Psychosis in a Time of Economic Crisis* (New York, NY: Fordham University Press, 2018); Leigh Claire La Berge, *Scandals and Abstraction: Financial Fiction of the Long 1980s* (Oxford: Oxford University Press, 2015); Nicky Marsh, *Money,*

Speculation, and Finance in Contemporary British Fiction (London: Continuum, 2007); Annie McClanahan, *Dead Pledges: Debt, Crisis, and Twenty-First-Century Culture* (Stanford, CA: Stanford University Press, 2016); Katy Shaw, *Crunch Lit* (London: Bloomsbury, 2015); and Alison Shonkwiler, *The Financial Imaginary: Economic Mystification and the Limits of Realist Fiction* (Minneapolis, MN: University of Minnesota Press, 2017).

11. Greta R. Krippner, *Capitalizing on Crisis: The Political Origins of the Rise of Finance* (Cambridge, MA: Harvard University Press, 2011), 4.

12. Cédric Durand, *Fictitious Capital: How Finance is Appropriating Our Future*, trans. David Broder (London: Verso, 2017), 1.

13. Kevin R. Brine and Mary Poovey, *Finance in America: An Unfinished Story* (Chicago, IL: University of Chicago Press, 2017), 3.

14. Simon Springer, Kean Birch, and Julie MacLeavy, "An Introduction to Neoliberalism," *The Handbook of Neoliberalism* (Abingdon: Routledge, 2016), 2.

15. William Davies, *The Limits of Neoliberalism: Authority, Sovereignty, and the Logic of Competition* (London: Sage, 2014), 21.

16. See Philip Mirowski, *Never Let a Serious Crisis Go to Waste: How Neoliberalism Survived the Financial Meltdown* (London: Verso, 2013), esp. ch. 2.

17. Key intellectual histories of neoliberalism are Mirowski, *Never* and Daniel Stedman Jones, *Masters of the Universe: Hayek, Friedman, and the Birth of Neoliberal Politics* (Princeton, NJ: Princeton University Press, 2012).

18. See e.g. Jamie Peck, Neil Brenner, and Nik Theodore, "Actually Existing Neoliberalism," *The Sage Handbook of Neoliberalism*, ed. Damien Cahill, Melinda Cooper, Martijn Konings, and David Primrose (London: Sage, 2018), 3–15.

19. Arjun Appadurai, *Banking on Words: The Failure of Language in the Age of Derivative Finance* (Chicago, IL: University of Chicago Press, 2015), 125.

20. Martijn Konings, *Capital and Time: For a New Critique of Neoliberal Reason* (Stanford, CA: Stanford University Press, 2018), 2.

21. On neoliberalism's putative demise, see e.g. David M. Kotz, *The Rise and Fall of Neoliberal Capitalism* (Cambridge, MA: Harvard University Press, 2015).

22. Tony D. Sampson, *Virality: Contagion Theory in the Age of Networks* (Minneapolis, MN: University of Minnesota Press, 2012), 104.

23. McClanahan, *Dead*, 25.

24. Ibid., 29.

25. Ibid., 26.

26. Fredric Jameson, "Postmodernism, or The Cultural Logic of Late Capitalism," *New Left Review* I 146 (1984), 53–92.

27. See Fredric Jameson, "Culture and Finance Capital," *Critical Inquiry* 24/1 (1997), 246–65; "The Aesthetics of Singularity," *New Left Review* 92 (2015), 101–32.

28. Fredric Jameson, *Postmodernism, or, The Cultural Logic of Late Capitalism* (London: Verso, 1991), 48.

29. Max Horkheimer and Theodor W. Adorno, *Dialectic of Enlightenment: Philosophical Fragments*, trans. Edmund Jephcott (Stanford, CA: Stanford University Press, 2002), 113.

30. Ibid., 105.

31. Ibid., 127–28.

32. Ibid.

33. Jameson, *Postmodernism*, 4.

34. Ibid., 63.

35. Ibid., 304–05.

36. Ibid., 48.

37. Jameson, "Culture and Finance Capital," 252.

38. Jameson, *Postmodernism*, 48.

39. Fredric Jameson, *The Political Unconscious: Narrative as a Socially Symbolic Act* (Ithaca, NY: Cornell University Press, 1981), 38–39.

40. Ibid., 40.

41. Rita Felski, *The Limits of Critique* (Chicago, IL: University of Chicago Press, 2015), 2, 6, 17–18.

42. Nico Baumbach, Damon R. Young, and Genevieve Yue, "For a Political Critique of Culture," *Social Text* 34/2 (2016), 7.

43. Susan Sontag, "Notes on 'Camp,'" *Against Interpretation and Other Essays* (London: Penguin, 2009), 275.

44. Jackie Stacey, "Wishing Away Ambivalence," *Feminist Theory* 15/1 (2014), 43; Carolyn Pedwell, "Cultural Theory as Mood Work," *New Formations* 82 (2014), 61.

45. See Robert Pfaller, *On the Pleasure Principle in Culture: Illusions without Owners*, trans. Lisa Rosenblatt (London: Verso, 2014), 100–103.

46. Leigh Claire La Berge and Quinn Slobodian, "Reading for Neoliberalism, Reading Like Neoliberals," *American Literary History* 29/3 (2017), 611, 608.

47. Evan Brier, "The Literary Marketplace," *Oxford Research Encyclopedia of Literature* (Oxford: Oxford University Press, 2017), http://literature.oxfordre.com/.

48. See e.g. Kevin J.H. Dettmar and Stephen Watt, eds., *Marketing Modernisms: Self-Promotion, Canonization, Rereading* (Ann Arbor, MI: University of Michigan Press, 1996); Lawrence Rainey, *Institutions of Modernism: Literary Elites and Public Culture* (New Haven, CT: Yale University Press, 1998); Catherine Turner, *Marketing Modernism Between the Two World Wars* (Amherst, MA: University of Massachusetts Press, 2003); and Ian Willison, Warwick Gould, and Warren Chernaik, eds. *Modernist Writers and the Marketplace* (London: Macmillan, 1996).

49. John B. Thompson, *Merchants of Culture: The Publishing Business in the Twenty-First Century*, 2nd ed. (Cambridge: Polity, 2012), 103.

50. Andrew Goldstone, "The Short Life of Publishing Tradition," *Arcade*, 6 June 2012, http://arcade.stanford.edu/blogs/short-life-publishing-tradition.

51. In addition to sources cited directly, my account of these transformations draws on Albert N. Greco, Clara E. Rodríguez, and Robert M. Wharton, *The Culture and Commerce of Publishing in the 21st Century* (Stanford, CA: Stanford University Press, 2007); Laura Miller, *Reluctant Capitalists: Bookselling and the Culture of Consumption* (Chicago, IL: University of Chicago Press, 2007); Claire Squires, *Marketing Literature: The Making of Contemporary Writing in Britain* (Basingstoke: Palgrave Macmillan, 2007); and Ted Striphas, *The Late Age of Print: Everyday Book Culture from Consumerism to Control* (New York, NY: Columbia University Press, 2009).

52. Randall Stevenson, *The Last of England?* (The Oxford English Literary History, vol. 12) (Oxford: Oxford University Press, 2004), 147.

53. See ibid., ch. 1; Margaret Doherty, "State-Funded Fiction: Minimalism, National Memory, and the Return to Realism in the Post-Postmodern Age," *American Literary History* 27/1 (2014), 79–101.

54. Stevenson, *Last of England?*, 145.

55. Michael Szalay, "The Author as Executive Producer," *Neoliberalism and Contemporary Literary Culture*, ed. Mitchum Huehls and Rachel Greenwald Smith (Baltimore, MD: Johns Hopkins University Press, 2017), 265. On the crisis of industrial profitability, see Robert Brenner, *The Economics of Global Turbulence: The Advanced Capitalist Economies from Long Boom to Long Downturn, 1945–2005* (London: Verso, 2006).

56. Szalay, "Author," 265.

57. Jeremy Rosen, *Minor Characters Have Their Day: Genre and the Contemporary Literary Marketplace* (New York, NY: Columbia University Press, 2016), 123.

58. See James F. English, *The Economy of Prestige: Prizes, Awards, and the Circulation of Cultural Value* (Cambridge, MA: Harvard University Press, 2005), esp. 10, 22.

59. Martin Paul Eve, *Literature Against Criticism: University English and Contemporary Fiction in Conflict* (Cambridge: Open Book, 2016), 132; emphasis in original.

60. Thompson, *Merchants*, 397; italics in original.

61. Ibid., 399; italics in original.

62. See e.g. Paul Delany, "Who Paid for Modernism?" *The New Economic Criticism: Studies at the Intersection of Literature and Economics*, ed. Martha Woodmansee and Mark Osteen (London: Routledge, 1999), 335–51.

63. On the logic of the field, see Thompson, *Merchants*, 11–12.

64. Sarah Brouillette, *Literature and the Creative Economy* (Stanford, CA: Stanford University Press, 2014), 208.

65. Timothy Aubry, *Reading as Therapy: What Contemporary Fiction Does for Middle-Class Americans* (Iowa City, IA: University of Iowa Press, 2011), 9–10.

66. "Too Much Sociology," *n+1* 16 (2013), https://nplusonemag.com/issue-16/the-intellectual-situation/too-much-sociology/.

67. Sarah Brouillette, "Neoliberalism and the Decline of the Literary," *Neoliberalism and Contemporary Literary Culture*, ed. Mitchum Huehls and Rachel Greenwald Smith (Baltimore, MD: Johns Hopkins University Press, 2017), 281.

68. Ibid.

69. *Literature in the 21st Century: Understanding Models of Support for Literary Fiction* (Arts Council England, 2017), 10–11; Thompson, Merchants, 403.

70. While the report focuses primarily on the United Kingdom, the data it includes from the United States suggest, if anything, an even more challenging set of conditions there (*Literature in the 21st Century*, 12).

71. See Zadie Smith, 'Two Paths for the Novel," *New York Review of Books*, 20 November 2008, www.nybooks.com/articles/2008/11/20/two-paths-for-the-novel/.

72. *Literature in the 21st Century*, 11.

73. Ibid., 18, 3.

74. See *Authors' Earnings: A Survey of UK Writers* (London: Authors' Licensing and Collecting Society, 2018), 4; *The Wages of Writing: Key Findings from the Authors Guild 2015 Member Survey* (New York, NY: Authors Guild, 2015), 5, 8.

75. *Literature in the 21st Century*, 46.

76. Ibid., 23.

77. Mark McGurl, *The Program Era: Postwar Fiction and the Rise of Creative Writing* (Cambridge, MA: Harvard University Press, 2009), 216, 24 (the latter quotation is from David Fenza, "A Letter from the AWP's Director," *Association of Writers and Writing Programs Program Director's Handbook* [2006], 1).

78. Ibid., 216.

79. Brouillette, "Neoliberalism," 281, 287.

80. Peter Boxall, *The Value of the Novel* (Cambridge: Cambridge University Press, 2015), 9.

81. See "MFA vs. NYC," *n+1* 10 (2010), https://nplusonemag.com/issue-10/the-intellectual-situation/mfa-vs-nyc/.

82. See Graham Huggan, *The Postcolonial Exotic: Marketing the Margins* (London: Routledge, 2001); Sarah Brouillette, *Postcolonial Writers in the Global Literary Marketplace* (Basingstoke: Palgrave Macmillan, 2007); Amitava Kumar, ed., *World Bank Literature* (Minneapolis, MN: University of Minnesota Press, 2003); Pascale Casanova, *The World Republic of Letters*,

trans. M.B. DeBevoise (Cambridge, MA: Harvard University Press, 2004); William Marling, *Gatekeepers: The Emergence of World Literature and the 1960s* (Oxford: Oxford University Press, 2016); Mads Rosendahl Thomsen, *Mapping World Literature: International Canonization and Transnational Literatures* (London: Continuum, 2008); Raphael Dalleo, ed., *Bourdieu and Postcolonial Studies* (Liverpool: Liverpool University Press, 2016); and Stefan Helgesson and Pieter Vermeulen, eds., *Institutions of World Literature: Writing, Translation, Markets* (Abingdon: Routledge, 2016).

83. Lucien Febvre and Henri-Jean Martin, *The Coming of the Book: The Impact of Printing 1450–1800*, trans. David Gerard (London: Verso, 1976), 109.

84. Nicholas Thoburn, *Anti-Book: On the Art and Politics of Radical Publishing* (Minneapolis, MN: University of Minnesota Press, 2016), 42.

85. For a prescient early account of this neoliberal collapsing of the notion of the popular into that of the market, see Stuart Hall, *The Hard Road to Renewal: Thatcherism and the Crisis of the Left* (London: Verso, 1988), esp. chs. 13 and 19.

86. Nicholas Brown, "Close Reading and the Market," *Literary Materialisms*, ed. Mathias Nilges and Emilio Sauri (New York, NY: Palgrave Macmillan, 2013), 158–59.

1 Market Metafiction and the Varieties of Postmodernism

1. Claire Squires, *Marketing Literature: The Making of Contemporary Writing in Britain* (Basingstoke: Palgrave Macmillan, 2007), 16.

2. Jeremy Rosen, *Minor Characters Have Their Day: Genre and the Contemporary Literary Marketplace* (New York, NY: Columbia University Press, 2016), 31.

3. Linda Hutcheon, *A Poetics of Postmodernism: History, Theory, Fiction* (London: Routledge, 1988), 224.

4. Patricia Waugh, *Metafiction: The Theory and Practice of Self-Conscious Fiction* (London: Routledge, 1984), 2.

5. Quoted in Randall Stevenson, *The Last of England?* (The Oxford English Literary History, vol. 12) (Oxford: Oxford University Press, 2004), 406.

6. See Jonathan Coe, *Like a Fiery Elephant: The Story of B.S. Johnson* (London: Picador, 2004), 187, 377ff.

7. B.S. Johnson, *Christie Malry's Own Double-Entry* (London: Picador, 2013), 12, 11, 16, 74; references hereafter noted parenthetically.

8. B.S. Johnson, *Aren't You Rather Young to Be Writing Your Memoirs?* (London: Hutchinson, 1973), 15.

9. Ibid., 123, 140.

10. Stevenson, *Last of England?*, 160, 430.

11. Quoted in ibid., 430.
12. See Jeffrey DeShell, R. M. Berry, Lance Olsen, and Matthew Kirkpatrick, "The Fiction Collective Story," www.fc2.org/about.html.
13. William McPheron, *Gilbert Sorrentino: A Descriptive Bibliography* (Elmwood Park, IL: Dalkey Archive Press, 1991), 37.
14. See Loren Glass, *Counterculture Colophon: Grove Press, the* Evergreen Review, *and the Incorporation of the Avant-Garde* (Stanford, CA: Stanford University Press, 2013).
15. Gilbert Sorrentino, *Mulligan Stew* (New York, NY: Grove, 1987), n.p.; emphasis in original; references hereafter noted parenthetically.
16. Abram Foley, "Ghosts from Limbo Patrum: Dalkey Archive Press and Institutional Literary History," *ASAP Journal* 1/3 (2016), 453.
17. In addition to Jameson's *Postmodernism*, see Andreas Huyssen, *After the Great Divide: Modernism, Mass Culture, Postmodernism* (Bloomington, IN: Indiana University Press, 1986); David Harvey, *The Condition of Postmodernity: An Enquiry into the Origins of Cultural Change* (Oxford: Blackwell, 1990), esp. ch. 3.
18. Larry McCaffery, "Avant-Pop: Still Life after Yesterday's Crash," *After Yesterday's Crash: The Avant-Pop Anthology* (London: Penguin, 1995), xvii–xviii.
19. DeShell, et al., "Fiction Collective."
20. Chris Kraus, *After Kathy Acker: A Biography* (London: Allen Lane, 2017), 118. Acker's shifting stance in relation to the literary marketplace is thus a key facet, I'd suggest, of the complexity and ambivalence that scholars have recently noted in her attitudes towards market systems more generally (see the variously angled accounts of Acker and neoliberalism in Michael W. Clune, *American Literature and the Free Market, 1945–2000* [Cambridge: Cambridge University Press, 2010], ch. 4; Alex Houen, *Powers of Possibility: Experimental American Writing Since the 1960s* [Oxford: Oxford University Press, 2012], esp. 165–69; Lee Konstantinou, *Cool Characters: Irony and American Fiction* [Cambridge, MA: Harvard University Press, 2016], 135–54).
21. Nicola Pitchford, *Tactical Readings: Feminist Postmodernism in the Novels of Kathy Acker and Angela Carter* (Lewisburg, PA: Bucknell University Press, 2002), 73.
22. Kathy Acker, *Literal Madness: Three Novels* (New York, NY: Grove, 1987), 219; references hereafter noted parenthetically.
23. Kathy Acker, "Critical Languages," *Bodies of Work* (London: Serpent's Tale, 1997), 84, 86.
24. Martin Amis, *Money: A Suicide Note* (London: Jonathan Cape, 1984). For an absorbing account of Amis's engagement with late twentieth-century finance,

see Nicky Marsh, *"Money's* Doubles: Reading, Fiction, and Finance Capital," *Textual Practice* 26/1 (2012), 115–33.

25. See Graham Fuller, "The Prose and Cons of Martin Amis," *Interview* 25/5 (1995), http://www.martinamisweb.com/pre_2006/fuller.htm.

26. Martin Amis, *The Information* (London: Flamingo, 1996), 63, 281; references hereafter noted parenthetically.

27. For an account of "l'affaire Amis," see Squires, *Marketing,* 115–18.

28. Paul D. Colford, "Publishers Find It Pays to Do Write Thing," *New York Daily News,* 11 December 2000, www.nydailynews.com/archives/money/pub lishers-find-pays-write-article-1.881649.

29. Quoted in Nicholas Dinofrio, "Multiculturalism, Inc.: Regulating and Deregulating the Culture Industries with Ishmael Reed," *American Literary History* 29/1 (2017), 101.

30. Quoted in ibid., 117.

31. Ibid., 124.

32. John K. Young, *Black Writers, White Publishers: Marketplace Politics in Twentieth-Century African American Literature* (Jackson: University Press of Mississippi, 2006), 120, 125, 120.

33. Ibid., 4.

34. Paul Beatty, *Slumberland: A Novel* (London: Harvill Secker, 2008), 162.

35. Rachel Farebrother, "'Out of Place': Reading Space in Percival Everett's *Erasure,*" *MELUS* 40/2 (2015), 117.

36. Percival Everett, *Erasure* (London: Faber and Faber, 2003), 65–66; references hereafter noted parenthetically.

37. See, in particular, Madhu Dubey, "Post-Postmodern Realism?" *Twentieth-Century Literature* 57/3–4 (2011), 364–71; Adam Kelly, "The New Sincerity," *Postmodern/Postwar – And After,* ed. Jason Gladstone, Andrew Hoberek, and Daniel Worden (Iowa City, IA: University of Iowa Press, 2016), 197–208; Konstantinou, *Cool,* esp. ch. 3; Robert L. McLaughlin, "Post-Postmodernism," *The Routledge Companion to Experimental Literature,* ed. Joe Bray, Alison Gibbons, and Brian McHale (New York, NY: Routledge, 2012), 212–23.

38. See Margaret Doherty, "State-Funded Fiction: Minimalism, National Memory, and the Return to Realism in the Post-Postmodern Age," *American Literary History* 27/1 (2014), 79–101.

39. Stephen J. Burn, "Second-Generation Postmoderns," *The Cambridge History of Postmodern Literature,* ed. Brian McHale and Len Platt (Cambridge: Cambridge University Press, 2016), 452.

40. One additional constituent element of that first generation of postmodernist fiction – which I don't address directly here, though it intersects in various ways with styles that I do consider – is the mode that Linda Hutcheon

famously terms "historiographic metafiction" (see Hutcheon, *Poetics*, esp. ch. 7).

41. See e.g. Konstantinou, *Cool*, ch. 3.
42. Mitchum Huehls and Rachel Greenwald Smith, "Four Phases of Neoliberalism and Literature," *Neoliberalism and Contemporary Literary Culture*, ed. Huehls and Smith (Baltimore, MD: Johns Hopkins University Press, 2017), 8.
43. Rachel Greenwald Smith, "Six Propositions on Compromise Aesthetics," *The Account* 3 (2014), https://theaccountmagazine.com/article/six-propositions-on-compromise-aesthetics.
44. David Foster Wallace, "E Unibus Pluram: Television and U.S. Fiction," *A Supposedly Fun Thing I'll Never Do Again: Essays and Arguments* (London: Abacus, 1998), 81.
45. McLaughlin, "Post-Postmodernism," 218–19; David Shields, *Reality Hunger: A Manifesto* (London: Penguin, 2011).
46. Konstantinou, *Cool*, 166, 181.
47. Ibid., 178–79, 166.
48. Dave Eggers, *A Heartbreaking Work of Staggering Genius* (London: Vintage, 2001), xxx; references hereafter noted parenthetically.
49. Though on Eggers's wider concerns with (his own) publicity and celebrity across his various activities, see Amy Hungerford, *Making Literature Now* (Stanford, CA: Stanford University Press, 2016), ch. 2.
50. Mark McGurl, "The Novel's Forking Path," *Public Books*, 1 April 2015, http://www.publicbooks.org/the-novels-forking-path/.
51. Ibid.
52. Andrew Hoberek, "Epilogue: 2001, 2008, and After," *The Cambridge History of Postmodern Literature*, ed. Brian McHale and Len Platt (Cambridge: Cambridge University Press, 2016), 501–02.
53. Andrew Hoberek, "Post-Recession Realism," *Neoliberalism and Contemporary Literary Culture*, ed. Mitchum Huehls and Rachel Greenwald Smith (Baltimore, MD: Johns Hopkins University Press, 2017), 237.
54. See Fredric Jameson, *Postmodernism, or, The Cultural Logic of Late Capitalism* (London: Verso, 1991), 3–5, 45–49; "The Aesthetics of Singularity," *New Left Review* 92 (2015), 103–04.
55. McGurl, "Novel's Forking Path."
56. Alex Christofi quoted in *Literature in the 21st Century: Understanding Models of Support for Literary Fiction* (Arts Council England, 2017), 10.
57. Mitchum Huehls, "Risking Complicity," *Arcade*, 9 November 2015, http://arcade.stanford.edu/content/risking-complicity.
58. Colson Whitehead, *Zone One* (London: Harvill Secker, 2011), 307; references hereafter noted parenthetically.

59. Huehls, "Risking."
60. Ibid.
61. See Ed Finn, *What Algorithms Want: Imagination in the Age of Computing* (Cambridge, MA: MIT Press, 2017), esp. 11–12, 97.
62. Stacey Mickelbart, "The Anhedoniast," *New Yorker* Page-Turner, 12 July 2011, https://www.newyorker.com/books/page-turner/the-anhedoniast.
63. Huehls, "Risking."
64. Mitchum Huehls, *After Critique: Twenty-First-Century Fiction in a Neoliberal Age* (Oxford: Oxford University Press, 2016), x.
65. See Annie McClanahan, *Dead Pledges: Debt, Crisis, and Twenty-First-Century Culture* (Stanford, CA: Stanford University Press, 2016), 16; Katy Shaw, *Crunch Lit* (London: Bloomsbury, 2015).
66. On the English tradition, see e.g. J. Russell Perkin, "John Lanchester's *Capital*: A Dickensian Examination of the Condition of England," *Journal of Modern Literature* 41/1 (2017), 100–17; on the American, see Alison Shonkwiler, *The Financial Imaginary: Economic Mystification and the Limits of Realist Fiction* (Minneapolis, MN: University of Minnesota Press, 2017), esp. intro. and chs. 1 and 5.
67. Shonkwiler, *Financial*, xvi.
68. Edward LiPuma, "Ritual in Financial Life," *Derivatives and the Wealth of Societies*, ed. Benjamin Lee and Randy Martin (Chicago, IL: University of Chicago Press, 2016), 62.
69. Sebastian Faulks, *A Week in December* (London: Hutchinson, 2009), 102–3.
70. C.K. Stead, *Risk* (London: MacLehose Press, 2012), n.p. (ebook).
71. Martha McPhee, *Dear Money* (New York, NY: Mariner, 2011), 337–38.
72. Paul Torday, *The Hopeless Life of Charlie Summers* (London: Weidenfeld and Nicolson, 2010), 1, 2, 3, 197.
73. Zia Haider Rahman, *In the Light of What We Know* (New York, NY: Farrar, Straus, and Giroux, 2014), 329, 264, 4–5.
74. Talitha Stevenson, *Disappear* (London: Virago, 2010), 26, 193; emphasis in original.
75. Aifric Campbell, *On the Floor* (New York, NY: Picador, 2012), 21, 61, 12, 73.
76. Jonathan Dee, *The Privileges* (New York, NY: Random House, 2010), 203.
77. Adam Haslett, *Union Atlantic* (New York, NY: Anchor, 2010), 282.
78. Ibid., 277–78.
79. Jean-Joseph Goux, *The Coiners of Language*, trans. Jennifer Curtiss Gage (Norman, OK: University of Oklahoma Press, 1994), 17.
80. Shonkwiler, *Financial*, xii.

81. McClanahan's *Dead Pledges* is a partial exception to the general exclusion of speculative/supernatural genres in this body of scholarship, devoting a chapter to a group of post-credit crisis horror films. There has, however, been little scholarly consideration of the role of the supernatural in contemporary financial *fiction* – surprisingly, given both the prevalence of novels that feature such elements and the attention that has been paid to the financial and economic dimensions of earlier novelistic manifestations of horror and the Gothic (see, in particular, Gail Turley Houston, *From Dickens to* Dracula: *Gothic, Economics, and Victorian Fiction* [Cambridge: Cambridge University Press, 2005]; Andrew Smith, *The Ghost Story, 1840–1920* [Manchester: Manchester University Press, 2010], esp. chs. 1–4). Also noteworthy is the special issue of *Journal of American Studies* (49/3 [2015]) on "Fictions of Speculation" edited by McClanahan and Hamilton Carroll. While the collection features articles on SF, thriller, crime, espionage, and apocalyptic genres, however, it only glancingly addresses the kinds of Gothic, magical, and occult modes that are my focus in Part II.

2 Trading in the As If: Fiduciary Exchangeability and Supernatural Financial Fiction

1. Ben Leach, "City Workers Turn to Psychics for Advice," *Telegraph*, 17 January 2009, www.telegraph.co.uk/finance/recession/4277426/City-workers-turn-to-psychics-for-advice.html; Catherine Mayer, "An Anxious London Flocks to Psychics," *Time*, 2 May 2009, www.time.com/time/world/article/0,8599,1894 843,00.html.

2. Peter Allen, "French Trader Jérôme Kerviel Used Clairvoyants to Predict Future," *Telegraph*, 15 February 2009, www.telegraph.co.uk/news/world news/europe/france/4632184/French-trader-Jerome-Kerviel-used-clairvoyants-to-predict-future.html.

3. Helena de Bertodano, "Meet Laura Day: The Financial Psychic of Wall Street Who Predicted Global Meltdown," *Telegraph*, 7 November 2008, www .telegraph.co.uk/news/worldnews/northamerica/3400109/Meet-Laura-Day-The-financial-psychic-of-Wall-Street-who-predicted-global-meltdown.html.

4. Laura Blumenfeld, "Voodoo Economics," *Washington Post Magazine*, 7 December 2008, www.washingtonpost.com/wp-dyn/content/gallery/2008/1 2/05/GA2008120501562.html.

5. Michael J. de la Merced, "For Psychic, Suit Came as Surprise," *New York Times*, 4 March 2010,www.nytimes.com/2010/03/05/business/05psychic.html.

6. Kerry Wills, Rebecca Rosenberg, and Tim Perone, "Praying for Almighty $$," *New York Post*, 10 October 2008, www.nypost.com/p/news/regional/item_UTQw9PJoYpvJuAEZl9PEaM.

7. Tony Carnes, "In Crisis, Wall Street Turns to Prayer," *Christianity Today*, 19 September 2008, www.christianitytoday.com/ct/2008/septemberweb-only /138–53.0.html.

8. See Gabriele M. Lepori, "Dark Omens in the Sky: Do Superstitious Beliefs Affect Investment Decisions?" *Social Science Research Network* (July 2009), http://papers.ssrn.com/sol3/papers.cfm?abstract_id=1428792; Brian M. Lucey, "Friday the 13th and the Philosophical Basis of Financial Economics," *Journal of Economics and Finance* 24/3 (2000), 294–301; Paul Whitfield, "Superstition Stalks the Market," *BBC News*, 25 October 2001, http://news.bbc.co.uk/1/hi/ programmes/working_lunch/1617969.stm.

9. See Caley Horan, "The Stars Ascendant: Financial Astrology and Market Rationality in the United States, 1970-Present," paper presented at Business History Conference, Columbus, OH, March 2013; Douglas Martin, "Money and Metaphysics: New-Age Wall Street," *New York Times*, 30 January 1994, www.nytimes.com/1994/01/30/nyregion/new-yorkers-co-money-and-metaphy sics-new-age-wall-street.html; Danny Penman, "City Looks to the Heavens for Answers," *Telegraph*, 19 March 2008, www.telegraph.co.uk/news/features/36359 65/City-looks-to-the-heavens-for-answers.html.

10. Quoted in Alan Jay Levinovitz, "The New Astrology," *Aeon*, 4 April 2016, https://aeon.co/essays/how-economists-rode-maths-to-become-our-era -s-astrologers.

11. See Caitlin Zaloom, *Out of the Pits: Traders and Technology from Chicago to London* (Chicago, IL: University of Chicago Press, 2006), 122.

12. Cf. "Cultural Economy and Finance," spec. section of *Economy and Society* 36/3 (2007), ed. Michael Pryke and Paul du Gay.

13. On Vanderbilt, see Molly McGarry, *Ghosts of Futures Past: Spiritualism and the Cultural Politics of Nineteenth-Century America* (Berkeley, CA: University of California Press, 2008), 97. On Morgan, see Howard M. Wachtel, *Street of Dreams – Boulevard of Broken Hearts: Wall Street's First Century* (London: Pluto, 2003), 138. On Schwab, see Gordon Thomas and Max Morgan Witts, *The Day the Bubble Burst: A Social History of the Wall Street Crash of 1929* (London: Penguin, 1980), 70–71.

14. See Liaquat Ahamed, *Lords of Finance: 1929, the Great Depression, and the Bankers Who Broke the World* (London: William Heinemann, 2009), 27–28.

15. Jackson Lears, *Fables of Abundance: A Cultural History of Advertising in America* (New York, NY: Basic Books, 1994), 44, 10.

16. Max Gunther, *Wall Street and Witchcraft: An Investigation into Extreme and Unusual Investment Techniques* (Petersfield, Hampshire: Harriman House, 2011).

17. J.G.A. Pocock, *The Machiavellian Moment: Florentine Political Thought and the Atlantic Republican Tradition* (Princeton, NJ: Princeton University Press, 1975), 441.

18. Iain Sinclair, *White Chappell, Scarlet Tracings* (London: Vintage, 1995), 39, 41.
19. David Graeber, *Debt: The First 5,000 Years* (New York, NY: Melville House, 2011), 18.
20. Nigel Dodd, *The Social Life of Money* (Princeton, NJ: Princeton University Press, 2014), 15–16; emphasis in original.
21. Karl Marx, *A Contribution to the Critique of Political Economy*, trans. S.W. Ryazanskaya, ed. Maurice Dobb (New York, NY: International Publishers, 1970), 119.
22. Jacques Derrida, *Specters of Marx: The State of the Debt, the Work of Mourning, and the New International*, trans. Peggy Kamuf (New York, NY: Routledge, 1994), 45.
23. See Marx's account of the effects on the value of money were the State to yield to the temptation to thrust "any arbitrarily chosen number of [banknotes] into circulation and to imprint them at will with any monetary denomination" (*Contribution*, 119–22).
24. Derrida, *Specters*, 42.
25. See Ole Bjerg, *Making Money: The Philosophy of Crisis Capitalism* (London: Verso, 2014), 167–92.
26. Philip Goodchild, *Theology of Money* (Durham, NC: Duke University Press, 2009), 132.
27. Arne De Boever, *Finance Fictions: Realism and Psychosis in a Time of Economic Crisis* (New York, NY: Fordham University Press, 2018), 13, 11
28. Karin Knorr Catina, "What is a Financial Market? Global Markets as Media-Institutional Forms," *Re-Imagining Economic Sociology*, ed. Patrik Aspers and Nigel Dodd (Oxford: Oxford University Press, 2015), 104–07.
29. Cédric Durand, *Fictitious Capital: How Finance is Appropriating Our Future*, trans David Broder (London: Verso, 2017), 66.
30. "What the Trader Said" *Independent*, 25 April 2010, www.independent.co.uk/news/business/news/what-the-trader-said-in-the-middle-of-complex-trades-without-understanding-them-1954288.html.
31. Annie McClanahan, *Dead Pledges: Debt, Crisis, and Twenty-First-Century Culture* (Stanford, CA: Stanford University Press, 2016), 28. See also Joshua Clover, "*Value | Theory | Crisis*," *PMLA* 127/1 (2012), 107–14; Annie McClanahan, "Investing in the Future: Late Capitalism's End of History," *Journal of Cultural Economy* 6/1 (2013), 78–93.
32. McClanahan, *Dead*, 42.
33. See e.g. Jens Beckert, *Imagined Futures: Fictional Expectations and Capitalist Dynamics* (Cambridge, MA: Harvard University Press, 2016), esp. 65, 107; Bjerg, *Making*, esp. 111.
34. Samuel Taylor Coleridge, *The Major Works*, ed. H.J. Jackson (Oxford: Oxford University Press, 2000), 314.

35. Catherine Gallagher, "The Rise of Fictionality," *The Novel, Vol. 1: History, Geography, and Culture*, ed. Franco Moretti (Princeton, NJ: Princeton University Press, 2007), 346–47.
36. A.J. Greimas and Joseph Courtès, "The Cognitive Dimension of Narrative Discourse," trans. Michael Rengstorf, *New Literary History* 7/3 (1976), 439.
37. Christine Gledhill, "Genre and Gender: The Case of Soap Opera," *Representation: Cultural Representations and Signifying Practices*, ed. Stuart Hall (London: Sage/Open University, 1997), 360–61.
38. Lauren Berlant, "Intuitionists: History and the Affective Event," *American Literary History* 20/4 (2008), 847.
39. Martha Woodmansee and Mark Osteen's introduction to their landmark collection of that name remains the best guide to the scope and key concerns of the field: see "Taking Account of the New Economic Criticism: An Historical Introduction," *The New Economic Criticism: Studies at the Intersection of Literature and Economics* (London: Routledge, 1999), 3–50.
40. For a nuanced consideration of the role of homology in the New Economic Criticism, see Osteen and Woodmansee, "Taking Account," 14–18.
41. Raymond Williams, *Marxism and Literature* (Oxford: Oxford University Press, 1977), 105–06.
42. E.g. Marc Shell, *The Economy of Literature* (Baltimore, MD: Johns Hopkins University Press, 1978), 39; Jean-Joseph Goux, *Symbolic Economies: After Marx and Freud*, trans. Jennifer Curtiss Gage (Ithaca, NY: Cornell University Press, 1990), 4.
43. Mary Poovey, *Genres of the Credit Economy: Mediating Value in Eighteenth- and Nineteenth-Century Britain* (Chicago, IL: University of Chicago Press, 2008), 2.
44. Ibid., emphasis in original.
45. Ibid., 300, 123.
46. Ibid., 286; emphases in original.
47. Ibid., 27, 298.
48. Ibid., 8.
49. Ibid., 123.
50. On the notion of "secular enchantment," see Joshua Landy and Michael Saler, eds., *The Re-Enchantment of the World: Secular Magic in a Rational Age* (Stanford, CA: Stanford University Press, 2009).
51. See Leah Price, *How to Do Things with Books in Victorian Britain* (Princeton, NJ: Princeton University Press, 2012). Of course, communal complements to the experience of solitary, absorbed reading also exist – in new forms – today (see Elizabeth Long, *Book Clubs: Women and the Uses of Reading in Everyday Life* [Chicago, IL: University of Chicago Press, 2003], esp. 2–11; Jim Collins,

Bring on the Books for Everybody: How Literary Culture Became Popular Culture [Durham, NC: Duke University Press, 2010], chs. 1–2).

52. Moniek M. Kuijpers, Frank Hakemulder, Katalin Balint, Miruna Doicaru, and Ed Tan, "Towards a New Understanding of Absorbing Reading Experiences," *Narrative Absorption*, ed. Hakemulder et al. (Amsterdam: John Benjamins, 2017), 34.

53. See Ken Gelder, *Popular Fiction: The Logics and Practices of a Literary Field* (London: Routledge, 2004); Anna Faktorovich, *Formulas of Popular Fiction: Elements of Fantasy, Science Fiction, Romance, Religious, and Mystery Novels* (Jefferson, NC: McFarland, 2014); Jodie Archer and Matthew L. Jockers, *The Bestseller Code: Anatomy of the Blockbuster Novel* (New York, NY: St Martin's Press, 2016).

54. Poovey, *Genres*, 8; emphasis in original.

55. Beckert, *Imagined*, 129.

56. Brooke Harrington, "The Capitalist's Imagination," *Atlantic*, 13 July 2016, www.theatlantic.com/business/archive/2016/07/the-capitalists-imagination/491009/.

57. There are several sustained and insightful engagements with *American Psycho*'s portrayal of its Reagan-era financial milieu, though with different emphases to the ones I offer here: see Amy Bride, "Byronic Bateman: the Commodity Vampire, Surplus Value, and the Hyper-Gothic in *American Psycho* (1991)," *Irish Journal of Gothic and Horror Studies* 14 (2015), 3–18; Richard Godden, "Fictions of Fictitious Capital: *American Psycho* and the Poetics of Deregulation," *Textual Practice* 25/5 (2011), 853–66; and Leigh Claire La Berge, *Scandals and Abstraction: Financial Fiction of the Long 1980s* (Oxford: Oxford University Press, 2015), ch. 3.

58. Bret Easton Ellis, *American Psycho* (London: Picador, 1991), 275, 330; references hereafter noted parenthetically.

59. Bret Easton Ellis, *Lunar Park* (London: Picador, 2005), 74; references hereafter noted parenthetically.

60. Richard Godden, "Bret Easton Ellis, *Lunar Park*, and the Exquisite Corpse of Deficit Finance," *American Literary History* 25/3 (2013), 591–92.

61. The novel is positively reviewed on Amazon.com and Amazon.co.uk (with around a third of reviewers giving it a five-star rating) (accessed 6 November 2018). Praise is consistently couched in terms of the novel's outstandingly (for many, surprisingly) absorbing and affecting qualities. As a number of other critics have done in recent years, I make use of such reviews at several points in this book in order to gain insights into readers' responses to specific aspects of texts I discuss. As Seth Studer and Ichiro Takayoshi rightly note, "the vast number of reader-authored reports that daily appear on the Internet provide a unique window into the reading habits of the 'ordinary'

reader" ("Franzen and the 'Open-Minded but Essentially Untrained Fiction Reader,'" *Post45*, 8 July 2013, http://post45.research.yale.edu/2013/07/fran zen-and-the-open-minded-but-essentially-untrained-fiction-reader/).

Amazon reviewers are of course self-selecting, and thus, as Timothy Aubry remarks, "what one discovers on Amazon may not be exactly what one would find in a random survey." Nevertheless, such a survey "would produce its own distortions, and so Amazon may be as useful an archive of contemporary reader responses as one might hope to locate." Aubry further cautions that "this venue shapes as well as reflects the tastes and inclinations of particular readers, since online visitors inevitably find themselves influenced by the reviews they discover there" (*Reading as Therapy: What Contemporary Fiction Does for Middle-Class Americans* [Iowa City, IA: University of Iowa Press, 2011], 176). That publicly visible reader responses on Amazon actively affect the marketability of the texts they evaluate makes them all the more relevant for this project; indeed, they are among the key contemporary means via which readers communicate to one another the extent to which particular books deliver or withhold desired aesthetic and affective experiences.

62. Anne Billson, *Suckers* (London: Pan, 1996), 139, 136; emphasis in original; references hereafter noted parenthetically.

63. Quoted in Carol Margaret Davison, introduction to *Bram Stoker's Dracula: Sucking Through the Century, 1897–1997* (Toronto: Dundurn Press, 1997), 22.

64. Quoted in James Procter, "Anne Billson," *British Council: Literature* web site, 2013, https://literature.britishcouncil.org/writer/anne-billson.

65. Candice Rodd, review of *Suckers* by Anne Billson, *Independent on Sunday*, 24 January 1993, www.independent.co.uk/arts-entertainment/book-review-new-blood-not-much-bite-suckers-anne-billson-pan-499-pounds-1480483.html.

66. Ibid.

67. Ibid.

68. See Paul Crosthwaite, "Animality and Ideology in Contemporary Economic Discourse: Taxonomizing *Homo Economicus*," *Journal of Cultural Economy* 6/ 1 (2013), 94–109.

69. Stephen Marche, "How Genre Fiction Became More Important Than Literary Fiction," *Esquire*, 11 March 2015, www.esquire.com/entertainment/books/a33599/genre-fiction-vs-literary-fiction/.

70. Stephen Marche, *The Hunger of the Wolf* (New York, NY: Simon & Schuster, 2015), 7–8; references hereafter noted parenthetically.

71. Stephen Marche, "The Obama Years," *Los Angeles Review of Books*, 30 November 2016, https://lareviewofbooks.org/article/the-obama-years/.

72. Jonathan Coe, *The Terrible Privacy of Maxwell Sim* (London: Viking, 2010), 18; references hereafter noted parenthetically.

73. Jonathan Coe, *Number 11* (London: Penguin, 2015), n.p. (ebook).

74. The overwhelming majority of reader reviews of Coe's novel on Amazon .co.uk and Amazon.com (accessed 6 November 2018) single out the ending for discussion, with many criticizing it as leaving them feeling let down, cheated, or (as one puts it) "mugged"; many of those who praise the novel overall feel obliged to defend the ending (or acknowledge its defects).

3 "The Occult Logic of 'Market Forces'": Iain Sinclair's Post-Big Bang London

1. Ian Jack, review of *The Last London* by Iain Sinclair, *New York Review of Books* 27 September 2018, www.nybooks.com/articles/2018/09/27/imploding-cool-london-iain-sinclair/; Sinclair McKay, review of *London: City of Disappearances* ed. by Iain Sinclair, *Telegraph*, 29 October 2006, https://www.telegraph.co.uk/culture/books/3656213/Londons-dreams-are-still-thick-with-fog.html.

2. Iain Sinclair, *Ghost Milk: Calling Time on the Grand Project* (London: Penguin, 2012), 90.

3. Iain Sinclair, *White Chappell, Scarlet Tracings* (London: Vintage, 1995), 197; references hereafter noted parenthetically.

4. See William St Clair, *The Reading Nation in the Romantic Period* (Cambridge: Cambridge University Press, 2004), chs. 3–4.

5. See Colin Nicholson, *Writing and the Rise of Finance: Capital Satires of the Early Eighteenth Century* (Cambridge: Cambridge University Press, 1994); Sandra Sherman, *Finance and Fictionality in the Early Eighteenth Century: Accounting for Defoe* (Cambridge: Cambridge University Press, 1996); Mary Poovey, *Genres of the Credit Economy: Mediating Value in Eighteenth- and Nineteenth-Century Britain* (Chicago, IL: University of Chicago Press, 2008).

6. See David Callaway, "London Booming after Big Bang," *Washington Post*, 26 May 1996, www.washingtonpost.com/archive/business/1996/05/26/london-booming-after-big-bang/e1b16274-0f48-4485-aed5-5b1c500ab434/.

7. Sean McCann and Michael Szalay, "Do You Believe in Magic: Literary Thinking after the New Left," *Yale Journal of Criticism* 18/2 (2005), 436.

8. Roger Luckhurst, "The Contemporary London Gothic and the Limits of the 'Spectral Turn,'" *Textual Practice* 16/3 (2002), 534.

9. Ibid., 541.

10. See e.g. Robert T. Tally Jr., *Utopia in the Age of Globalization: Space, Representation, and the World System* (New York, NY: Palgrave Macmillan, 2013), 84, 87.

11. Sinclair, *Ghost*, 90.

12. McCann, and Szalay, "Do You Believe," 460.

13. Iain Sinclair, *Downriver (Or, The Vessels of Wrath): A Narrative in Twelve Tales* (London: Granta, 2002), 66, 93, 111, 357; references hereafter noted parenthetically.

14. On the "intense commodification of . . . magical realism in the world-literary market" in the decades following the Boom, and its accommodation to and by "the tastes of metropolitan cultural elites," see Warwick Research Collective, *Combined and Uneven Development: Towards a New Theory of World-Literature* (Liverpool: Liverpool University Press, 2015), 80.

15. Sara Upstone, *Spatial Politics in the Postcolonial Novel* (Farnham, Surrey: Ashgate, 2009), 96.

16. Randy Martin, "After Economy: Social Logics of the Derivative," *Social Text* 114 (2013), 85. See also, Max Haiven, *Cultures of Financialization: Fictitious Capital in Popular Culture and Everyday Life* (Basingstoke: Palgrave Macmillan, 2014), 150–54.

17. See Steve Pile, *Real Cities: Modernity, Space, and the Phantasmagorias of City Life* (London: Sage, 2005), 68.

18. Peter Ackroyd, "Canary Wharf Pier," Royal Institute of British Architects London *Dark Waters* exhibition web site (2008), www.darkwaters.org.uk/piers/canary-wharf-pier/.

19. Niall Martin, *Iain Sinclair: Noise, Neoliberalism, and the Matter of London* (London: Bloomsbury, 2015), 112.

20. Tony Norfield, *The City: London and the Global Power of Finance* (London: Verso, 2016), n.p. (ebook).

21. Luckhurst, "Contemporary," 538.

22. Anon., review of *Downriver, Kirkus Reviews*, n.d., www.kirkusreviews.com/book-reviews/iain-sinclair-2/downriver-or-the-vessels-of-wrath-2/.

23. The question of artistic autonomy is an important concern of Brian Baker's study *Iain Sinclair* (Manchester: Manchester University Press, 2007), esp. ch. 1.

24. Kirsten Seale, "Iain Sinclair's Excremental Narratives," *M/C Journal* 8/1 (2005), http://journal.media-culture.org.au/0502/03-seale.php.

25. Iain Sinclair, *Lights Out for the Territory: 9 Excursions in the Secret History of London* (London: Granta, 1997), 136; references hereafter noted parenthetically. Where required, I employ the abbreviation *LO*. Iain Sinclair, "A Note on the Press," in Jeffrey M. Johnson, *The Works of Iain Sinclair: A Descriptive Bibliography and Biographical Chronology, 1943–1987* (London: Test Centre, 2018), item A071, n.p.

26. Johnson, *Works*, item A071, n.p.

27. Iain Sinclair and Kevin Jackson, *The Verbals* (Tonbridge: Worple, 2003), 124, 129, 138, 134, 124, 129.

28. Robert Sheppard, *Iain Sinclair* (Tavistock: Northcote House, 2007), 7–8.

29. See Barry Eichengreen and Peter Temin, "The Gold Standard and the Great Depression," *Contemporary European History* 9/2 (2000), 183–207.

30. Ole Bjerg, *Making Money: The Philosophy of Crisis Capitalism* (London: Verso, 2014), 112.

31. Ibid.

32. Jean-Joseph Goux, *The Coiners of Language*, trans. Jennifer Curtiss Gage (Norman, OK: University of Oklahoma Press, 1994), 17.

33. Bjerg, *Making*, 93, 98. See Karl Marx, *A Contribution to the Critique of Political Economy*, trans. S.W. Ryazanskaya, ed. Maurice Dobb (New York, NY: International Publishers, 1970), 154–55; Jean-Joseph Goux, *Symbolic Economies: After Marx and Freud*, trans. Jennifer Curtiss Gage (Ithaca, NY: Cornell University Press, 1990), 28.

34. See Will Self, Iain Sinclair, and Kevin Jackson, "Psychogeography," *Literary London Journal* 6/1 (2008), www.literarylondon.org/london-journal/marc h2008/sinclair-self.html.

35. Ibid. See also Merlin Coverley, *Psychogeography* (Harpenden, Hertfordshire: Pocket Essential, 2010), 51–54.

36. See Self, Sinclair, and Jackson, "Psychogeography."

37. This is the kind of literature churned out by the publisher at the centre of Umberto Eco's *Foucault's Pendulum* (1988). Like *Lights Out for the Territory*, Eco's novel hovers between satirizing such writing and tapping into its (demonstrably marketable) pleasures and satisfactions.

38. On this acquaintance, see Sinclair and Jackson, *Verbals*, 89.

39. Laura Miller, "The Da Vinci Con," *New York Times*, 22 February 2004, www .nytimes.com/2004/02/22/books/the-last-word-the-da-vinci-con.html?_r=0.

40. Richard Leigh obituary, *Telegraph*, 30 November 2007, www.telegraph.co.uk /news/obituaries/1570965/Richard-Leigh.html.

41. Sinclair and Jackson, *Verbals*, 14.

42. "The Iain Sinclair Interview," *Londonist*, n.d. http://londonist.com/2005/06/ the_iain_sincla.

43. See Sinclair and Jackson, *Verbals*, 75; Self, Sinclair, and Jackson, "Psychogeography."

44. Sinclair and Jackson, *Verbals*, 75.

45. Stuart Jeffries, "On the Road," *Guardian*, 24 April 2004, www .theguardian.com/books/2004/apr/24/featuresreviews.guardianreview14.

46. Coverley, *Psychogeography*, 119; Jeffries, "On the Road."

47. Jeffries, "On the Road."

48. Michael Baigent, Richard Leigh, and Henry Lincoln, *The Holy Blood and the Holy Grail* (London: Arrow, 1996), 37, 35, 38, 37.

49. Ibid., 315.

50. Ibid., 255.

51. Ibid., 335, 336, 338.
52. Ibid., 338.
53. See Hayden White, *Metahistory: The Historical Imagination in Nineteenth-Century Europe* (Baltimore, MD: Johns Hopkins University Press, 1973).
54. Sinclair and Jackson, *Verbals*, 58–59.
55. Ibid., 59, 14.
56. Jeffries, "On the Road."
57. Tobias Carroll, "Witches, Demons, Mystics: When Writers Cross the Supernatural Line," *Literary Hub*, 30 October 2015, https://lithub.com/witches-demons-mystics-when-writers-cross-the-supernatural-line/.
58. Robert Bond, *Iain Sinclair* (Cambridge: Salt, 2005), 135.
59. See John Clark, "London Stone: Stone of Brutus or Fetish Stone – Making the Myth," *Folklore* 121/1 (2010), 38–60.
60. The temple was returned to its original location as part of the redevelopment of the site as Bloomberg's European headquarters, which opened in 2017.
61. Jean-Joseph Goux, "Cash, Check, or Charge?" trans. John R. Barberet, *The New Economic Criticism*, ed. Martha Woodmansee and Mark Osteen (London: Routledge, 1999), 117.
62. Goux, *Coiners*, 149.
63. Iain Sinclair, interview with Rupert M. Loydell, *The Argotist Online*, 2006, www.argotistonline.co.uk/Sinclair%20interview.htm.
64. Sinclair's strategies thus lend weight to Nicholas Brown's provocative claim that while genre writing would appear to be "the quintessential art commodity," it is in fact the case that the "very thing that invalidates" such writing "in relation to modernist autonomy – 'formulas,' Adorno called them – opens up a zone of autonomy within the heteronomous space of cultural commodities," since precisely the existence of such "rules" cries out for their "subversion" ("Close Reading and the Market," *Literary Materialisms*, ed. Mathias Nilges and Emilio Sauri [New York, NY: Palgrave Macmillan, 2013], 161).
65. J.K. Galbraith, *Money: Whence it Came, Where it Went* (London: Deutsch, 1975), 18–19.
66. Ibid., 4.
67. Karl Marx, *Capital: A Critique of Political Economy*, vol. 1, trans. Ben Fowkes (London: Penguin, 1990), 230.
68. On metaphors of excavation and disinterment in critical practice – of a kind literalized by Sinclair in *Lights Out* – see Rita Felski, *The Limits of Critique* (Chicago, IL: University of Chicago Press, 2015), ch. 2.
69. Eve Kosofsky Sedgwick, "Paranoid Reading and Reparative Reading; or, You're So Paranoid, You Probably Think This Introduction is About You," *Novel Gazing: Queer Readings in Fiction*, ed. Eve Kosofsky Sedgwick (Durham, NC: Duke University Press, 1997), 19.

70. Paul Ricoeur himself contrasts a hermeneutics of suspicion with a hermeneutics of "faith" or "trust" (central to biblical exegesis and religious phenomenology), which aims at the "restoration" or "recollection" of a true or "just" meaning (see *Freud and Philosophy: An Essay on Interpretation*, trans. Denis Savage [New Haven, CT: Yale University Press, 1970], 28–32). Sinclair's method differs, however, to the extent that it wants to believe in meanings that are not simply imagined to dwell, ready to be restored, in the world or in some other text, but which his own writing is openly in the process of embroidering into being.

71. The reference appears to be to Canto LXXXIX of *The Cantos of Ezra Pound* (New York, NY: New Directions, 1996), 591.

72. Fredric Jameson, *The Political Unconscious: Narrative as a Socially Symbolic Act* (Ithaca, NY: Cornell University Press, 1981), 60.

73. See ibid., esp. "Conclusion: The Dialectic of Utopia and Ideology." On critics' tendency to neglect Jameson's concern with the utopian dimensions of cultural artefacts, see Carolyn Lesjak, "Reading Dialectically," *Criticism* 55/2 (2013), 246, 250.

4 The Price Is Right: Market Epistemology, Narrative Totality, and the "Big Novel"

1. Slavoj Žižek, *The Ticklish Subject: The Absent Centre of Political Ontology* (London: Verso, 2000), 340.

2. Ibid., 340.

3. Ibid., 339.

4. Ibid.

5. Ibid., 341.

6. Philip Mirowski and Edward Nik-Khah, *The Knowledge We Have Lost in Information: The History of Information in Modern Economics* (Oxford: Oxford University Press, 2017), 7.

7. Žižek, *Ticklish*, 339.

8. Adam Smith, *An Inquiry into the Nature and Causes of the Wealth of Nations*, vol. 2 (London: W. Strahan and T. Cadell, 1776), 35.

9. Michel Foucault, *The Birth of Biopolitics: Lectures at the Collège de France, 1978–1979*, trans. Graham Burchell (Basingstoke: Palgrave Macmillan, 2008), 278–79.

10. Eleanor Courtemanche, *The "Invisible Hand" and British Fiction, 1818–1860: Adam Smith, Political Economy, and the Genre of Realism* (Basingstoke: Palgrave Macmillan, 2011), 3, 12, 14, 13.

11. See Jennifer Wicke, "*Mrs. Dalloway* Goes to Market: Woolf, Keynes, and Modern Markets," *Novel* 28/1 (1994), 5–23; Carey James Mickalites,

Modernism and Market Fantasy: British Fictions of Capital, 1910–1939 (Basingstoke: Palgrave Macmillan, 2012).

12. Wicke, "*Mrs. Dalloway*," 20, 11.
13. Ibid., 12.
14. See Courtemanche, "*Invisible Hand,*" 10–17 and ch. 4.
15. F.A. Hayek, "The Use of Knowledge in Society," *American Economic Review* 35/4 (1945), 519–20.
16. Ibid., 525; emphasis in original.
17. Ibid., 521.
18. Ibid., 527.
19. See Thomas Frank, *One Market Under God: Extreme Capitalism, Market Populism, and the End of Economic Democracy* (London: Vintage, 2002).
20. Charles Dickens, *The Mystery of Edwin Drood*, ed. Margaret Cardwell (Oxford: Oxford University Press, 2009), 119; Virginia Woolf, *Mrs Dalloway*, ed. David Bradshaw (Oxford: Oxford University Press), 3–4.
21. Don DeLillo, *Players* (London: Vintage: 1991), 132.
22. Philip Mirowski, *Never Let a Serious Crisis Go to Waste: How Neoliberalism Survived the Financial Meltdown* (London: Verso, 2013), 298.
23. See, principally: Paul A. Samuelson, "Proof That Properly Anticipated Prices Fluctuate Randomly," *Industrial Management Review* 6/2 (1965), 13–32; Eugene F. Fama, "Random Walks in Stock Market Prices," *Financial Analysts Journal* 21/5 (1965), 55–59, and "Efficient Capital Markets: A Review of Theory and Empirical Work," *Journal of Finance* 25/2 (1970), 383–417. For an overview of the emergence of the EMH, see Donald MacKenzie, *An Engine, Not a Camera: How Financial Models Shape Markets* (Cambridge, MA: MIT Press, 2006), esp. 57–105.
24. Hirokazu Miyazaki, "The Temporalities of the Market," *American Anthropologist* 105/2 (2003), 258, 259.
25. Samuelson, "Proof," 41.
26. Leo Melamed with Bob Tamarkin, *Escape to the Futures* (New York, NY: John Wiley & Sons, 1996), 170.
27. Milton Friedman, "The Case for Flexible Exchange Rates," *Essays in Positive Economics* (Chicago, IL: University of Chicago Press, 1953), 157–203.
28. Mirowski, *Never*, 268.
29. Ibid., 265–66.
30. See John Quiggin, *Zombie Economics: How Dead Ideas Still Walk Among Us* (Princeton, NJ: Princeton University Press, 2010), ch. 2.
31. Mirowski, *Never*, 267.
32. Ibid., 268.
33. Jonathan Clarke, Tomas Jandik, and Gershon Mandelker, "The Efficient Markets Hypothesis," *Expert Financial Planning: Investment Strategies*

from Industry Leaders, ed. Robert C. Arffa (New York, NY: Wiley, 2001), 129.

34. Burton G. Malkiel, *A Random Walk Down Wall Street*, 8th ed. (New York, NY: W.W. Norton, 2003), 126.

35. Thomas E. Copeland and Daniel Friedman, "The Effect of Sequential Information Arrival on Asset Prices: An Experimental Study," *Journal of Finance* 42/3 (1987), 763.

36. Justin Fox, *The Myth of the Rational Market: A History of Risk, Reward, and Delusion on Wall Street* (New York, NY: HarperCollins, 2009), 232.

37. Mirowski and Nik-Khah, *Knowledge*, 70–71; italics in original.

38. Ibid., 71.

39. Andrew W. Lo, "Why Animal Spirits Can Cause Markets to Break Down," *Financial Times*, 21 July 2009, www.ft.com/cms/s/0/a38cb79a-758c-11de-9e d5-00144feabdco.html#axzz2wIpMBuJQ.

40. Frank, *One Market*, xiv.

41. Ibid., xii.

42. Edward Mendelson, "Encyclopedic Narrative: From Dante to Pynchon," *MLN* 91/6 (1976), 1267–75.

43. Tom LeClair, *In the Loop: Don DeLillo and the Systems Novel* (Urbana and Chicago, IL: University of Illinois Press, 1987).

44. Tom LeClair, *The Art of Excess: Mastery in Contemporary American Fiction* (Urbana and Chicago, IL: University of Illinois Press, 1989).

45. Stefano Ercolino, *The Maximalist Novel: From Thomas Pynchon's* Gravity's Rainbow *to Roberto Bolaño's* 2666, trans. Albert Sbragia (London: Bloomsbury, 2014); Nick Levey, *Maximalism in Contemporary American Literature: The Uses of Detail* (Abingdon: Routledge, 2017).

46. Frederick R. Karl, *American Fictions, 1980–2000: Whose America Is It Anyway?* (Bloomington, IN: Xlibris, 2001), ch. 3.

47. Brian McHale, *The Cambridge Introduction to Postmodernism* (Cambridge: Cambridge University Press, 2015), 72–79.

48. Mark McGurl, *The Program Era: Postwar Fiction and the Rise of Creative Writing* (Cambridge, MA: Harvard University Press, 2009), esp. 42–46, 62–67.

49. Douglas Coupland, "Convergences," review of *Gods Without Men* by Hari Kunzru, *New York Times*, 8 March 2012, www.nytimes.com/2012/03/11/boo ks/review/gods-without-men-by-hari-kunzru.html.

50. James Wood, "Human, All Too Inhuman," *New Republic*, 24 July 2000, https://newrepublic.com/article/61361/human-all-too-inhuman.

51. Jacket copy, LeClair, *Art of Excess*.

52. Wood, "Human."

53. For a recent, and especially clear, alignment of the maximalism of Pynchon, DeLillo, Wallace, and others with a conspiratorial mindset, see Ercolino, *Maximalist*, ch. 7 ("Paranoid Imagination").

54. Thomas Pynchon, *Gravity's Rainbow* (London: Vintage, 2000), 124; references hereafter noted parenthetically.

55. See Melamed, *Escape*, 3–59; Nathan Guttman, "Leo Melamed Retraces Path of Escape From Nazis to Japanese Port," *Forward*, 27 July 2014, http://forw ard.com/news/200802/leo-melamed-retraces-path-of-escape-from-nazis-to/.

56. Melamed, *Escape*, 169.

57. The critical literature on *Gravity's Rainbow* is vast, but previous studies have not – to the best of my knowledge – situated the novel in relation to the concepts of market efficiency entering into public circulation in the United States in the late 1960s and early 1970s. For an excellent discussion of the novel's more general concern with markets, see Eric Cassidy, "Cyberotics: Markets, Materialism, and Method in Pynchon and Deleuze," *Pynchon Notes* 34–35 (1994), 107–28. Doug Haynes also touches on some of my concerns here in tracing an iconography of gold through Pynchon's novel (though without relating it directly to the contemporaneous unravelling of the Bretton Woods accords): see "'Gravity Rushes Through Him: *Volk* and Fetish in Pynchon's Rilke," *Modern Fiction Studies* 58/2 (2012), esp. 322–27.

58. See LeClair, *Art*, ch. 4.

59. William Gaddis, *J R* (London: Penguin, 1993), 95; references hereafter noted parenthetically.

60. Michael W. Clune, *American Literature and the Free Market, 1945–2000* (Cambridge: Cambridge University Press, 2010), 23. Naturally, given *J R*'s subject matter, concerns relating to money and financial capitalism have figured prominently in critical responses (see e.g. the reading by Marsh, cited below; for another recent example, see Ralph Clare, "Family Incorporated: William Gaddis's *J R* and the Embodiment of Capitalism," *Fictions Inc.: The Corporation in Postmodern Fiction, Film, and Popular Culture* [New Brunswick: Rutgers University Press, 2014], ch. 5). Surprisingly, however, Clune's is the only analysis to pay sustained attention to the ways in which the novel's "encyclopedism" or "systematicity" is entangled with an understanding of financial markets in terms of their capacity to process information (though Stephen Schryer touches on this idea in "The Aesthetics of First- and Second-Order Cybernetics in William Gaddis's *J R*," *Paper Empire: William Gaddis and the World System*, ed. Joseph Tabbi and Rone Shavers [Tuscaloosa: University of Alabama Press, 2007], 86). While Clune and Schryer position the novel in relation to intellectual movements (Hayekian economics; Wienerian cybernetics) that rose to prominence in the 1940s, I argue that the novel can

revealingly be read in light of the more historically proximate emergence and dissemination of the EMH in the 1960s and 1970s.

61. Nicky Marsh, "'Hit Your Educable Public Right in the Supermarket Where They Live': Risk and Failure in the Work of William Gaddis," *New Formations* 80/81 (2013), 189.

62. James Wood, "Tell Me How Does It Feel?" *Guardian*, 6 October 2001, www .theguardian.com/books/2001/oct/06/fiction.

63. Anon. review of *Three Farmers on Their Way to a Dance*, *Kirkus Reviews*, August 1985, www.kirkusreviews.com/book-reviews/richard-powers-2/three-farmers-on-their-way-to-a-dance/.

64. Richard Powers, *Three Farmers on Their Way to a Dance* (HarperCollins, 1992), 144; references hereafter noted parenthetically.

65. Peter Knight, "Reading the Ticker Tape in the Late Nineteenth-Century American Market," *Journal of Cultural Economy* 6/1 (2013), 56–58.

66. Richard Powers, *Plowing the Dark* (London: Vintage, 2002), 120, 121; references hereafter noted parenthetically.

67. See Franzen's interview with Stephen J. Burn, *Paris Review* 195 (2010), www .theparisreview.org/interviews/6054/the-art-of-fiction-no-207-jonathan-franzen.

68. Jonathan Franzen, *Strong Motion* (New York: Picador, 1992), 209; references hereafter noted parenthetically.

69. Several valuable readings of *The Pale King* in relation to neoliberalism and post-1970s financial capitalism have appeared, though none explores the notion of the informationally efficient market whose centrality to the novel I argue for here. See Richard Godden and Michael Szalay, "The Bodies in the Bubble: David Foster Wallace's *The Pale King*," *Textual Practice* 28/7 (2014), 1273–322; Jeffrey Severs, "'Blank as the Faces on Coins': Currency and Embodied Value(s) in David Foster Wallace's *The Pale King*", *Critique* 57/1 (2016), 52–66; Stephen Shapiro, "From Capitalist to Communist Abstraction: *The Pale King*'s Cultural Fix," *Textual Practice* 28/7 (2014), 1249–71.

70. Editor's Note to David Foster Wallace, *The Pale King: An Unfinished Novel* (London: Penguin, 2012), x; references hereafter noted parenthetically.

71. Marshall Boswell has made insightful links between *The Pale King*'s "Author here" interventions and the novel's "dramatization of information overload," though without addressing how these elements are bound up with notions of market efficiency, or with the novel's understanding of its position in relation to the literary marketplace (see "Author Here: The Legal Fiction of David Foster Wallace's *The Pale King*," *English Studies* 95/1 [2014], 25–39).

72. Garth Risk Hallberg, "David Foster Wallace 1962–2008," *The Millions*, 14 September 2008, www.themillions.com/2008/09/david-foster-wallace-196 2-2008_14.html.

73. Garth Risk Hallberg, *City on Fire* (London: Vintage, 2015), 274; references hereafter noted parenthetically.
74. See e.g. Jed Rasula, "Textual Indigence in the Archive," *Postmodern Culture* 9/3 (1999); Luc Herman and Petrus van Ewijk, "Gravity's Encyclopedia Revisited: The Illusion of a Totalizing System in *Gravity's Rainbow*," *English Studies* 90/2 (2009), 167–79.
75. See e.g. Levey, *Maximalism*, 28–29.
76. See, in particular, Leslie Marmon Silko, *Almanac of the Dead* (New York: Simon and Schuster, 1991); Karen Tei Yamashita, *Tropic of Orange* (Minneapolis: Coffee House Press, 1997) and *I Hotel* (Minneapolis: Coffee House Press, 2010); and Zadie Smith, *White Teeth* (London: Hamish Hamilton, 2000).
77. Garth Risk Hallberg, "Is Big Back?" *The Millions*, 8 September 2010, www .themillions.com/2010/09/is-big-back.html.

5 Fully Reflecting: Knowing the Mind of the Market in DeLillo and Kunzru

1. For readings of this kind, see Steffen Hantke, "'God Save Us from Bourgeois Adventure': The Figure of the Terrorist in Contemporary American Conspiracy Fiction," *Studies in the Novel* 28/2 (1996), esp. 232–35; John Johnston "Generic Difficulties in the Novels of Don DeLillo," *Critique* 30/4 (1989), esp. 267–69.
2. Alessandra De Marco, "'Morbid Tiers of Immortality': Don DeLillo's *Players* and the Financialisation of the USA," *Textual Practice* 27/5 (2013), 8.
3. Don DeLillo, *Players* (London: Vintage: 1991), 13, 99, 82, 109, 119, 183; references hereafter noted parenthetically.
4. Interview with Adam Begley, *Paris Review* 128 (1993), www.theparisreview.org /interviews/1887/the-art-of-fiction-no-135-don-delillo.
5. McKenzie Wark, *Virtual Geography: Living with Global Media Events* (Bloomington, IN: Indiana University Press, 1994), 176, 178.
6. Eugene Fama, "Efficient Capital Markets: A Review of Theory and Empirical Work," *Journal of Finance* 25/2 (1970), 383.
7. Jean Baudrillard, *The Ecstasy of Communication*, trans. Bernard Schutze and Caroline Schutze (New York, NY: Semiotext(e), 1988), 21–22, emphasis in original.
8. Ivan Ascher, *Portfolio Society: On the Capitalist Mode of Prediction* (New York, NY: Zone, 2016), 48.
9. See Harvey Cox, *The Market as God* (Cambridge, MA: Harvard University Press, 2016), 29–32.
10. Anne Longmuir, "Genre and Gender in Don DeLillo's *Players* and *Running Dog*," *Journal of Narrative Theory* 37/1 (2007), 133, 140.

11. Felix Salmon and Jon Stokes, "Algorithms Take Control of Wall Street," *Wired*, 27 December 2010, www.wired.com/magazine/2010/12/ff_ai_flashtrading/.

12. Scott Patterson, *Dark Pools: The Rise of AI Trading Machines and the Looming Threat to Wall Street* (New York, NY: Random House, 2012), 297–98; emphasis in original.

13. Kunzru discusses his leftist political self-identification in Max Haiven, "Hari Kunzru on Networks, the Novel, and the Politics of the Author," *Public Books* (2013), www.publicbooks.org/hari-kunzru-on-networks-the-noveland-the-politics-of-the-author/.

14. See, in particular, Fredric Jameson, *Postmodernism, or, The Cultural Logic of Late Capitalism* (London: Verso, 1991), ch. 1.

15. Haiven, "Hari Kunzru."

16. Hari Kunzru, *Gods Without Men* (London: Hamish Hamilton, 2011), 73; references hereafter noted parenthetically.

17. See Franco Moretti, *Distant Reading* (London: Verso, 2013).

18. Walter Benjamin, *Illuminations*, ed. Hannah Arendt, trans. Harry Zorn (London: Pimlico, 1999), 246.

19. Hirokazu Miyazaki, "The Temporalities of the Market," *American Anthropologist* 105/2 (2003), 261; emphasis in original.

20. Haiven, "Hari Kunzru."

21. Jameson, *Postmodernism*, 38.

22. Amitava Kumar, "Hari Kunzru on *Gods Without Men*," *Paris Review*, 6 March 2012, www.theparisreview.org/blog/2012/03/06/hari-kunzru-on-%E2%80%98gods-without-men%E2%80%99.

23. Christopher Sorrentino, "Rocky Horror Show," review of *Gods Without Men* by Hari Kunzru, *Book Forum*, February/March 2012, www.bookforum.com/inprint/018_05/8885.

24. Julian Stallabrass, "A View from the Fish Tank," www.blackshoals.net/text pages/stallabrassText.html.

25. Roland Barthes, "The Reality Effect" (1968), in *The Rustle of Language*, trans. Richard Howard (Berkeley, CA: University of California Press, 1989), 148; italics in original.

26. Stallabrass, "View."

27. Alberto Toscano, "Gaming the Plumbing: High-Frequency Trading and the Spaces of Capital," *Mute*, 16 January 2013, www.metamute.org/editorial/articles/gaming-plumbing-high-frequency-trading-and-spaces-capital.

28. Theodor W. Adorno and Walter Benjamin, *The Complete Correspondence, 1928–1940*, ed. Henri Lonitz, trans. Nicholas Walker (Cambridge: Polity, 1999), 283–84.

29. Haiven, "Hari Kunzru."

30. Alice Jardine, *Gynesis: Configurations of Woman and Modernity* (Ithaca, NY: Cornell University Press, 1985), 25.

31. Ibid., 25, 73.

32. Mary Anne Doane, *Femmes Fatales: Feminism, Film Theory, Psychoanalysis* (New York, NY: Routledge, 1991), 68.

33. See Randy Martin, *Knowledge Ltd: Toward a Social Logic of the Derivative* (Philadelphia: Temple University Press, 2015), 27–33.

34. Ibid., 23.

35. Haiven, "Hari Kunzru."

36. Ibid.

37. Jonathan Franzen, "Mr Difficult: William Gaddis and the Problem of Hard-to-Read Books," *New Yorker*, 30 September 2002, www.newyorker.com/magazine/2002/09/30/mr-difficult.

38. Rachel Greenwald Smith, *Affect and American Literature in the Age of Neoliberalism* (Cambridge: Cambridge University Press, 2015), 42.

39. Interview with Stephen J. Burn, *Paris Review* 195 (2010), www.theparisreview.org/interviews/6054/the-art-of-fiction-no-207-jonathan-franzen.

40. Amazon.co.uk (accessed 6 November 2018).

41. Haiven, "Hari Kunzru."

6 Putting Everything on the Table: Markets and Material Conditions in Twenty-First-Century Fiction

1. Tao Lin, *Taipei* (Edinburgh: Canongate, 2013), 191; references hereafter noted parenthetically.

2. See Lin's characterization of his style in these terms in Brandon Tietz, "The Way of Tao," *The Cult*, 12 May 2010, http://chuckpalahniuk.net/interviews/tao-lin.

3. Ian Sansom, review of *Taipei* by Tao Lin, *Guardian*, 4 July 2013, www.theguardian.com/books/2013/jul/04/taipei-tao-lin-review.

4. Something of a generational touchstone, *Back to the Future* is also invoked in relation to the temporal experiments of Ben Lerner's *10:04* (discussed later in this chapter), furnishing its title and receiving multiple references.

5. Richard Doyle, *Wetwares: Experiments in Postvital Living* (Minneapolis, MN: University of Minnesota Press, 2003), 84.

6. On the "public epitext," see Gérard Genette, *Paratext: Thresholds of Interpretation*, trans. Jane E. Lewin (Cambridge: Cambridge University Press, 1997), ch. 13.

7. On varying definitions of autofiction, see Hywel Dix, *The Late-Career Novelist: Career Construction Theory, Authors, and Autofiction* (London: Bloomsbury, 2017), esp. ch. 7.

8. Ann Friedman, "Who Gets to Speak and Why: A Conversation with Chris Kraus," *The Cut*, 22 June 2017, www.thecut.com/2017/06/chris-kraus-in-conversation-with-ann-friedman.html.
9. Chris Kraus, *I Love Dick* (London: Tuskar Rock Press, 2015), 224, 148; references hereafter noted parenthetically.
10. Tao Lin, interview with Ben Lerner, *The Believer* (2014), www.believermag.com/exclusives/?read=interview_lerner_2.
11. Dix, *Late-Career*, 163.
12. Mark Banks, ."Autonomy Guaranteed? Cultural Work and the 'Art–Commerce Relation,'" *Journal for Cultural Research* 14/3 (2010), 262, 252.
13. Colin MacCabe, Christopher Roth, Ben Lerner, and Akshi Singh, "A Song for Politics: A Discussion with John Berger," *Critical Quarterly* 56/1 (2014), 3.
14. The impact of Jameson's account of the cultural logic of late capitalism on Lerner's thinking is explicitly evident in "Damage Control: The Modern Art World's Tyranny of Price," *Harper's*, December 2013, https://harpers.org/archive/2013/12/damage-control/?single=1.
15. Lin, interview with Lerner.
16. Karl Smith, "Time Is a Flat Circle," *Quietus*, 8 February 2015, http://thequietus.com/articles/17190-ben-lerner-interview-1004-leaving-atocha-station-poetry-time-knausgaard; Lin, interview with Lerner.
17. Smith, "Time."
18. Ben Lerner, *10:04* (London: Granta, 2014), 116–17; references hereafter noted parenthetically.
19. Ben Lerner, *Leaving the Atocha Station* (London: Granta, 2013), 101.
20. Adam Kelly astutely notes the importance of the responses Ben receives from his social circle during this episode – in addition to the demands of the market and of a notion of modernist autonomy ("Autonomy, Economy, Sincerity: Ben Lerner and Contemporary Aesthetics," paper delivered at Northumbria University, September 2016).
21. Smith, "Time."
22. Emily Temple, "Ben Lerner on the Porous Boundaries of Literature, Truth, and Plagiarism," *Literary Hub*, 4 May 2017, https://lithub.com/ben-lerner-on-the-porous-boundaries-of-literature-truth-and-plagiarism/.
23. Theodore Martin, "The Dialectics of Damage: Art, Form, Formlessness," *nonsite.org* 18 (2015), http://nonsite.org/feature/9500. Martin's essay is a response to Jennifer Ashton's reading of *10:04* in "Totaling the Damage: Revolutionary Ambition in Recent American Poetry," *nonsite.org* 18 (2015), http://nonsite.org/feature/totaling-the-damage. I share Martin's view that, while ingenious, Ashton's attempt to show how *10:04* models an "aesthetics of resistance" to capital and the market elides some of the contradictions and tensions with which the novel is shot through.

24. Randy Martin, "Taking an Administrative Turn: Derivative Logics for a Recharged Humanities," *Representations* 116 (2011), 158.

25. John B. Thompson, *Merchants of Culture: The Publishing Business in the Twenty-First Century*, 2nd ed. (Cambridge: Polity, 2012), 203, 204.

26. Ibid., 141.

27. As Lerner has acknowledged, at the time of writing *10:04* his first novel had in fact already sold more than 10,000 copies (in late 2015, sales figures reportedly stood at around 30,000) (see Boris Kachka, "Ben Lerner on *10:04*, His Second Hall-of-Mirrors Semi-Memoir," *Vulture*, 28 August 2014, www.vulture.com/2 014/08/ben-lerner-interview-1004.html; John Freeman, "Ben Lerner Is Apprehensive: John Freeman Profiles The Newly Minted MacArthur Fellow," *Electric Literature*, 25 November 2015, https://electricliterature.com/b en-lerner-is-apprehensive-john-freeman-profiles-the-newly-minted-macarthur -fellow-a3f33d9bfed6).

28. Thompson, *Merchants*, 197–98.

29. Ibid., 194–95, 209.

30. Daniel Katz, "'I Did Not Walk Here All the Way from Prose': Ben Lerner's Virtual Poetics," *Textual Practice* 31/2 (2017), 325.

31. R. Martin, "Taking," 160.

32. T. Martin, "Dialectics."

33. Ibid.

34. Ibid.

35. Pieter Vermeulen, "How Should a Person Be (Transpersonal)? Ben Lerner, Roberto Esposito, and the Biopolitics of the Future," *Political Theory* 45/5 (2017), 662.

36. Smith, "Time"; Kachka, "Ben Lerner."

37. John Guillory, *Cultural Capital: The Problem of Literary Canon Formation* (Chicago, IL: University of Chicago Press, 1993), 326.

38. Tellingly, among submissions to a conference on "The Contemporary" at Princeton in 2016 Lerner was the most frequently mentioned author and *10:04* the most referenced text (see Sarah Chihaya, Joshua Kotin, and Kinohi Nishikawa, "'The Contemporary' By the Numbers," *Post45*, 29 February 2016, http://post 45.research.yale.edu/2016/02/the-contemporary-by-the-numbers/; Christopher Patrick Miller, "Letters from 'The Contemporary,'" *Post45*, 1 November 2016, http://post45.research.yale.edu/2016/11/letters-from-the-contemporary-christo pher-patrick-miller-november-1/#_ftn5).

39. Ben De Bruyn, "Realism 4°. Objects, Weather, and Infrastructure in Ben Lerner's *10:04*," *Textual Practice* 31/5 (2017), 957.

40. Ibid., 958.

41. Teju Cole, *Open City* (London: Faber & Faber, 2012), 45; references hereafter noted parenthetically.

42. Renamed in 2014 as Brookfield Place.
43. Ian Baucom, *Specters of the Atlantic: Finance Capital, Slavery, and the Philosophy of History* (Durham, NC: Duke University Press, 2005), 38.
44. Ibid., 53, 30.
45. Ibid., 144, 24, 52.
46. Aleksander Hemon, interview with Teju Cole, *Bomb*, 1 April 2014, https://bombmagazine.org/articles/teju-cole/; Baucom, *Specters*, 36.
47. Hemon, interview with Cole.
48. Walter Johnson, *River of Dark Dreams: Slavery and Empire in the Cotton Kingdom* (Cambridge, MA: Harvard University Press, 2013), 10.
49. Baucom, *Specters*, 53.
50. "About the Museum," www.moaf.org/about.
51. Leigh Claire La Berge, *Scandals and Abstraction: Financial Fiction of the Long 1980s* (Oxford: Oxford University Press, 2015), 39.
52. Christina Sharpe, *In the Wake: On Blackness and Being* (Durham, NC: Duke University Press, 2016), 5.
53. Ibid., 17–18, 13.
54. On Taylor and the origins of AT&T, see Alan Singer, "Nineteenth-Century New York's Complicity with Slavery: Documenting the Case for Reparations," *Redress for Historical Injustices in the United States: On Reparations for Slavery, Jim Crow, and Their Legacies*, ed. Michael T. Martin and Marilyn Yaquinto (Durham, NC: Duke University Press, 2007), 289–90.
55. Sharpe, *In the Wake*, 13.
56. Madhu Krishnan, "Postcoloniality, Spatiality, and Cosmopolitanism in the *Open City*," *Textual Practice* 29/4 (2015), 685, 691.
57. Rebekah Cumpsty, "Sacralizing the Streets: Pedestrian Mapping and Urban Imaginaries in Teju Cole's *Open City* and Phaswane Mpe's *Welcome to Our Hillbrow*," *Journal of Commonwealth Literature* (forthcoming), 6.
58. See *The New York African Burial Ground: Unearthing the African Presence in Colonial New York* (Washington, DC: Howard University Press/US General Services Administration, 2009), 94.
59. Baucom, *Specters*, 61–62.
60. Sharpe, *In the Wake*, 13.
61. Ibid., 14.
62. Teju Cole, "Natives on the Boat," *Known and Strange Things* (London: Faber & Faber, 2016), 20.
63. Teju Cole, "The White Savior Industrial Complex," *Known and Strange*, 349, 345.

64. David Harvey, *A Brief History of Neoliberalism* (Oxford: Oxford University Press, 2005), 27, 28–29.

65. Ibid., 29.

66. Ibid.

67. Ibid., 92, 29–31.

68. Ibid., 93, 74.

69. Sharpe, *In the Wake*, 15.

70. Teju Cole, "Black Body," *Known and Strange*, 14.

71. In addition to Huggan, cited below, see, in particular, Sarah Brouillette, *Postcolonial Writers in the Global Literary Marketplace* (Basingstoke: Palgrave Macmillan, 2007) and Chris Bongie, *Friends and Enemies: The Scribal Politics of Post/Colonial Literature* (Liverpool: Liverpool University Press, 2008).

72. Graham Huggan, *The Postcolonial Exotic: Marketing the Margins* (London: Routledge, 2001), 25–26; italics in original.

73. Cole, "Natives," 19, 18.

74. Cole, "White Savior," 344–345, 347.

75. Teju Cole, "In Place of Thought," *Known and Strange*, 75.

76. Pieter Vermeulen, "Reading Alongside the Market: Affect and Mobility in Contemporary American Migrant Fiction," *Textual Practice* 29/2 (2015), 278, 282, 283.

77. Lily Saint, "From a Distance: Teju Cole, World Literature, and the Limits of Connection," *Novel* 51/2 (2018), 325.

78. Aaron Bady, interview with Teju Cole, *Post45*, 19 January 2015, http://post45 .research.yale.edu/2015/01/interview-teju-cole/.

79. Cole, "White Savior," 344.

80. Bruce Robbins, *The Beneficiary* (Durham, NC: Duke University Press, 2017), 5, 6.

81. Brady, interview with Cole.

82. Steve Paulson, "Finding My Way into a New Form: An Interview with Teju Cole," *The Millions*, 5 July 2017, https://themillions.com/2017/07/finding-way-new-form-interview-teju-cole.html.

83. Hemon, interview with Cole.

84. Emma Brockes, interview with Teju Cole, *Guardian*, 21 June 2014, www .theguardian.com/culture/2014/jun/21/teju-cole-every-day-thief-interview.

7 Between Autonomy and Heteronomy: Exchanging Capital in Zink, Cohen, and Heti

1. See Kathryn Schulz, "Outside In," *New Yorker*, 18 May 2015, www .newyorker.com/magazine/2015/05/18/outside-in; Adam Vitcavage, "I'm Not

Entirely Demented: *The Millions* Interviews Nell Zink," *The Millions*, 5 October 2016, themillions.com/2016/10/millions-interviews-nell-zink.html.

2. Matthew Jakubowski, "Purity of Essence: One Question for Nell Zink," *Paris Review Daily*, 8 December 2014, www.theparisreview.org/blog/2014/12/08/p urity-of-essence-one-question-for-nell-zink/.

3. Joe Fassler, "Writing for an Audience of One," *Atlantic*, 4 October 2016, www.theatlantic.com/entertainment/archive/2016/10/writing-for-an-audience-of-one /502700/.

4. See e.g. Schulz, "Outside"; Ella Cory-Wright, "'I Don't Need Tricks': An Interview with Nell Zink: Novelist & Literary Sensation," *Culture Whisper*, https://ellacorywright.com/2017/06/05/i-dont-need-tricks-an-interview-with -nell-zink-novelist-literary-sensation/.

5. Fassler, "Writing."

6. Pierre Bourdieu, *The Rules of Art: Genesis and Structure of the Literary Field*, trans. Susan Emanuel (Cambridge: Polity, 1996), 217–18.

7. Fassler, "Writing"; italics in original.

8. See the account in Schulz, "Outside."

9. Paula Cocozza, "Nell Zink: The Cuckoo of Bad Belzig," *Guardian*, 17 June 2015, www.theguardian.com/books/2015/jun/17/nell-zink-the-cuckoo-of-bad-belzig.

10. Hannah Ellis-Petersen, "Nell Zink: There's a Clear Distinction between Taking Your Career Seriously and Taking Your Writing Seriously," *Guardian*, 4 January 2015, www.theguardian.com/books/2015/jan/04/nell-zink-jonathan-franzen-clear-distinction-taking-career-seriously-writing-seriously.

11. Schulz, "Outside."

12. Jakubowski, "Purity."

13. See Ellis-Petersen, "Nell Zink."

14. Ibid.

15. Ibid.

16. Schulz, "Outside."

17. See Ellis-Petersen, "Nell Zink."

18. Frances Chiem, "Danielle Dutton's Paper Bodies," *Seattle Review of Books*, 15 April 2016, www.seattlereviewofbooks.com/writers/frances-chiem/.

19. Keith Gessen, interview with Nell Zink, *Bomb*, 15 September 2016, https://bombmagazine.org/articles/nell-zink/.

20. Sianne Ngai, *Our Aesthetic Categories: Zany, Cute, Interesting* (Cambridge, MA: Harvard University Press, 2012), 5, 15, 30, 33.

21. Ibid., 1, 30.

22. Ibid., 14, 11.

23. Ibid., 9.

24. Schulz, "Outside"; Ellis-Petersen, "Nell Zink."

25. Vitcavage, "I'm Not Entirely."
26. Gessen, interview with Zink.
27. Vitcavage, "I'm Not Entirely"; Nell Zink, "'The Gears Meshed; the Cuckoo Spoke' – Nell Zink on *Nicotine*," 7 October 2016, *Harper Reach*, www.harperreach.com/gears-meshed-cuckoo-spoke-nell-zink-nicotine/.
28. Gessen, interview with Zink; Vitcavage, "I'm Not Entirely"; Cocozza, "Nell Zink."
29. Cocozza, "Nell Zink."
30. Ngai offers a pertinent discussion of such devices and their relations to human labour in "Theory of the Gimmick," *Critical Inquiry* 43/2 (2017), esp. 472–74.
31. Ngai, *Our Aesthetic*, 3.
32. Gessen, interview with Zink; Vitcavage, "I'm Not Entirely."
33. Vitcavage, "I'm Not Entirely."
34. Ibid.
35. Ibid.
36. See Hal Foster, "Postmodernism: A Preface," *The Anti-Aesthetic: Essays on Postmodern Culture*, ed. Hal Foster (Port Townsend, WA: Bay Press, 1983), xi–xii.
37. Vitcavage, "I'm Not Entirely."
38. Ngai, *Our Aesthetic*, 8, 1, 27.
39. Ibid., 11.
40. Nell Zink, *Nicotine* (New York, NY: Ecco, 2016), 107, 179 (see also e.g. 106–08, 115, 222, 256, 280, 283); references hereafter noted parenthetically.
41. See Moira Weigel's examination of the economic dynamics of contemporary courtship in *Labor of Love: The Invention of Dating* (New York, NY: Farrar, Straus, and Giroux, 2016).
42. Nell Zink, "Writing for Rejection," *n+1*, 24 February 2017, https://nplusonemag.com/online-only/online-only/writing-for-rejection/.
43. See the various discussions of Adorno's thinking on aesthetics in Helen Zink, *Portable Music and the Scalable Self: Performativity in Music Journalism and Interdisciplinary Music Analysis*, PhD Thesis, University of Tübingen, 2009, https://publikationen.uni-tuebingen.de/xmlui/handle/10900/46326.
44. Fassler, "Writing."
45. Gessen, interview with Zink.
46. Hannah Beckerman, "Nell Zink: 'Franzen Leaned on Me, Pressured Me, Encouraged Me,'" *Guardian*, 2 October 2016, www.theguardian.com/books/2016/oct/02/nell-zink-nicotine-interview-meet-author.
47. See Gessen, interview with Zink.
48. Beckerman, "Nell Zink."
49. Freia Anders and Alexander Sedlmaier, "Introduction: Global Perspectives on Squatting," *Public Goods versus Economic Interests: Global Perspectives on the History of Squatting* (New York, NY: Routledge, 2017), 17.

50. Loretta Lees, Tom Slater, and Elvin Wyly, preface to *Gentrification* (New York, NY: Routledge, 2008), xv, xvii.
51. Dan Duray, interview with Joshua Cohen, *Bomb*, 9 June 2015, https://bomb magazine.org/articles/joshua-cohen/.
52. Alexandra Alter, "Nothing to Hide and Nowhere to Hide It in Joshua Cohen's Internet Novel," *New York Times*, 12 June 2015, www.nytimes.com/2015/06/13/ books/nothing-to-hide-and-nowhere-to-hide-it-in-joshua-cohens-internet-novel .html; Matt Seidel, "The Promised Land: Joshua Cohen," *Publishers Weekly*, 5 June 2015, www.publishersweekly.com/pw/by-topic/authors/profiles/article/ 67032-the-promised-land-joshua-cohen.html.
53. Alter, "Nothing."
54. Christian Lorentzen, "A Nice Jewish Boy's Naughty Big Novel," *New York Observer*, 31 March 2010, http://observer.com/2010/03/a-nice-jewish-boys-naughty-big-novel/.
55. Joshua Cohen, "When Writers Put Themselves Into the Story," *Atlantic*, 16 June 2015, www.theatlantic.com/entertainment/archive/2015/06/by-heart-joshua-cohen-dostoyevsky/395978/.
56. Mukti Khaire, *Culture and Commerce: The Value of Entrepreneurship in Creative Industries* (Stanford, CA: Stanford University Press, 2017), xii, 29; italics in original.
57. Bourdieu, *Rules*, 217.
58. For Bourdieu's fullest elaboration of this point, see "The Production of Belief: Contribution to an Economy of Symbolic Goods," *The Field of Cultural Production: Essays on Art and Literature*, ed. Randal Johnson (Cambridge: Polity, 1993), ch. 2 (on "symbolic bankers," see p. 77).
59. Ben Bush, interview with Joshua Cohen, *Rumpus*, 3 July 2015, emphasis in original, http://therumpus.net/2015/07/the-rumpus-interview-with-joshua-cohen/.
60. Duray, interview with Cohen.
61. I follow the novel in referring to the author character as Josh and the other character named Joshua Cohen as "Principal." I refer to the actual author as Cohen.
62. Joshua Cohen, *Book of Numbers* (London: Vintage, 2016), 1.521 (the novel's pagination, inspired by binary notation, consists of part number and page number: the first part is denoted 1; the second 0; and the third 1); references hereafter noted parenthetically.
63. Ironically, Josh will later review Norman G. Finkelstein's controversial 2000 study *The Holocaust Industry: Reflections on the Exploitation of Jewish Suffering* during a brief stint as a book critic (1.26–27).

64. Cohen discusses Adorno's anxieties about art's "cooption by a rapacious mass-market" in "On Adorno on Music," *Forward*, 30 September 2009, https://forward.com/culture/115564/on-adorno-on-music/.

65. Joseph Vogl, "The Ascendancy of Finance: Toward a Concept of Seignorial Power," trans. Mareile Pfannebecker, *Credo Credit Crisis: Speculations on Faith and Money*, ed. Laurent Milesi, Christopher John Müller, and Aidan Tynan (London: Rowman and Littlefield, 2017), 26.

66. See Richard Barbrook and Andy Cameron, "The Californian Ideology," *Mute* 1/3 (1995), www.metamute.org/editorial/articles/californian-ideology.

67. Nicholas Brown, "Close Reading and the Market," *Literary Materialisms*, ed. Mathias Nilges and Emilio Sauri (New York, NY: Palgrave Macmillan, 2013), 165, n. 30.

68. Adam Rivett, "Internet Age Captured in Joshua Cohen's *Book of Numbers*," *Australian*, 12 September 2015, www.theaustralian.com.au/arts/review/internet-age-captured-in-joshua-cohens-book-of-numbers/news-story/80949d4a3241f6d a62e6f26331472026.

69. Duray, interview with Cohen.

70. Ibid.

71. Ibid.

72. For a cogent analysis and critique of the ideology of "disruption," see Stuart Hogarth, "Valley of the Unicorns: Consumer Genomics, Venture Capital, and Digital Disruption," *New Genetics and Society* 36/3 (2017), 250–72.

73. Luc Boltanski and Ève Chiapello, *The New Spirit of Capitalism*, trans. Gregory Elliott (London: Verso, 2018), 39, 504.

74. Sarah Brouillette, *Literature and the Creative Economy* (Stanford, CA: Stanford University Press, 2014), 14.

75. Steven Poole, *Guardian*, 3 July 2015, www.theguardian.com/books/2015/jul/03/book-of-numbers-joshua-cohen-review.

76. Mark Sarvas, *New York Times Book Review*, 2 July 2015, www.nytimes.com/2015/07/05/books/review/book-of-numbers-by-joshua-cohen.html.

77. Lisa Zeidner, *Washington Post*, 10 June 2015, www.washingtonpost.com/entertainment/books/book-of-numbers-by-joshua-cohen-tmi/2015/06/10/f23c71 bo-0ba3-11e5-95fd-d580f1c5d44e_story.html?utm_term=.88794b351c07.

78. Accessed 6 November 2018.

79. Duray, interview with Cohen.

80. Bush, interview with Cohen.

81. Quoted in Richard Ellmann, *James Joyce*, revised ed. (Oxford: Oxford University Press, 1983), 521.

82. See e.g. Julie Sloan Brannon, *Who Reads* Ulysses? *The Rhetoric of the Joyce Wars and the Common Reader* (New York, NY: Routledge, 2003).
83. Joshua Cohen, "First Family, Second Life: Thomas Pynchon Goes Online," *Harper's*, October 2013, emphases in original, https://harpers.org/archive/20 13/10/first-family-second-life/.
84. Joshua Cohen, "A Bloomsday Celebration," *Daily Beast*, 15 June 2010, www .thedailybeast.com/a-bloomsday-celebration-by-joshua-cohen-author-of-witz.
85. Cohen, "First Family."
86. Sarvas, *New York Times Book Review*.
87. Thomas Morton, "Talking Books in a Bathhouse with the Intimidatingly Brilliant Joshua Cohen," *Vice*, 16 June 2015, www.vice.com/en_uk/article/q bx8ex/cohen-for-a-schvitz-0000661-v22n6.
88. Jonathon Sturgeon, "The Evolution of the Internet Novel, 1984 to Present: A Timeline," *Flavorwire*, 19 June 2015, http://flavorwire.com/523568/the-evolution-of-the-internet-novel-1984-to-present-a-timeline.
89. Review in *Details*.
90. Adam Kirsch, *Tablet*, 4 June 2015, www.tabletmag.com/jewish-arts-and-culture/books/191355/joshua-cohen-adam-kirsch-book-of-numbers.
91. Tim Groenland, *Irish Times*, 8 December 2015, www.irishtimes.com/culture/books/joshua-cohen-portrait-of-the-author-as-a-monkey-tied-to-a-typewriter-and-cctv-1.2458896.
92. Boris Kachka, *New York*, 14 June 2015, http://nymag.com/arts/all/to-do-201 5-6-17/.
93. Kyle Chayka, *Rolling Stone*, 21 July 2015, www.rollingstone.com/culture/features/the-great-american-internet-novel-is-here-inside-book-of-numbers-20150721.
94. Review in *Details*.
95. In the United States, publishers typically bill as "national bestsellers" books that have appeared on a bestseller list in at least one periodical with national distribution.
96. Sheila Heti, *How Should a Person Be?* (London: Harvill Secker, 2013), 123; references hereafter noted parenthetically.
97. Peter Wollen, "Death (and Life) of the Author," *London Review of Books*, 5 February 1998, www.lrb.co.uk/v20/n03/peter-wollen/death-and-life-of-the-author.
98. While this emphasis on literature's instrumental capacities is out of step with prevailing conceptions of literary value, it has precedents in the history of aesthetic thought. Indeed, Joseph North has recently argued that the very foundations of academic literary criticism lie in attempts by early twentieth-century critics (notably William Empson and – especially – I.A. Richards) to orientate the discipline away from a concern with pure aesthetic value (a

concern that goes back ultimately to Kant) and towards "an aesthetic theory that emphasized the usefulness, rather than the glorious uselessness, of the work of art." This project, North suggests, rested on the conviction that readers of literature are looking, above all else, "for something to go on with, something that will help them live their lives," and hence that criticism should conceive of itself as "helping readers, each from their own specific material situations, to use the aesthetic instruments of literature to cultivate their most useful practical capabilities" (*Literary Criticism: A Concise Political History* [Cambridge, MA: Harvard University Press, 2017], 77, 6, 15).

99. The classic critique is Christine Battersby, *Gender and Genius: Towards a Feminist Aesthetics* (London: Women's Press, 1989).

100. David Naimon, "A Conversation with Sheila Heti," *Missouri Review* 35/4 (2012), 112.

101. John Barber, "How Should a Novel Be? Don't Ask Sheila Heti," *Globe and Mail*, 13 April 2013, www.theglobeandmail.com/arts/books-and-media/boo k-reviews/how-should-a-novel-be-dont-ask-sheila-heti/article11134050/.

102. *Library Journal* review, 15 March 2006.

103. Barber, "How Should."

104. Naimon, "Conversation," 117.

105. See Rachel Sagner Buurma and Laura Heffernan, "Notation after 'The Reality Effect': Remaking Reference with Roland Barthes and Sheila Heti," *Representations* 125 (2014), 92.

106. See Kelly C. George, "Self-Help as Women's Popular Culture in Suburban New Jersey: An Ethnographic Perspective," *Participations: Journal of Audience & Reception Studies* 9/2 (2012), 26.

107. Naimon, "Conversation," 113.

108. Rebecca Wigod, "A Bounty of Fall Book Releases," *Vancouver Sun*, 25 September 2010, www.pressreader.com/canada/vancouver-sun/2010092 5/284245231692316.

109. Christopher Fenwick, "How Should a Person Be?" *The Point*, 2014, thepoint mag.com/2014/criticism/how-should-a-person-be.

110. Jessica Ferri, "'The Culture Decides What It Wants': Sheila Heti on Writing, Youth, and Beauty," *The Awl*, 14 June 2010, emphases in original, www.theawl.com/2012/06/the-culture-decides-what-it-wants-sheila-heti-on-writing-youth-and-beauty/.

111. Joanna Biggs, "It Could Be Me," *London Review of Books*, 24 January 2013, www.lrb.co.uk/v35/no2/joanna-biggs/it-could-be-me.

112. Ferri, "Culture."

113. Naimon, "Conversation," 112; Barber, "How Should."

114. Kat Stoeffel, "The Problem Child: Why Won't America Publish Sheila Heti's Second Novel?" *New York Observer*, 16 December 2010, http://obser

ver.com/2010/12/the-problem-child-why-wont-america-publish-sheila-hetis
-second-novel/2/.

115. Ibid.; Barber, "How Should."
116. Stoeffel, "Problem."
117. Ferri, "Culture"; emphasis in original.
118. Barber, "How Should."
119. https://houseofanansi.com/products/how-should-a-person-be.
120. Sarah Boesveld, "Toronto Author Sheila Heti Wants to be More Than the Voice of the 'Now' Generation," *National Post*, 14 July 2012, http://national post.com/news/canada/toronto-author-sheila-heti-wants-to-be-more-than-the-voice-of-the-now-generation.
121. Stoeffel, "Problem."

Coda: Basic Income, or, Why Barbara Browning's *The Gift* Is Not a Gift

1. Barbara Browning, *The Gift (Or, Techniques of the Body)* (Minneapolis, MN and New York, NY: Coffee House Press/Emily Books, 2017), 127, 147, 201; references hereafter noted parenthetically.
2. Tao Lin, interview with Ben Lerner, *The Believer* (2014), www.believermag.com /exclusives/?read=interview_lerner_2.
3. John B. Thompson, *Merchants of Culture: The Publishing Business in the Twenty-First Century*, 2nd ed. (Cambridge: Polity, 2012), 156; Lee Konstantinou, "Lewis Hyde's Double Economy," *ASAP Journal* 1/1 (2016), 141.
4. Konstantinou, "Lewis Hyde's," 141.
5. Germany and, especially, Norway are known for their extensive support for writers and literary culture more generally: on the exemplary Norwegian case, see Wendy Griswold, *Regionalism and the Reading Class* (Chicago, IL: University of Chicago Press, 2008), ch. 5.
6. Karl Marx and Frederick Engels, *The German Ideology*, ed. C.J. Arthur, 2nd ed. (London: Lawrence & Wishart, 1974), 109; John Guillory, *Cultural Capital: The Problem of Literary Canon Formation* (Chicago, IL: University of Chicago Press, 1993), 338; emphasis in original.
7. As Guillory notes, however, while such a state would be genuinely utopian in its thorough democratization of access to the means of "artistic" production, one could hardly expect recognition for the artefacts so produced to be distributed equally: "cultural producers would still compete to have their products read, studied, looked at, heard, lived in, sung, worn, and would still accumulate … 'prestige' or fame" (*Cultural*, 339).
8. Chris Kraus, *After Kathy Acker: A Biography* (London: Allen Lane, 2017), 123, 130.

9. Peter Frase, *Four Futures: Visions of the World after Capitalism* (London: Verso, 2016), n.p. (ebook).

10. See Aaron Bastani, *Fully Automated Luxury Communism: A Manifesto* (London: Verso, 2019). For a clear articulation of the sceptics' position, see Daniel Zamora, "The Case against a Basic Income," trans. Jeff Bate Boerop, *Jacobin*, 28 December 2017, www.jacobinmag.com/2017/12/universal-basic-income-inequality-work.

11. Frase, *Four Futures*; Nick Srnicek and Alex Williams, *Inventing the Future: Postcapitalism and a World Without Work* (London: Verso, 2015), n.p. (ebook); emphasis in original; Robert Meister, "Liquidity," *Derivatives and the Wealth of Societies*, ed. Benjamin Lee and Randy Martin (Chicago, IL: University of Chicago Press, 2016), 173.

12. Quoted in Heather Stewart, "Tory MP Condemns Universal Basic Income 'On Moral Grounds,'" *Guardian*, 28 December 2017, www.theguardian.com/money/2017/dec/28/tory-mp-condemns-universal-basic-income-on-moral-grounds.

13. Srnicek and Williams, *Inventing*, n.p.

Index

9/11, 138, 163, 237

absorption, 73, 80–81, 82, 86, 104, 114
Acker, Kathy, 45–46, 190, 259–60
  My Death My Life by Pier Paolo Pasolini, 45–46
Ackroyd, Peter, 89, 97, 102
Adorno, Theodor, 12–13, 46, 176
Africa, 33, 208, 209, 210–11
  conventional representations of, 194, 212–17
Afropolitanism, 216
alchemy, 89, 94, 102, 107, 110, 121–23
Amazon, 21, 62, 258
  reader reviews, 85, 90, 183, 244
ambivalence, 15–17, 62, 82, 112, 156
Amis, Martin, 46–47, 97, 190
  Information, The, 46–47
  Money, 46
animality, 86–87, 119
Appadurai, Arjun, 10
Arts Council, 20, 25
Aubry, Timothy, 23
austerity, 25, 259
Autofiction, 189–90, 192
autonomy, 5–6, 193, 220, 241–42, 259–61
  and contemporary capitalism, 243–44
  and modernism, 12–15, 18–20
  politics of, 28–29
avant-garde, 5–6, 23, 43, 45, 220, 248, *See also* modernism
Avant-Pop, 44–46, 53, 59, 82

Baigent, Michael, Richard Leigh, and Henry Lincoln, 111–16
  Holy Blood and the Holy Grail, The, 112–14
Bank of England, 72, 119, 125
Banks, Mark, 193
Barthes, Roland, 51, 174
Baucom, Ian, 205–6, 209
Baudrillard, Jean, 160
Beatty, Paul, 50
Becker, Gary, 225

Beckert, Jens, 81–82
behavioural economics, 11
Benjamin, Walter, 129, 145, 170–72, 176
Berlant, Lauren, 78
Big Bang (UK financial services), 94, 101, 103
Billson, Anne
  Suckers, 85–86
Bjerg, Ole, 109
Black Monday Crash, 1987, 138–39
blogging, 192, 217
Boltanski, Luc and Ève Chiapello, 243
Bourdieu, Pierre, 4–7, 23, 220, 234–35, *See also* symbolic capital
Boxall, Peter, 26
Bretton Woods system, 10, 75, 109, 135–36, 142
Brier, Evan, 18
Brouillette, Sarah, 23, 24, 26, 27, 243
Brown, Dan, 111, 121
Brown, Nicholas, 28–29, 241–42
Browning, Barbara
  Gift, The, 256–59
Burn, Stephen J., 54

Campbell, Aifric
  On the Floor, 65
Canary Wharf, 101–5, 205
Clune, Michael, 143–44
Coe, Jonathan, 79
  Terrible Privacy of Maxwell Sim, The, 88–90
cognitive mapping, 169, 172, 175
Cohen, Joshua
  Book of Numbers, 220, 234–46
  Witz, 233–34
Cole, Teju
  Open City, 204–17
conspiracy, 111, 129
  and the encyclopedic/systems novel, 141, 164
counterculture, 72, 94–96, 139, 231
Courtemanche, Eleanor, 132
creative writing programmes, 26–27, 217
credit crunch. *See* global financial crisis, 2007–8

critique, 38, 126, 172
  versus postcritique, 16–17, 62
culture industry, 12–13, 238
Cumpsty, Rebekah, 209

De Boever, Arne, 66, 75
De Bruyn, Ben, 203
Dee, Jonathan
  Privileges, The, 65
Defoe, Daniel, 93–94
DeLillo, Don, 140, 143, 150
  Players, 155–67
derivatives, 10, 76, 94, 101, 188, 197–98, 201,
  See also hedging
Derrida, Jacques, 74–75, 178
Dickens, Charles, 134
disruption, ideology of, 243–44
Dix, Hywel, 192
Docklands (London). *See* Canary Wharf
Donofrio, Nicholas, 48
dot-com boom, 57–58, 230, 240–41
Doyle, Richard, 188
Durand, Cédric, 8, 76

efficient market hypothesis, 134–39, 156–57,
  158–59, 171
  popularization of, 155
  temporality of, 162–63
Eggers, Dave
  Heartbreaking Work of Staggering Genius, A,
  55–58
Ellis, Bret Easton
  American Psycho, 82–83, 86
  Lunar Park, 83–85
encyclopedic novel, 139–41, *See also* systems novel
  and anti-encyclopedism, 151–52
  and gender, 152–53, 164–67, 178
English, James, 22
Eve, Martin Paul, 22
Everett, Percival
  Erasure, 50–53
experimental fiction, 25–26, 40–44, 45,
  52–53, 245
  market constraints on, 23
  state support for, 20

Fama, Eugene, 134, 138, 158, *See also* efficient
  market hypothesis
Farebrother, Rachel, 50
Faulks, Sebastian
  Week in December, A, 63
Felski, Rita, 16
Fiction Collective, 22, 42, 45
fictional contract, 77–78, 84, 98, 113, 149,
  182–83, 187

fiduciary exchangeability, 73, 80, 82, 91,
  115, 125
Financial Revolution, 78, 89, 93
financialization, 75, 96, 206
  and neoliberalism, 8–11
Finn, Ed, 62
Foster, Hal, 224
Foucault, Michel, 132
fractional-reserve banking, 124
Frank, Thomas, 133, 139
Frankfurt School, 12, 53, 226, 238, *See also*
  Adorno, Theodor; Horkheimer, Max
Franzen, Jonathan, 25, 219, 220–22
  "Mr Difficult", 182–83
  Corrections, The, 53, 182
  Strong Motion, 146–47
Friedman, Milton, 135

Gaddis, William, 182, 246
  J R, 143–44
Galbraith, John Kenneth, 124–25
Gallagher, Catherine, 77
genre writing, 21–22, 25–26, 78
  genre turn, 58–60, 87, 97, 126
  popular, 28, 43–45, 82, 224
  speculative/supernatural, 63–66, 81, 82–91
gentrification, 99, 219, 231–32
gift exchange, 232, 257
global financial crisis, 2007–8, 7, 10–11, 71, 76, 77,
  178–79
  effects on the publishing industry, 24–26,
  60, 192
  in fiction, 62–65, 87, 88–89, 179–81, 257
globalization, 5, 203
Goldstone, Andrew, 19
Goodchild, Philip, 75
Gothic, 44, 74, 82, 85, 95
Goux, Jean-Joseph, 66, 109, 119–20
Graeber, David, 74, 257
Guillory, John, 203, 259

Haider Rahman, Zia
  In the Light of What We Know, 64
Haiven, Max, 101
Hallberg, Garth Risk, 153
  City on Fire, 150–51
Harvey, David, 44, 211–12
Haslett, Adam
  Union Atlantic, 65–66
Hayek, Friedrich, 133–34, 143
hedging, 197–203, *See also* derivatives
hermeneutics
  of speculation, 31, 125
  of suspicion, 125, 126
heteronomy, 220, 237–38

Heti, Sheila
  How Should a Person Be?, 247–55
  Ticknor, 250
High-Frequency Trading, 167–68
Hoberek, Andrew, 58–59
Holocaust, the, 236
homology, 78–79, 80
Horkheimer, Max, 12–13
Huehls, Mitchum, 54, 60–62
Huggan, Graham, 27, 212–13
Hutcheon, Linda, 38
Huyssen, Andreas, 44

infinity list, 146, 148, 151, 168, 174

Jameson, Fredric, 194
  methodology of, 15, 126
  on cognitive mapping, 169, 172
  on postmodernism, 12, 13–15, 18,
    44, 59
Jobs, Steve, 240, 241–42
Johnson, B.S., 90
  *Aren't You Rather Young to be Writing Your
    Memoirs?*, 41
  Christie Malry's Own Double-Entry,
    40–41
  Unfortunates, The, 40
Johnson, Walter, 206
Joyce, James, 47, 107, 244–46, 250
  Finnegans Wake, 106
  Portrait of the Artist as a Young Man, A,
    106
  Ulysses, 19

Katz, Daniel, 201
Keynes, John Maynard, 132, 133
Khaire, Mukti, 234
Knight, Peter, 144
Knorr Catina, Karin, 75–76
Konings, Martijn, 10–11
Konstantinou, Lee, 55–56, 259
Kraus, Chris, 45, 259–60
  I Love Dick, 190–92
Krippner, Greta, 8
Krishnan, Madhu, 209
Kunzru, Hari, 153
  Gods Without Men, 167–84

La Berge, Leigh Claire, 17, 66,
  207
labour, 133, 157, 223, 225, 233
LeClair, Tom, 143
Lerner, Ben, 192, 257
  10:04, 194–204
  Leaving the Atocha Station, 194, 195

Lin, Tao, 1–2
  Taipei, 187–89
LiPuma, Edward, 63
literary fiction, 25–26, 54, 60–62, 63, 97
literary marketplace, 3, 17–29, 48, 182, 247,
  See also publishing industry
London, 27, 92, 112, 117–18, 123
  financial services in, 85, 89, 93–94, 100–5,
    116–17
Luckhurst, Roger, 95, 103

magical realism, 97–106, 116
Major, Clarence, 49
Malkiel, Burton, 137, 155
Marche, Stephen
  Hunger of the Wolf, The, 86–88
market. *See also* literary marketplace
  and gender, 86, 225, 252–53
  financial, 11–12, 15–16, 75–77, 105, 129–31,
    134–39, 155–81
  model of literary value, 55, 79, 183
market logic, 4, 9, 21, 23, 194–95,
  256, 261
market metafiction, 3, 37–62, 82–91, 99,
  150, 193, 196–203, 213–15, 227–52,
  256–58
market reading, 29
Marsh, Nicky, 144
Martin, Niall, 102
Martin, Randy, 101, 179, 197, 201
Martin, Theodore, 197, 201–2
Marx, Karl, 46, 74, 109, 124, 259
McCaffery, Larry, 45
McCann, Sean, 95–96
McClanahan, Annie, 11, 62, 66, 76–77
McGurl, Mark, 26, 58
McLaughlin, Robert, 55
McPhee, Martha
  Dear Money, 64
Meister, Robert, 260
Melamed, Leo, 135–36, 142
Mendelson, Edward, 141
metafiction, 39–44, 53, 55, 150, 195, *See also* market
  metafiction
Mickalites, Carey James, 132
Mirowski, Philip, 9, 136–37, 139
Mithraism, 118–21
Miyazaki, Hirokazu, 171
modernism, 5, 40, 106–7, 132–33, 244–45, 250–51,
  See also avant-garde
  and autonomy, 12–14, 18, 196
  and the publishing industry, 18–20
money, 74–75, 124–25, 238–39
  fiat, 75, 109, 239
  metallic, 113, 115, 124, 239

metallism, 65–66, 108–9, 118–24
representative, 74
Morrison, Toni, 48–49, 51

National Endowment for the Arts, 20, 42, 258
Naylor, Gloria, 49
neoliberalism, 9–10, 17, 29, 59, 133, *See also*
    efficient market hypothesis; market
    and financialization, 10–11
    and literature, 54–55
    and structural adjustment programmes,
        211–12
    challenges to, 11
    Pierre Bourdieu on, 4–7
network, 133, 172, 203
    and narrative form, 172–73, 182
New Economic Criticism, 78–79, 109
New Sincerity, 55, 58, 190
New York, 27, 259
    financial services in, 204–5, 207–8, 209,
        211–12
Ngai, Sianne, 222–25
Nik-Khah, Edward, 139
Norfield, Tony, 103

Occupy Wall Street, 197, 257, 258
oil crisis (1973), 20, 42, 211
orientalism, 213–14

patronage, 23, 26, 219
periodization, 3–4, 8, 13, 54
Poovey, Mary, 78–79
postirony, 55, 58, 190
postmodernism, 12, 66, 92
    and post-postmodernism, 38, 54
    and race, 48–53
    and the market, 13–14, 37–62, 82, 245
    of resistance/reaction, 224
poststructuralism, 51, 76
Powers, Richard, 153
    Ploughing the Dark, 145–46
    Three Farmers on Their Way to a Dance, 144–45
precarity, 27, 183, 225
privilege, 27, 56, 183, 195, 203–4, 215–17
pseudohistory, 111, 114, 121
psychogeography, 89, 110–12, 119
publishing industry, 18, 43, 47, 198, 199–201, 212,
        234, 253–54, *See also* literary marketplace
    and literary agents, 2, 199, 221
    and race, 48–53
    and the media, 192, 222, 233
    independent presses and, 1, 22, 23, 26, 42,
        45, 254
    literary prizes and, 22
    modernism and, 18–20

nonprofit presses and, 258–59
    restructuring of, 6, 20–27, 41–42, 98
Pynchon, Thomas, 246
    Gravity's Rainbow, 141–43, 152

Random House, 2, 19, 20, 49, 52, 56, 234, 236
realism, 40, 53, 201–2, 226
    and finance, 62–63, 66
    and New Sincerity/postirony, 53–54, 55
    as a genre, 25
Reed, Ishmael, 48
Rosen, Jeremy, 37

Saint, Lily, 214
Samuelson, Paul, 134, 135, *See also* efficient market
        hypothesis
Sapphire, 51
Sedgwick, Eve Kosofsky, 124
self-help writing, 251–52
Sharpe, Christina, 208, 210, 212
Shaw, Katy, 62, 66
Shields, David, 55
Shonkwiler, Alison, 63, 66
Silicon Valley, 239, 240, 243
Sinclair, Iain, 73, 89–90, 92–97
    Downriver, 97–107
    Lights Out for the Territory, 107–26
    White Chappell, Scarlet Tracings, 93–94
slavery, 205
    history of, 205–8
    legacy of in the present, 208–10
Slobodian, Quinn, 17
Smith, Adam, 87, 131–32, 152
Smith, Rachel Greenwald, 54–55, 183, 197
Smith, Zadie, 25, 54, 112, 153
Sontag, Susan, 16
Sorrentino, Gilbert
    Mulligan Stew, 42–44
squatting, 231
Squires, Claire, 37
Srnicek, Nick, 261
Stead, C.K.
    Risk, 64
Stevenson, Randall, 20, 42
Stevenson, Talitha
    Disappear, 64
structural adjustment programmes, 211–12
Sukenick, Ronald, 42
superstition, 71–72
suspension of disbelief, 55, 73, 77, 226
symbolic capital, 5, 22, 198, 199, 202–3, 235, 247
systems novel, 139–41, 143, 146, 150, 172, 182–83,
        See also encyclopedic novel
    and gender, 152–53, 164–67, 178
Szalay, Michael, 20, 95–96

Thompson, John B., 19, 22–23, 198, 200, 259
Torday, Paul
  Hopeless Life of Charlie Summers, The, 64
Toscano, Alberto, 175
transcoding, 14–15

Universal Basic Income, 260–61
usefulness
  of literature, 248, 252–53, 254

Vermeulen, Pieter, 27, 214
Vogl, Joseph, 239
Volcker shock, 211

Wallace, David Foster, 246
  "E Unibus Pluram: Television and U.S. Fiction", 55
  Infinite Jest, 147
  Pale King, The, 147–50

Wark, McKenzie, 157
Waugh, Patricia, 40
welfare state, 5, 20, 24–25, 259–60
White, Hayden, 114
Whitehead, Colson
  Zone One, 60–62, 87
Wicke, Jennifer, 132
Wideman, John Edgar, 50
Williams, Alex, 261
Williams, Raymond, 78
Wilson, Colin, 111
Wood, James, 140, 144
Woolf, Virginia, 132, 134, 256
Wright, Richard, 51

young adult fiction, 224
Young, John K., 49

Zink, Nell, 218–27
  Nicotine, 227–33
Žižek, Slavoj, 129–30